MODERN
SYSTEMS OF
GOVERNMENT

To my son Cyrus

MODERN SYSTEMS OF GOVERNMENT

Exploring the
Role of
Bureaucrats
and Politicians

Ali Farazmand

Editor

SAGE Publications
International Educational and Professional Publisher
Thousand Oaks   London   New Delhi

For information address:

SAGE Publications, Inc.
2455 Teller Road
Thousand Oaks, California 91320
E-mail: order@sagepub.com

SAGE Publications Ltd.
6 Bonhill Street
London EC2A 4PU
United Kingdom

SAGE Publications India Pvt. Ltd.
M-32 Market
Greater Kailash I
New Delhi 110 048 India

Printed in the United States of America

Library of Congress Cataloging-in-Publication Data

Modern systems of government: Exploring the role of bureaucrats and
    politicians / editor, Ali Farazmand.
      p. cm.
    Includes bibliographical references (p.) and index.
    ISBN 0-7619-0608-8 (cloth : acid-free paper). — ISBN
    0-7619-0609-6 (pbk. : acid-free paper)
    1. Bureaucracy. 2. Public administration. 3. Politicians.
    4. Comparative government. I. Farazmand, Ali.
    JF1501.M63 1997
    350—dc21   96-51224

97 98 99 00 01 02 03 10 9 8 7 6 5 4 3 2 1

Acquiring Editor:	Peter Labella
Editorial Assistant:	Frances Borghi
Production Editor:	Astrid Virding
Production Assistant:	Denise Santoyo
Book Designer/Typesetter:	Christina Hill
Cover Designer:	Candice Harman
Indexer:	Juniee Oneida
Print Buyer:	Anna Chin

Contents

Preface

The political and administrative history of human civilization from the ancient empires and city-states to the modern nation-states reveals a central feature of governance in all societies: the relationship between the administrative or bureaucratic elites and the political elites, the higher level civil servants and politicians, and the elected and nonelected officials. This relationship at the highest level of government in different political systems, including the ancient monarchies and the modern parliamentary and presidential systems of governance, has produced various manifestations in performance, character, and outcomes.

The significance of understanding the centrality of the governance and administration relationship can be explained in many ways, and it may even be argued that this relationship between bureaucrats and politicians is the heart of modern governance, just as it has always been, because both the administrative and the political elites' personal characters, standards, conduct, and professionalism set the tone for the entire system of government and its institutions in daily contacts with citizens and society. The way these two groups of governing-administrative elites work together affects the entire citizenry's attitudes toward government and administration. A good, cooperative relationship between the two reinforces the legitimacy of the temporal government and its effectiveness, whereas a hostile and noncooperative relationship tends to undermine both institutional capacity for effective governance and the legitimacy of the government in general.

Governance and administration have always been together, one being indispensable to the other. However, this relationship has not been without tension. In fact, the tension between democracy as a form of government and bureaucracy as an institution of administrative governance has been a persistent dilemma in modern political systems. What is significant at this time is the severity of tension since the 1970s, which has characterized, and to a great extent paralyzed, modern governments, especially in the United States and other industrialized countries. Antibureacracy sentiment and bureaucrat bashing have reached an epidemic level. Once again, the ancient questions of governance and administration, bureaucracy and politics, bureaucrats and politicians, and professionalism and responsive government have surfaced dramatically. What has been overlooked is that institutional capability, which is secured through professionalism, is central to effective governance. Good, effective governance requires competent administration by professional bureaucrats. A cooperative, supportive relationship between political elites and administrative elites would foster effective governance and responsiveness as well as accountability, whereas a hostile and destructive relationship between the two would certainly have an undermining effect, with possible consequences for political system legitimacy.

This book was born out of two major conference panels organized by the editor and Fred Riggs, in Chicago and Washington, D.C., in 1992 and 1993, for the American Political Science Association (APSA). Original papers were presented on the themes of governance, professionalism, and the role of professional bureaucracy and bureaucrats in modern parliamentary and presidential systems of government. Additional papers were subsequently solicited for inclusion in this volume. Various countries have been covered to represent both developed and developing nations.

This book could not have completed without the cooperation of the contributors, who always responded to my requests. Although this was a time-consuming process, they always cooperated despite busy schedules, and I am extremely grateful to them all. I would also like to thank Sage Publications for pursuing this project, and the individuals at Sage whose cooperation and suggestions made the book what it is. My special appreciation goes to Senior Editor Peter Labella, who reviewed the manuscript and made suggestions for improvement. My thanks also go to such individuals as Frances Borghi, assistant editor; Astrid Virding, production editor; and Janet Brown, freelance copy editor, who worked efficiently to produce this book.

Introduction

Bureaucrats and Politicians
in Comparative Perspective

Ali Farazmand

The relationship between bureaucrats and politicians has always been a central issue of governance from the dawn of civilization. This relationship between bureaucracy and politics and bureaucrats and politicians, as an independent variable, may even explain the degree of success or failure in governing empires, nation-states, and city-states. It may even be argued that this relationship is the heart of modern governance, for the administrative elite's and political elite's leadership, standards, and behavior set the tone for all institutions of governments. Their relationship at the highest level of government is an example for all who work in governments, and affects the attitudes of citizens toward their governments. The administrative history of the ancient empires and city-states reveals ample evidence on the centrality and importance of a cooperative relationship between bureaucratic elites and political elites (Farazmand forthcoming). A good relationship reinforces the legitimacy of each party, while a bad or conflictual relationship tends to undermine the legitimacy of governments in general and regimes in particular. Both governance and administration have always lived inseparably together, one being indispensable to the other. But there has also been a tension between democracy as a form of governance and bureaucracy as an institution of administration (Waldo 1981). This tension has never been so severe as it has been since the 1970s, especially in the United States, where the antibureaucracy movement and bureaucrat bashing have reached an epidemic level (Goodsell 1994; Farazmand 1989b). The entire history of human civilization contains the twin aspects of civilization and administration, governance and administration, politicians and bureaucrats. Does this mean a dichotomous relationship between politics and administration is inevitable? Or does this mean that governance cannot exist without administration or bureaucracy? The answer appears too be "no," but good and effective governance requires competent administration, and competent administration requires a good degree of professionalism. The implications of these terms and concepts are discussed extensively throughout this book.

Theoretical Setting

The rapid growth of modern governments around the world—due to a number of factors beyond the scope of discussion in this introduction (see Farazmand 1996)—has resulted in a continuing expansion of the modern administrative state assigned to perform a wide range of governmental functions from economic development to social welfare. Consequently, the largess and professionalization of the administrative state and the public bureaucracy around the world have created resentment and opposition in various segments of society including critics from academia, citizens, and politicians, who have considered the growth of bureaucracy as a threat to democracy. This has, since the 1970s, resulted in a continuous attack on the bureaucracy and civil service around the world, causing drastic downsizing, restructuring of the public sector, reconfiguration of public-private sectors boundaries, massive privatization of public enterprises, and adoption of private-sector management systems in public organizations. The U.S. Civil Service Reform Act of 1978 is a prime example of this new development in modern governance and administration. Subsequently, the role of government in society and the role of bureaucracy in governance have been questioned by conservative, and some liberal, politicians all over the globe, and this global movement has been led by the United States and Britain. This late twentieth-century phenomenon has altered the relationship between bureaucracy and politics and bureaucrats and politicians and their appointees. This timely debate—on the relationship between the two groups central to the effectiveness of modern governance under different political systems—has captured the attention of all concerned in academia and government as well as among citizens.

The academic discussions of the relationship between bureaucrats and politicians, as well as the other related concepts and issues mentioned above, are extremely varied and contain competing and contending tendencies or approaches. One approach is to consider absolute control of bureaucracy and bureaucrats by elected politicians in representative democracies. This approach also extends to almost all political systems of governance, whether authoritarian or democratic, monarchies or elected democracies, socialist or capitalist. According to this approach, the necessity to maintain political control by politicians over the bureaucracy and bureaucrats is indisputable, for the nonelected career bureaucrats, if not controlled, may pose a threat to political authority or democracy. In fact, Max Weber himself was ambivalent about the role of bureaucracy and expressed concern about the danger of "overtowering" bureaucracy in society (Weber 1946: 228). Such an approach tends to promote a separation of politics from administration, leading to a dichotomous relationship between politicians and administrators or bureaucrats, the first being policymakers and the second being policy implementers or bureaucrats. Most of the proponents of this approach are found in the discipline of political science (Finer 1941; Mosher 1968; Wilson 1989). For developing nations, the proponents also argue, maintaining firm political control over bureaucracy is essential for nation building and achieving national developmental goals. Unless controlled, the bureaucracy and bureaucrats would stifle development and cause a major obstacle in nation building (Huntington 1968). By extension, the leaders of major revolutions in the contemporary world have expressed similar concerns and arguments, for example, in the Bolshevik Revolution (Lenin 1971), the Iranian Revolution of 1978-1979 (Farazmand 1989a), and Nicaragua's Sandinista Revolution (Riposa 1996). The problem for the revolutionary leaders has been how to abolish the bureaucratic machinery of the old regime and create a new and trusting administrative system.

The second approach makes the opposite point and rejects the politics-administration dichotomy, arguing instead for a dual political as well as administrative role for the bureaucracy. This approach treats bureaucrats as integral parts of the policy process and governance in general. The relationship between bureaucrats and politicians is mixed and interactive, fluid and integrative, not dichotomous or hierarchical. According to this approach, bureaucrats and politicians should and must work together, and their relationship should be cooperative, not adversarial, to promote efficient and effective administration and governance (Riggs 1994; Rockman 1996). There is little to fear from bureaucrats, who are seen as professional administrators or civil servants whose active role in society and politics would promote social change, justice, and fairness, and whose professional role can serve the general public interest. This approach tends to promote the utility of bureaucracy, considers the possible reconcilability of bureaucracy and democracy, and contends that public administration theory is political theory also (Waldo 1981, 1986; Levine 1985; Heclo 1977; Long 1949, 1952).

A possible third approach, which is developing and gaining increased attention, is to treat high-level bureaucrats with some autonomy vis-à-vis politicians in the administrative system of governance. Recognizing the responsibility and limits of bureaucratic power, this approach tends to empower the bureaucratic elite and higher career civil servants against partisan and other political abuses of politicians in power. Proponents argue that the constitutionally empowered higher level civil servants can promote broad general public interests and prevent politicians' potential abuses of power and privilege in serving powerful particularistic and big business interests (Friedrich 1940; Farazmand forthcoming; Goodsell 1994; Rohr 1986). Proponents argue for enhancing the power of the career administrators as "actors in the governing process" (Wamsley et al. 1987: 43, 1992).

Each of the above three approaches offers a wealth of academic information with policy and practical implications. However, what is often ignored or overlooked is the fact that these approaches have often been considered in conflict as *the* only right approach in public administration and governance. The first approach fails to recognize the expertise and experience of the career bureaucrats (Peters and Rockman 1996: 4). Consequently, the conflictual relationship between the often hostile and suspicious politicians, on the one hand, and professional and experienced bureaucrats/higher level civil servants, on the other, has eroded the quality of modern governance and undermined the governing ability of politicians polarized by ideological, political, and economic tendencies. This problem has caused a general diminution of legitimacy for modern governments in the eyes of citizens, who seem to have lost confidence in and become more disenchanted with their governments (Waldo 1981; Lipset 1987; Farazmand 1989b; Rosen 1986; Levine 1988). The fact is that all these approaches or tendencies can be complementary and benefit of public administration and the modern systems of governance, whether presidential or parliamentary, democratic or authoritarian, developed or developing.

Themes of the Book

This book is organized around the major themes of professionalism, bureaucracy, governance, and the relationship between career bureaucrats/

higher level civil servants and political appointees/politicians under presidential and parliamentary systems. These broad themes are discussed by all contributors throughout the book. However, some chapters devote more attention to some themes than others. Therefore, the major themes of professionalism, bureaucracy, and governance are analyzed in the context of bureaucrats' and politicians' relationship in the broadest scope. This is followed by a discussion of each of these concepts and themes in the contexts of presidential and parliamentary systems. Therefore, the chapters of this book are divided into three parts, moving from the broader themes to the application of the themes to the specific political systems. Along with the main themes emerge a number of others, including the politics-administration dichotomy; the professional state, democracy, and bureaucracy; corruption, civil service reform; the politicization of bureaucracy, the professionalization of bureaucracy; bureaucratic power, political power; administrative or bureaucratic discretion; separation of powers, and restructuring, reinventing, or shrinking the modern state; and replacing the welfare state.

Professionalism, Bureaucracy, and Modern Governance

The first set of general themes in this book focuses on the concept of professionalism of the bureaucracy and its implications for modern governance. Several divergent theories or tendencies emerge in the discussion. One theory treats bureaucracy and professionalization of bureaucracy as a danger to democracy and representative government. Proponents of this theory (Finer 1941; Meier 1987; Mosher 1968; Wilson 1986) contend that nonelected professional administrators, and the professional bureaucracy in general, not only play a policy implementation role in the governance process but also make policy decisions that they should not. Therefore, there is a growing danger to democracy and representative government. The threat of professionalization of the bureaucracy involves the danger of creating the "professional state" (Mosher 1968) and the "bureaucratic state" (Wilson 1989). Consequently, professionalism is viewed by critics as a hindrance to democratic governance. Of course, public choice theorists are among the strong opponents of a professional bureaucracy that is motivated by budget-maximizing bureaucrats who seek to further their personal and professional interests in the policy process (Downs 1965; Niskanen 1971; Ostrom 1973).

Countering this argument are a host of proponents of a professionalism that builds institutional competence; has expertise equipped with professional standards and criteria that safeguard the constitutional principles and values of fairness, individual rights, and broad societal public interests;

and prevents partisan political and personal abuse of powers by politicians who seek to enhance the interests of powerful, particularistic interest groups (Goodsell 1994; Newland 1987; Friedrich 1940, 1960; Farazmand 1989b; Rockman 1996).

Unfortunately, there has been a hostile relationship between experienced career civil servants who are professionals with professional standards to serve the general public interest regardless of partisan or personal interests of particular groups in society, on the one hand, and the "transients" assigned to leadership positions in government bureaucracy who are appointed according to partisan, personal, and politico-economic criteria to implement specific ideological and politic-economic policies aimed at special interest group interests, on the other. This problem has been acute, particularly in the presidential systems in which political appointees come and go frequently, with short tenure of office, but swiftly pursue the policy agenda of regimes in power, which are often in conflict with legal, constitutional, and professional requirements, values, and standards. As Peters and Rockman (1996: viii) note, "The conflict between the responsibility of the civil service in the highest sense of protecting the interests and the accountability of the civil service to higher legal authority provides one of the fundamental tensions in modern democracies."

The issues of professionalism and professional bureaucracy in modern public administration and governance occupy a central place in the discussion of all chapters in this book. Part I of this book is entirely devoted to this broad theme. Five theoretical and empirical chapters focus on the matters of professionalization of bureaucracy, bureaucratic power, and governance. Fred Riggs, Ali Farazmand, Renu Khator, Fred Thayer, and Matthew Holden present extensive analyses of these issues and their implications for public administration and politics.

Bureaucrats and Politicians in Presidential Systems

Part II of the book focuses on the relationship between politicians and bureaucrats in presidential systems of government. System separation denotes the possible distinction between the relationship of politicians and their political appointees, on the one hand, and the career bureaucrats/civil servants, on the other, under the two different political systems of governance. A presidential system is generally characterized by a strong executive power, often vested in the president, with strong constitutionally granted authority, whereas the parliamentary system generally has a stronger legislature whose majority party leader is also the chief executive leader or prime minister or chancellor. Therefore, the nature of the relationship between the bureaucratic elite and political elite may very well be different under the two political systems. Generally, there is greater harmony in the relationship between the two administrative groups under the parliamentary systems, but this may not always be the case.

The chapters in this part, by David Rosenbloom, Francis Rourke, Paul Van Riper, and Lawrence Graham, discuss the separation of powers in the U.S. constitutional system of government, the professionalization and role of the federal bureaucracy in U.S. politics and administration, and the role of transients and career bureaucrats in Latin America, Europe, and Africa.

Bureaucrats and Politicians in Parliamentary Systems

Not all parliamentary systems are alike, just as not all presidential systems are not alike. For example, postrevolutionary Iran represents both a semipresidential and semiparliamentary system with additional institutional arrangements based on Islamic principles; Brazil represents a semipresidential system, as Graham discusses in his chapter in this book; and France represents both strong presidential and parliamentary systems.

Part III, with Chapters 10 and 11, addresses in detail the theoretical and empirical aspects of parliamentary systems of governance, particularly in Continental Europe, and the relationship between bureaucrats and politicians in those democracies. Here, Guy Peters makes an extensive comparative analysis of the different political systems in Europe and the United States, while Francis Terry focuses his analysis on the United Kingdom.

The Shrinking/Downsizing State?

One of the most important issues of modern governance is the shrinking or downsizing of state by governments around the world. This is a trend that has far-reaching consequences locally and globally, and its roots are found in economics, politics, and ideology as well as managerial and organizational efficiencies. The modern state began to grow tremendously by the 1920s and the scope and functions of its activities have expanded beyond imagination. The modern state has been transformed into a strong interventionist state to solve market failure and market imperfection problems, to provide public goods, to provide for the safety and security of sovereign nations, to mediate among conflicts and claims in society, to defend its citizens, to provide various opportunities for the population, to perform redistributional and social welfare functions, to maintain stability, to enhance the regimes in power or sustain them, and so on. Consequently, the modern state has become large and includes a large bureaucracy with multifunctional activities that can have far-reaching consequences for its involvements in policy making as well as policy development and administration. The professionalization of the bureaucracy has also meant major growth in the scope and functions of public administration in the modern time. However, citizens' disenchantment and dissatisfaction with the ever expanding role of the state and bureaucracy in all spheres of society and individual life, along with growing budget deficits and higher taxation, have caused major concern regarding the role of government in society in general and the role of the bureaucracy in particular. Various ideological trends, especially from the conservative Right, have produced a major force for fundamental changes in the structure and functions of the modern governments in the United States and Britain—two major industrial powers with strong global leadership capable of influencing a strategic policy of governmental restructuring around the globe. For example, the World Bank has allocated more than $20 billion to implement a policy of privatization around the world. This global, strategic policy of governmental restructuring has included retrenchment, downsizing of personnel and civil service, privatization, commercialization or marketization, contracting out and shrinking governmental functions, and promotion of private business enterprises. There is a major political ideology behind this global strategic policy as well as major consequences for modern governance and public administration. The concluding chapter in this book is by Bert Rockman, who presents a succinct analysis of this phenomenon in late twentieth-century governance.

The above introductory notes suggest the importance and centrality of a professional administrative system for the effective and responsive governance of modern society. A cooperative and supportive relationship between politicians and bureaucrats in this new web of the political-administrative system is extremely important. Ideologically based statements and other policy decisions mean nothing unless they are implemented by competent and responsible administrators who are also part of the guidance process of governance. And competence rests on professionalism, which is itself based on standards of fairness, quality, and responsiveness, all in the service of the general public interest. Professionalism is also a solid safeguard against various forms of political corruption, including the initiation of marketized government operations.

We hope this book will fill any gaps in the literature on the relationship between bureaucrats and politicians in modern governance and public administration. This book can be used as a primary or supplementary text in the areas of public personnel administration, conceptual foundations and scope of public administration, comparative public policy, bureaucratic politics, and government as well as seminars on bureaucracy and politics at graduate and undergraduate levels. It can also be a resource for libraries, researchers, teachers, and students in government, political science, and public administration as well as policy designers and policy-making officials.

References

Downs, Anthony. (1965) *Inside Bureaucracy.* Boston: Little, Brown.

Farazmand, Ali. (1989a) *The State, Bureaucracy, and Revolution in Modern Iran: Agrarian Reform and Regime Politics.* Westport, CT: Praeger.

———. (1989b) "Crisis in the U.S. Administrative State." *Administration & Society,* 21, 2: 173-199.

———. (1996) "Introduction: The Comparative State of Public Enterprise Management." In Ali Farazmand, ed., *Public Enterprise Management.* Westport, CT: Greenwood.

———. (Forthcoming) "Administration of the Persian Achaemenid World-State Empire: Implications for Modern Public Administration." *International Journal of Public Administration.*

Finer, Herman. (1941, Summer) "Administrative Responsibility in Democratic Government." *Public Administration Review,* 1: 335-350.

Friedrich, Carl. (1940) "Public Policy and the Nature of Administrative Responsibility." In Carl Friedrich and Edward Mason, eds., *Public Policy 1940.* Cambridge, MA: Harvard University Press.

———. (1960) "The Dilemma of Administrative Responsibility." In Carl Friedrich, ed., *Responsibility,* pp. 189-202. New York: Liberal Arts Press.

Goodsell, Charles. (1994) *The Case for Bureaucracy: A Public Administration Polemic.* 2nd ed. Chatham, NJ: Chatham House.

Heclo, Hugh. (1977) *A Government of Strangers: Executive Politics in Washington.* Washington, DC: Brookings Institution.

Huntington, Samuel. (1968) *Political Order in Changing Society.* New Haven, CT: Yale University Press.

Lenin, V. Illich. (1971) *State and Revolution.* New York: International Publishers.

Levine, Charles. (1985) "Where Policy Comes From: Ideas, Innovations, and Agenda Choices." *Public Administration Review,* 45: 255-258.

———. (1988) "Human Resources Erosion and the Uncertain Future of the U.S. Civil Service: From Policy Gridlock to Structural Fragmentation." *Governance,* 1: 115-143.

Lipset, S. M. (1987, Spring) "The Confidence Gap During the Reagan Years, 1981-1987." *Political Science Quarterly:* 1-23.

Long, Norton. (1949) "Power and Administration." *Public Administration Review,* 9: 257-264.

———. (1952, September) "Bureaucracy and Constitutionalism." *American Political Science Review,* 46: 808-818.

Meier, K. J. (1987) *Politics and the Bureaucracy: Policy Making in the Fourth Branch of Government.* 2nd ed. Monterey, CA: Brooks/Cole.

Mosher, Frederick C. (1968) *Democracy and the Public Service.* 2nd ed. New York: Oxford University Press.

Newland, Chester. (1987) "Public Executives: Imperium, Sacerdotium, Collegium? Bicentennial Leadership Challenges." *Public Administration Review,* 47, 1: 45-56.

Niskanen, William R. (1971) *Bureaucracy and Representative Government.* Chicago: Aldine-Atherton.

Ostrom, Vincent, Jr. (1973) *The Intellectual Crisis of Public Administration in America.* University, AL: University of Alabama Press.

Peters, Guy, and Bert Rockman, eds. (1996) *Agenda for Excellence: Administering the State 2.* Chatham, NJ: Chatham House.

Riggs, Fred. (1994) "Bureaucracy: A Profound Puzzle for Presidentialism." In Ali Farazmand, ed., *Handbook of Bureaucracy,* pp. 97-148. New York: Marcel Dekker.

Riposa, Gerry. (1996) "Public Enterprises in Nicaragua." In Ali Farazmand, ed., *Public Enterprise Management.* Westport, CT: Greenwood.

Rockman, Bert. (1996) "Conclusion." In Guy Peters and Bert Rockman, eds., *Agenda for Excellence: Administering the State 2,* pp. 163-177. Chatham, NJ: Chatham House.

Rohr, John. (1986) *To Run a Constitution.* Lawrence: University Press of Kansas.

Rosen, B. (1986) "Crisis in the U.S. Civil Service." *Public Administration Review,* 46, 3: 195-215.

Waldo, Dwight. (1981) *The Enterprise of Public Administration.* Novato, CA: Chandler & Sharp.

————. (1986) "Bureaucracy and Democracy: Reconciling the Irreconcilable." In *Current Issues in Public Administration.* 3rd ed., pp. 455-469. New York: St. Martin's.

Wamsley, Garry, and associates. (1987). "Public Administration and the Governance Process: Refocusing the American Dialogue." In R. C. Chandler, ed., *A Centennial History of the American Administrative State.* New York: Free Press.

Wamsley, Garry, Charles Goodsell, John Rohr, Orion White, and James Wolf. (1992) "A Legitimate Role for Bureaucracy in Democratic Government." In Larry Hill, ed., *The State of Public Bureaucracy,* pp. 59-86. New York: M. E. Sharpe.

Weber, Max. (1946) *From Max Weber: Essays in Sociology.* H. H. Gerth and Wright Mills, trans. and eds. New York: Oxford University Press.

Wilson, James Q. (1989). *Bureaucracy.* New York: Basic Books.

PART

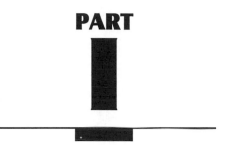

Professionalism, Bureaucracy, and Modern Governance

The first set of general themes in this book focuses on the concept of professionalism of the bureaucracy and its implications for modern governance. As discussed in the general introduction, there are several competing theories on the role of a professional bureaucracy in public administration and governance. One theory treats bureaucracy and the professionalization of bureaucracy as a danger to democracy and representative government. The second tendency or theory defends professionalization and the role of the professional bureaucracy as a necessary institution for effective governance. This approach argues that a government that cannot administer efficiently and effectively is a bad government. Only a government equipped with professional competence is a good and effective government. Accordingly, a cooperative and supportive relationship between politicians and their appointees, on the one hand, and the appointed career bureaucrats, especially the higher civil servants, on the other, is imperative in the administration of modern systems of governance. Still another theory further argues that as guardians of the Constitution and the general public interest, or "common good," the senior professional bureaucrats or administrators should be granted some sort of constitutional empowerment to veto any politicians' decisions or actions deemed against the interests of the general public and that serve particular powerful private interests. Supporters of this approach cite a variety of reasons for such an empowerment of professional bureaucracy and bureaucratic actions.

Although the issues of professionalism and professional bureaucracy in modern public administration and governance occupy a central place in the discussions in all chapters in this book, Part I discusses this broad theme in detail. Five theoretical and empirical chapters focus on the matters of professionalization of bureaucracy, bureaucratic power, and governance. In Chapter 1, Fred Riggs sets a theoretical and conceptual tone for the issues of professional bureaucracy and bureaucratic power, and their implications for governance of modern political systems under parliamentarism and presidentialism. Riggs develops a typology of bureaucratic power from powerless to dominant, at the two ends of the continuum, with the powerful and semipowered bureaucracies in between. To Riggs, professionalization of bureaucracy can potentially endanger the political systems of governments. Riggs' s typology provides a framework for analysis of the relationship between bureaucrats and politicians. He argues that coups and "crashes" take place when the political regime in power loses legitimacy as a result of many direct factors as well as from "bureaucratic fatigue," which refers to disenchanted and frustrated bureaucrats who look for a power alignment against the regime, contributing to its sudden fall or "crash." These bureaucrats simply submit to the new regime or, if dominant, will dominate the polity and take over the government. Because the military is also included in the discussion of bureaucracy, the military-civilian alignment is often seen as the strategy that civilian bureaucracy uses in crashing the regime in question. Therefore, according to Riggs, in political systems with powerful bureaucracies—in most developing countries as well as Eastern Europe and the formerly communist countries—bureaucrats tend to engage in coalition building and use their professional expertise as a basis of power in coups d'état that cause regime collapse.

Such a conceptual argument raises a broad question, among others, about the general relationship between bureaucratic elites and political elites among nations. But Riggs asserts that professionalism has contributed to the strong power position of bureaucracy and bureaucrats—both civilian and military—who find their power base to be an instrument in administration and governance processes. Rejecting the traditional myth of a politics-administration dichotomy, Riggs argues that career administrators are engaged in a variety of ways in politics and the policy-making process, but he also fears that unless bureaucratic power is curtailed, it can pose a serious threat to the democracy so cherished by representative governments. His major concern is that powerful professional bureaucracies tend to take independent actions against constitutional political systems and the regimes they find unworkable; this theme is elaborated throughout his chapter. He finds this problem mostly in presidential systems of governance in which a "powerful" bureaucracy is in charge of an administration staffed by trained professionals. In presidential systems, the relationship between the higher level civil servants and the top bureaucrats, political appointees, and elected officials is an uneven one: Career bureaucrats have professional expertise, experience, and long-term tenure. Political appointees come to office because of patronage or partisan and political/personal preferences; although their tenure of office is generally short, their job is to provide organizational and policy leadership for the bureaucracy in charge of administration. When the bureaucracy is "powerful," bureacrats tend to form alliances with the military bureaucratic elite and cause a crash in the regime they are unhappy with.

To Riggs, presidential systems of governance are more vulnerable to breakdown from powerful bureaucracies than are parliamentary systems. However, the only exception in presidential systems is the United States, which has a "semipowered" bureaucracy, not a powerful one. This is a reason for the survival of the American presidential system, even though most if not all other presidential systems in the contemporary world have failed. Parliamentary systems, according to Riggs's typology, have generalist bureaucracies that are strong and efficient but are also controlled well by the dominant political party in parliament; therefore, it is easier to exercise control over these mandarin bureaucrats, who can move from one agency to another and provide stability and continuity to the government and administration.

Chapter 2, by Ali Farazmand, counters many of Riggs's arguments regarding the threat of bureaucrats and professional bureaucracy in causing regime collapse, particularly in modern developing nations. Citing the ancient cases of the Persian Empire and other powers as well as the later Ottoman Empire, Farazmand analyzes professionalism and the professional state in a historical context that shows the ancient origins of modern public administration and governance. He discusses the Chinese, Assyrian, Persian, and Roman empires, and focuses on the "world-state Achaemenid Persian Empire" in some detail, in which the bureaucracy was professionalized by training and experience and held a highly powerful and esteemed position in governance and society. The bureaucracy was indispensable for effective governance. Professionalization of the bureaucracy and administration increased effectiveness of governance in the empire; at the same time, the bureacracy showed tendencies of overpowering the weak political authorities of the king whenever it could. However, the centralization of the professional bureaucracy was geared more to effective governance and efficient administration than it was a threat to the regime itself. Never did the bureaucracy attempt to break the system down and "crash" it for self-interest, either when it was dominant or when it was fatigued. The bureaucratic elite was not separable from the political and economic elite of the nobility.

Analyzing the political economy of the modern U.S. bureaucracy and its professionalization, as well as the role of public bureaucracy in developing countries, whether presidential or parliamentary systems, in some detail, Farazmand argues that bureaucratic elite engaging in coalition-building strategies to bring down the American presidential system would be a suicidal exercise; there is no incentive for the bureaucratic elite to crash a regime it is a leading part of it. Further, he argues that the bureaucratic elites in developing nations enjoy little or no autonomy of their own and are integral parts of the ruling elites—economic and political as well as administrative—and thus their attempt to engage in coups d'état to crash the regimes in power would not be the major determining factor in the process of regime breakdown. Most developing countries have only nominally independent systems; they are highly dependent politically and economically on the Western superpowers, particularly the United States. The strategic elites, including the administrative and bureaucratic elites, are also dependent on the foreign powers for their material benefit, power, positions, and privileges. Farazmand argues that it is the dominant foreign powers—in addition to internal revolutions or a combination of both, such as Iran under the shah—that actually cause the breakdowns and crashes of the regimes considered unfriendly or challenging (Iran under Premier Mussadegh in 1953, Egypt under Nasser, Indonesia under Sukarno in the 1960s, and Chile under Allende in the 1970s). Their local bureaucratic elites act only in accordance with the interests of the strategic elites whose goals and actions are in harmony with foreign powers, including the multinational corporations protected by their governments. If the Cuban regime under Castro breaks down sometime in the future, it would be because of the system's internal deficiencies plus the overwhelming external political, economic, financial, propaganda, and military pressures of the United States and its allies who have kept Cuba under continuous blockade; it would not be crashed by the Cuban bureaucracy, no matter how disenchanted it might be. Nevertheless, evidence shows that in popular revolutions, the lower echelons of the bureaucracy, alienated and repressed by an unpopular regime, have a tendency to join the revolutionary movements. Examples include Iran during the revolution of 1978-1979, Nicaragua, and the Philippines.

Farazmand also contends that Western European governments have not experienced frequent regime breakdowns in part because that they are not highly dependent on or influenced by external powers, and their bureaucracies are major actors in the policy processes. Farazmand further argues that professionalization of modern public administration is no threat to democracy. In fact, he points out that professionalization of bureaucracy should be increased to prevent corruption and abuse of power by politicians and political elites, who are often motivated to further their own personal interests as well as those of the powerful—big business—interests. Farazmand concludes that parliamentary bureaucracies are more powerful and effective and are more in harmony with their legislative parliaments in policy making and administration; the professionalization of bureaucracy in these systems has benefited the process of modern governance, not hindered it. A professional bureaucracy can contribute to a more effective checks-and-balance system of governance and serve the general public interest better than a less powerful or nonprofessional and patronage-based one.

In Chapter 3, Renu Khator puts Riggs's conceptual and theoretical points to an empirical test by raising a number of hypotheses with India as a case study. A former British colony and a country with ancient administrative and cultural traditions, India was divided into two nations in 1947: India and Pakistan. Focusing on the issues of professionalism and the role of the bureaucracy in governance, Khator argues against Riggs's thesis and shows that India has had a powerful bureaucracy and a stable political system, with no regime breakdown or crashes, whereas Pakistan has experienced several such breakdowns since partition. After discussing in detail the nature of the U.S. and Indian bureaucracies, Khator concludes that the Indian bureaucracy has maintained a low-level professional status with a strong mandarin system checked by the cultural and social forces of the society. Pakistan's bureaucracy, on the other hand, has experienced a shifting alliance with the military, which can be explained by external factors (à la Farazmand) as well as domestic factors. In general, Khator tends to support much of Riggs's theses about parliamentary and presidential systems and the role of their bureaucracies in modern governance.

The fourth chapter, by Fred Thayer, focuses on the two civil service reforms of 1883 and 1978 in the United States. His argument is that the original mission of the civil service reform of 1883 was to be a "watchdog, the moral guardian of governmental decision making," "not . . . solely to improve government 'efficiency.' " He states that, indeed, the Pendleton

Act of 1883 "actually was the full equivalent of a constitutional amendment, even though there was no way to describe it as such." In a nutshell, Thayer's first point is that the Civil Service Reform of 1883 was a measure to abolish the rampant spoils system and ensuing political corruption that was crippling the political system and the government. The reform established an institution of professional civil servants to prevent massive corruption, to limit the partisan political abuse of government employees for personal and partisan purposes, and to promote efficiency in the administration of modern governance. The Hatch Act of 1939 was also a reinforcing measure toward professionalization to get rid of corruption by politicians—by both political parties—and to control many governmental operations. Professional civil servants would be able to question the ethical, moral, and legal bases of decisions made by politicians and patronage appointees.

Thayer's second major argument is that the Civil Service reform Act of 1978 and the Clinton Administration's National Performance Review measures—not to mention Reagan's sweeping measures—have basically crippled the federal civil service, and the professional bureaucracy, once a guardian of the patronage corruption, has been reduced to an institutional arrangement for personal and partisan benefit. Carter's CSRA was a major step toward making the federal bureaucracy more like a business enterprise system of hiring and firing, making it much easier to fire bureaucrats deemed undesirable. Job security gave professional civil servants—especially higher level civil servants—the ability to function professionally and guard the constitutional system of values. "Now that job security has been largely stripped away, the guardians are powerless." Thayer's argument has significant implications for the relationships between politicians and bureaucrats as well as for modern governance and administration. His contribution completely rejects Riggs's thesis, discussed earlier. A crippled or hollow professional bureaucracy would be used as an instrument of political, economic, and moral corruption in the constitutive system of modern governance, and this would work against democracy, not in favor of it, as can be seen in the current political fervor.

In Chapter 5, Matthew Holden makes a profound contribution to administrative theory in general and bureaucratic theory and professionalism in particular. His discussions focus on the centrality of administration and administrative discretion in modern governance. Administration, he states, consists in the exercise "discretion about the actual use of information, money, and force." "The centrality of administration to power is . . . a fundamental. . . . [N]o one over succeeds in power . . . without control of administration." Holden hits the core issue of modern governance: To govern effectively and efficiently, one needs a strong, competent, and professional administration, not only at the top level of the bureaucracy but also—and perhaps more important—at the field level. Professor Holden identifies bureaucrats as "the administrative political actors" who also include "field administrators operating in the territory away from the physical center of government—the capital—as well." Citing the lack of adequate academic attention to field administration research, Holden makes a major contribution to our knowledge of public administration and political science, in general, and to the relationship between politicians and bureaucrats in modern systems of governance, in particular.

Coups and Crashes:
Lessons for Public Administration

Fred W. Riggs

Bureaucratic Excesses and Fatigue

When bureaucrats feel pushed to the wall and see no solutions to their problems within the confines of constitutional rules and customary norms, they may, in desperation, choose one of two contradictory options. The first involves a suspension of the rules and the imposition of bureaucratic domination—as commonly seen in contemporary *coups d'état*. The alternative reaction involves surrender—the abandonment of efforts to cope with current administrative problems—a choice that can contribute to regime *crashes*. I shall call the first *bureaucratic excesses* and the second *bureaucratic fatigue*. Both of these responses are based on extreme forms of bureaucratic frustration, as when officials cannot understand or carry out the tasks expected of them and/or when great insecurities and stress result from inadequate rewards, both objective and subjective, for their efforts.

Excessive responses include efforts to seize power and suspend the normal rules for running a government, as manifested in a constitution and public laws. The first sense of excess as defined in *Webster's New Universal Unabridged Dictionary (WD2)* involves "action or conduct that goes beyond the usual, reasonable or lawful limit." Bureaucratic excesses occur when civil servants support military officers in their efforts to seize power and set aside the normal constraints imposed by responsible governments, leading to arbitrary actions, corruption, and even apathetic neglect of duty.

By contrast, *fatigue,* as this word is used in physiology, means "the decreased ability of an organism . . . to function because of prolonged exertion" *(WD2)*. In mechanics, the same term is used to characterize the breakdown of materials (as in an airplane) caused by continuing and intolerable strains. Bureaucratic fatigue occurs when officials become totally exhausted—it refers to a collective pathology that goes beyond the kind of *burnout* to which individual bureaucrats are so often subject. As described by Robert K. Merton, heavily disciplined bureaucrats stress "conformance with regulations" and develop "rigidities and an inability to adjust readily" (1957: 199). Such tendencies are sharply aggravated under single-party rule and contribute to regime breakdowns like those that occurred in the Soviet Union.

The coup d'état. Bureaucratic excess is evident in the frequent coups that have occurred in many Third World states since they achieved their independence as all the modern empires collapsed after World War II. The phenomenon has been analyzed extensively to discover both its causes and what can be done to prevent further coups or reestablish constitutional government. See Finer (1976), Janowitz (1977), Kennedy (1974), Linz and Stepan (1978), Stepan (1988), Taylor and Hudson (1983), and Thompson (1973). Most research on coups and military rule has been carried out by scholars primarily interested in political phenomena. An exception can be found in the work of Ferrel Heady (1995) He offers, for public administration, a typology of various kinds of *bureaucratic-prominent political regimes* (pp. 332-394). Although not all of them are *bureaucratic polities* as I understand this phenomenon, we would agree that bureaucrats play a prominent political role in all of them, and our two typologies overlap.

In addition to analysis of the causes and consequences of coups, political scientists and public administrationists may also view them as an intellectual challenge: What can we learn from them? If we view coups and crashes as *teachers,* we will find, I think, that they can be quite instructive. They will contribute to comparative governance a better understanding of what enables any democratic regime to survive, to administer public policies effectively, and also, more specifically, to see why our truly exceptional American regime has not suffered the kind of breakdown that has been universally experienced by all other presidentialist systems of government.

How exceptional the American experience has been becomes apparent, I think, when it is contrasted with the fate (as of 1985) of 30 other presidentialist regimes, all of which had experienced coups by then. This contrasts with some 43 parliamentary regimes, of which only 13 (39%) had suffered coups before 1985. Data can be found in Riggs (1993, table I). Consider also the fact that, among the industrialized countries, all those with stable democratic governments except the United States are parliamentary in form: The United States is the only industrialized country to maintain a presidentialist regime for an extended period of time. It has not experienced a constitutional collapse for more than 200 years despite acute crises such as the Civil War, a major depression, and two world wars.

To explain the American exception, we must ask how, despite the inherent contradictions and fragility of a constitutional regime based on the separation of powers, the U.S. government has managed to retain control over its bureaucracy. One of the reasons, among the many that may be offered, is surely the inability of American public officials (military and civil) to band together to seize power and replace the formal political institutions of constitutional government—that is, the relative powerlessness of bureaucracy in the United States.

Moreover, the unique design of the American career services, by contrast with the prevalence of patronage systems in other presidentialist regimes, permits a relatively high level of administrative competence to prevail in America, thereby reducing, though not fully overcoming, the public's antipathy toward government. Even when bureaucratic performance is viewed as a purely administrative phenomenon, without political significance, the fact is that wretched public administration undermines public confidence in government and contributes to the growth of the popular discontents that sustain coups d'état. Although coups are typically viewed as the precursors of *military rule*, a more useful understanding of these sad events sees them as *bureaucratic* revolts leading to political domination by appointed government officials, both military and civil—a state of affairs properly characterized as a *bureaucratic polity*.

Bureaucracy. I use *bureaucracy* here to mean a collectivity that includes all the appointed officials of a state: military as well as civil, transients as well as long-termers, higher as well as lower level personnel, and those in state and local government as well as those in central (national) government. It includes cabinet officers (if they are not elected members of parliament), generals and colonels, high-level managers and directors, lowly civil servants and soldiers. This concept is required for the comparative study of coups.

Because of radical differences in the way different bureaucracies are organized, it is impossible to make meaningful comparisons if we limit our concept of bureaucracy to any subset of appointed officials or to the unique features of a particular bureaucracy, like the American system. Just as we use *fruit* to characterize and compare a wide variety of edible plants, such as plums, bananas, and lemons, so we need a generic concept for the many types of bureaucracy found in different countries if we want to make comparisons between them. A definition based on the specific features of any one system, like the American, cannot support comparisons with other varieties of bureaucracy, any more than one can compare apples and oranges. However, with a generic concept, like fruit, one can easily compare those that have only one seed with those that have many, those that are sweet with those that are sour, the segmented with the nonsegmented, and so on. Just as we can compare apples and oranges as two kinds of fruit, so we can distinguish between different kinds of bureaucracy, but only after identifying a generic concept that applies to all of its many varieties.

To illustrate, we can easily characterize the components of a bureaucracy as central versus local, higher level versus lower level, civil servants versus military officers, careerists versus transients, partisan versus nonpartisan, and so on. But when we use *bureaucracy* to mean any specific subset of bureaucrats, comparisons that involve other subsets of the same concept cannot be made. No doubt, when the context clearly indicates that a particular subset is intended, *bureaucracy* can be used imprecisely for that subset, just as one may casually use *fruit* to refer to an apple. However, here I shall use *bureaucracy* only for the broad category that includes all appointed officials serving a particular government, including many subtypes and diverse components.

No doubt, the word *bureaucracy* also has some other meanings, but we can easily identify them by using different terms. For details, see Albrow (1970), Beetham (1987), and Riggs (1979).

The most important of these senses, for present purposes, was its original meaning, as suggested by its etymology: It was coined in the eighteenth century—in parallel with *aristocracy, monarchy,* and *democracy*—to mean a type of political system dominated by appointed officials. A modern use of the word in this sense can still be found in Lasswell and Kaplan (1950: 209-210). However, this usage is extremely rare and, I believe, confusing. Consequently, I will call any such system a *bureaucratic polity*. Essentially, every coup creates or re-creates a bureaucratic polity (Riggs 1966; Girling 1981). Consequently, this is a necessary concept for use in this chapter but we risk misleading each other if we use *bureaucracy* in its original sense.

Sometimes *bureaucracy* refers to an institution in which officials are employed—what may be called a government *organization* or a *public agency.* Sociologists often use *bureaucracy* to refer to a particular kind of organization, such as one that manifests the properties identified by Max Weber in his ideal type—we could call them *Weberian organizations.*

When one speaks of a bureaucratic organization, one often has in mind a particular kind of organizational design or phenomenon, such as one that stresses hierarchic authority rather than polyarchic or matrix structures. This concept might better be called a *machine bureaucracy,* following the usage found in Mintzberg (1983: 163-187). Economists sometimes use *bureaucracy* for governmental organizations by contrast with market-oriented corporations. All these concepts are important, but we can distinguish them more clearly by using the italicized synonyms mentioned above rather than the word *bureaucracy.*

In public administration, *bureaucracy* is often used as a synonym for *public administration,* including both the function of implementing government policies and the organizations responsible for this activity. The word is also found in popular usage as a term for organizational pathologies: "unnecessary complications, constraining standardization, the stifling of individual personality" (Crozier 1963: 1). I prefer to use *bureaupathology* for this concept, following Thompson (1976: 90-91). Whenever I need to refer to any of these additional meanings of *bureaucracy,* I will avoid using this word, substituting one of the unambiguous synonyms mentioned above.

Bureaucratic polities. As noted above, the original sense of bureaucracy has become increasingly important but the word is no longer used in this sense. Moreover, because military officers alone can command the means of violence needed for a successful coup, we tend to think of the regimes they form as *military.* However, we need to remember that military officers are bureaucrats and that some civil servants usually support the military officers who stage a coup. Without their support, moreover, military officers typically cannot govern effectively.

Remember that both civil and military personnel are adversely affected by a government's failure to govern well: Their status and security depend on the regular provision of salaries, pensions, and other perquisites of office. Of course, not all bureaucrats (military or civil) support every coup—many remain aloof waiting to see what will happen, and many nonofficials (private citizens, merchants and bankers, landlords and peasants, doctors, professors, and students, and so on) may also rally to support or oppose a coup. The concept of a "bureaucratic polity" merely means that some appointed (not elected) officials (military and civil) play a leading role in creating and maintaining a bureaucratic polity.

Actually, the promoters of a coup are typically only a small cabal of activists working secretly inside the framework of a much larger bureaucracy. Sometimes, during a major crisis, they are able to mobilize enough support to overthrow the constitutional organs of government and to seize power in the expectation that, thereby (under the leadership of the military), they will be able to restore stable government and safeguard their official privileges.

No doubt, different observers draw conflicting lessons from this experience, but I offer the hypothesis that most modern bureaucracies are powerful enough to seize power whenever the constitutionally authorized system of government cannot cope effectively with a major crisis. The coup need not result from greed or ambition—rather, the primary cause is the inability of a regime to cope with severe crises and meet the minimal requirements or expectations of the body of officials (public bureaucrats) whom they have appointed.

Such failures may also be viewed as the result of a regime's inability to control or lead the bureaucracy. The unsatisfactory levels of administrative *performance* that result contribute to so much dissatisfaction with government that coup leaders normally count on widespread popular support for their seizure of power. The explosive mixture of popular and bureaucratic discontent often combines to fuel revolutionary movements promoting violent political transformations. However, before such movements can succeed, the organizers of a military coup usually win the support of threatened social and economic elites who, normally, back bureaucratic rule as less of a threat to their own interests than popular revolution.

Regime crashes. Bureaucratic fatigue, by contrast, does not lead to coups; party-dominated bureaucrats become too demoralized and passive to be able to organize any coherent or energetic response. Instead, they fail to act, and this failure becomes, then, a motor for the crash of regimes. No doubt, internal contradictions within the ruling party and widespread popular discontent were the direct causes of the recent crises that led to the collapse of the communist regimes in Eastern Europe and the Soviet Union—the classic cases, now, of political crashes.

Crash is not currently used in this political sense, but it has the closely related meaning of "to fail suddenly, as a business or an economy" *(American Heritage Dictionary [AHD]).* Until the recent crash of the Soviet polity and the East European regimes, it was scarcely a phenomenon calling for analysis. Now, however, we need the concept of a sudden more or less violent collapse of a political regime brought about by its internal dynamics rather than by any external force such as a foreign conquest, a political revolution, or a military coup. The concept of a political crash, based on the experiences of the former Soviet Union and Yugoslavia, now seems to be so important that we need a convenient term for it. Until someone suggests a better synonym, let me refer to it as a *crash*.

The immediate reason for a crashing single-party regime is, I believe, the inability of its ruling party to handle serious crises. However, an underlying reason is surely the administrative incapacity of its bureaucracy and the massive popular discontents that such failures fuel. I believe that bureau fatigue is the underlying reason. It explains the inherent incapacity of officials in a single-party regime to carry out their administrative responsibilities with energy and creative imagination. Such regimes cannot tolerate a politically effective legislature, nor, I believe, can they permit their bureaucrats to exercise real leadership and to control enough resources to carry out their duties effectively and with enthusiasm. When all initiative is concentrated in the central organs of the ruling party, the independent exercise of power outside those organs is suppressed.

Admittedly, this is a speculation based on limited knowledge. Until the breakdown of the U.S.S.R., it has been difficult to gain a realistic understanding of how party officials and bureaucrats interacted at the working level. However, a remarkable collection of Russian local-government records captured by the Germans and subsequently transferred to American authorities give us some revealing details. The captured material was analyzed by Merle Fainsod (1958) and it shows, in detail, how party leaders struggled to impose their policies and preferences on local bureaucrats and how these demoralized officials reacted, often seeking to obstruct the implementation of party directives.

For example, a "closed letter" from Rumyantsev, first secretary of the *obkom bureau* in the Smolensk region, that was circulated in 1934, called attention to "unhealthy and disgraceful symptoms which exist in a number of organizations: . . . administrative excesses . . . cheating in workers' wages, embezzlement and peculation . . . insensitive reactions of many Party organizations to these disorders and crimes" (Fainsod 1958: 105-106). This glimpse into the Soviet system of local administration depicts the powerlessness and extreme frustrations of local officials under single-party rule as well as the many expedients used by them to resist unworkable expectations and, at the same time, to exploit the system for their personal benefit.

We can also understand, I think, why public officials in such cases lack the cohesiveness and energy to seize power by means of a coup d'état. Actually, the officials in Fainsod's account organized informally, in "family circles," to obstruct program goals. The administrative failures that resulted help us to understand why an increasingly hungry and angry population should so passively accept the collapse of their government.

Preconditions for success. If we assume that the extremes of bureau excess (as shown in coups) and bureau fatigue (as revealed by crashes) are not surprising, then should we not focus our attention on the preconditions for bureaucratic vigor? Do they not require regimes that can maintain effective control over their bureaucrats while simultaneously giving them enough support to enable them to administer successfully? Effective control is needed to prevent bureaucratic excesses, but bureau power is also required to enable officials to manage creatively and effectively.

To formulate more precise and testable theories relating to the intermediate degrees of control and empowerment required for administrative success and the maintenance of democratic government, we need, I think, to be clear about three basic variables relevant to all *bureaucracies*. Please remember that I use this word for the set of all appointed officials (military and civil, career and transient) found in any system of government—a truly generic concept. These generalizations will not be relevant if we use the word only for a particular kind of bureaucrat (like apples); rather, they require a general concept that applies to all the varieties (like fruit).

Bureaucratic Power, Performance, and Cohesiveness

The three bureaucratic variables noted above are *power, performance,* and *cohesiveness*. They are closely linked to and affect each other. Because these terms are also subject to ambiguities and limitations, I shall discuss each in turn.

Note first, however, the fundamental difference between the properties of a single entity and those of an aggregate of entities. Although the same terms are often applied to both, they have to be understood in a different way. An individual or an organization, for example, can take action directly so as to exercise power or to accomplish a goal. By contrast, an aggregate cannot.

However, members of an aggregate—such as a "bureaucracy," a set of officials—have a power potential to the degree that they can mobilize for collective action. We may, for example, think about the sum of their separate actions. To the degree that individuals in a class affect a government's decisions, they can be said to have power. In this sense, we often speak of "farmers," "workers," "capitalists," "doctors," or "legislators" as exercising power. Such aggregated power, however, differs from the power that the same individuals can exercise through such formal organizations as the Grange, the AFL, the NAACP, the NAM, or the AMA. Bureaucrats can exercise power both individually and collectively, but we need to distinguish between these levels when thinking about this matter.

Power. The degree to which bureaucrats, as a collectivity, exercise power over nonbureaucrats within the government where they are employed varies significantly. To make this point more concretely, we need to identify the nonbureaucrats who, in any modern government, are organized through a constitutive system.

I claim that all modern organizations have two main parts: a polyarchic mechanism designed to articulate their collective preferences and a hierarchic apparatus established to implement these goals. Traditional (premodern) organizations may have had one of these parts, but they did not have both—or, at least, they could not link them effectively. Hierarchic structures were pervasive in premodern civilizations, and polyarchic ones were normal among "simpler" peoples, that is, those without cities.

By contrast, in all modern states, viewed as a single organization, citizens constitute their members and (in principle) act polyarchically to constitute the representative organs of governance. By contrast, they typically rely on a hierarchic apparatus composed of bureaucrats (or a staff) to implement their policies. No doubt, the distinction is never clear-cut and we find polyarchic elements in any bureaucracy and hierarchic aspects of representative systems. Moreover, many social structures—including courts of law, families, clubs, informal organizations, gangs, even heads of state—fall outside these basic components. However, these deviations from the ideal type and additional elements should not blind us to the basic structure, which also requires a linking mechanism in the form of a chief executive or cabinet.

Constitutive systems. The polyarchic (representative) machinery designed to translate citizen preferences into authoritative mandates for action has three main components: an elected assembly, an electoral system, and a party system. We need to see them as parts of a whole. Curiously, we can readily identify these three parts of a representative system but we lack an accepted term for the whole that includes all its parts. More than a quarter century ago, I proposed the term *constitutive system* to identify this gestalt (Riggs 1969: 243-246) but my suggestion has not been generally accepted. Those who find this phrase unacceptable may prefer *representative system,* but I have resisted this equivalent term because it is easily confused with *representative government,* a concept that includes the bureaucracy as well as the constitutive system. Moreover, it unnecessarily and misleadingly excludes authoritarian constitutive systems; although constitutive systems are designed to promote democracy, they can also be perverted to support single-party dictatorships.

The core component of any representative (constitutive) system is an *elected assembly,* as found in a congress, parliament, or soviet; note that even under single-party dictatorships, the formality of an elected assembly is required to legitimize the authority of the ruling party. Clearly, elected assemblies can exist only on the basis of elections, so an *electoral system* is a necessary part of any representative system. Because elections cannot be held unless candidates come forward and "stand for election," some machinery is obviously necessary to serve this function. Normally, this machinery takes the form of one or more political parties, that is, a *party system,* but in small-scale systems, nonpartisan elections may also be organized.

I chose the term *constitutive system* because it presupposes a constitution (whether written or unwritten) that links its citizens (members), as constituents, to the polity (organization) as a whole. I proposed this term because constitutive systems are, in fact, constitutive for all modern states and formal organizations. However, anyone who finds this term awkward or confusing is invited to use and recommend a better one—*representative system* is a possible synonym, as noted above. The concept is needed here to identify the political context that coups and crashes can destroy. It is important to remember that, although an elected assembly is the core component of a constitutive system, it is only a component—the system also includes electoral and party systems and their relationships to each other.

Whatever term one uses for this concept, it is an idea that can help one understand all *modern* organizations (including states). However, this involves defining *modern* in a specific way. The word is confusing because of its various possible meanings, especially when it is used to mean *contemporary.* Many contemporary organizations are not "modern" in the sense that, by definition, they have both a constitutive (representative) system and a bureaucracy.

For example, contemporary bureaucratic polities created by a coup d'état are dominated by appointed officials (military officers) who are not accountable to a representative assembly. Bureaucratic polities are, therefore, not *modern* according to the way we are using this term here, although they are quite contemporary. A more precise term would be *tonic,* an expression that suggests countervailing forces. Resistance to neologisms led me to abandon this proposal, which I spelled out long ago in Riggs (1969: 248, 301), but I'm not sure *modern* is preferable.

The point is that we need to recognize that most contemporary organizations (including states) have both a constitutive system and a bureaucracy as basic components and we need to be able to talk about them as they relate to each other. To do so, we may give a new meaning to a familiar word, like *modern,* or use a neologism, like *tonic.* Unless we accept such a term, however, we will continue to handicap ourselves when we try to analyze the basic structure of most contemporary formal organizations or states.

Finally, let us remember that both traditional and modern political systems are legitimate insofar as their members (subjects or citizens) accept the exercise of political authority as right and proper. This was clearly true in small-scale polities based on consensus, but it was also true of monarchies in which royal authority had a supernatural basis, as explained in convincing detail by Hocart (1927). As a result of secularization and democratization, however, the citizens of a modern polity accept the legitimacy of the state only when they are represented by elected officials in the making of public policies. However, because constitutive systems may work in quite different ways, we need to identify them and understand the consequences of the main options.

Types of constitutive systems. Although constitutive systems can support democratic governance, they are also found in authoritarian regimes. A single-party (closed) system that gives voters no meaningful choice among rival candidates for election is necessarily authoritarian. Its ideology may range from far right to far left, but its citizens are always required (by definition) to cast all their votes for persons nominated by leaders of the ruling party. This party also selects the head of government and claims to exercise authority on behalf of all the people. Their leaders speak of "democratic centralism," and "people's democracy," thereby obscuring our understanding of democracy.

The "myth" of popular sovereignty, however, undergirds all constitutive systems just as much as a myth of supernatural sovereignty drives traditional monarchies. We do not need to believe in such myths to see what an important role they play. No doubt, the degree to which legitimizing myths correspond to reality varies between wide extremes. Although never fully achieved, constitutional democracy becomes possible, I believe, only when the electoral system is open in the sense that competing political parties are integral to the system, that is, they do nominate candidates and the elected office holders exercise authentic power. The most important difference between types of constitutive systems, therefore, reflects the distinction between closed and open systems.

However, open constitutive systems also vary in a fundamental way according to the rule that determines how the head of government is selected. In parliamentary systems, the elected assembly must approve the chief executive (and cabinet) and may discharge the government on a vote of no confidence. Whether the head of state is an elected president or a hereditary monarch does not change the definitive character of a parliamentary system.

By contrast, in regimes based on the separation of powers, the president (as head of government) is elected separately from members of the assembly. This basic difference creates the *separation of powers* that is distinctive of presidentialism and contrasts with the *fusion of powers* typical of parliamentarism. This structural difference explains why power is fused in the former but separated in the latter; although the "separation of powers" may be mentioned in a constitutional charter, its existence is determined by the design of the constitutive system rather than the language of a document.

Other consequences follow from this structural difference. The head of government in parliamentary systems holds office for an indeterminate term because no-confidence votes can occur at any time, but without such a possibility, presidentialist regimes need to elect their head of government for a fixed term. This distinction also affects the role of head of state. In parliamentary systems, the two roles must be sharply differentiated—it would be disruptive to combine them because that would entail the possibility of making the head of state politically accountable. Consequently, the head of state must have either an indeterminate term (as a hereditary monarch) or a fixed term, as an elected president.

By contrast, when the head of government is chosen by a popular election, it would be difficult to separate the two roles and hold a separate election for the head of state. Consequently, it is typically (perhaps necessarily?) true that in presidential regimes the head of government also serves as the head of state. This practice unintentionally undermines the legitimacy of all presidentialist regimes because, inescapably, political controversies caused by the exercise of the functions of head of government override and invalidate the legitimizing functions of a head of state.

In parliamentary republics, the elected head of state may exercise substantial powers. Consequently, we cannot distinguish between presidentialist and parliamentary systems on the basis of how their heads of state are chosen or the duration of their tenure in office. Actually, such a president may also serve as head of government so long as the elected assembly is supportive. The crucial point is that when the assembly majority dissents, someone able to win its support needs to be named as head of government—the French Fifth Republic provides the salient example.

Because parliamentary republics (by contrast with constitutional monarchies) do elect their head of state for a fixed term and call him or her a "president," the two kinds of systems are easily confused, especially because the term *presidential* can be used for parliamentary systems. To make the necessary distinction clearly, I use the admittedly awkward term *presidentialist* to identify only those systems that follow the separation-of-powers principles.

However, even this word can be confusing because it is sometimes used to refer to an *imperial* presidency, as in the contrast between Franklin D. Roosevelt and Calvin Coolidge. One might say that the former was *presidentialist* but the latter was not. Anyone who uses *presidentialist* in this way may prefer to specify *separation of powers* to designate what I mean here by *presidentialist.* However, the crucial difference arises from the right of a parliamentary assembly to discharge the government on a vote of no confidence, a right denied to the congress in presidentialist systems, where, of course, there is the right of impeachment, which, however, can be used only to attack presidents accused of major crimes, not to oust a government because of policy differences.

There are, no doubt, important differences among presidentialist regimes as there also are between different kinds of parliamentary systems. We must not, however, permit these variations to hamper our perception of the properties of pure presidentialist and parliamentary regimes, a theme I have discussed in much more detail in Riggs (1994a). My goal here is not to talk about these systems as such but to consider how they affect bureaucratic behavior and power.

My basic premise is that the fusion of powers in parliamentary systems enables them to establish and maintain effective control over bureaucracies that are both more powerful politically and more effective administratively than those that presidentialist regimes can manage. By contrast, because of the separation of powers, presidential systems are inherently limited in their ability to manage a bureaucracy (see Riggs 1993, 1994a). Because this conclusion contradicts a widely held belief among American political scientists, I will discuss it at more length.

The context of bureaucracy. The separation of powers in presidential regimes, as noted above, fundamentally affects the way bureaucratic power is exercised. In such regimes, bureaucrats often find themselves in a double bind, compelled to split their loyalty between the two main branches of

powerless	semipowered	powerful	dominant

Figure 1.1 Imaginary Continuum of Bureaucratic Power

government and, frequently also, contradictory court decisions founded in the judicial branch. The resulting cross-pressures drive bureaucrats to frustration and uncoordinated action, which often enough leads to the arbitrary exercise of power and, in severe cases, to the seizure of power by means of a military coup d'état.

When bureaucrats seize power, the constitutive system is automatically overridden. Appointed officials, led by military officers, typically dominate the government, ruling by fear and coercion without benefit of the legitimacy created in modern governments by a constitutive system. The possibility of bureaucratic domination shows that we are not dealing with a simple dichotomy between "powerful" and "powerless" bureaucracies but with a continuum on which more levels can be imagined. The scale presented in Figure 1.1 may help to clarify this point.

In this figure, two terms are added to the powerful-powerless dichotomy: namely, *semipowered* and *dominant*. Normally, in functioning democracies, a powerful bureaucracy shares power (de facto, though, not de jure) with the constitutive system. A dominant bureaucracy, by contrast, is one that effectively monopolizes power and suspends the constitution, even though a nominal "constitutive system" may exist, formalistically but ineffectively.

No bureaucracy is completely powerless, but the condition may be approximated in single-party regimes where the dominant party monopolizes policy decisions and public officials serve purely instrumental functions. However, because party officers in these states typically hold many posts in the public bureaucracy, it is not easy to distinguish between bureaucratic *experts* and party activists, the *reds*. Quite often their positions and roles overlap or merge.

When we omit the extremes of bureaucratic domination and powerlessness, we see that in democratic regimes, bureau power can fluctuate between intermediate degrees of power: that is, between being powerful and being semipowered. This difference may well be crucial for the survival of democracy. I believe that we need to investigate both the causes and the consequences of these variations, and the contexts in which different levels of bureau power are appropriate or sustainable.

Performance. Most students of public administration are preoccupied with issues concerning bureaucratic performance. This concept includes a range of values starting with efficiency and effectiveness (the traditional norms) but also embracing such matters as commitments to impartiality, social justice, legality, civility, sensitivity, and professional norms. Although these properties no doubt vary independently of each other so that a given bureaucracy (or bureaucratic agencies) may do well on some but not on others, we need an overarching concept that, roughly speaking, can include all of them.

We might distinguish between *satisfactory* and *unsatisfactory* performance of administrative tasks. These words are awkward, however, because they hinge on subjective norms that can be highly variable. More objective terms, although ones that also presuppose a set of values, are *effective* and *ineffective,* terms that subsume the qualities that public administration specialists admire and deplore in the conduct of bureaucrats. However, I cannot disaggregate them here by paying separate attention to all the overlapping and competing values that public administration specialists study when analyzing bureaucratic performance.

As with the powerful-powerless dichotomy, these terms represent contraries, opposites on a scale of variation in which most cases would have to be characterized at intermediate levels, from 3 to 7, let us say, on a scale from 0 to 10. Unfortunately, no familiar words come to mind to characterize this central and usual property. Our language typically dichotomizes variables and provides no convenient intermediate terms: How do you speak of a glass of water that is half *full* or half *empty* without using one of the polar words?

Although *so-so* is only a colloquialism, it suggests what I have in mind better than *average, modest, fair, passable,* or even *sufficing* or *satisficing.* I shall use it therefore to mean that a bureaucracy's administrative performance is neither effective nor ineffective but just so-so. My guess is that in any evaluation of administrative performance, most public officials would come nearer to the "so-so" than to the "effective" or "ineffective" levels. Admittedly, I am unhappy about this term and would welcome suggestions for a better one: Please propose one!

Cohesiveness. So little has been written about cohesiveness that I am diffident about discussing it. Yet, clearly, when bureaucrats are able to join together to seize power, as they do in all bureaucratic polities, they demonstrate a high level of cohesiveness. Subsequently, no doubt, intrabureaucratic conflicts often lead to a decline of cohesiveness and succeeding coups. By contrast, the uncohesiveness associated with bureaucratic fatigue and crashes will prevent coup attempts from succeeding.

In viable democratic regimes, the degree of bureaucratic cohesiveness varies between these dysfunctional extremes. There must be enough cohesiveness so that officials can cooperate both to achieve their principled goals and also to protect their expedient interests against the adverse pressures of those who, inescapably, think their conduct is oppressive or arbitrary. I assume that most bureaucrats, having worked hard to obtain a public post, also have an interest in retaining and even enhancing the status and rewards of public office. To the degree that bureaucrats act cohesively, their joint efforts may be used both to protect their self-interests and also to advance the public interest—or the "special interests" of some segments of the public.

An analogy might be drawn with the situation among industrial workers who may or may not be able to form and support trade unions. Preoccupation with their personal careers as well as status envy may block cooperation among officials—or they may not know each other intimately enough to share personal concerns that, if made public, might impede their career prospects. In the United States, the professional norms and associations to which many bureaucrats belong, plus the dispersal of power among competing government programs and agencies reflected in the emergence of "iron triangles," stand in the way of bureaucracywide cooperation for any shared concerns—a point discussed below. Moreover, the formation of unions for government employees probably focuses attention on concrete benefits that can be negotiated with the state and, thereby, helps abort the formation of cabals designed to seize state power.

To discuss this subject, we need terms for different degrees of cohesiveness. Words such as *strong, potent, firm, solid, robust,* and *fit* come to mind. None of them is specific to the bureaucratic situation. The best, for present purposes, may be *strong* and its antonym, *weak.* We also lack an unambiguous term for the intermediate status of being neither strongly nor weakly cohesive. Could we speak of something that is *in between* or *intermediate* on a scale of "cohesiveness"?

These terms are, no doubt, cumbersome to use when talking about what is, surely, the most common situation. A better term might be *elastic.* It suggests something that is not resistant yet can also push back. The word also has positive connotations. Pending a better suggestion, therefore, I shall use *elastic* to characterize any bureaucracy that has a dormant capacity to organize in support of its interests, but is unlikely to do so until very hard-pressed. Instead, it will use its latent cohesiveness to unite in support of principled goals associated with its public service functions.

The American bureaucracy is highly "elastic." It has been well characterized by James Q. Wilson (1989: 60), who explains that "professionals" in American government agencies are more likely to accept the "standards of the external reference group than the preferences of the internal management." The dispersed orientation and loyalties of American bureaucrats make them less cohesive than virtually all other bureaucracies in viable democratic polities.

Nevertheless, the desire and ability of these officials to work together in innumerable professional associations demonstrates their capacity to be cohesive. American officials are not so incohesive as are those in countries suffering from bureau fatigue where anomie among officials prevails. The institutionalized structures of governance in the United States discourage pan-bureaucratic cohesiveness yet they encourage officials to participate in voluntary organizations that cut across public-private boundaries. The American Society for Public Administration and the National Academy of Public Administration give us two examples of how bureaucratic elasticity works in this country.

The ecological perspective. All three bureaucratic variables—power, performance, and cohesiveness—are *relative* or *context-dependent*. One cannot determine the degree to which they may be present by looking only at the internal features of bureaucracy; we must also take into account the context in which they occur. Consequently, an *ecological perspective* is needed, one in which relations between the variables and interactions between bureaucrats and their environment are taken into account.

As to their internal linkages—the most salient involves power and performance—in general, they vary directly with each other. The more powerful a bureaucracy, the more effectively it can perform. However, there is a ceiling beyond which increased power leads to dominance and a radical drop in administrative effectiveness. The ceiling, of course, is that point at which the constitutive system loses control and is overwhelmed by a coup d'état. A completely powerless bureaucracy, by contrast, suffers from fatigue and the collapse of its administrative capabilities, contributing to regime crashes.

The relation between cohesiveness and the other two variables is more complex. A dominant bureaucracy has to be cohesive to gain power, but it may subsequently lose it. A bureaucracy without any cohesiveness is powerless. I expect the most effective bureaucracies to be elastic, but among them the less powerful are also less cohesive, and the more powerful, more cohesive. However, these are broad speculations and we need a lot more information to support them or make them more precise.

Relations between a bureaucracy and its external environment affect all three variables. This is conspicuously true of bureaucratic power because its extent depends on the degree to which the constitutive system with which a bureaucracy is linked can exercise reciprocal or controlling power.

We have a kind of "tipping the scales" situation. One ounce added to the weight of A might tip the scales against B if the two are almost evenly matched, but, if not, it could make no difference at all. Similarly, a bureaucracy that would be completely powerless in one country might have overwhelming power in another. The different kinds of constitutive systems vary greatly in their capacity to create and manage bureaucracies, as discussed below under the heading "Structural Linkages."

A similar ecological interdependency also affects the two other variables discussed above. Thus the level of performance of any bureaucracy might appear to be something that could be determined by direct inspection, yet the environment of action needs to be taken into account. For example, a police department that could maintain peace and order in one community might prove quite inadequate in another. Consequently, performance levels should be evaluated in the context of variable thresholds that determine how much work of what kind is required for success.

The extent to which bureaucrats in a given country are able, cohesively, to organize themselves for collective action also varies situationally. The more they feel threatened by external events, the more they might exert themselves to meet the challenge. Such an adventitious matter as the emergence of charismatic leaders and the character of their ambitions might radically transform the capacity of a bureaucracy to take collective action in support of its interests.

In an ideal situation, where bureaucrats are respected and rewarded for their work, they may well organize to promote professional or policy goals but not to enhance their power as bureaucrats. By contrast, to the degree that they feel threatened or insecure, officials have more reasons to establish networks and structures designed to promote their collective (or class) interests as bureaucrats. The distinctively American style of bureaucratic elasticity mentioned above clearly depends on the exceptional form of presidentialism found in the United States—a theme explored below under the heading "Functionaries as Specialists."

Hyperanimated and inanimate bureaucracies. Once established, bureaucracies easily become self-animated organizations capable of furthering their own expedient goals and egocentric norms. To the degree that they are cohesive, creating their own intrabureaucratic "informal organizations" and political leadership, they can mobilize the bureaucracy as political actors promoting their own expedient interests. However, when they openly organize formally as trade unions, my guess is that they do not intend to seize power—the format of a union implies acceptance of "management" as a bargaining partner rather than any intention to replace it.

When bureaucratic interests are ignored by the constitutive system, however, bureaucrats become *hyperanimated:* Under military leadership, they organize secretly to displace the constitutive system and impose their own domination. This has happened today in many countries that are ruled by appointed officials who have seized power through a coup d'état. Such cases dramatize the process of hyperanimation and its result, coup-based bureaucratic excesses and political domination.

The opposite phenomenon can emerge under a single-party dictatorship in which the party directorate (a "politburo"), using the slogan, "democratic centralism," seeks not only to dominate the constitutive system as a whole but also to impose harsh control over all bureaucrats. Its "political commissars"—that is, party activists associated with or even sharing appointments with public officials—are able to control the bureaucracy.

Carried to extremes, such control is suffocating—the bureaucracy becomes inanimated. It cannot administer effectively and it easily falls victim to bureaucratic fatigue. It can never dominate its polity, but it can undermine its viability simply by failing to administer well enough to meet the minimal needs of the population. Although mass protests may result, the more immediate cause of such a regime's failure is neither a revolutionary movement nor a coup. Rather, it is a political crash caused by the failure of party leaders to sustain their own enthusiasm for the system. Their internal schisms can ultimately precipitate its collapse.

The disintegration of the Communist Party regimes in Eastern Europe and the Soviet Union provide evidence of the internal contradictions that can compel party leaders in such regimes to abandon power. The fate of the abortive Soviet coup of August 1991 also shows how impotent that bureaucracy was when it sought to impose its domination over the U.S.S.R. Even its ability to command nuclear weapons of mass destruction proved useless. This failed coup seems to support the proposition that bureaucratic fatigue and inanimation, rather than bureaucratic excesses, are associated with the breakdown of single-party regimes.

Further evidence that an inanimated bureaucracy cannot organize a successful coup may be found in the current history of single-party regimes in the Third World. As of 1985, of 34 such regimes, 29 (or 85%) had retained power since their creation, by contrast with the larger number of successful coups in new states striving to create democratic constitutional government (Riggs 1993, Table I). Admittedly, 5 (15%) of the single-party regimes that existed before then had been overthrown by coups (Riggs 1991: 500), but none of them collapsed because of the internal disintegration of their ruling parties.

To explain this apparent anomaly, I think that in the five single-party regimes where coups did succeed, the dominant party was not well institutionalized; it had become, instead, the facade for a dominant personality whose failings or death precipitated a collapse. Put differently, a weak authoritarian regime cannot really dominate its bureaucracy; the "ruling party" may, in such circumstances, be little more than a front for the governing elite. Moreover, the powerful bureaucracies inherited from imperial powers were usually "indigenized" by local activists who preferred careers in public office to roles in the ruling party. When seriously abused by a dominant party, they were sometimes able to capture power.

Animated bureaucracies. Ideally, of course, bureaucrats remain subject to the direction and control of the constitutive system that animates them. However, they do acquire superior knowledge and expertise within the areas of their specialized experience and competence. Effective public administration, therefore, requires not only that the technical qualifications of bureaucrats be used in public administration but also that appointed officials be enabled to help shape public policy through the constitutive system. Can we not refer to them as *animated bureaucracies?* To be effective administratively, they need to exercise real power without becoming politically dominant—they cannot be either inanimated or hyperanimated.

Consider that the legitimate interests of bureaucrats as members of a state who share in its sovereign rights ought to be satisfied. They have their own personal needs as do all citizens in a democracy. The general public, therefore, should recognize its obligation to support bureaucrats as a matter of social justice. More important, however, they should also recognize that bureaucrats must be well rewarded and honored to sustain their morale and enthusiasm. Failure to do so will adversely affect the zest required by officials if they are to serve as effective administrators. Consequently, every constitutive system faces the problem of how best to animate its bureaucracy—to keep it under effective control while granting it enough power to enable public officials both to satisfy their personal needs and also to contribute their expertise and knowledge to the formation and execution of public policies.

Within limits, therefore, the more powerful a bureaucracy is, the more effective will be its administrative performance. At the low end of powerlessness and bureau fatigue—as we now find in single-party dictatorships— a bureaucracy becomes essentially inanimate and unable to implement the policies for which it has responsibility. However, at the high end of political domination—as seen in bureaucratic polities created in the wake of military coups—self-indulgent officials not subject to extrabureaucratic controls also become ineffective administrators.

In this perspective, only democratic constitutive systems are able to animate bureaucracies enough to assure effective public administration while also retaining political control over them. To be *democratic*—in the minimal sense intended here—the constitutive system needs to have a politically potent elected assembly. Otherwise, a pliant or "rubber-stamp" legislature will endorse whatever policies the head of government promulgates: Autocracy will result. However, to maintain an independent assembly, a multiparty system is needed; if one party can dominate the constitutive system, it can also control the assembly. This means that whoever controls the ruling party is also able to dominate both the legislature and the bureaucracy.

Structural linkages. If we accept this premise, then we need to compare the two main types of open (democratic) constitutive system with reference to their capacity to animate a bureaucracy. My hypothesis is that parliamentary regimes can control their bureaucracies more effectively than can presidentialist ones—that is, the fusion of powers in cabinet government is more likely to succeed than the separation of powers found in presidentialist systems. To test this hypothesis, of course, we need to take into account all the regimes based on the separation of powers, not just the exceptional case of the United States.

Consider first that in parliamentary regimes, the fusion of powers in a government that is directly accountable to parliament permits its constitutive system to focus its efforts to animate the bureaucracy within the cabinet as the main channel for linking the constitutive system with the bureaucracy. Career officials in parliamentary regimes can be cohesively organized and they can exercise substantial influence over cabinet members and public policy without thereby jeopardizing the ability of the constitutive system to maintain effective political control over public policy. This mechanism also permits the bureaucracy to become animated as servants of the polity's general interests, not just of a congeries of separately organized special interests. Moreover, in this context, bureaucrats have much less need for direct contact with members of parliament than do public officials in presidentialist regimes, and MPs also have few incentives for consulting directly with bureaucrats (Aberbach et al. 1981: 233-235).

Parliamentary regimes, therefore, are usually able to manage and integrate their bureaucracies well enough to animate them as public administrators without losing political control over them. They can focus their attention on management issues without worrying too much about how to retain power over their own appointed officials. Put differently, the capacity of parliamentary regimes to retain control over their bureaucracies is great enough to allow substantial flexibility; they can afford to permit their bureaucracies to be powerful enough to optimize administrative performance without running the risk of regime collapse.

By contrast, the separation of power that results from the presidentialist rule that the chief executive is separately elected for a fixed term and is not accountable to the congress leads to divided authority over the bureaucracy. Appointed officials must be concurrently accountable to diverse congressional committees and presidential appointees, to say nothing of a hierarchy of courts. In short, there is no focus of executive power in the constitutive system of a presidentialist polity. Instead, the authority to govern is dispersed among at least three major branches of government— or, more realistically, among the many subcenters of power that arise within these branches.

Specialists on public administration in America sometimes recognize the adverse effects of the separation of powers on bureaucratic performance, pointing to the split loyalties and values that typically put officials into ambiguously uncomfortable positions and generate internal contradictions and turf battles between rival agencies and incompatible policies (Rosenbloom 1983). In this perspective, however, bureaucratic politics is viewed as a purely internal or intrabureaucratic problem rather than as a result of the presidentialist context. The possibility that frustrated officials, led by military officers, will join forces to revolt and seize power from the elected politicians is not even considered.

The Blacksburg perspective. Far from worrying about how to maintain control over public officials, a more typical reaction to the problems caused by the separation of powers involves a belief that the authority of American career administrators ought to be enhanced. A classic expression of this view can be found in the Blacksburg Manifesto, which proclaims that, to improve public administration, we need to enhance bureaucratic power in America. It claims that "the Public Administration needs to assert, but also to be granted, its propriety and legitimacy as an institution. . . . the value and legitimacy of the Public Administrator as an actor in the governing process" should be enhanced (Wamsley et al. 1990: 43).

Unfortunately, the manifesto fails to recognize the countervailing need of a divided presidentialist polity to keep the bureaucracy weak enough to avoid the potential threat of bureaucratic domination. Preoccupation with the administrative consequences of bureaucratic weakness in America has led, in this perspective, to demands for more bureaucratic power.

It also leads, of course, to explanations of bureaucratic behavior and internal contradictions. A leading example can be found in the writings of

John Rohr, who has closely examined the implications of the constitutional separation of powers for public administration in the United States. He writes that "the Public Administration exercises all three powers in a subordinate capacity . . . by choosing which of its constitutional masters it will favor at a given time on a given issue" (Rohr 1986: 182). In this perspective, one can explain the contradictory strategies pursued by animated bureaucrats seeking to cope with the deep frustrations generated by the division of powers.

In his more recent work, Rohr compares the contemporary French and American political systems, hoping thereby to shed more light on American public administration (Rohr 1995). Because of the persistence of some basic parliamentary features in the French Fifth Republic, I believe the French are able to maintain effective control over a far more powerful bureaucracy than is possible in the American system. However, Rohr cannot, I think, fully explain these differences without adding a systematic comparison with some other presidentialist regimes. The distinctive features of the American exception become explicable only in such a context. Otherwise, what we see are striking differences that cannot convincingly be explained.

The handicaps that impede the capacity of all presidentialist regimes, because of the separation of powers, to maintain effective and coordinated control over their bureaucracies apply to the United States. What is atypical in the American case, I believe, is not the design of its constitutive (representative) system but the exceptional weakness of the American bureaucracy. For historical reasons, it has evolved in a unique way that has continuously limited its power potential.

Students of public administration in the United States have felt no need to explain this weakness because, when the only explicit comparisons they make are with parliamentary regimes, they see no reason to consider bureaucrats as potential rulers. They cannot imagine that an administrative apparatus designed to implement public policies could ever become politically dominant. After all, we normally try to explain why things differ from what we might assume to be normal, ignoring the considerations that lead us to believe in these assumptions.

Predictably, however, a constitutional system based on the separation of powers will surely collapse in the face of major crises unless, somehow, it can reduce the power position of its bureaucrats enough so that they cannot organize to seize power. Simultaneously, it must also empower appointed officials enough to enable them to administer effectively; otherwise, bad administration will provoke popular alienation and lead to widespread support for revolutionary action or a military coup. Seen in this light, the challenge facing every presidentialist constitutive system is how to animate a bureaucracy without losing control over it, how to enhance performance by elevating the bureaucracy's power position without thereby jeopardizing regime survival: how, indeed, to avoid the twin risks of bureaucratic excess and fatigue demonstrated by coups and crashes.

I fully agree with the Blacksburg premise that a more empowered bureaucracy in the United States could perform better, administratively. However, the manifesto fails to consider the other horn of our dilemma—a more powerful bureaucracy could also threaten American democracy by seizing power in a coup d'état or even by an invisible revolution during which career officials would gradually extend their effective control over elected politicians. The experience of other presidentialist regimes demonstrates, I believe, that enhanced bureaucratic power, important as it may be for the improvement of public administration, can also undermine the viability of an extremely fragile formula for running a democracy. In short, the degree of tolerance for bureaucratic power is far greater in parliamentary than in presidentialist regimes.

I use *tolerance* here not to mean "permissiveness" but in another sense of the word; it can also mean "permissible deviation" from a standard or norm *(AHD)*. The range of variation in bureaucratic power that will not endanger a parliamentary system is much greater than the range that is compatible with the maintenance of presidentialism. This means, of course, that a more empowered bureaucracy, as a stronger administrative performer, is compatible with parliamentarism, but it may well be incompatible with the survival of democratic presidentialism. One of the great problems facing government in America, therefore, is how to enhance bureaucratic power and performance without thereby jeopardizing the survival of democracy in a presidentialist regime that is inescapably weakened by its reliance on the principle of the separation of powers.

Other factors. No doubt there are other factors that also affect the interactions between a constitutive system and its bureaucracy. They include many geographic, historical, cultural, economic, and social forces that can have significant influence. The most familiar distinctions are those between the North and the South, between the industrialized and industrializing countries. This theme is too complex and contingent on other variables to justify additional comment in the limited space available here.

However, I would like to mention the fact that, throughout the Third World, European imperialism, which led to the formation of the new states, also created powerful bureaucracies as instruments of imperial rule. Foreign rulers had no reason to help dependent peoples establish institutions for self-government, that is, constitutive systems. Consequently, when imperialism collapsed and independence finally came, for whatever combination of reasons, the new states inherited entrenched bureaucratic institutions without viable constitutive systems. The effort to create such systems on the eve of independence usually floundered. Logically, one might therefore have expected bureaucratic dominance to occur promptly and uniformly in all of these states.

The remarkable fact, however, is that in some of them, newly established constitutive systems have been able to work and to achieve moderately effective control over their bureaucracies. Single-party regimes did so quite successfully, though at a high cost in terms of bureaucratic performance (fatigue). By contrast, the new presidentialist regimes have universally, at different times, suffered catastrophic failures, usually based on bureaucratic dominance (excess) secured by a coup d'état. Parliamentary systems have had intermediate degrees of success. These historical events attract attention to the significant differences between regime types in all modern states. Thus history is not just an explanation; it highlights structural issues that require further analysis and corrective action.

Explanatory Variables:
Distribution, Tenure, Functions

In addition to all the external factors that affect bureaucratic behavior, we need to think about some important variations in the design of bureaucracies that significantly affect their political power, administrative performance, and internal cohesiveness. Among them are the following:

1. the distribution of authority,
2. the tenure and duties of public officials, and
3. the composition of the bureaucracy as a whole.

Distribution. Clearly, in unitary states the national bureaucracy is much larger than it is in federal systems, where many public officials are employed by state and local governments. The bureaucratic fragmentation attributable to federalism means that the U.S. national bureaucracy is necessarily weaker than its counterparts in unitary states, where virtually all public officials are employed by the central government. The fact that most other presidentialist regimes are unitary, not federal, means that their bureaucracies, by comparison with that of the United States, are more powerful.

Similarly, the more a state relies on private organizations to implement public policies—defense contractors, health insurers, communications companies, industrial corporations, and voluntary associations, for example—the less officials are needed by comparison with states in which bureaucrats perform all or most of these functions (Sharkansky 1979). In the American case, heavy reliance on the private sector to perform public functions substantially reduces the number of public officials. By contrast, in many other presidentialist regimes, a larger proportion of governmental functions are performed by bureaucrats, thereby greatly enhancing their power position.

Bearing in mind the relatively greater ability of parliamentary regimes to control their bureaucracies, for reasons explained above, I conclude that they can typically afford a unitary form of government and minimal reliance on the private sector without risking bureaucratic domination. Presidentialist regimes that do so, however, jeopardize their own survival.

Tenure. By *tenure* I refer to the duration of appointments held by bureaucrats. A broad distinction can be made between *transients* and *long-termers.* Clearly, transients are far less able to mobilize bureaucratic power than are long-termers, both because they have a much lower stake in their appointments and because they have too little time to create the interpersonal networks that are required for the cohesive exercise of bureaucratic power.

In the United States, an exceptionally large number of partisan *in-and-outers* and nonpartisan *consultants* who hold temporary appointments in government substantially weaken the bureaucracy. To the degree that they hold senior posts in government, they block the promotion of careerists who might otherwise replace them. Because only highly placed career officials are able to organize coups, reliance on transients helps to explain the weakness of bureaucratic power in the United States. Perhaps even more important, transients have no reason to form cohesive intrabureaucratic networks because their temporary status leads them to focus on the private networks with which they expect to associate after their short terms in public office end. Taken together, these considerations help us to explain the ability of the essentially fragile presidentialist system in the United States to survive.

By contrast, the ratio of long-termers to transients is higher, I believe, in all other modern governments. As noted above, the constitutive system in parliamentary regimes is able to maintain discipline over these long-term bureaucrats, but in presidentialist regimes the viability of such control is highly precarious. Given that careerism has greatly increased in the American bureaucracy, despite the continuance in office of many transients, our explanation of the U.S. exception will be incomplete unless we look carefully at their special characteristics.

All long-term bureaucrats are not the same in their performance and power potential. The basic distinctions concern their mode of recruitment and their subsequent careers. A primary contrast involves the difference between *patronage* and *merit* systems. Among the latter, a fundamental distinction concerns *generalist* versus *specialist* orientations. These variables give us a threefold typology of *retainers, mandarins,* and *functionaries* whose potential for power, performance, and cohesiveness varies significantly, both reflecting and affecting the dynamics of their constitutive systems as I shall now explain.

Retainers as patronage appointees. The premodern Western mode of bureaucratic recruitment typically involved the appointment of relatives, favorites, or partisan supporters with little or no formal consideration of their technical and educational qualifications and without any planned system of tenure to give them job security. Admittedly this is an oversimplification. Earlier systems often involved the sale of office and ascriptive linkages between social classes, religious orders, and bureaucratic functions. Under feudalism, offices became hereditary, passing from fathers to sons. For more details, see Barker (1944: 1-34) and Gladden (1972: 141-187).

What I have in mind here is the widespread reliance on retainers that prevailed throughout Europe in the eighteenth century. Patronage appointees typically retained their posts indefinitely without, however, transforming them into hereditary offices, as found under feudal conditions. This rule also prevailed in the new American republic, under the Federalists and Jeffersonians, during the first 40 years of its existence. According to Leonard White, "The spirit of the Federalist system favored continuity of service from the highest to the lowest levels . . . No property right in office was ever established or seriously advocated, but permanent and continued employment during good behavior was taken for granted" (White 1951: 369).

However, job security in the public service was abridged in the United States by the rotation system as it was inaugurated by President Andrew Jackson in 1829. Concerning this change, White tells us that, contrary to a widespread belief, Jackson "did not introduce the spoils system . . . [but] he did introduce *rotation* into the federal system" (1954: 4-5). Further observations on retainerism and rotation in the American bureaucracy can be found in Riggs (1994b: 67-68).

Strangely, despite the ubiquity of job retention under patronage systems, we lack a generally accepted term for the practice. In European monarchies, the personal retainers or servants of a king or lord often assumed governmental administrative functions and were still called *retainers*. We may, therefore, also use this word to refer to patronage appointees in a republic whenever they remain in office indefinitely. Until a better term is proposed, therefore, I shall use *retainer* to refer, specifically, to partisan appointees in a bureaucracy who retain their positions indefinitely. Ironically, we keep the word *servant* to refer to "public servants"—but this phrase lacks the explicit sense of continuity in office denoted by *retainer.*

When an entrenched bureaucracy is constituted primarily of retainers, it can become very powerful. Although, because of long-term experience in office, some retainers become proficient administrators, the lack of preappointment qualifications often hampers administration. Moreover, because of the absence of tenure rooted in legal safeguards, many retainers feel quite insecure and anxious about their job security. Predictably, therefore, retainers have strong reasons to establish networks and support structures that will help them keep their positions. As a result, retainer bureaucracies, through the years, become quite cohesive and politically powerful.

Retainer bureaucracies generally prevailed in Europe during much of the nineteenth century and they remain entrenched throughout Latin America. However, in Europe and North America, retainerism has been largely—though by no means completely—replaced. Actually, merit criteria and examinations were introduced into Europe as early as the eighteenth century. In Prussia, candidates for appointment to the judicial service were recruited from among persons who had passed written and oral exams. "By 1700 such examinations had already been introduced for military judges and judicial councillors" (Gladden 1972: 162). Gradually, the principle was extended to other positions.

> As early as 1727 Frederick William established a chair in Cameralism at Halle and Frankfurt to give instruction in "the principles of agriculture and police . . . and also the efficient administration and government of towns." Successful candidates were expected to serve in the departments on an unpaid basis . . . before receiving a definite appointment. (Gladden 1972: 162)

However, the most decisive and comprehensive reforms in modern bureaucracies involved the appointment of career generalists on the basis of the Chinese mandarin model. Evidence for this claim is summarized in Riggs (1994b, note 3, p. 70, and 1994c). The establishment of the British mandarinate is fully explained in Chapman (1970: 21-29) and details of the Chinese connection are elaborated in Teng (1943: 296-300). After explaining a similar pattern in France, Mattei Dogan (1975: 4) observes: "If through some miracle a group of mandarins from the Imperial Court could come to Paris . . . they could act like genuine French mandarins except for losing their sumptuous silk robes."

Mandarins as generalists. The basic scheme of recruiting generalist administrators—through competitive written examinations based on academic, literary, and legal prowess; giving them tenure in office; rotating them among different agencies and parts of the country; and distinguishing an elite cadre or class as the core of the bureaucracy from the mass of lower level officials—goes back some 2,000 years. It provided the basis for maintaining centralized control over vast Chinese empires, and it was greatly admired by servants of the British East India company working in Canton. Faced with huge difficulties in their efforts to govern a distant Indian Empire, the British instituted a mandarin counterpart known as the Indian Civil Service. Subsequently, when the retainer bureaucracy floundered in England, they were able to establish a second counterpart there, notably in their Administrative Class.

Because of the decline of the Manchu empire in the nineteenth century, however, it became impolitic to mention the Chinese precedent: E. N. Gladden (1972: 313) just touches on it when he writes: "Some speakers in the Commons ridiculed the idea that modern progressive Britain should have anything to learn from the administrative practices of a China that was so backward and, as they erroneously thought, primitive." Representative Thomas A. Jenkes, an early advocate of American civil service reform, included the chapter "Civil Service in China" in his influential report to Congress in 1868. The contemporary British experience, however, received much more attention than its Chinese prototype in the United States (Van Riper 1958: 64; Teng 1943: 306).

A more important consideration arises from the fact that mandarin bureaucracies typically gain so much power that they can dominate any regime. Indeed, all traditional monarchies experienced great difficulty in their efforts to retain control over mandarin bureaucracies. No doubt this was why they preferred to rely on patronage appointees whose personal loyalty to the rulers could be counted on. The most exceptional feature of the Chinese empire may well have been its capacity to dominate a mandarin bureaucracy.

Even though the Chinese were able to maintain such control more successfully than any other premodern empire, they also experienced dynastic collapses and intervening times of feudal chaos whenever the capacity of a ruling dynasty to control the bureaucracy failed (Kracke 1953: 36). These breakdowns, however, were not caused by *coups* or *crashes,* as these terms have been used in this chapter. Alternatively, as in the Mameluke dynasties of Egypt, rebellious officials replaced a ruling sultan with one of their own leaders, thereby perpetuating the authority of that office—they did not presume to govern through a military junta. For more details, see Riggs (1991: 491-492).

To understand the power potential inherent in any mandarin bureaucracy, consider how easy it is for career generalist administrators to establish personal networks that enhance their power position while simultaneously acquiring the competence required to coordinate and execute public policies and programs. Traditionally, they also had upper-class backgrounds and connections because the high cost of preentry education at private universities prevented poorer citizens from qualifying. I believe that their power to act autonomously, as augmented by long experience in government service and their upper-class associations, has enabled mandarin burcaucracies to combine a high level of administrative capability with great power. In short, the power potential of any mandarinate is quite high and it correlates directly with administrative capabilities.

However, the link between power and performance in a mandarin bureaucracy presupposes the ability of a constitutive system to maintain the upper hand politically so as to sustain its effective control over the bureaucracy. In the parliamentary systems found in all industrialized democracies except the United States, the fusion of powers through the cabinet enables governments, even when they change frequently, to retain such control. The basic reasons are elaborated above in the section headed "Structural Linkages." By contrast, to understand the relative political weakness of the U.S. career bureaucracy, we need to understand how it differs from a mandarin system.

Functionaries as Specialists

A third type of long-term bureaucrat became established in the United States following the careerist reforms launched by the Pendleton Act of 1883. Although American public administration tends to view the resulting *career* system as "normal," it is actually exceptional. Other countries in recent years have sometimes imitated or emulated this model—typically with more or less vigorous prodding by American advisers or even superior authority (as in the Philippine case)—but I believe that no other country has spontaneously developed a specialist career service like that in the United States. No doubt mandarin systems do employ specialists at lower bureaucratic levels but their access to top-level posts is blocked by the elite class of generalists. American careerists face no such ceiling. However, they confront partisan transients at the top, a type of official whose capacity to exercise bureaucratic power is virtually nil. The unique features of the American career services can now be explained.

The essential principles of what can be called the *American type* of career system are so familiar that they scarcely need to be described here.

However, it is useful to remind readers about its structural differences from mandarin systems. In the United States, specialists recruited through open exams at all levels enter and remain, for the most part, throughout their careers in their own program fields. Unlike mandarins, American careerists cannot join the bureaucracy as members of a rotating elite class. Instead, they start up separate career ladders that reinforce their specializations and professional competence in selected program or policy domains. They may also be joined at any time by outsiders who enter the government service through open recruitment procedures based on position classification.

It is proper to call such people *functionaries*—although we normally do not use this term and it has a somewhat different meaning in France. Functionaries, I believe, can never be converted into mandarins, as the abortive effort, through the Senior Executive Service—established under the Civil Service Reform Act of 1987—has clearly demonstrated (Riggs 1994c). Only a total career experience, from early entrance as generalists through frequent rotations between program fields and center to field postings can create a mature class of powerful, integrative, and effective mandarins.

The history of the Pendleton Act of 1883 and its specific provisions requiring appointees to pass "practical" entrance exams that would equip entrants to perform specific services is well known (Van Riper 1958: 60-95; Hoogenboom 1961: 215-222; White 1958: 278-302). Its stipulation that recruits must be drawn from all the states enhanced the influence of the land grant colleges that had already been established under the Morrill Act of 1862. Professional schools that could equip their graduates to take the newly prescribed entrance examinations evolved from them, generating powerful state universities. A symbiotic relationship developed between these schools and their alumni, who began to monopolize functionary positions in the career services. The Ivy League colleges that would have prepared future mandarins, had the British model been followed, were bypassed until they, also, created their own professional schools in competition with the state institutions.

As Van Riper tells us, it was the British model that inspired the reformers whose support led to enactment of the Pendleton Act. However, opposition to what was seen as the essential elitism of that model, with its Oxbridge bias, long blocked the reformers. It was not until after the American plan for "practical," nonacademic exams and "national," not regional, recruitment had been devised that enough political support could be mobilized to secure passage of the act.

Partisanship and bureaucracy. Equally important for winning acceptance of the Pendleton Act was its commitment to a nonpartisan career service. Career officials were to be formally barred from contributing money or supporting electoral campaigns, and certainly they could not retain their offices if they themselves became candidates for an elective office. Perhaps unconsciously, the authors of the Pendleton Act also understood that partisanship in office might enhance the powers of a career bureaucracy and make it more difficult to control. Whether or not they understood that possibility, I believe it to be true in any presidentialist (separation-of-powers) regime.

By contrast, parliamentarism provides a strong enough basis for control over a career bureaucracy so that their members may engage in partisan activities and even run for election to a public office without jeopardizing the regime. For some details on this practice in Europe, see Peters (1988: 152), Birnbaum (1982: 50), and Suleiman (1984: 118-130). According to Suleiman (1984),

> The law in France poses no hindrance to the civil servant who wishes to enter politics . . . While he is a candidate for an elective office, he neither resigns nor takes a leave of absence . . . When he is elected to a local office, he continues to exercise his function as a civil servant. (p. 119)

> The French civil servants have essentially succeeded in taking out the element of risk associated with the political career. The extraordinary facility with which they are able to move into and out of politics, the possibility of campaigning without resigning their positions, the liberty of testing the terrain, of joining political movements . . . If they do not succeed they can simply return to their corps. (p.128)

To give American civil servants permission to run for public office would, by contrast, jeopardize the precarious ability of a regime based on the separation of powers to control career bureaucrats. Americans see the French practice as "extraordinary" because they do not understand the greater capacity of its parliamentary (or semiparliamentary) regime to maintain effective control over the bureaucracy.

French observers, however, might regard the American ban on political careers for civil servants as "extraordinarily" inflexible. Indeed, we not only prohibited political careers for career officials but barred them from exercising rights possessed by all other citizens: that is, to make political contributions and to participate in partisan campaigns. The Hatch Acts of 1939 and 1940 even extended these prohibitions against partisan political activity to noncareer public employees except for those in top policy-making positions.

The basic significance of the "politics-administration" dichotomy amounted to this: Career officials (functionaries) were to be nonpartisan, but transient in-and-outers could be partisan. Although designed to "depoliticize" career bureaucrats, the American career system actually empowered them to become nonpartisan promoters of professional norms. They became increasingly committed to programs and standards that became entrenched or institutionalized through a host of professional associations in which bureaucrats mingled as colleagues with their private sector counterparts and with the faculty and students of professional schools.

These unofficial extrabureaucratic organizations subtended the formal structures of the constitutive system, augmenting it in unexpected ways, especially as manifested in subgovernments ("iron triangles") through which career officials were able both to exercise power and to gain support for their programs and policies. James Q. Wilson (1989: 60) points to this phenomenon when he writes about the prevalence of "professionals" in the American bureaucracy who receive "important occupational rewards from a reference group whose membership is limited to people who have undergone specialized formal education and have accepted a group-defined code of proper conduct." Reciprocally, of course, professionals in the bureaucracy could use these outside "reference groups" to win support for their own programs and policies.

Paradoxically, while the professionalization of the career services in the United States empowered functionaries in their own niches, it undermined the cohesiveness of the bureaucracy as a whole. Unlike the mandarins found in other polities, they do not associate or identify with each other in such a way as to enhance their collective power as bureaucrats. Incidentally, this makes the American bureaucracy a convenient scapegoat for politicians, who often blame "bureaucrats" for problems that arise because they do, indeed, promote policies whose separate constituencies and purposes often conflict with each other and with the priorities of elected politicians. Because their formal posture as "nonpolitical" (i.e., nonpartisan) officials enjoins them from publicly defending their policies and counterattacking their critics, American career officials have little choice but to endure these humiliations.

The integrative roles performed by mandarins in most parliamentary systems are supposed, in the American case, to be undertaken by partisan transients—a role inherited from the spoils system as it evolved prior to the Pendleton Act. However, as mentioned above, transients are inherently incapable of exercising bureaucratic power and their partisanship (both to parties and to programs) thwarts whatever inclinations they may have to play synthesizing functions to promote the general public interest.

Heterogeneity. In historical perspective, we can now see that the fragile presidentialist regime in the United States has never been threatened by the kind of cohesive bureau power manifested in the coups that have terminated, at various times, almost all of the other presidentialist regimes. The risk of growing bureau power in the United States was aborted twice, though never, I think, with any conscious understanding of its real character. The first time occurred in 1829 when the Jacksonian revolution blocked the incipient growth of retainer power and institutionalized the rotation of transients in public office, and the second in 1883 when the Pendleton Act, while instituting careerism, avoided the risks involved in creating a mandarin bureaucracy.

The incompatibility of a mandarin bureaucracy and presidentialism has been revealed in recent years by the Korean and Vietnamese experience. In both countries, presidentialist regimes, established under American sponsorship, were overthrown and replaced by military coups in 1961 and 1963, respectively. Both countries had developed their indigenous mandarinates under Chinese tutelage, and their subsequent French and Japanese masters had built on these traditions when they established their imperial rule. Although the first elected presidents of these two countries relied heavily (and clumsily) on patronage appointees, they could not establish effective control over their bureaucracies. South Korea has now moved toward the reestablishment of an open presidentialist regime, but it remains to be seen whether it will succeed and how long it can last. A personal interpretation of the contemporary Korean experience can be found in Riggs (1995). As for the South Vietnamese mandarin bureaucracy, a good account can be found in Dang (1966. 170-204).

At an earlier time, the first Chinese Republic also failed, though for rather different reasons. It did have a mandarin background, of course, but most of the imperial bureaucrats had already vanished when the empire collapsed: The mandarin tradition was irrelevant except in the sense that the administrative vacuum that followed led to a period of anarchy and the rise of competing warlords. The presidentialist constitution of the first republic promptly failed, however, when President Yuan Shih Kai, the former commander of a modernized Manchu imperial army, usurped power in 1913 and tried, vainly, to establish a new empire. The regime crisis stemmed from the seizure of power by the president, not by a military junta. No doubt Yuan did command the most effective army in China at that time, but even that army was far too weak to control the whole country.

By contrast, all the nineteenth-century presidentialist regimes in Latin America inherited their relatively weaker retainer bureaucracies from Spain and Portugal. Despite their presidentialist constitutions, they were generally able to avoid coups until well into the twentieth century. The Philippines provides an exceptional test case. Its Spanish colonial bureaucracy was based on patronage and retainerism (Corpuz 1957). Its first experiment with presidentialism in the 1890s (the so-called Malolos Constitution) failed because of a radical internal class cleavage within its congress, and President Aguinaldo (anticipating Yuan Shih Kai) seized power as commander of the revolutionary forces. However, they were not a disciplined army and, ultimately, they could not prevent the American conquest that followed.

Under American rule, exceptionally, a functionist bureaucracy came into existence concurrently with the Philippine Congress and a replica of American presidentialism. Following independence, Filipino nationalists grew disgusted with the separation-of-powers formula and established a constitutional convention that designed a parliamentary system. However, in 1971, when they were about to promulgate it, President Ferdinand Marcos, with military support, suspended the existing constitution and established a presidential autocracy with a purely formalistic parliamentary facade of his own design. After the restoration of presidentialist democracy under President Corazon Aquino, several abortive coup attempts were made against the new regime. My conclusion is that although presidentialism failed in the Philippines, the American-style functionist and patronage-based bureaucracy lacked the power needed to seize power as retainer bureaucracies have done in almost all other presidentialist regimes. A summary account of the Filipino bureaucracy can be found in De Guzman et al. (1988).

The first example of a failed presidentialist regime was perhaps that of the Second French Republic, although it probably had a quasi-mandarin bureaucracy, formed under the auspices of Emperor Napoleon Bonaparte. The republic of 1848 collapsed when its first president, Louis Napoleon, in profound conflict with congress, usurped power with the help of the armed forces and subsequently launched the Second Empire in 1852. The classic examples of toppled presidentialist regimes have occurred in this century in Latin America where retainer bureaucrats have supported military coups. As noted earlier, their motives for organizing informally to defend their interests and their administrative failures contributed, respectively, to their power potential and also to the popular discontents that fueled support for the rejection of whatever regime was in power.

By contrast with other presidentialist regimes, the semipowered federal bureaucracy of the United States is more heterogeneous and proportionally smaller. It combines transients and long-termers in an unstable mixture that prevents the rise of cohesive bureau power. Among the transients, we find not only partisan in-and-outers but a host of nonpartisan consultants performing tasks that, in other countries, would be carried out by career bureaucrats. Although most of the long-termers are functionaries, some are also retainers who have been "blanketed" into the classified services by executive fiat.

More important, however, the careerists themselves are heavily oriented toward organized constituencies, legislative committees, and professional associations that block the formation of any kind of pan-bureaucratic cohesive organization which would empower American officials to effect radical changes in the constitutional system. The very heterogeneity of this mixed bureaucracy also creates intrabureaucratic tensions that inhibit collegial coordination among appointed officials. Nevertheless, the administrative capabilities of professionalized career bureaucrats and in-and-outer transients have been sufficiently strong to maintain, though sometimes precariously, enough popular support for the regime to keep it viable.

America's Semipowered Bureaucracy

The perception of American public officials as a semipowered bureaucracy not only seems to contradict the antibureaucratic slogans so often heard in political campaigns today, but it also differs from much academic writing. Indeed, most of the research on bureaucratic politics in America focuses on the extent to which public officials influence and help shape public policy. Good examples can be found in Rourke (1984) and Lewis (1977). Actually, within their policy domains, bureaucratic influence prevails. However, segmented power in dispersed niches does not add up to cohesive bureau power that could be potent enough to topple a constitutive system.

Widespread popular acceptance of the notion that politics and administration are and ought to be divorced reinforces this perspective because it leads to the assumption that bureaucrats are, or should be, powerless. When empirical research reveals that they are, in fact, semipowered, this comes as a surprise if not a shock. However, if American government were studied in a comparative perspective—as, unfortunately, it is not—we would start with the contrary premise that all bureaucracies are powerful, and that officials in virtually all democratic regimes exercise more cohesive power than American officials do.

Once this perception gains support, a follow-up question would inquire into the consequences of its semipowered status for the bureaucratic role in American governance. I believe these include the historical fact that a highly fragile (presidentialist) system of government has been able to persist in the United States. By contrast, in all other presidentialist polities, more powerful bureaucracies, homogeneously rooted in retainer power, have not been effectively controlled by their constitutive systems, have performed less effectively as administrators, and have been able to seize power when they saw that their own interests, as bureaucrats, were seriously threatened.

Academic implications. The approach taken above has, I believe, important implications for political science.

For *comparative politics,* it raises questions about the constitutional requisites for more effective public administration and also the role of bureaucratic power as it affects regime stability. Comparisons will show, I believe, that mandarin bureaucrats can exercise power and be excellent administrators in parliamentary systems, but their presence threatens the survival of presidentialist democracies. However, retainer bureaucracies can also undermine presidentialist regimes for two complementary reasons: first, by becoming too powerful and, second, by providing ineffective public administration. Such findings will also explain why a semipowered heterogeneous and professionalized bureaucracy in the United States has been able to link its so-so administrative achievements with system survival, steering a middle course between bureaucratic excesses and fatigue.

For *comparative public administration,* this approach explains why countries that are dominated by a ruling bureaucratic elite (both military and civil) experience not only oppression but also ineffective public administration. We can test the proposition that increasing bureaucratic power correlates with increasing administrative effectiveness, subject to a ceiling imposed by the capacity of democratic regimes to maintain effective control over their bureaucracies. Failure to maintain such control can lead to bureaucratic domination (imposed during a coup d'état) with resultant oppression and administrative incompetence.

At the opposite extreme, we can study the link between bureaucratic powerlessness and unsatisfactory public administration, as revealed in the countries that have experienced political crashes. If these hypotheses are true, then we can see how decisively constitutional differences in political systems affect administrative performance. These differences include not only contrasts between democratic and authoritarian regimes but also an understanding of why a powerful mandarin bureaucracy can serve parliamentary regimes without destroying them, but such a bureaucracy would annihilate any presidentialist regime. Again, contrasts based on the coups that signalize bureaucratic excess, and the crashes that can accompany bureaucratic fatigue, provide a frame of reference for significant comparisons.

Specialists on *American government* may also come to see that if we want to maintain our presidentialist Constitution, then we have no choice but also to retain a semipowered bureaucracy based on the internal contradictions caused by bureaucratic heterogeneity and a relatively small and highly dispersed functionary career system. The study of coups and crashes will help us understand some of the most perplexing problems confronting the American people.

Admittedly, the views advanced here are hypothetical and even controversial. However, I believe that comparative research, taking the polar extremes of bureaucratic domination and powerlessness into account, will help us to understand not only some of the paradoxes and weaknesses of public administration in America but also how they enable our precarious type of democracy to persist. The approach offered here will, I think, explain the truly exceptional character of American public administration and help us see governments in the rest of the world through less ethnocentric glasses. By understanding ourselves better—thanks to coups and crashes—we shall also enhance our understanding of the rest of the world.

References

Aberbach, Joel D., Robert D. Putnam, and Bert A. Rockman. (1981) *Bureaucrats and Politicians in Western Democracies*. Cambridge, MA: Harvard University Press.

Albrow, Martin. (1970) *Bureaucracy*. New York: Praeger.

Barker, Ernest. (1944) *The Development of Public Services in Western Europe, 1660-1930*. London: Oxford University Press.

Beetham, David. (1987) *Bureaucracy*. Milton Keynes, United Kingdom: Open University Press.

Birnbaum, Pierre. (1982) *The Heights of Power: An Essay on the Power Elite in France*. Chicago: University of Chicago Press.

Chapman, Richard A. (1970) *The Higher Civil Service in Britain*. London: Constable.

Corpuz, Onofre D. (1957) *The Bureaucracy in the Philippines*. Manila: University of the Philippines, Institute of Public Administration.

Crozier, Michel. (1963) *The Bureaucratic Phenomenon*. Chicago: University of Chicago Press.

Dang, Ngiem. (1966) *Viet-Nam: Politics and Public Administration*. Honolulu: East-West Center Press.

De Guzman, Raul P., Alex B. Brillantes, Jr., and Arturo G. Pacho. (1988) "The Bureaucracy." In Raul P. De Guzman and Mila A. Reforma, eds., *Government and Politics of the Philippines*, pp.180-206. Singapore: Oxford University Press.

Dogan, Mattei. (1975) "The Political Power of the Western Mandarins." In M. Dogan, ed., *The Mandarins of Western Europe*, pp. 3-24. New York: John Wiley.

Fainsod, Merle. (1958) *Smolensk Under Soviet Rule*. New York: Vintage.

Finer, Samuel. (1976) *The Man on Horseback: The Role of the Military in Politics*. Middlesex, United Kingdom: Penguin.

Girling, John L. S. (1981) *The Bureaucratic Polity in Modernizing Societies*. Singapore: Institute of Southeast Asian Studies.

Gladden, E. N. (1972) *A History of Public Administration*. Vol. 2. London: Frank Cass.

Heady, Ferrel. (1995) *Public Administration: A Comparative Perspective.* 5th ed. New York: Marcel Dekker.

Hocart, A. M. (1927) *Kingship.* London: Oxford University Press.

Hoogenboom, Ari. (1961) *Outlawing the Spoils: A History of the Civil Service Reform Movement, 1865-1883.* Urbana: University of Illinois Press.

Janowitz, Maurice. (1977) *Military Institutions and Coercion in the Developing Nations.* Chicago: University of Chicago Press.

Kennedy, Gavin. (1974) *The Military in the Third World.* London: Duckworth.

Kracke, E. A. (1953) *Civil Service in Early Sung China, 960-1067.* Cambridge, MA: Harvard University Press.

Lasswell, Harold D., and Abraham Kaplan. (1950) *Power and Society.* New Haven, CT: Yale University Press.

Lewis, Eugene. (1977) *American Politics in a Bureaucratic Age.* Cambridge, MA: Winthrop.

Linz, Juan, and Alfred Stepan, eds. (1978) *The Breakdown of Democratic Regimes.* Baltimore: Johns Hopkins University Press.

Merton, Robert K. (1957) *Social Theory and Social Structure.* Glencoe, IL: Free Press.

Mintzberg, Henry. (1983) *Structure in Fives: Designing Effective Organizations.* Englewood Cliffs, NJ: Prentice-Hall.

Peters, B. Guy. (1988) *Comparing Public Bureaucracies.* Tuscaloosa: University of Alabama Press.

Riggs, Fred W. (1966) *Thailand: The Modernization of a Bureaucratic Polity.* Honolulu: East-West Center Press.

———. (1969) "The Structures of Government and Administrative Reform." In Ralph Braibanti, ed., *Political and Administrative Development,* pp. 220-324. Durham, NC: Duke University Press.

———. (1979) "Shifting Meanings of the Term 'Bureaucracy'." *International Social Science Journal,* 32: 563-584.

———. (1991) "Bureaucratic Links Between Administration and Politics." In Ali Farazmand, ed., *Handbook of Comparative and Development Public Administration,* pp. 485-509. New York: Marcel Dekker.

———. (1993) "Fragility of the Third World Regimes." *International Social Science Journal,* 136: 199-243.

———. (1994a) "Conceptual Homogenization of a Heterogeneous Field: Presidentialism in Comparative Perspective." In *Comparing Nations: Concepts, Strategies, Substance,* pp. 72-152. Oxford: Basil Blackwell.

———. (1994b) "Bureaucracy and the Constitution." *Public Administration Review,* 54, 1: 65-72.

———. (1994c) "Bureaucracy: A Profound Perplexity for Presidentialism." In Ali Farazmand, ed., *Handbook on Bureaucracy,* pp. 97-148. New York: Marcel Dekker.

———. (1995) "Korean Economic Growth in a Global Context: Cultural, Political and Administrative Aspects." Chung-hyun Ro, ed., *Korea in the Era of Post-Development and Globalization,* pp. 153-220. Seoul: Korea Institute of Public Administration.

———. (1996) "Viable Constitutionalism and Bureaucracy: Theoretical Premises." *Journal of Behavioral and Social Sciences,* 2: 1-35 (Tokyo: Toikai University, Research Institute of Social Sciences).

Rohr, John A. (1986) *To Run a Constitution.* Lawrence: University Press of Kansas.

———. (1995) *Founding Republics in France and America: A Study in Constitutional Governance.* Lawrence: University Press of Kansas.

Rosenbloom, David H. (1983) "Public Administrative Theory and the Separation of Powers." *Public Administration Review,* 43, 3: 219-227.

Rourke, Francis E. (1984) *Bureaucracy, Politics, and Public Policy.* 3rd ed. Boston: Little, Brown.

Sharkansky, Ira. (1979) *Wither the State.* Chatham, NJ: Chatham House.

Stepan, Alfred. (1988) *Rethinking Military Politics.* Princeton, NJ: Princeton University Press.

Suleiman, Ezra N. (1984). "From Right to Left: Bureaucracy and Politics in France." In E. N. Suleiman, ed., *Bureaucrats and Policy Making.* New York: Holmes & Meier.

Taylor, Charles L., and Michael C. Hudson, eds. (1983). *World Handbook of Political and Social Indicators.* 3rd ed. New Haven, CT: Yale University Press.

Teng, Ssu-Yu (1943) "Chinese Influence on the Western Examination System." *Harvard Journal of Asiatic Studies,* 7: 267-312.

Thompson, Victor. (1976) *Bureaucracy and the Modern World.* Morristown, NJ: General Learning Press.

Thompson, William R. (1973) *The Grievances of Military Coup-Makers.* London: Sage.

Van Riper, Paul P. (1958) *History of the United States Civil Service.* Evanston, IL: Row, Peterson.

Wamsley, Gary, et al. (1990) "Public Administration and the Governance Process." In Gary Wamsley et al., eds., *Refounding Public Administration,* pp. 31-51. Newbury Park, CA: Sage.

White, Leonard D. (1951) *The Jeffersonians.* New York: Macmillan.

———. (1954). *The Jacksonians.* New York: Macmillan.

———. (1958) *The Republican Era.* New York: Macmillan.

Wilson, James Q. (1989) *Bureaucracy: What Government Agencies Do and Why They Do It.* New York: Basic Books.

Professionalism, Bureaucracy, and Modern Governance: A Comparative Analysis

Ali Farazmand

This chapter addresses four major issues related to professionalism, bureaucracy, and governance in modern societies, with particular emphasis on the U.S. bureaucracy: First is a background discussion of the professional state in ancient and modern times. Second is an analysis of the professionalization of the American bureaucracy and civil service. Third is a brief analysis of the political economy of the U.S. bureaucracy and administrative state. Then the relationship between bureaucracy and political systems or regimes is analyzed comparatively, with implications for modern governance. The latter is a particular attempt to challenge Riggs's recent (1993, 1994a, 1994b) arguments that the U.S. bureaucracy is semipowered, which makes it difficult or impossible for bureaucrats to engage in coalition building with the military to dominate the society and cause the breakdown of the

American presidential system. This chapter also challenges Riggs's argument that bureaucracy in parliamentary systems is more powerful and more cohesive than the U.S. bureaucracy, therefore providing more harmony with the parliament and the executive branch represented by a president or prime minister. Further, a stronger challenge is raised here against Riggs's assertions concerning bureaucracy and political systems in twentieth-century developing nations, whether parliamentary or presidential.

Background of the Professional State

Professionalization of government institutions, particularly the bureaucracy, dates back to ancient time. From the time of empire building, almost all states have sought to improve their ability to govern effectively. This has been particularly the case with the military and in the maintenance of law and order. The role of experts and professionally trained officials in state functions has been recognized by political authorities from ancient time. Administration and civilization are the inseparable twins, both contributing to the other's development. From the dawn of the political history, certain large empires promoted a highly specialized, differentiated, and functionally competent bureaucracy as the core of the states in governing their territories. The bureaucracies held a powerful position in these societies (Farazmand forthcoming-a; Nash 1969).

Although the Egyptian and Chinese bureaucracies were very much controlled by the monarch, their systems developed a tendency toward professionalization through functional specialization and structural differentiation based on some education, training, and, in the case of the Chinese, some form of merit entrance examination for the civil service system (Eisenstadt 1963). The Assyrian empire was a bureaucratic empire with maximum rigidity and inflexibility; it was efficient but brutally uprooting and highly displacing in nature. Its officialdom reached a high mark of political dominance, and the system survived a long time until the empire fell forever in 612 B.C. to the emerging Medes, a young and vigorous group of Aryan people who already held Asia and whose conquest of Assyria in the west set the stage for a global expansion. The Median empire was governed by a professionalized, competent state gaining maturity through a long process of learning and structural differentiation that evolved both in society at large and in the administration of the empire (Farazmand 1991a, 1994b, forthcoming-b; Ghirshman 1954; Olmstead 1948). The Medes were the first in history who adopted the concept of "state" and "turned the concept into a reality " (Ghirshman 1954: 127). But that concept was even more rigorously realized by the Achaemenid Persians, whose "One World-State" empire governed virtually the entire known world of antiquity.

The Median state was notorious for its internal managerial efficiency and administrative effectiveness, and the societies under the Medes became increasingly professionalized (Frye 1963, 1975; Ghirshman 1954). The fall of the Median empire to the Achaemenid Persians under Cyrus II, grandson of the Median king in power, left a rich legacy to the Persians, who were destined to change the course of political history. When Cyrus the Great took over the Median empire, he inherited a highly competent, profession-alized, functioning administrative state. The Median administrators learned a great deal from the Assyrian bureaucrats during a long period of contact with them, but their competence evolved mainly through training, a new philosophy of good administration, and a novel mission they were seeking to accomplish: a sound administrative system for a mighty empire led by a novel, Aryan people (Farazmand forthcoming-b).

Professionalization of the Median bureaucracy and state was promoted by the principles of apprenticeship, training, the arts of statecraft, merit and technical qualifications for jobs, and the rigidity of professional "closeness as a guild" by "men of pen." This professional state and its rank-and-file bureaucrats enjoyed a position of power and influence in society.

The Achaemenids under Cyrus the Great, Darius the Great, and Xerxes the Great King, as well as other Persian kings, achieved what the Medes aspired to but did not have the chance to do: administration of virtually the entire known world. In a single generation, the Achaemenid Persians built a world-state empire unknown to the world before. While Cyrus the Great was a military genius, a charismatic political leader, and a skilled statesman, Darius was also a great administrator and organizer. Under his rule, the administration of the entire Persian empire was reorganized and reformed—in legal/justice administration, in taxation and financial man-agement, in communication, and in personnel administration—to high standards. The Universal Laws of the Empire were applied to the remotest areas. The financial system was based on the capacity of trained, expert officials; semiprofessionalized general bureaucrats; and professional spe-cialists who constituted the core of the highly centralized bureaucracy of the Empire. Recruitment was based on merit and experience gained through apprenticeship and training as well as on patronage. Loyalty was central to the system, but competency was highly esteemed and recognized. Persians were subsidized for production of male children for future lead-ership cadres in the gigantic administrative system (Cook 1983; Frye 1975; Farazmand forthcoming-b). The bureaucracy followed wherever the mili-tary went. The central office of the bureaucracy headed by the prime minister, *hazarpati,* was informed of almost everything that happened in the *satrapies,* large territories—often composed of several nations or kingdoms—that were headed by a governor, or *satrap,* who acted like a mini-king in his territory (Farazmand 1991a, forthcoming-b; Olmstead 1948).

Administration of a vast empire like that of the Achaemenids was a challenge that few could conceive of. But the Persians have gained a historic reputation of being "good" or "excellent administrators." This reputation originated under the Medes, continued in the Achaemenid period, and was perfected 600 years later under the Sasanid Empire. Its realization was possible through the notorious bureaucracy of the state, which was managerially efficient and politically and administratively effective. For 200 years, the bureaucracy and the military constituted the backbone of the Empire, but it was also the prosperous economy and the high principle of tolerance so characteristic of the Persians that held the Empire together. The Persian gold, the military, and the bureaucracy, together with the skilled diplomacy, held the Empire intact. Darius the Great quickly realized that without a sound economy and a fair legal system, there would be no peace, and without a lasting peace the Empire would always face formidable challenges from within as well as from outside. This would also come from the bureaucracy, which might find its position and privileges threatened. But the king had many novel institutions of control, and countercontrol, that enabled him to maintain effective control over the bureaucracy (for details, see Farazmand 1991a, 1994b, forthcoming-b).

The professionalization of the bureaucracy led increasingly to its high position in society, and it was transformed gradually into a contender for power, not vis-à-vis the Great King to whom it was both loyal and subordinate, of course, but in general. The more excessive the bureaucratization of the Empire, as time passed, the greater the possibilities for bureaucratism and abuse of power around the Empire. This was compounded by the excessive taxation, which incrementally produced a degree of mass disaffection with the administration and its bureaucracy. The eventual fall of the Empire to the young Alexander was a surprise, for the Persian military was formidable and the bureaucracy was professionalized to a great extent, and both never expected to be challenged. But it was the political and popular attitudes that had already changed the perception of the power of the Empire (Farazmand 1994b; Cook 1983; Frye 1975).

The Persian bureaucracy was intact during the reign of Alexander the Great, who was advised to marry a Persian and stay in Persia proper if he aspired to rule Persians; he did that and was himself Persianized also. The decentralized Parthian Empire of Persia for 467 years (240 B.C.-227 A.D.) adopted the bureaucracy it inherited, but centralization and professionalization were held subordinate to the powerful patronage system that prevailed. The rivalry, hostility, and cooperation between Parthia and Rome led the two superpowers of the ancient world to political and military claims for global domination. Neither paid much attention to professionalization of its state, although Rome fared better in this matter (Debevoise 1938; Farazmand 1994b).

However, professionalization of the state bureaucracy and administrative system of the Persian Empire reached its high mark during the Sasanid Empire. Sasanid bureaucracy achieved a high degree of structural differentiation, specialization, and centralization, all corresponding to the social differentiation and stratification (Eisenstadt 1963). The bureaucracy also achieved a high position of power, and bureaucrats gained high status in society, both formally and informally. Their power position was not to be taken lightly by the kings, and the people, but it was kept subordinate to the sovereign political authority. Yet centralization of the bureaucracy and its high power position posed a threat to the noble families and the aristocracy, which found it a serious challenge to their privileged position in society (Cook 1983; Olmstead 1948). The conflict between the increasingly professionalized, rational bureaucracy, on the one hand, and the nobility and feudal aristocracy, on the other, was detrimental to the political system in general, a factor that was at times capitalized on by Romans, unsuccessfully though, for the Sasanid Persians in all groups and classes were extremely patriotic and nationalistic, claiming superiority, and certainly not inferiority, in the civilizational groups. The bureaucracy gained an upper hand over the aristocracy during the latter part of the Empire.

The Sasanid Empire, like the Achaemenid, was at its zenith when it unexpectedly fell to a culturally inferior, undisciplined, bedouin people of the Arab peninsula, who spread Islam by conquest. Again, overtaxation, excessive bureaucratization and bureaucratism, as well as religious orthodoxy and rigid social stratification of the society contributed to a general dissatisfaction among the masses, particularly the peasantry. This led to a gradual erosion of the system's legitimacy, which ultimately resulted in the fall of the Empire to the Islamic forces in 651 A.D. Subsequently, the Islamic empire adopted almost entirely the Persian system of administration, and the Persian bureaucracy continued to cooperate as the principal institution of governance under Islamic rule (Cook 1983; Frye 1963, 1975; Olmstead 1948; Eisenstadt 1963; Farazmand 1991a, forthcoming-b). The Persian state tradition and administrative system were also entirely adopted by the Ottoman Empire, as well as by the following Persian Safavids, who then introduced the merit system as well as declared Shi'ism the state religion of Persia or Iran (Farazmand 1996; Savory 1980).

Several generalizations can be made about the professionalization of the bureaucracy under the Persian Empire. First, it was generally professionalized by both experience and training, although not by modern standards. Second, both Achaemenid and Sasanid bureaucracies were highly centralized. Third, both systems were managerially efficient and administratively and politically effective. Fourth, they both were politically instrumental to the effective governance of the vast Empire. Fifth, both bureaucracies gained a high power position and tended to overpower the society. Sixth, both left legacies that may be found today in almost the entire Middle and Near East and perhaps, by extension, in the Western world. Seventh, the contributions that the Persian bureaucracy and the Byzantine/ Roman bureaucracy have made to modern governance and organization/ administrative theory deserve significant attention but have been unstudied, with some exceptions (see the author's edited symposium, "Civilization and Administration," a collection of articles on ancient empires and city-states in the *International Journal of Public Administration*, December 1997).

The Roman/Byzantine bureaucracy produced a good degree of professionalism. Its bureaucratic state was, however, more repressive than the Persian. But its political and military effectiveness produced significant orientations that were both self-serving and excessive (Eisenstadt 1963).

The professionalization of the European empires during the past several centuries is also to be noted for its significant contributions to modern concepts of bureaucracy. Particular attention must be paid to the French and Prussian, as well as the British, systems whose highly developed bureaucracies contributed to a large extent to the concepts of the modern state and bureaucracy. The modern concepts of state and professionalization of bureaucracy ought to be studied carefully in connection with the Scientific and Industrial Revolutions and the ensuing transformation of global mercantilism into modern capitalism, a system far superior to the system of capitalism that existed in the ancient time.

But the French, Prussian, British, and other empires did not invent bureaucracy and the professional state; they made improvements in them. All modern states have inherited and learned from those in the distant past, the ancient great civilizations and their administrative systems. The Ottomans maintained, with minor modifications, the Persian traditions of bureaucracy and state for a long time, from the Middle Ages to the twentieth century. Similarly, the Europeans learned from the Romans (who had learned a great deal from Persians), the Greeks, and others. Upon preparing a proposal to reform the U.S. civil service system in the late nineteenth century, the reformers considered the Ottoman and Chinese civil service systems as well as the French, German, and British systems (Rohr 1993; Van Riper 1993). These historical traditions have been passed on to the modern states with their economic systems of advanced capitalism and the rapidly advancing technology that requires increased levels of specialization, professionalization, and social and political control. The nature of modern governance requires a complex system of social organization and administration that is capable of maintaining the political system by balancing capitalism and the social and ecological ills it produces.

Professionalization of the
American Bureaucracy

The American administrative state may actually have reached fledgling status in the 1880s (Skowronek 1982; Rosenbloom 1993). The professionalization of the American bureaucracy began with the passage of the Pendleton Act of 1883, which reformed the U.S. civil service system, and with the creation of a number of regulatory organizations in the American state. Experts on American governments tend to overstate the extent to which the United States was "stateless" throughout the nineteenth century (Stillman 1991); the state has existed in America since its inception as an independent republic. Before then, it was a colonially controlled state. A socioeconomically oriented elite emerged with U.S. independence. The government by "gentlemen" (White 1926; Mosher 1982 [1968]; Rosenbloom 1993) was clearly dominated by the upper-class elite. Selection was from the upper social and economic class; "dismissal was rare, and office was conceptualized essentially as a form of property, and in some instances it was passed down in families" (Rosenbloom 1993: 1, 1971).

The "Jacksonian Revolution" was cognizant of the relationship between political dominance and the public. Its attempt to broaden the social representation in the public service by recruiting from the "common man" and by rotation of office was a political strategy to strengthen democracy and responsiveness. The Jacksonian patronage system, however novel, was abused to the point of excessive corruption, which led to the outcry from the reform movement. The excessive corruption in the 1860s prompted the Congress to pass a civil service law, in 1871, which, however, had to be abandoned because of a lack of funding.

The primary objective of the 1883 Civil Service Reform Act was to abolish the rampant corruption that pervaded the system. Its introduction of the merit system based on job-related qualifications and competitive examination was a major step toward professionalization of the civil service in the United States. At that time, professionalization was a new phenomenon for both the civil service and the organizations of the private sector. However, the 1883 Pendleton Act and the Civil Service Commission were mainly ignored by federal agencies until the early twentieth century. The merit system actually only became operational this century.

Nevertheless, the stage was set for professionalization of the federal bureaucracy. Why? What was the main rationale behind it? Was not the danger of professional experts/bureaucrats making policy decisions considered? It is difficult to believe that it was not. Then, why was it allowed? I will come back to these questions later. But suffice it to say here that it was both necessary and inevitable. It was necessary because something had to be done about the corruption, and the public was fed up with the system. Also, it was necessary because there was a need for stability in office and for a strong "state" in society. It was inevitable because the economic system of capitalism needed a government that would be able to respond to the capital's call for policies that could support and ensure capital accumulation and protect the interests of the privileged, considered to be the leaders of the nation.

Woodrow Wilson's (1887 [1941]) article "The Study of Administration" also set the foundations of the American state to move toward a managerially biased ideology of separating politics from administration. Wilson (1992: 18) wrote, "The field of administration is the field of business. It is removed from the hurry and strife of politics." He proposed a *businesslike* administration and bureaucracy in which bureaucrats should stay away from politics. Similarly, Frank Goodnow (1900) perpetuated this orthodoxy of businesslike administration by arguing that "politics has to do with policies and or expressions of the state will. Administration has to do with the execution of these policies" (1992: 25).

The doctrines of the political-administrative dichotomy, of the businesslike managerial ideology, and of "neutral competence" pervaded American public administration for decades until they were shattered by the powerful argument that politics cannot and should not be separated from administration (Waldo 1948; Appleby 1949; Dahl 1947). Waldo's (1948) argument that public administration theory is political theory was both theoretically sound and empirically verifiable. The New Deal era produced a monument of cases that would test his and other's arguments (Piven and Cloward 1971). In pursuit of the above doctrines, major structural reorganizations and process rearrangements were made in the federal bureaucracy, and significant measures were taken to professionalize the American bureaucracy. The decades of the 1930s through the 1970s experienced serious efforts to professionalize the federal bureaucracy and public administration in America.

The rise and largess of the bureaucratic/administrative state in the United States was not unchallenged. Indeed, the judiciary and the Congress, as well as intellectuals and academicians, reacted to the phenomenon. It is beyond the scope of this chapter to discuss this phenomenon. But suffice it to say here that the judiciary's response was one of initial hostility followed by cooperation, "partnership" with administration, and eventual self-bureaucratization (Rosenbloom 1987, 1986; Nachmias and Rosenbloom 1980). The congressional reaction also has resulted in the bureaucratization of its own structure and process (Nachmias and Rosenbloom 1980). Others have reacted differently.

The challenges shattering the orthodox doctrines of politics-administration dichotomy and neutral competence by Waldo and others resulted in an "identity crisis" in the field. However, despite these arguments that public administration theory was also political theory, the study of bureaucracy in political science was largely ignored and left to the sphere of sociology and public administration. Waldo's *Administrative State* (1948) set the tone for a new doctrine to be established, a politically oriented theory of organizing and administering society and the economy. Waldo's arguments were based on two points: that public administration has significant political theoretical elements and implications, and that public administration theory is also political theory. Although the first has been accepted by now as a fact, the second has yet to be realized, but "the latter perspective is more profound and innovative than is usually appreciated" (Marini 1993: 415).

How would Professor Wilson view the status of public administration today? In an imaginary interview with George Graham (1993), Wilson states,

> Broaden your perspective to include all stages of the process of administering the nations's affairs from beginning to end. Actively enlist members of Congress and other legislators in your own ranks. You can broaden their perspectives and they can broaden yours. You will have to take the initiative. . . . The policy of improving administration by strengthening the chief executive, integrating the structure, and teaching "management" as a set of techniques has passed the point of diminishing returns. The vein has yielded some rich ore in results; but it is running out. (Graham 1993: 502)

The growth and professionalization of the American bureaucracy, first, was in part due to the political need to respond to the demands and pressures raised by the lower classes and the underprivileged; it was a reactive response of the system to the social pressures challenging system legitimacy during the 1930s and 1960s. Second, it was due to the growing need to promote professional competence by attracting talented and competent personnel to the government bureaucracy; this was done in competition with the private sector. Further, professionalization of the bureaucracy occurred as a result of the increasingly dominant role of the U.S. federal government both domestically and internationally. Domestically, federal interventions in state and local affairs and economy through grants administration and social welfare functions occurred to maintain the system as well as promote the infrastructure, which in turn enhanced the capacity of the private sector to grow. In the international sphere, U.S. interventions in developing countries increased dramatically, not to mention the role they played in World War II and the wars that have followed.

The internationalization of the U.S. government—military, security, and economic powers—necessitated a huge bureaucracy staffed with professional experts in a variety of fields. Therefore, to manage an internationalized economy and political-security affairs, the U.S. bureaucracy was an ideal form of organization as well as a desirable one; its effectiveness has been proven with the characteristics outlined by Max Weber. Elsewhere (1994c), I have argued that as a result of the changing global conditions and the ever expanding American economic, political, and administrative roles under the New World Order, there is an emerging global bureaucracy and public administration that will be both elite oriented and professionalized.

Because of public dissatisfaction with the performance of both government and corporate leaders/elites in the 1970s, the U.S. bureaucracy began to receive severe criticism from almost all directions. Professionalization of the American bureaucracy was feared by both politicians and experts on American governments—from the Left to the Right—for its intrusion into private life, for being unaccountable to the public, for its involvement in policy making, and for overpowering the legislative and other legitimate institutions of a democratic society. It was also criticized for being too big and inefficient. Almost every president and office seeker in America has criticized the bureaucracy before and during election (Rosenbloom 1993; Henry 1995).

The second landmark legislation reforming the U.S. civil service system and bureaucracy, after the Pendleton Act, was passed under the Carter presidency. It was a major step toward both professionalization of the bureaucracy *and* reinforcement of the "businesslike" ideology or the doctrine preaching efficiency as a central objective of the civil service system. The businesslike doctrine or ideology of the U.S. bureaucracy and public administration, already quite strong, was further reinforced by the Civil Service Reform Act of 1978. Its provisions contributed to the further professionalization of the federal bureaucracy. But it also opened the door for politicization of the system, as was done fully under the Reagan Administration in the 1980s.

The U.S. bureaucracy under the Reagan presidency was politicized and its professional competence redirected toward stronger security-military and economically elite sectors; it became more particularistic and elite oriented than ever before. How did the Reagan group manage to more effectively control the bureaucracy than the Carter group did? This is an important question on the "position of bureaucracy" that requires a separate essay.

The Political Economy
of the American Bureaucracy

As a dominant mode of economic organization of society, modern capitalism necessitated a bureaucratic system of administration that goes hand in hand with, is an integral part of, and is an essential by-product of it. As Weber (1946) correctly observed, bureaucracy and capitalism are inseparable from each other, and "everywhere the modern state is undergoing bureaucratization" (Weber, in Rourke 1986b: 69). Also, to Marx (1984a [1967]), bureaucracy is a by-product and an instrument of class rule by capitalism. Although to Weber the ideal-type bureaucracy is the most efficient form of organization for the administration of economy and society, to Marx it is the most demeaning form of organization, resulting in both work and self-alienation for individual human beings, as well as being a repressive instrument of class domination (1984; also in Tucker 1978).

Foreseeing continually bureaucratizing societies, Weber (1946) also stated that "whether the power of bureaucracy within the polity is universally increasing must here remain an open question" (1986: 68). The "indispensability" of officialdom and the power position of the bureaucracy is questionable in the sense that bureaucracy cannot replace political authority. According to Weber (1986: 68), the slaves were indispensable to the wealth accumulation of the master, but they were not powerful and not decisive. Similarly, bureaucrats are not decisive even though they are indispensable to the maintenance of political and economic systems. Empirical evidence of revolutions around the globe seems to support this claim (more on this later). The fact is that bureaucracy can be and is an instrument of power for class and other forms of rule in society. "Once it is fully established, bureaucracy is among those social structures which are the hardest to destroy. . . . Bureaucracy has been and is a power instrument of the first order—for the one who controls the bureaucratic apparatus"

(Weber 1986: 67). And where the "bureaucratization of administration has been completely carried out, a form of power position is established that is practically unshatterable" (p. 67).

The 1871 Civil War in France and the Russian and Iranian Revolutions of 1917 and 1978-1979 are good cases to test Weber's propositions. Both revolutions had to deal with established and powerful bureaucratic-autocratic states with which both regimes were identified; the regimes and the states were considered synonymous, and any challenge to the state was considered a challenge to the regimes (Farazmand 1989a; McDaniel 1991). The proletariat abolished the state and bureaucracy of the absolute monarchy in France but later fell victim to its own failure to completely wipe out the political power now outside of Paris; it did not foresee the possibility of the Prussian ruling power coming to the aid of the French. The result was a disaster for the proletariat, who in a few months had succeeded in establishing a popular and unbureaucratic system of administration (Marx, 1984).

Bureaucracy was hard to abolish for the revolutionary leaders of Russia and Iran, after both revolutions. In fact, Lenin (1971) himself clearly stated that it would be impossible to abolish a bureaucracy already well entrenched in society and part of the old regime. A similar problem was faced by the new revolutionary leaders in Iran. Indeed, the established bureaucratic state of Iran was found to be instrumental to the new regime, but both Russian and Iranian revolutionary leaders significantly altered the power structure of the bureaucracy in both countries: The bureaucratic elite at all levels was completely replaced by the new young revolutionaries, whose competence in bureaucratic order was minimal but whose political and ideological energy was inexhaustible. The bureaucracy was brought under complete control, although the process of the bureaucratic system remained an obstacle to the swift policy implementation required and demanded by the new political authority. Control over the bureaucracy was established by creation of a multitude of parabureaucratic and revolutionary organizations charged with policy implementation and popular action. This was also done by debureaucratization of the society, a process that took years but did accomplish the political objectives (for details, see Farazmand 1989a, 1991b). Similar observations have been made about the Philippine, Cuban, and Nicaraguan bureaucracies after their revolutions (see, for example, Carino 1994).

The political culture that is dominant in the United States has perpetuated the myth that America is "stateless." This is not the place to analyze this question fully, but it may be argued well that this political belief is in part a product of corporate ideology and the private enterprise system. This prevailing view (the myth) has even been established in the American political science and public administration traditions. Generally, American theorists and politicians refer to the concept of state in other nations, and they reject the idea of state in the United States.

The concept of state should not be confused with the concepts of administrative state, hallow state, the welfare state, and so on, which have appeared in the American public administration literature during the last half century; it is a broader concept that deals with the whole society and its economic, social, and political system. The point is that state has existed in the United States ever since its conception, and the bureaucracy has been an instrument of the power elite, although it may not have been as coherently formed as elsewhere in the world. And, in fact, control of the bureaucracy has been overly accomplished ever since its largess began (Rosenbloom 1993; Henry 1995).

The growth of the professional bureaucracy in the United States has deeper roots and rationales that are often overlooked or ignored by social scientists, including political and administrative scientists. A fact of historical development is that modern capitalism has resulted in an increasing need for professionalism, expertise, specialization of functions, and standards for performance to achieve high efficiency in work organizations. The growth and advance of capitalism and the advance in technology have contributed to increased differentiation of roles in society and in organizations. Consequently, we have observed an explosion of professions in modern organizations, including public, private, and corporate sectors. The professionalization of bureaucracy in public and private sectors has had consequences, a subject that is beyond the scope of this chapter. However, professions and professionalism have meanings, not all of which may apply to modern bureaucracy. One example is the autonomy that professionals have traditionally tended to enjoy. Is this characteristic present in modern professionalism? Is it present in professional bureaucrats? I would argue that it is not. The professionals—trained or experienced experts in various fields or disciplines—in modern bureaucracies, private and public alike, are not autonomous, because their autonomy has been limited or severely restricted by both governments and corporate sector elites.

As mentioned earlier, the growth and professionalization of the U.S. bureaucracy have been both imperative and inevitable. I say "inevitable" because the growth and expansion of capitalism as an economic system of organization requires a modern state equipped with a competent administration of governance. It requires a bureaucratic apparatus that is functional to the survival and maintenance of the system and, indeed, to the continued accumulation of capital as well as its expansion. The corporate sector needs a strong bureaucracy to assist the business elite in achieving this goal. It is also "imperative" because the modern state and its huge, rational, professional bureaucracy must absorb major functions that the business sector does not perform—"social welfare functions." The modern state must also absorb the social costs to society of the corporate-business sector—pollution, externalities, market failures, unemployment, and so on (MacPherson 1985; Gilbert 1983; Domhoff 1990). The New Deal policies of the 1930s and the social welfare policies of the 1960s are two examples that relate to this point.

Another imperative for the growth and professionalization of modern bureaucracy is capitalism's requirement/need for a professional middle class as a major consumer class; the middle class is considered the backbone of modern capitalism and the survival of its political system (Huntington 1968). The professional middle class is also politically and administratively easier to control than the peasantry or the blue-collar working class, which is potentially threatening to the capitalists. The bureaucratic middle class offers expertise, skills, and knowledge that are indispensable to the functioning of the capitalist system. The bureaucratic middle class is also dependent on the capitalists for jobs, promotions, and material privileges. Additionally, the bureaucratic professionals who work for the government—particularly in security and military sectors—are completely dependent on the government.

The professional bureaucratic class is essential to the power elite in that it provides the system with the managerial capability that is needed for both capital accumulation and the maintenance of political and social order. The managerial elite therefore serves the power elite in the best possible way, for it provides the elite a variety of shields that make the elite invisible (see Farazmand 1994a; Scott and Hart 1989). It is therefore essential for capitalism to encourage the growth of a professional bureaucracy. The dilemma, however, is that the professional middle class may at some point challenge the power elite by withholding its expertise and knowledge. This is unlikely—although some (Scott and Hart 1989) argue to the contrary—as long as the system is stable and provides them with the opportunity to grow and keep busy. The bureaucratic state therefore is the institutional channel to promote and protect the system as well as provide opportunities for professions and encourage professionalization of the bureaucratic class.

The above statement leads us to a broader question: What is the status of the state in society? Is it dependent on capital, labor, and so on? Is the state autonomous of forces in society? What is the role of the state and, by extension, of its bureaucracy in society? These questions cannot be answered fully here, but several schools of thought have attempted to answer the autonomy question. The school of state autonomy or "statism" represented by Theda Skocpol (1985) asserts that through its various pluralistic institutions, the state is capable of exercising independent power vis-à-vis other forces in society. It severely criticizes both the Marxist and the pluralist schools for being "reductionist," for ignoring or underestimating the importance of state activities and power (1985; see also Gibbs 1991 and Domhoff 1990).

Closely related to the pluralist model, the bureaucratic politics school emphasizes the role of bureaucracy and the power it is capable of acquiring and exercising in society; it tends to dominate the policy process as well as its implementation (Mosher 1982; Wilson 1986). The instrumentalist model as well as the structural Marxist school have similar arguments: that the state is not autonomous, and that it is dependent on the business interests and on the ruling class (Baran and Sweezy 1966; Poulantzas 1969; Chomsky 1985). But a variation in this school exists that seems to accept the "relative autonomy of the state" (Poulantzas 1969; Miliband 1969). Abandoning his earlier pluralist view, Charles Lindbloom (1977) seems to have joined the structuralist school. He argues that business occupies a privileged position in society because it has the ability to cease investing, which would wreck the economy and bring down the government (see Gibbs 1991 for more on this). Regardless of whichever model is accepted concerning the power of the state and its bureaucracy in society, it is clear that bureaucracy and its professionalism are instrumental to both capital and society (Miliband 1969).

The growth of the bureaucratic, professional state in the United States raised serious questions about its ability to manipulate political authority and to exercise power that is not democratically entrusted in it. In other words, the bureaucracy's involvement not only in policy implementation but also in policy making was feared by the critics as undemocratic, with significant consequences for representative democracy based on election. The idea is that because appointed officials are secure in their positions through civil service system protection, these unelected bureaucrats should not be making policy decisions that should only be made by elected officials. Represented by Mosher (1968, 1982), Rourke (1986a), Wilson (1986), and others, including especially the conservative public choice theorists (Buchanan and Tullock 1962; Ostrom 1973), critics have sounded the alarm that bureaucracy is out of control and must be brought under democratic control. The Left has also been critical of the role of the bureaucracy as being too powerful in repressing the working and lower classes. To the Left (too many to list), bureaucracy and its professionalism serves only the upper, ruling class. Still others have criticized bureaucracy for producing alienation and demeaning work organizations (Thayer 1981).

The criticism against bureaucracy from all sources at least indicates that bureaucracy has become powerful and is a force to be reckoned with, as well as being a threat to democratic rule. What are not often mentioned, or at least are overlooked, are some fundamental facts: that the civilian bureaucracy in charge of the social welfare functions and provision of public services must be distinguished, and separated, from the military-security bureaucracies that are most prevalent and pervasive in all societies but are least paid attention to in the general analyses of bureaucracy. Almost all political systems maintain a huge bureaucracy—security and military or paramilitary in nature—that performs the key functions of system maintenance and regime enhancement (Farazmand 1982; Eisenstadt 1963).

The second important point that has been overlooked in the literature is the elite—political, social, and economic—orientation of the upper echelon of the bureaucracy, whether civilian or security and military. In harmony with the interests and goals of the established political and economic elites, the bureaucratic/administrative elite leads a bureaucracy that must not only maintain but also enhance the system in place. The elite orientation of the bureaucracy is antidemocratic, for the mass of ordinary people have little control over the key decisions that are made in both public and private sectors (Farazmand 1993, 1994a; Scott and Hart 1989). It is in this context that the role of bureaucracy in relationship to the political system/regime should be carefully examined and understood.

The above discussion leads us to the last topic of this chapter, the relationship between burcaucracy and political systems/regimes.

Bureaucracy and Modern Governance

Public bureaucracy has been indispensable to governance and to political systems ever since the era of empire building in ancient times. Civilization and administration began and have lived together; one without the other has been almost impossible (Waldo 1992; Farazmand forthcoming-b). But not all governments have been bureaucratic and relied on bureaucracy for governance. However, those that haven't have been an exception, not the rule (Nash 1969; Heady 1996).

Generally, bureaucracy plays a major political role of maintaining and enhancing the political and economic system or regime in power. Bureaucracy also plays an essential role in economic and national development. This has been the case in both developed and developing nations. In the United States, the creation of the U.S. post office was to provide jobs and services and to promote economic development. Similarly, in the 1930s and 1960s, the expansion of the administrative state was to promote economic development, the infrastructure, and the like, as well as to maintain and enhance the political and economic system by performing major social welfare functions (Farazmand 1982, 1989a, 1989b; Parenti 1988; MacPherson 1985).

Fred Riggs, in his recent writings (1993), has made a forceful argument that the American professionalized bureaucracy is semipowered and this has caused the survival of the American presidential system. The bureaucracy has to satisfy diverse interest groups, therefore it cannot amass the power to engage in a coup d'état to topple the presidential regime in power—hence the survival of the regime. Riggs further argues that the bureaucracy in parliamentary systems is powerful but it is a generalist bureaucracy, therefore the parliament has a better control over it. Yet the bureaucracy is capable of exercising more power than in the United States. His further argument is that most of those developing countries adopting the U.S. presidential system of governance have experienced system breakdown and failed because of the powerful position the bureaucracy holds in these societies. Further, the bureaucracy will join military coups d'état to change a regime with which they are dissatisfied.

This is a powerful argument that Riggs has been making, and it deserves serious empirical attention. However, Riggs's argument has serious problems. The following is an outline of the problems that challenge his propositions.

First, the U.S. bureaucracy has become professionalized mainly during the twentieth century while its presidential system has existed for two centuries.

Second, to argue that the U.S. bureaucracy is not powerful or is semipowered seems an understatement. The bureaucracy achieved full status during the late nineteenth century, and by early this century it was fully in place. The question then remains: Why did the bureaucracy not topple the political system and the regime in power during the severe recessions that the U.S. economy and society experienced as well as the crises it suffered? The answer seems to be what I argued earlier: The bureaucracy is an instrument of power and, also, it has self-interest in perpetuating itself. However, the bureaucratic elite often works in harmony with the political and economic/business elite. In addition, the bureaucracy is controlled by the power elite. Nevertheless, the possibility of the lower echelon members of the bureaucracy joining system or regime challengers is considerable. The lower class members do have the potential to join the oppositional forces or the counterelite in times of serious crises threatening system or regime legitimacy.

This potential existed and to some extent manifested itself during the early 1930s when alternative systems of economy and politics were considered in society (Rosenbloom and Shafritz 1985). Once it felt the threat, the established elite's response was to "neutralize" the potential political threat of the bureaucratic forces that might have joined militant labor; "neutral competence" was both a business, corporate ideology as well as a political ideology to protect the American bureaucracy from being affected by the fallout of the Bolshevik Revolution in Russia and from becoming radically politicized. The concept of neutral competence was also to protect public employees from being abused by partisan interests. The reality is that public employees have always had political preferences and their partisan preferences cannot be eliminated, but their behaviors can be controlled in modern bureaucratic organizations (Farazmand 1989b).

There is another reason the U.S. presidential system has survived: It has survived due to its relative democratic representativeness, however elite in nature. The political culture in America has evolved differently than in other nations. America is a young nation with a young and vigorous people; it has a long way to go to mature historically. By contrast, most nations of the world have a longer history of nationhood and culture. The United States became a powerful nation economically and militarily in a very short period of time. Combined with relative internal participation and economic prosperity, this has enabled the country to move externally for expansion and economic and political leadership at a global level, which has benefited the internal system and, relatively speaking, satisfied its people. Should this have happened otherwise, the survival of the political system would have been in question also.

Still another explanation may be given about the U.S. bureaucracy and its presidential survival. The chief executive, the president, has gained an upper hand over the Congress since World War II. The dominant executive position of the president has contributed tremendously to the ability of the chief executive to control the bureaucracy and to use it to its advantages vis-à-vis the legislature. This has had serious ramifications for the democratic process, for the legislative representative body has been weakened in favor of the presidency (Rosenbloom 1993).

Second, by contrast, the parliamentary systems of government have greater control over the executive and appear to be more representative and democratic than the dominant-executive systems such as the one in the United States. Postcommunist Russia is now undergoing a serious struggle between the parliament as the representative institution of democratic governance and the elected chief executive, Yeltsin, who had little more than 50% votes at large, has aspired to become a strong executive able to dictate to the legislative body. The threat to democracy is as serious in Russia as that experienced in the United States. One of the major implications of a dominant presidency is its ability to dominate the policy process and veto popular legislation passed by the parliament and, more seriously, to promote particularistic, big business interests at the expense of the common people's interests. Charges of the Imperial Presidency under Nixon and Reagan are not too few (see, for example, Newland 1983, 1987; Rosenbloom 1993). The state and its bureaucracy are powerful in the United States, but they are not autonomous. They serve the more powerful interests, and because the corporate business interests enjoy more privileges than any other groups in society, the business interests are more powerful (Lindbloom 1977).

The power position of bureaucracy—however generalist it may seem according to Riggs—has been tempered by the legislative strength and the control the power elite maintains over it. Also, the bureaucratic elite has been given real authority, to an extent that it can even veto executive actions, as is the case in France (Rohr 1993). This is done in the general public interest. The French bureaucrat has the knowledge of both the law and the processes by which the law must be implemented. The argument that the bureaucracy in parliamentary systems is powerful and in harmony with the parliament is not an exaggeration. But what is also interesting is that bureaucracy in European nations appears to be more representative and more articulative of diverse interests than it is in the United States and many other nations.

Why has the bureaucracy not engaged in overthrowing the regimes in Europe? One explanation appears to be that, after all, the bureaucracy is controlled by the representative body. Another reason is that the bureaucracy is a major part of the policy process, not outside of it, and therefore it is also responsible for policy outcomes and consequences. Also, the political system is independent and capable of being externally exploitative while internally responsive and satisfying. Most European nations fall in this category. Like the United States, they have been, first as colonial powers and then as neocolonialists or imperialists, able to extract substantial profits in their external adventures and operations in developing nations, profits that have benefited the internal interest groups, including their bureaucracies. The incentive for the bureaucratic elite to topple the system or regime may prove fatal to its position. The state in European market economies is also powerful, but it is not autonomous. Its power depends to a great extent on how much it serves the interests of the more powerful groups, the business elite.

Third, the situation in developing and underdeveloped nations is significantly or completely different. These nations generally fall under the three categories: the formerly colonial nations, those never colonized, and those recently created as nation-states. (The former socialist or communist nations are not included here.)

All of these nations of the developing world have experienced several common phenomena. Almost all of them lack a well-developed market system comparable to the advanced capitalist nations of the West. Some have tried but could not compete with the powerful economies of the West. In the age of colonialism and now imperialism in which the dominant powers of the West—Europe and the United States—have politically, militarily, and economically dominated these nations, the interventions of the Western powers in the affairs of these countries have created an entirely different situation in them.

In the market-based economic systems of these nations, the indigenous, nationalist economic power bases have gradually been eroded and eventually replaced by the multinational corporations of the developed imperialist and colonial powers of the West. This has happened during the last two centuries but mainly in this century. As a consequence of extensive foreign intrusion, the nationalists—both economic and political power bases—have lost their positions to the outside international corporations backed by their military and political states that have intervened by force and diplomacy whenever their interests have either been threatened or cut off. Chile in the 1970s and Iran in the 1950s are but two examples of this phenomenon; in both cases, the United States intervened through the domestic military elites.

Because the economies of these nations have been integrated and are dependent on the Western-based multinational corporations and their powerful states, the political systems in these countries have remained shaky, dependent, and fragile. Their fragility is not due to the powerful bureaucracies that exist in them. Rather, these political systems and regimes are too often extremely corrupt and repressive. Ironically, they are backed by the democratic states of the West, for they provide some stability and market opportunities for the international capital. Therefore, the struggle between the popular forces organized with the common goal of overthrowing these repressive regimes and the political authority that possesses the monopoly of coercive power at its disposal has continued ever since the colonialization period. In modern times, these struggles are on all fronts—military, political, cultural, administrative, and bureaucratic as well as economic.

The political regimes in most developing nations, whether parliamentary or presidentialist, are not truly independent; they are largely dependent on the international forces of the dominant West. The elites are often Western educated with Western values that are in conflict with the indigenous, traditional values of their societies. The political regimes, to survive, often lean on the external, international governments. This puts them in an odd position vis-à-vis their own populations, which they are supposed to represent and serve. Because most of them are also corrupt and hold a monopoly on their nations' political power and economic resources, they become unpopular among their masses. The Pahlavi regime in Iran, the Somoza regime in Nicaragua, the Marcos regime in the Philippines, the Batista regime in Cuba, and others are but a few examples. To rule, these regimes depended heavily on their military and bureaucratic institutions as well as international supporters.

The bureaucratization of society served these regimes in their economic exploitation of resources and political control of their populations. But bureaucratization also serves as an instrument of capitalist development and growth of the elites. The military is always ready to intervene whenever popular demands get out of hand and popular pressures threaten regime stability and survival. The military elite seizes power with external support or even by its instigation—generally from the dominant Western governments and the multinational corporations that they represent. The military elite as well as the bureaucratic elite have externally oriented attitudes, often subordinating the domestic indigenous interests to the interests of international capital and its governments. There has in this century developed a powerful class of "comprador bourgeois" composed of the military, bureaucratic, and economic sectors in developing countries. This new class of dependent bourgeoisie is a powerful agent of dominant foreign powers and plays a fundamental role in the domestic politics, economics, and administration of developing nations. Broadly speaking, it is a change agent of Western capitalism and international capital in the Third World.

Because of the increasing dependence of these regimes on externally oriented elites, the systems in developing and underdeveloped nations face continuous crises of legitimacy and collapse. Most of them face popular revolts or revolutions by lower and middle classes. The role that the bureaucracy plays in these revolutionary processes is complex and may differ from case to case. Generally, the bureaucracy is conservative, antirevolutionary, and resists radical change; its central focus is continuity and stability. But its rank and file, the lower echelon members, often find themselves caught between the two powerful blocs, one of which is the masses, which demand services and responsiveness. The popular culture exists in contradiction to the bureaucratic culture. The other bloc is the political authority of the regime and the bureaucratic elite that demands obedience, stability, competence, performance, and regime representation. As a result, it is not surprising that a major part of the intelligentsia in developing nations is cultivated among the professional, middle-class bureaucrats who are closer to the masses but have to carry out the not-so-popular policies of the regime in power.

The result is that in times of revolution, the lower bureaucracy often joins the movements against the regime. This action by the bureaucracy therefore is not because the bureaucracy is powerful and able to sieze political power and cause system or regime breakdown. On the contrary, it is the bureaucratic elite that tends to perform its externally oriented duties of resisting popular pressures or revolutions and may become a victim of its elite orientation or fall to the revolution (e.g., Iran, Russia, Cuba, and elsewhere)—exceptions aside, of course. So the argument that bureaucracy in developing societies is powerful, dominates the political systems, and causes regime breakdown appears to be an exaggerated and overstated proposition about the bureaucratic role and politics in society.

The external role of the United States, Britain, France, and other powerful nations must be regarded as a major independent variable in why these political regimes and systems are fragile and break down frequently— and not the role of their bureaucracy in these nations. Similarly, the former colonial powers of Spain and Portugal left formidable legacies in the bureaucracies and political systems of the Latin and Central America that pervaded the bureaucratic attitude, structure, and behaviors in these nations (Hopkins 1994; Felker 1993). The bureaucracies in these nations are powerful, but they are not autonomous: They serve powerful, dominant interest groups, and most of these powerful groups are the business, military, and administrative elites that have, over time, become highly external oriented. This trend is even likely to be accentuated in the foreseeable future under the New World Order in which a global bureaucracy and public administration is emerging with its central office in the United States and key international locations around the globe. It will be both professionalized and hierarchically ordered with commanding structures in the United States and Europe (for more on this, see Farazmand 1994b).

The above discussion demonstrates why Riggs's assumptions and arguments fail to match the realities of bureaucratic theory and politics. I intend to discuss Riggs's arguments in a separate essay with a more detailed empirical analysis. Until then, I end my discussion here.

References

Appleby, Paul. (1949) *Policy and Administration*. University, AL: University of Alabama Press.

Baran, Paul, and Paul M. Sweezy. (1966) *Monopoly Capital*. New York: Monthly Review Press.

Buchanan, James, and Gordon Tullock. (1962) *The Calculus of Consent*. Ann Arbor: University of Michigan Press.

Carino, Ledivina. (1994) "A Subordinate Bureaucracy: The Philippine Civil Service up to 1992." In Ali Farazmand, ed., *Handbook of Bureaucracy*, Chap. 39, pp. 603-616. New York: Marcel Dekker.

Chomsky, Noam. (1985) *Turning the Tide*. Boston: South End.

Cook, J. M. (1983) *The Persian Empire*. New York: Schocken.

Dahl, Robert. (1947) "The Science of Public Administration: Three Problems." *Public Administration Review*, 7: 1-11.

Debevoise, N. C. (1938) *A Political History of Parthia*. Chicago: University of Chicago Press.

Domhoff, William. (1990) *The Power Elite and the State: How Power Is Made in America*. New York: Aldine de Gruyter.

Eisenstadt, S. (1963) *The Political Systems of Empires*. New York: Free Press.

Farazmand, Ali. (1982) *Bureaucratic Politics: Development System Maintenance? A Study of Administrative Theory*. Ph.D. dissertation in Public Administration, Maxwell School of Citizenship and Public Affairs, Syracuse University, Syracuse, NY.

———. (1989a) *The State, Bureaucracy, and Revolution in Modern Iran: Agrarian Reform and Regime Politics*. New York: Praeger.

———. (1989b) "Crisis in the U.S. Administrative State." *Administration & Society*, 21, 2: 173-199.

———. (1991a) "State Tradition and Public Administration in Iran in Ancient and Contemporary Perspectives." In Ali Farazmand, ed., *Handbook of Comparative and Development Public Administration*, Chap. 19, pp. 255-270. New York: Marcel Dekker.

———. (1991b) "Bureaucracy and Revolution: The Case of Iran." In Ali Farazmand, ed., *Handbook of Comparative and Development Public Administration*, Chap. 55, pp. 755-767. New York: Marcel Dekker.

———. (1993) "Elite Theory of Organization: A Conceptual Model." Paper presented at the Annual Symposium of the Public Administration Theory Network, California State University—Hayward, July.

———. (1994a) "Organization Theory: An Overview and Appraisal." In Ali Farazmand, ed., *Modern Organization*, Chap. 1, pp. 3-54. Westport, CT: Praeger.

———. (1994b) "Bureaucracy, Bureaucratization, and Debureaucratization in Ancient and Modern Iran." In Ali Farazmand, ed., *Handbook of Bureaucracy*, Chap. 43, pp. 675-686. New York: Marcel Dekker.

———. (1994c) "The New World Order and Global Public Administration: A Critical Essay." In Jean-Claude Garcia-Zamor and Renu Khator, eds., *Public Administration in the Global Village*, Chap. 3, pp. 61-81. Westport, CT: Praeger.

———. (1996) "Religion and Politics in Contemporary Iran: Shia Radicalism, Revolution, and National Character." *International Journal on Group Rights*, 3: 227-257.

———., ed. (Forthcoming-a) "Symposium: Civilization and Administration: Contributions of Ancient Civilizations of the East to Modern Governance." (Special issue) *International Journal of Public Administration*, 20, 12.

———. (Forthcoming-b) "Administration of the Persian Achaemenid World-State Empire: Implications for Modern Public Administration." *International Journal of Public Administration*, 20, 12.

Felker, Lon. (1993) "The Spanish and Portuguese Empires and Their Administrative Legacies." Paper presented at the 1993 American Society for Public Administration's National Training Conference, San Francisco, July.

Frye, Richard. (1963) *The Heritage of Persia*. New York: World.

———. (1975) *The Golden Age of Persia*. New York: Harper & Row.

Ghirshman, R. (1954) *Iran From the Earliest Times to the Islamic Conquest*. New York: Penguin.

Gibbs, David. (1991) "Private Interests and Foreign Intervention: Toward a Business Conflict Model." Paper presented at the 1991 Annual Conference of the American Political Science Association, Washington, DC, August.

Gilbert, Neil. (1983) *Capitalism and the Welfare State: The Dilemmas of Social Benevolence*. New Haven, CT: Yale University Press.

Goodnow, Frank. (1900) *Politics and Administration: A Study in Government*. New York: Russell & Russell.

———. (1992) "Politics and Administration." In Jay Shafritz and Albert Hyde, eds., *Classics of Public Administration*. 3rd ed., pp. 25-28. Pacific Grove, CA: Brooks/ Cole.

Graham, George. (1993) "How Professor Wilson Would Rate Public Administration Today." *Public Administration Review*, 53, 5: 486-502.

Heady, Ferrel. (1996) *Public Administration: A Comparative Perspective*. 4th ed. New York: Marcel Dekker.

Henry, Nicholas. (1995) *Public Administration and Public Affairs*. 6th ed. Englewood Cliffs, NJ: Prentice Hall.

Hopkins, Jack. (1994) "Administration of the Spanish Empire in the Americas." In Ali Farazmand, ed., *Handbook of Bureaucracy*, pp. 17-27. New York: Marcel Dekker.

Huntington, Samuel. (1968) *Political Order in Changing Society*. New Haven, CT: Yale University Press.

———. (1991) *The Third Wave: Democratization in the Late Twentieth Century*. Norman: University of Oklahoma Press.

Lenin, V. I. (1971) *State and Revolution*. New York: International Publisher.

Lindbloom, Charles. (1977) *Politics and Markets*. New York: Basic Books.

MacPherson, C. B. (1985) *The Rise and Fall of Economic Justice*. New York: Oxford University Press.

Marini, Frank. (1993) "Leaders in the Field: Dwight Waldo." *Public Administration Review*, 53, 5: 409-418.

Marx, Karl. (1984a) "Beyond Bureaucracy. The Paris Commune." In Frank Fischer and Carmen Sirianni, eds., *Critical Studies in Organization and Bureaucracy*, pp. 40-48. Philadelphia: Temple University Press. Reprinted from the *Writings on the Paris Commune*, by Karl Marx and Friedrich Engels, edited by Hal Draper (New York: Monthly Review Press, 1971), 69-78

———. (1984b) "The Spirit of Bureaucracy" In Frank Fischer and Carmen Sirianni, eds., *Critical Studies in Organization and Bureaucracy*, pp. 40-41. Philadelphia: Temple University Press. Reprinted from Loyd Easton and Kurt Guddat, eds., *Writings of the Young Marx on Philosophy and Society*, pp. 185. Garden City, NY: Doubleday, 1967, pp. 185-187.

McDaniel, Tim. (1991) *Autocracy, Modernization, and Revolution in Russia and Iran*. Princeton, NJ: Princeton University Press.

Miliband, Ralph. (1969) *The State in Capitalist Society*. London: Weidenfeld & Nicolson.

Mosher, Frederick. (1968) *Democracy and the Public Service*. (2nd ed., 1982). New York: Oxford University Press.

———. (1982) *Democracy and Public Service*. New York: Oxford University Press.

Nachmias, D., and D. Rosenbloom. (1980) *Bureaucratic Government: USA*. New York: St. Martin's.

Nash, Gerald. (1969) *Perspectives on Administration: The Vistas History and Method*. Tuscaloosa: University of Alabama Press.

Newland, Chester. (1983) "A Mid-Term Appraisal—the Reagan Presidency: Limited Government and Political Administration." *Public Administration Review,* 43, 1: 45-56.

———. (1987) "Public Executives: Imperium, Sacerdotium, Collegium? Bicentennial Leadership Challenges." *Public Administration Review,* 47, 1: 45-56.

Olmstead, A. (1948) *History of the Persian Empire: The Achaemenid Period.* Chicago: University of Chicago Press.

Ostrom, Vincent, Jr. (1973) *The Intellectual Crisis of Public Administration in America.* University, AL: University of Alabama Press.

Parenti, Michael. (1988) *Democracy for the Few.* 5th ed. New York: St. Martin's.

———. (1989) *The Sword and the Dollar: Imperialism, Revolution, and the Arms Race.* New York: St. Martin's.

Piven, F. F., and R. Cloward. (1971) *Regulating the Poor.* New York: Pantheon.

Poulantzas, Nicos. (1969) "The Problem of the Capitalist State." *New Left Review,* 58: 73.

———. (1978) *State, Power, Socialism.* London: New Left Books.

Riggs, Fred. (1993) "Fragility of the Third World Regimes." *International Social Science Journal,* 136: 199-243.

———. (1994a) "Bureaucracy: A Profound Puzzle for Presidentialism." In Ali Farazmand, ed., *Handbook of Bureaucracy,* Chap. 7, pp. 97-146. New York: Marcel Dekker.

———. (1994b) "Global Forces and the Discipline of Public Administration." In Jean-Claude Garcia-Zamor and Renu Khator, eds., *Public Administration in the Global Village,* Chap. 1, pp. 17-44. Westport, CT: Praeger.

Rohr, John. (1993) "Public Administration and the French State: A Review Essay." *Public Administration Review,* 53, 5: 473-479.

Rosenbloom, David. (1971) *Federal Service and the Constitution.* Ithaca, NY: Cornell University Press.

———. (1986) "The Judicial Response to the Rise of the Administrative State." In F. Lane, ed., *Current Issues in Public Administration.* 3rd ed., pp. 129-150. New York: St. Martin's.

———. (1987) "Public Administrators and the Judiciary: The New Partnership." *Public Administration Review,* 47, 1: 75-83.

———. (1993) *Public Administration: Understanding Management, Politics, and Law in the Public Sector.* 2nd ed. New York: Random House.

Rosenbloom, D. H., and J. M. Shafritz. (1985) *Essentials of Labor Relations.* Reston, VA: Reston.

Rourke, F. E. (1986a) "The Presidency and the Bureaucracy." In F. Lane, ed., *Current Issues in Public Administration,* 3rd ed., pp. 71-89. New York: St. Martin's.

———., ed. (1986b) *Bureaucratic Power in National Policy Making,* 4th ed. Boston: Little, Brown.

Savory, R. (1980) *Iran Under the Safavids.* Cambridge: Cambridge University Press.

Scott, William G., and David K. Hart. (1989) *Organizational Values in America.* New Brunswick, NJ: Transaction.

Seidman, Harold. (1970) *Politics, Position, and Power.* New York: Oxford University Press.

Skocpol, Theda. (1985) "Political Response to Capitalist Crisis: Neo-Marxist Theories of the State and the Case of the New Deal." *Politics and Society,* 10, 2: 155-201.

Skowronek, Stephen. (1982) *Building a New American State.* New York: Cambridge University Press.

Stillman, Richard. (1991) *A Preface to Public Administration.* New York: St. Martin's.

Thayer, Fred. (1981) *An End to Hierarchy and Competition.* 2nd ed. New York: Watts.

Tucker, Robert C., ed. (1978) *The Marx-Engels Reader.* New York: Norton.

Van Riper, Paul. (1993) "The Pendleton Act of 1883 and Professionalism in the U.S. Public Service." Paper presented at the American Political Science Association Meeting in Washington, DC, September.

Waldo, Dwight. (1948) *The Administrative State.* New York: Ronald. (2nd ed., New York: Holmes and Meier, 1984).

———. (1992) *The Enterprise of Public Administration: A Summary View.* Novato, CA: Chandler & Sharp.

Weber, Max. (1946) *From Max Weber: Essays in Sociology.* H. H. Gerth and C. Wright Mills, trans. and eds. New York: Oxford University Press.

———. (1984) "Bureaucracy." In Frank Fischer and Carmen Sirianni, eds., *Critical Studies in Organization and Bureaucracy,* pp. 24-39. Philadelphia: Temple University Press. Reprinted from H. H. Gerth and C. Wright Mills., eds. and trans., *From Max Weber: Essays in Sociology* (1946), Oxford University Press. (1973), Hans H. Gerth.

———. (1986) "Essay on Bureaucracy." In Francis Rourke, ed., *Bureaucratic Power in National Policy Making.* 4th ed., pp. 62-73. Boston: Little, Brown.

White, Leonard. (1926) *Introduction to the Study of Public Administration.* New York: Macmillan.

Wilson, James Q. (1989) "The Rise of the Bureaucratic State." In Francis Rourke, ed., *Bureaucratic Power in National Policy Making,* pp. 125-148. Boston: Little, Brown.

Wilson, Woodrow. (1941, December) [1887] "The Study of Administration." *Political Science Quarterly,* 56: 481-506.

———. (1992) "The Study of Administration." In Jay Shafritz and Albert Hyde, eds., *Classics of Public Administration.* 3rd ed., pp. 11-24. Pacific Grove, CA: Brooks/ Cole.

Professionalism in Bureaucracy: Some Comparisons Based on the Indian Case

Renu Khator

Fred W. Riggs (1994b) contends that the American bureaucracy harbors an exceptional degree of professionalism and that this professionalism is responsible for the stability of the American presidential system. The objective of this chapter is, first, to formulate some conceptual and operational hypotheses based on Riggs's arguments and, then, to put these hypotheses to test in a comparative setting.

For the purpose of testing, I have selected India as a case study. The use of India as a testing ground is justified on several grounds: First, India has one of the world's most complex and developed public service systems. In the eighteenth and nineteenth centuries, it served as a laboratory for the British to experiment with new ideas that were to later become the bulwark of not only the British system but also of most British colonies. Second, India has a parliamentary system where, in exact contrast to the American presidential system, political power is purposefully concentrated in a single office. Even though the Indian political system is modeled after the British, its administrative system is a hybrid of the British legacy and its own social and cultural heritage. Thus the Indian case study will offer us an opportunity not only to test the independent effect of the parliamentary system (as Riggs contends) but also the intervening effect of other possible variables that may have been overlooked so far.

Third and last, India, having been partitioned in 1947 into India and Pakistan, provides a unique opportunity to evaluate the impact of historical factors (professionalism being one of them) on bureaucratic developments. In 1947, India and Pakistan were left with common baggage: the same history, the same culture (to a large extent), the same political system (established by the British India Act of 1935), and, indeed, the same bureaucracy. Yet their postindependence experiences differed greatly: India remained a parliamentary government while Pakistan suffered several coups d'état and political overthrows during the same time period.

The "Professionalism" Argument

Fred W. Riggs's professionalism argument is based on a long chain of logical axioms. Several excellent arguments form the nexus of his thesis. To begin with, Riggs claims that presidential and parliamentary systems are inherently different—not only that they are different but one is a rule and the other an exception. Riggs notes that most industrialized countries are parliamentary in the sense that their political power is not separated into compartments of executive, legislative, and judiciary. The United States, in contrast, is a presidential system. The direct influence of these countries is apparent: Today, most ex-colonies of Great Britain have some form of parliamentary system while the countries freed from the grip of the United States resemble the American presidential system. To the United States's dismay, the postcolonial history of these countries proves that the parliamentary model is more appropriate to their surroundings than the presidential model. In the past three decades, a significantly larger number of presidential than parliamentary systems have been taken over by military rulers or dictatorships (Riggs 1993).

This leads Riggs to his second argument, that is, parliamentary systems have a greater degree of resilience than presidentialist systems. He empirically tested this hypothesis in a 1993 study and claimed that out of the 76 Third World political systems in his population framework, the survival rate for parliamentary system was 69% (30 out of 43) while it was only 9% (3 out of 30) for presidential systems. In 1978, Juan Linz also argued that parliamentary systems were more likely than presidentialist regimes to produce stable democracies. This line of logic leads us to our first hypothesis:

> *Hypothesis 1:* Parliamentary systems have a better survival capability than presidential systems.

Why are parliamentary systems more stable? Riggs concedes that one of the most important internal challenges to a political system comes from its bureaucracy. Bureaucracy, over a time period, becomes more knowledgeable, more expert, more cohesive, and more assertive. Often it becomes the single most organized organization. Although curbing the ambitions and powers of such an organization is a daunting task, a parliamentary system, due to its single most important characteristic, that is, consolidation of political power, is more capable of controlling such a bureaucracy than its presidential counterpart is. The parliamentary system is more cohesive and can provide a unified front to counterbalance bureaucracy's power. In other words, one can say that cohesiveness of the parliamentary system (concentration of all powers in the hands of the cabinet and subsequently the prime minister) helps in preventing the emergence of a parallel bureaucratic power system. This is not to say that bureaucracies are not powerful in a parliamentary system; in most cases, they are. However, the thrust of Riggs's argument is that they are unable to become dominant enough to develop their own independent political agenda. In Riggs's (1993) words,

> Among representative governments, those that set a fixed term for the head of government (presidentialist regimes institutionalizing the separation of executive, legislative and judicial powers) are much more vulnerable to breakdowns via a coup d'état than are regimes in which a governing cabinet is subject to discharge by a no-confidence legislative vote (i.e. parliamentary regimes having fused executive/legislative powers). This may be explained by the greater capacity of parliamentary regimes to maintain control over their bureaucracies and, as a result, to sustain higher administrative performance levels so that both public officials and the general public are more likely to trust them and voluntarily respect their authority.

Consolidation of power in a parliamentary system protects its political players from the multiple and cross-pressures of a presidential system. Riggs notes in his writings that presidential regimes divide powers based on functions—executive, legislative, and judicial. This functional division puts the bureaucracy in an awkward position of trying to serve several masters simultaneously. This arrangement also promotes feelings of frustration and mistrust among bureaucrats who, in turn, become eager to support a military coup and popular rebellion against the existing political system. I derive my second conceptual hypothesis from this argument.

Hypothesis 2: A parliamentary system is better able to control its bureaucracy than a presidential system because of the consolidation of powers permitted by it.

Because the survival of a political system depends on its ability to control its bureaucracy, it becomes critical for us to analyze the patterns of interaction between the two. Do bureaucracies operate under different rules in a presidential versus a parliamentary system? Are they organized on different premises? Are the general rules of the game different? To answer these questions, Riggs brings in the distinction between mandarin and retainer bureaucracies. A mandarin bureaucracy is a bureaucracy of generalists in which recruitment is based on competitive examinations; training is geared toward serving the public; and the job environment offers immunity from social, political, and occupational pressures. A bureaucracy with mandarin characteristics is common in parliamentary systems In contrast, a retainer bureaucracy is a norm in presidential regimes. The retainer bureaucracy consists of bureaucrats who are partisan, recruited on the basis of their party loyalty, and retained for an indefinite term. Due to its politicized nature, the retainer bureaucracy can pose a formidable challenge to its political masters. Despite these dangers, presidential systems must live with retainer bureaucracies because they are compatible with their political arrangements.

At this point, Riggs raises his most critical question: Why is the U.S. bureaucracy not like other retainer bureaucracies? What would have been the consequences had the United States kept a retainer bureaucracy? Historically, monarchies always had retainer bureaucracies that served on their kings' whims and fancies. However, this situation changed as European countries began to embrace the concept of a popularly elected government. To make the bureaucracy serve the interest of the people rather than of the royalty, countries were forced to slowly neutralize their bureaucracies and transform them from retainer to mandarin organizations.

Of interest, the United States has neither the mandarin nor the retainer bureaucracy. Its bureaucracy is truly unique. Riggs calls it a professional bureaucracy—born of the failure of the rotation system introduced by President Andrew Jackson. The Jacksonian system of bureaucracy failed because it placed undue importance on the loyalty of civil officials and the temporality of their terms. The outcome of this failed attempt was the Pendleton Act of 1883. The Pendleton Act established a new system of recruitment where recruits were selected through a nonpolitical and non-partisan merit system. This system proved successful, albeit tensions and controversies regarding the nature of recruits—nonpolitical versus political—have continued to this day.

The United States is also exceptional in the sense that it was able to transform its bureaucracy from a retainer to a professional organization. Despite the provision of meritorious recruitment, the U.S. bureaucracy is far from being mandarin in character. American bureaucrats, rather than being generalists—a fundamental requirement of a mandarin bureau-cracy—are specialists and professionals. Riggs (1994a) distinguishes three types of bureaucrats: professionals (who uphold the standards of their professions), professionalists (who have the skills to put the public mission before their profession's mission), and professionists (who perceive public service as a profession in itself, that is, mandarins). Bureaucrats in a parliamentary system are professionists, while bureaucrats in the United States are professionals.

Why and how could the U.S. political system, despite being fragmented in nature, succeed in controlling its bureaucracy? How could the political system remain internally unchallenged? Answers to these questions, Riggs contends, lie in the level of professionalism that the American bureaucracy exhibits. The American administrative system, having emerged as an antithesis to the rotation system, resulted in an arrangement that attracted and rewarded specialists. Today, civil servants in America are professionals and feel more bound by the norms and standards of their independent professions than their bureaucratic organizations. They identify more readily with professional colleagues than with superiors and compatriots. James Q. Wilson (1989) notes that the tendency of the American bureau-crats is to strive to live up to their professions' standards. This dilutes the oneness of their civil mission, because their feelings of satisfaction and frustration come from their own professions rather than from the civil services. In addition, high-ranking bureaucrats tend to be transients who have neither the time nor the motivation to induce a single, common mission in the organization.

The consequences of this high level of professionalism are both positive and negative. On one hand, it provides stability and tranquillity to the political system by undermining the power of the bureaucracy. On the other hand, it makes bureaucratic coordination nearly impossible. Riggs (1994a) points to U.S. foreign policy as a case in point. He claims that there are not one but many foreign policies in America. Lack of coordination has resulted in haphazardness, wastefulness, and incoherence in foreign policy.

The argument of the high level of professionalism in the United States leaves us with two additional hypotheses:

> *Hypothesis 3:* The level of professionalism is higher in the United States than is generally found in parliamentary regimes.
>
> *Hypothesis 4:* The low level (or lack) of professionalism in a mandarin bureaucracy is responsible for promoting its unified identity.

These hypotheses, to be externally valid, need to be tested on a larger scale involving several systems. However, my intent in this chapter is to begin the process by testing in one logical setting, that is, India. I hope that the breadth being sacrificed by the use of a single-country study can be compensated for by the depth that it allows.

The Indian Bureaucracy:
A Testing Ground

This section operationalizes the conceptual hypotheses formed earlier. Hypothesis 1 requires a comparative analysis based on several cases, which is clearly beyond the scope of this single case study. Regrettably, this hypothesis has to be left here with the hope that another comparative study in the future will be able to shed some light on it. However, Hypotheses 2, 3, and 4 can be operationalized to fit this specific case study. (They are still referred to with their original numbers.)

> *Hypothesis 2:* The Indian political system is able to control its bureaucracy because of the inherent consolidation of political powers.

(Of course, this hypothesis in itself makes two other assumptions: first, that the Indian system is able to control its bureaucracy, and, second, that the Indian system allows consolidation of political powers.)

> *Hypothesis 3:* The Indian bureaucracy is not as professional as the U.S. bureaucracy.
>
> *Hypothesis 4:* Lack of professionalism in the Indian bureaucracy is responsible for its seemingly unified position.

The Indian bureaucracy was the brainchild of the British, who wanted to devise a mechanism to keep this jewel colony under the Empire's effective control (Jain 1990; Kennedy 1987). It was established to serve this very specific purpose. It was not to be a political institution and not to reflect the political interests of those who were placed under its administrative control. Neither was it meant to be sensitive to the social and cultural needs of those people. In fact, one may argue that one of its tasks under the British raj was to undermine the political, social, and cultural identity of Indians. Considering this purpose, it is no wonder that the British considered the Weberian bureaucracy with its rational, neutral, and hierarchical characteristics to be the most suitable model for India.

Bureaucracy and the
Consolidation of Political Powers

India is a constitutional democracy with federalism and parliamentarianism as its two guiding principles. The political system in India is a replica of the British system, nonetheless there are three important differences that give it an independent character. These differences are critical for the organization and functioning of the bureaucracy. First, unlike Great Britain, India does not have a two-party system. It has at least four national parties (that contest and win elections in more than two states) and a long list of regional parties (Hardgrave and Kochanek 1993). Despite this diversity, the country has been governed by a single party, the Congress Party, for most of its history. In the parliamentary model, the two-party system plays an important role. Because all the powers are concentrated in a single office, some internal check on this office is necessary. The opposition party, which in a two-party system is almost parallel in strength, is supposed to serve this very function.

In India, the omnipotent presence of the Congress Party produces a different power equation. It tilts the balance of power in favor of the political system. In a one-party-dominant system, when the same people return to power, bureaucrats find that their role as being the stabilizing force during the times of transition is no longer needed. This also means that they do not get the opportunity to exploit the vacuum created by the political system due to transitions (from one party government to another).

Second, the Indian political system is federal. In contrast to the British unitary system, it must accommodate the priorities and needs of 25 states. States in India have a separate social and cultural identity and are often eager to assert it. This leads to a very complex environment for the bureaucracy, for it must absorb the pressures coming from various directions: the center, the states, and the sociocultural interactions among the states.

Third, and last, the judiciary in India is relatively independent. In Great Britain, the judiciary is subordinate to the parliament in the sense that it cannot challenge laws passed by the parliament. In contrast, the Indian Constitution allows a separate Supreme Court with a right to judicial review.

In sum, political power in India is not as concentrated in the office of the prime minister as is often assumed; state governments remit pressures and the judiciary poses its own control. At the same time, power is not as fragmented as in the United States. The absence of a rival opposition party makes it possible for the prime minister to exert control on the states and also to undermine the judiciary. The prime minister also has several means to control the states. He or she is given the power to appoint state governors. This power becomes particularly important when state legislatures are controlled by the opposition.

It must be noted that the Indian bureaucracy was compatible with the needs of the political system at the time of the British. In fact, the administrative system worked so well that Indian leaders (as well as Pakistani leaders) decided to adopt it without modifications in 1947. The name of the bureaucratic system was, of course, changed from the Indian Civil Services (ICS) to the Indian Administrative Services (IAS) to give it a new image. Applauding the role of the bureaucracy, Sardar Patel, one of the 10 masterminds behind India's independence, once said,

> I wish to place on record of this House that if during the last two or three years, most of the members of the Services had not behaved patriotically and with loyalty, the Union would have collapsed . . . you will not have a united India, if you do not have a good All India Service which has the independence to speak out its mind, which has a sense of security that you will stand by your word. (quoted in Vepa 1978: 131)

Thus, in the Indian Constitution adopted in 1950, the place of the bureaucracy was not only preserved but also glorified. According to Article 311 of the Constitution, a civil servant cannot be dismissed without a show-cause notice. Organizationally, there are several layers and sections of the bureaucracy. The Indian Administrative Services (IAS), at the apex of this organization, provides leadership and vision. This is an elite group of civil servants who are placed at all—federal, state, and local—levels of key administrative positions. According to the statistics, out of a total of 3.7 million bureaucrats, 5,047 were IAS officers in 1984. The overall rate of growth in the Indian bureaucracy parallels the growth in other countries: Approximately 1 million new bureaucratic positions are created every 15 years. Its strength stood at 1.7 million in 1956, 2.8 million in 1971, and 3.7 million in 1984 (Mehta 1989: 30). Because IAS officers are the ones who give direction and tone to the bureaucracy, this study will primarily focus on them; however, whenever necessary, we will break the pattern and delve into "other" bureaucratic norms and patterns.

In the following section, I will focus on two key characteristics of the Indian bureaucracy: broad-based recruitment and the oath of neutrality. These are considered important for the functioning of the political-bureaucratic dichotomy in India.

Recruitment. Recruitment practices in the Indian bureaucracy are the products of British experimentation. In 1833, T. B. Macaulay drafted Clause 87 of the East India Charter Act (under which the country was being governed by the British at that time) that opened service in the Indian bureaucracy to all races without discrimination. Despite this, the practice of preferential treatment toward British citizens was in existence. The practice of preferential treatment continues to exist even today, albeit in a different form and involving different groups. Scholars argue that the IAS examination is meant to tap and train elite. Rules dictate that anybody between the ages of 21 and 24 (for the protected classes, the upper limit is 28) can appear in the written examination specifically held for the recruitment to IAS ranks. Successful candidates must, then, go through another layer of tests, called a test of personality. After this rigorous process, only 100 recruits remain from a pool of more than 30,000 (Vepa 1978: 133).

The elitist nature of the Indian bureaucracy has been a topic of intense research among scholars. Subramaniam (1971) and Sharma (1978) studied the demographic characteristics of higher civil servants and concluded that they come from the urban, salaried, and professional middle class. Thus, even though the entrance criterion is egalitarian, the outcome is decisively selective. Most of the recruits come from the top 10% of the population— the population that is urban, salaried, and professional. Needless to say, this selective population has a greater access to the schools (privately owned and English medium) that are better equipped to provide an IAS-type education.

Does elitism affect bureaucratic disposition? Does it increase or decrease bureaucratic power? According to some, elitism has caused alienation in India. It has resulted in feelings of mistrust and aloofness among bureaucrats. It has adversely affected the public's perception of bureaucracy. Bureaucrats are viewed as maladjusted, lacking in dedication, corrupt, and authoritarian. In fact, people of all classes and regions consider it a pastime to share horror stories of their bureaucratic encounters. Ironically, even the privileged class, despite having the largest representation in the bureaucracy, mistrusts it. According to Samuel J. Eldersveld et al. (1968), the urban, educated, high-status people distrust public administrators more than the rural, poor, and uneducated. It is not an uncommon practice, even for politicians, to blame bureaucrats in public. This negative public image necessarily counterbalances the power of the Indian bureaucracy.

Indian bureaucrats, because of their aloof and elitist orientations, are less likely to get involved in politics. They lack the mass appeal necessary to be able to lead a revolution or to rebel against politicians, as has been the case in many developing countries. They are a liability rather than an asset to the military, should the military decide to take control of the popular political system.

Oath of neutrality. Bureaucrats in India are supposed to be neutral. According to Dwivedi and Jain (1985: 81),

> The Central Services Conduct Rules forbid a government servant to be a member of or be otherwise associated with any political party or any organization and in fact require him to prevent every member of his family from taking part in, subscribing in aid of, or assisting in any other manner in movement or activity which is directly or indirectly deemed to be subversive of the government.

They can vote but cannot talk about it. However, the system to ensure neutrality is not perfect. Politics in India seems naturally to draw aspiring bureaucrats, particularly after they retire from the service life. Many go into politics; some even form their own political parties and seek elections. The Swatantra Party was home to several top bureaucrats including C. C. Desai, N. Dandekar, H. M. Patel, and Lobo Prabhu.

Still, neutrality is essential to the Indian bureaucracy. Almost all parliamentary systems have mandarin (generalist, neutral) bureaucracies. Bureaucratic neutrality makes the transfer of power between parties smooth. Furthermore, it provides continuity and stability in a system where politicians' terms are unpredictable. In India, during the years of chaos (the time of partition in 1947), political turmoil (Emergency Years from 1975 to 1977), and leadership uncertainty (following Indira Gandhi's and then Rajiv Gandhi's deaths in 1984 and 1991, respectively), it was the bureaucracy that held the country together through its iron will (Hardgrave 1984; Hardgrave and Kochanek 1993).

Two questions must be raised in this context: How is this neutrality assured? And what are its implications for the political-bureaucratic dichotomy? To answer the first question, we must examine the recruitment system. Bureaucrats in the IAS are appointed for life based on their exceptional performance in a set of written and oral examinations. Once recruited, they are formally trained to be "neutral." The training of new officers is extensive. Upon recruitment, they are required to attend a formal training institution specially designed for this purpose for a period of six months. Curriculum for this training is carefully crafted and covers several areas including political theory, constitution, public administration, law, economics, history, culture, and Hindi. This is to build a common, generalist-oriented value system. The formal training program is followed by a field training program of 12 months in a designated state. Finally, recruits return for another refresher course lasting seven months at their host training institution before assuming the responsibilities of a sub-division officer (Misra 1986: 250).

An interesting aspect of the IAS, which is the core of the administrative services in India, is that recruits are bound to stay within the state to which they have been assigned. Some, of course, move to the central level, but as long as they stay at the state level, they cannot be transferred to another state. Additionally, rules require that not more than 50% of the recruits are assigned to their home state. This practice is to assure neutrality in recruits by diluting the possibility of them exploiting their own or their families' political connections. This also undermines the regional and linguistic identities of the recruits.

To answer the second question of what the implications of neutrality are for the political-bureaucratic dichotomy, let us examine the pressures and protection that this system creates for individual bureaucrats. Neutrality indeed increases the power base of bureaucrats. When bureaucrats are political appointees (in a rotational system), their tenure in office is dependent on the pleasure of their political masters because the source of power for rotational bureaucrats is political loyalty.

In contrast, the source of power for a mandarin bureaucracy (such as in India) is expertise and knowledge. Over a long time period, mandarins garner enough administrative expertise (despite their generalist orientation) to carve out an independent niche in the political system. Through their expertise, they are able to become indispensable and therefore powerful players in the political game. The ultimate expression of this power was seen several years ago when Indian ministers (political masters) resorted to *dharana* (strike) to make their own bureaucrats listen to them (Vepa 1978: 59).

Furthermore, neutrality makes bureaucrats less accountable because it allows them to escape from responsibility. The system allows them to implement a policy without having to worry about its consequences. More often than not, bureaucrats' performance is measured by the degree to which implementation has been carried out rather than the level to which goals have been met. In an earlier study of social forestry (1991), I had revealed that even when the process of implementation was followed to the fullest extent, the goals went largely unfulfilled.

Is India's bureaucratic neutrality real? Some scholars claim that the Indian bureaucracy is not actually neutral but instead is deeply politicized. Bhambhri (1971) claims that bureaucrats exercise more political power than is permitted under the law. The distinction between politics and administration is particularly blurred at the district level (Kothari and Roy 1969). As a district magistrate (an IAS post), an administrator exercises enormous political power. A vivid portrayal of the original district magistrate (under the British) is depicted in the following quote:

He is the great Sahib whose nod is to be obeyed—before whom all the great people of the village bow. He is the mighty one to whom the most flowery languages and ornate titles apply. He, or those who obey him, orders the life of the people of India and next to the creator and the laws of nature he comes in the hierarchy of arbitrary powers. Those above him are too remote from the life of the people to be anything but indefinite gleams, those below him are outwardly and visibly his servants. (quoted in Vepa 1978: 44)

This is a true portrayal of the district magistrate under the British. The powers of the district magistrate have been significantly reduced since then through administrative reform programs. Nonetheless, in the minds of many illiterate, poor, and rural people, this image still holds true.

Although bureaucratic power seems to be omnipotent at the local level, its glamor is significantly reduced at the top level. The political system at this level has its own way of exerting influence. Paul Brass (1990) feels that senior appointments are important tools in the hands of the politicians who can use them to curb bureaucratic fancies. Mrs. Gandhi used this privilege and gave important appointments to officers who were loyal to her ideals and goals. After Gandhi's loss of power in the 1977 elections, the Janata government replaced most of the old guard with their own cronies. Gandhi loyalists were either transferred or thrown out of the power circle. According to Brass (1990: 52),

The post-independence structure of political-bureaucratic relationships has consequently been fundamentally transformed in the direction of a patrimonial regime in which the political leadership selects officers who are personally loyal, who serve their narrow political interests, and who expect reciprocal preferments in return.

The above discussion, while insightful, fails to lead us toward any conclusive pattern of power relationship between the bureaucracy and its supposedly higher-up political masters. It seems that bureaucracy is able to thwart policy process by challenging political leaders in many cases. However, in other cases, politicians are able to assert their preferences when dealing with bureaucrats. From this discussion, it is difficult to assess whether or not the political system is in a controlling position; however, it is clear that the bureaucracy is not in the mandarin-style controlling position. The consolidation of political power in the office of the prime minister provides only a partial explanation for the political-bureaucratic dichotomy in India. The other part of the explanation may lie in the conditions that make such a consolidation possible. In India's context, one-party dominance assures consolidation of political power—a phenomenon we will explore later. In brief, we do not have definite grounds to accept or reject Hypothesis 2.

Professionalism in the Indian Bureaucracy

The identity of the Indian bureaucracy lies in its mandarin, generalist nature. Civil servants take an oath of commitment to the Constitution, and constitutional principles provide norms and conditions for their behavior in public. Unlike the United States, where civil servants are bound by the norms and standards of their individual professions (Wilson 1989), the primary norms and standards for Indian civil servants are specified in the civil service regulations. It is expected that upon joining, bureaucrats will put these standards before any other professional obligations and will draw their strength and charter from them.

The term *professionalism* has a specific meaning in India. Professionalism encompasses the ideas of neutrality, sincerity, and integrity. L. P. Singh, then Home Secretary and a member of the IAS himself, defines the term in a paper published in 1973 as "dedicated service to the people, the promotion of the welfare and happiness of the citizen and respect for his feelings and susceptibilities and principles of fairness and integrity in all his dealings" (quoted in Misra 1986: 328). Being professional thus means being beyond the norms and conditions of all narrow vested interests, whether engineering or law or medicine. In fact, Lord Macaulay, who was responsible for designing the basic recruitment policy for senior civil servants, reaffirmed this broad definition of professionalism by saying,

> Men who have been engaged up to one and two and twenty in studies which have no immediate connection with the business of any profession

and the effect of which is merely to open the mind will generally be found in the business of any profession to be superior to men who have at 18 or 19 devoted themselves to the special studies of their calling.

This particular notion of professionalism is accepted and promoted in India through various means. To begin with, professionals in other fields, particularly in medicine, are openly discouraged from entering the Indian Administrative Services. The government believes that "their professional experience need not be wasted in a purely administrative career" (Vepa 1978: 134). The administrative part of public administration seems to be reserved for the people coming from the liberal arts, particularly with a background in history or economics. In general, physicians and lawyers are expected to contribute to the goals of the government in other ways. However, these "other ways" ensure that they will be professionals and not "administrators." The distinction between the two is carefully drawn and painstakingly preserved.

Even though the so-called professionals do not enter the Indian Administrative Services, several thousands of them serve in the public sector and are civil servants. Their entry to the service comes from a different route. Engineers take a separate engineering examination. Physicians apply directly for job openings in the government sector. Both, however, are expected to be public professionals rather than public administrators. The term used to identify them is *technocrat* (the same is true in Pakistan; see Kennedy 1987). In terms of hierarchy, technocrats, despite their specialized knowledge and expertise, are placed below generalists.

The IAS entrance criteria also discourage people with professional degrees from entering the administrative ranks. Professional degrees typically require more time and a specialized focus. The age limit of 21 through 24 is a disincentive for profession-bound people. Because examinations are based on "general" knowledge, those who acquire their bachelor's degree in liberal arts and pursue a master's degree in one of the "preferred" fields are more often than not better prepared for competition.

The training that follows IAS recruitment further adds to antiprofessionalism. The training, as arranged, neutralizes whatever little commitment a recruit may have toward his or her professional society. The focus during the training is on developing a profession of "public administration." Needless to say, all of this time is spent on training in general administration. Indeed, it is possible for an officer to specialize in social administration, general administration, financial administration, and so on but only after he or she has spent at least 10 years in the service (Misra 1986: 247).

In sum, the IAS entrance criteria and training do not favor professional degree holders. When such people (whom I shall also refer to as technocrats) enter the service—whether through a separate route or through direct recruitment—they find that their professional experience does not carry much administrative worth. They are typically subjected to the superior authority of a generalist, who supposedly possesses better skills to make administrative decisions. For a long time, salary differentials were also astounding: The salary of a technocrat was not even at par with the salary of a generalist. The perks and status that came with a generalist position also surpassed the ones that were attached to a specialist position. In addition, their chances of promotion to positions such as secretary were also very low.

The Indian government, over the decades, has made several attempts to entice professional degree holders into administrative positions. During the 1960s, the Administrative Reforms Commissions (ARC) indicated a strong preference for inducting experts in the secretariat and other levels of government. An inquiry into the British bureaucracy and the subsequent report by the Fulton Committee upholding the merits of experts in decision-making positions made an impact in India as well. Another factor that helped the cause of technocrats was the advent of development administration in the 1970s. Development administration demanded a group of bureaucrats who, more than being neutral and generalists, were committed and knowledgeable about the technical aspect of administration.

Although the government has tried to narrow the gap between generalists and technocrats, the fact still remains that the system values technocrats less than it values generalists. In recent years, technocrats themselves have been ignoring government jobs because the average opportunity and income for a technocrat is far higher (sometimes more than double) in the private sector than in the public sector. This fact alone demoralizes the technocrats in the public sector.

A study by Richard P. Taub (1969), even though somewhat outdated, sheds light on the attitudinal patterns of Indian bureaucrats. To compare the background, attitudes, and working behavior of IAS officers and their technocrat (engineer) counterparts in the government service, Taub asked the sample population (bureaucrats and local elite) to identify "high status" people in the area. He found that even when engineers were earning as much as their IAS counterparts, not one person mentioned them as being "high status" people. In the same study, Taub asked respondents to declare their reasons for joining the service. Five out of twelve engineers said that they had never thought of joining the service; they were forced into it by family or friends. On the other hand, 21 out of 28 IAS officers (generalists) said that they were either forced into it by their family (7) or by the limited choices available to pursue a career (14). Obviously, no engineer said that the public service was the only alternative.

Thus one finds that professionalism as defined in the United States is neither accepted nor promoted in India. Although thousands of technically skilled people work in the public sector, they are marginalized in the process of decision making and administration. Technocrats adhere to the norms and standards of the civil services more readily than they do to the norms and standards of their specialized professions. They consider this necessary to serve the "public" and to satisfy the demands placed on them by their generalist supervisors. Based on this information, we are inclined to accept Hypothesis 3, that the Indian bureaucracy is not as professionalized as its American counterpart.

Professionalism:
A Source of Bureaucratic Identity

The acceptance of Hypothesis 3 brings us to the last link in Fred W. Riggs's argument, that it is because of nonprofessionalism that the Indian bureaucracy offers a unified identity (Riggs argues that in the United States it is the high level of professionalism that weakens the monolithic identity of the bureaucracy). First of all, we must assume that a unified bureaucracy is a bigger threat to a political system than an American-style fragmented bureaucracy. We also need to remind ourselves that a unified bureaucracy is necessary for cohesion in policy making (something that Riggs feels does not exist in the United States).

Is the bureaucracy in India unified? I would argue that despite their training as "professionals in the field of public administration," Indian bureaucrats do not possess a single identity or a common purpose or a cohesive culture. Several factors—social, cultural, and political—are responsible for this. According to R. B. Jain (1991), the sociopolitical structure of India affects the administrative system. He identifies two factors—caste and religion—as being particularly important for bureaucratic disposition. They, according to him, lead to dysfunctionalism by promoting unhealthy practices, including ethnoexpansionism, sons-of-the-soil, and authoritarianism.

Caste, a social hierarchical system, divides people into four major and several hundred minor groups (subcastes). Even though the government has made serious attempts to desegregate the society, caste boundaries are still carefully maintained and obeyed. Casteism entered the civil services in the 1940s when the government decided to create a quota for underprivileged castes. Emerging as a temporary solution, caste-based quotas had soon become a permanent condition. In past decades, quota size has increased, creating a feeling of discontent and frustration among higher caste people. The higher castes feel that they are being discriminated against (a) because entrance criteria for reserved seats are lower and (b) because competition for these seats is less fierce. These feelings have left a permanent scar. At the very least, they are prohibiting bureaucrats from developing a unified identity. Despite concentrated efforts to neutralize new recruits, the organization is marred by caste identities (Dwivedi and Jain 1985: 56-57).

Other than caste, religion also undermines the emergence of a unified identity among officers (Jain 1991). Because an officer works in a milieu full of social and religious fervor, his behavior must necessarily become culture-bound or else he risks social disapproval (58). India has 82% Hindus, 11% Muslims, 2% Sikhs, and fewer than 2% Christians. Although there are no reserved seats for religious minorities, religious identities certainly affect bureaucratic behavior.

In several of my studies on environmental management in India, I have found a forceful influence of social factors on bureaucratic practices (Khator 1992, 1994). Although my research was not intended to specifically study the bureaucratic phenomenon, its presence became evident as I evaluated individual programs. I found that there were specific ways in which social preferences found expression in administrative decision making. Bureaucratic discretion was often used to tilt policies in favor of the social elite (whether they were religious leaders, fellow caste persons, or people belonging to the economically privileged class). In social forestry, a program funded by the World Bank, I found that seeds and saplings distributed free of charge under the program went mostly to upper-caste farmers (Khator 1991). Social preferences were asserted through bureaucratic discretion available in the form of transfer and promotion of junior officials.

The question of morality does not arise in this context. According to Dwivedi and Jain (1985: 59), "When the upper castes assume bureaucratic office, their aim is not merely to expand their ranks through favoritism, but also to invest their caste values with a quality that they consider will be acceptable to other groups, castes and communities."

Thus, although the lack of professionalism exists in India, it does not have a decisive impact on the bureaucracy. Based on Riggs's theory, lack of professionalism in Indian bureaucracy should have created an environment conducive to the development of a single identity. However, that is not the case in India. The thing that prohibits such an identity from developing is the complexity of the Indian society. The divisive forces of the society are able to penetrate the otherwise "neutralized" bureaucracy and affect its members' behavior. If we compare the Indian situation with that of the United States, we can conclude that although both countries have obtained the same outcome (the subdued nature of the bureaucracy), the means to achieve this outcome have been different. In the United States, as Riggs contends, it is the high level of professionalism that has led to the fragmented identity among bureaucrats, while in India, it is the social cross-pressure that has resulted in the split identity. Thus we reject Hypothesis 4 that it is the lack of professionalism that is responsible for the bureaucracy's unified position in India.

Conclusion

Paradoxically, we find that the two factors—party dominance and social heterogeneity—that were most responsible for India's political stability (stability in the sense of not having been overthrown by the bureaucracy) are also the ones that are most criticized by Indian scholars. The dominant party system is instrumental in promoting a unified political front. Otherwise, the parliamentary system of India would have been more fragmented than the ideal model (the British). India has an independent judiciary and a federalist structure of government, both of which are capable of diffusing parliament's power. So far, this diffusion has not hurt India because the same party has been in power for most of the time. The presence of one party, and the degree of continuity resulting from it, have made political control of bureaucracy possible in a system that was not designed for it. The power base of a mandarin bureaucracy (which is known to develop over a period of time because of its permanency, expertise, and generalist outlook) has been undermined in India by the continuity of the political elite.

Social heterogeneity also plays a positive role by creating parallel subidentities within the singular bureaucratic identity. The evolution of a bureaucratic identity—independent from the identity given to it by the political system—is a prerequisite for bureaucratic rebellion or revolution. Because the Indian bureaucracy lacks a singular identity, the chances of bureaucratic rebellion are low. According to Taub (1969: 190), "Their attitude toward religion and caste to some extent put them out of touch with both the people and the people's representatives, their own superiors."

At this point, we should ask the question of how and why Pakistan experienced political upheavals and military overthrows when it, too, inherited the same "iron steel" bureaucracy as did India. Even though India and Pakistan share the same historical heritage, it would be misleading to assume that they were ideologically identical or that they shared the same expectations. Furthermore, their situations were not the same: Pakistan lost its founding father, Jinnah, within a few months of its inception; its political system lacked stability in the infancy itself; Liyakat Ali Khan died shortly thereafter, creating a serious political vacuum; and Pakistan received only a small share of bureaucratic resources from British-held India. Several Muslim bureaucrats chose to stay in India, which forced Pakistan to make special arrangements to recruit a large number of officers through emergency means. Unfortunately, these emergency means meant bypassing the mandarin safeguards, including the examination system. New recruits hired during the times of need did not go through the rigors of neutralizing training. They were, in all reality, political appointees. Thus, for Pakistan, the emergency situation called for the transformation of a mandarin bureaucracy into a retainer bureaucracy. This, coupled with the vacuum in the political leadership, led naturally to the formation of the new Pakistani bureaucracy, which was quite different than its Indian counterpart.

The political vacuum in Pakistan was further thickened by the uncertainty surrounding the arrangement of political power. As the pendulum swung between parliamentary and presidentialist arrangements, the bureaucracy was left uncontrolled. In the end, the whole situation gave the political system less of a chance to present a unified front. It was clearly unable to check the power of a politicized bureaucracy.

The bureaucratic system in Pakistan also suffered from abnormal practices. In the early 1970s, Prime Minister Bhutto started a lateral recruitment program. The intent of the program was to increase efficiency by recruiting experts. The program eventually became a liability, as the system was unable even to find suitable work for these people. When the program collapsed a few years later, some of the recruits were without charge (Kennedy 1987).

In brief, the Pakistan bureaucracy had sufficient room and motivation to develop a character of its own. Its independence was intimidating to politicians. The extent of its independence was evident from the fact that Bhutto's administrative reforms of 1973 were almost entirely directed at increasing and formalizing the political influence over the bureaucracy. During Zia's 11 years of rule, bureaucratic powers were somewhat curtailed, although not by the political system but by the military. In his attempt to militarize the system, Zia recruited military personnel to fill bureaucratic positions.

Today, Pakistan, like India, has a mandarin bureaucracy. Nonetheless, its generalist base is not as strongly established as India's. Several reasons account for this discrepancy. First, the pattern of power arrangements has been confusing in Pakistan; the pendulum keeps swinging between a strong executive and a strong legislature. Second, frequent military takeovers have allowed the bureaucracy and the military to develop a common identity. Third, the credibility of the "mandarin" bureaucracy is constantly assaulted by special programs, arrangements, and emergency provisions. Despite these differences, one must admit that the role of professionals is the same in Pakistan as it is in India. In both countries, generalists are preferred over specialists; they are in a position to develop a consolidated identity that can be a threat to the political system. In the Indian context, however, the generalists' power is undermined by social and cultural divisions. Such divisions also exist in Pakistan, but they do not hamper the consolidation of bureaucratic identity. What fuels the bureaucratic bandwagon in Pakistan is its close alliance with the military.

Thus the level of professionalism in the Indian bureaucracy is low. Whether this is responsible for the stability of the political system is unclear. It is clear, however, that despite its low level of professionalism, the Indian bureaucracy is not a unified, cohesive, and powerful entity. I would argue that the social fabric of India does not allow such a bureaucracy to emerge.

References

Bhambhri, C. P. (1971) *Bureaucracy and Politics in India*. Delhi, India: Vikas.

Brass, Paul R. (1990) *The Politics of India Since Independence*. Cambridge: Cambridge University Press.

Dwivedi, O. P., and R. B. Jain. (1985) *India's Administrative State*. New Delhi, India: Gitanjali.

Eldersveld, Samuel J., et. al. (1968) *The Citizen and the Administration in a Developing Democracy: An Empirical Study in Delhi State.* Reading, MA: Scott, Foresman.

Hardgrave, Robert L. (1984) *India Under Pressure: Prospect for Political Stability.* Boulder, CO: Westview.

Hardgrave, Robert L., and Stanley A. Kochanek. (1993) *India: Government and Politics in a Developing Nation*. San Diego, CA: Harcourt Brace Jovanovich.

Jain, R. B. (1990) "Policy Actors: Bureaucrats, Politicians and Intellectuals." *International Social Science Journal*, 123: 31-47.

———. (1991) "Inter-Relationships Between Socio-Political Structure and Public Administration in India." In Hartmut Elsenhans and Harald Fuhr, eds., *Administration and Industrial Development*. New Delhi: National Book Organization.

Kennedy, Charles H. (1987) *Bureaucracy in Pakistan*. Karachi, Pakistan: Oxford University Press.

Khator, Renu. (1991) *Environment, Development, and Politics in India*. Lanham, MD: University Press of America.

————. (1992, November-December) "State Autonomy and Environmental Challenge in India." *Political Chronicle.*

————. (1994) "Bureaucracy and the Environmental Challenge in a Comparative Perspective." In Ali Farazmand, ed., *Handbook on Bureaucracy.* New York: Marcel Dekker.

Kothari, Shanti, and Ramashray Roy. (1969) *Relations Between Politicians and Administrators at the District Level.* New Delhi: Indian Institute of Public Administration and the Centre for Applied Politics.

Linz, Juan. (1978) "The Perils of Presidentialism." *Journal of Democracy,* 1, 1: 51-69.

Mehta, Prayag. (1989) *Bureaucracy, Organizational Behavior, and Development.* New Delhi: Sage.

Misra, B. B. (1986) *Government and Bureaucracy in India.* Delhi, India: Oxford University Press.

Riggs, Fred W. (1993) "Fragility of the Third World Regimes." *International Social Science Journal,* 136: 199-243.

————. (1994a) "American Public Administration in the Global Context." In Jean-Claude Garcia Zamor and Renu Khator, eds., *Public Administration in the Global Village.* Westport, CT: Praeger.

————. (1994b) "Bureaucracy: A Profound Perplexity for Presidentialism." In Ali Farazmand, ed., *Handbook on Bureaucracy.* New York: Marcel Dekker.

Sharma, G. B. (1978) "Social Composition of Indian Bureaucracy." In Ramesh K. Arora et al., eds., *The Indian Administrative System,* pp. 200-223. New Delhi: Associated Publishing House.

Subramaniam, V. (1971) *Social Background of India's Administrators.* New Delhi: Ministry of Information and Broadcasting, Publications Division.

Taub, Richard P. (1969) *Bureaucrats Under Stress.* Berkeley: University of California Press.

Vepa, Ram K. (1978) *Change and Challenge in Indian Administration.* New Delhi, India: Manohar.

Wilson, James Q. (1989) *Bureaucracy: What Governments Do and Why They Do It?* New York: Basic Books.

The U.S. Civil Service: 1883–1993 (R.I.P.)

Frederick C. Thayer

This chapter is about the political lynching of the U.S. civil service, which, for practical purposes, has now died because its members can no longer be expected to perform the tasks originally assigned them. The civil service was not invented in 1883 solely to improve government "efficiency," a widely publicized myth designed to obscure history. The original mission of the civil service was to be the ethical watchdog, the moral guardian of governmental decision making. No, the Founding Fathers did not envision a professional administrative corps when they produced the U.S. Constitution, but neither did they anticipate the political party system that stood outside the constitutional framework, corrupting those within it. By the 1880s, it had become overwhelmingly clear that a new structure *within* government was needed to replace the unplanned cancerous growth that had come to control politicians, elections, voters, and much of government spending.

The 1883 law that created a civil service, the Pendleton Act, actually was the full equivalent of a constitutional amendment, even though there was no way to describe it as such. The political parties were an unplanned and ugly part of the political system, but not of the *constitutional* system, hence they cannot even now be directly targeted. The Pendleton notion was that not only would an independent agency make decisions about hiring but, given the advantage of job security, civil servants would be able to ask questions about the ethical standards that elected and patronage officials were using in their decision-making processes. Obviously, those without job security are in no position to challenge their bosses. Now that job security has been largely stripped away, the guardians are powerless. Given the unbelievably huge amounts of funds that politicians are now compelled to raise, there can be little doubt that, under more pressure than ever to "help" their supporters, politicians are quite aware of the benefits of having a hollow civil service whose remaining members will be kept quiet the old-fashioned way—by threats of firing.

The argument to follow is straightforward:

• If there is to be any discussion of the *legitimacy* or *founding* of "the administrative state," it must be centered on public law that, unless or until overthrown or replaced, is a part of the Constitution. Miscellaneous "orders" or "reports" cannot confer the same legitimacy.

• We cannot find the legitimizing concepts for a professional administrative structure in the Constitution, just as we should not blame the Founders for not anticipating the ultimately corrupting "spoils" systems that emerged in the nineteenth century, which many politicians and students of government still consider absolutely essential to the political system. Patronage appointees, it is still argued, are needed to get out the vote and perform other political chores that are more important than the official duties they are paid to perform. The selling of jobs and the collection of "kickbacks" from patronage appointees have not disappeared, but we cannot blame Jefferson or Madison for not looking ahead.

• While the great expansion of Franklin Roosevelt's New Deal in the 1930s had much to do with institutionalization of the modern presidency, the same New Deal was, until the passage of the Hatch Acts in 1939 and 1940, the basis of a personal spoils machine that substituted for the wholly unified Democratic Party that Roosevelt might have preferred but did not have. Patronage-driven political machines always have thrived on poverty and destitution, when people who need jobs will do whatever they are told to do, and businesses without business will do whatever they can to secure government contracts. Roosevelt simply took advantage of the situation, and there is little reason to fault him for using normal political methods. The Hatch Acts of that time were both necessary and perhaps more important than Roosevelt's famous Committee on Administrative Management. The "Brownlow Committee" set the stage for the modern presidency, but the "institution" of the presidency is more traceable to World War II than to that committee.

• The "bashing of bureaucrats" has become a staple of contemporary politics, successfully erasing the stature that the civil service was accorded until long after World War II. Although all presidential candidates now "run against the bureaucracy," the important *law* is the Civil Service Reform Act (CSRA) of 1978, designed primarily to make it easier to fire civil servants and to provide for direct partisan control of the civil service. The clearly intended outcome was to make it more difficult for civil servants to ask the questions they are supposed to ask. Although President Jimmy Carter initiated the CSRA, with the help of many academic experts in public administration, the "reform" became wholly bipartisan because all politicians relished the likelihood that they would gain more direct control over allocation decisions. In modern political jargon, distributing the "spoils" is known as "micromanagement."

• Predictably, the weakening of the civil service was followed by an increase in corruption involving the federal government. In the 1980s, there were significant scandals involving the Departments of Defense and Housing and Urban Development, not to mention the constant corruption, usually involving direct bribery, associated with state and local governments, almost always in connection with "privatization" and "contracting out."

• Building upon the CSRA, the Clinton Administration's "reinvention" was designed to quickly remove many civil servants (as this is written, the desired number is nearing 300,000), thereby generating "savings" that could be used to finance other programs. The driving force was a "zero-sum" bipartisan budget policy requiring that any *new* program be financed by cuts in *existing* programs. The "reinvention" initiative, however, was set up to get rid of civil servants, not patronage appointees who are instructed only to distribute rewards as their bosses specify. This threat of an endless wave of terminations, together with repeated announcements that any who express "cynicism" about the program will quickly be eliminated, has made the civil service virtually powerless.

The saddest part of this retreat from history is that academics who study such things and were among the leading reformers in the nineteenth century have given way to the contemporary academics of political science and public administration who have produced a mountain of literature condemning civil servants and, with the help of some old myths, have been content to forget about the systemic nature of political corruption. Not having advanced beyond a "good men versus bad apples" theory of corruption, they applaud the "reinvention" of a spoils system in an era when abundant supplies of ready cash make it inevitable that there will be an increase in corruption. They are well rewarded by the research grants available to the cheerleaders for "innovation."

Law as Legitimacy

In his 1994 presidential address to the American Political Science Association, Charles O. Jones proposed "more concentrated study of lawmaking." Describing it as "the core decision-making process of a democratic state," he added that

> lawmaking for any one issue is a trackable process as legislators, executives, bureaucrats, judges, and others variably participate in statute-making, rule-and-standard setting, administrative and executive interpretation, and court decision-making, which, combined, constitute the legitimate base for public policy. The authorizing processes of lawmaking are therefore interactive with the initiating and executing processes of policymaking . . . Statutes . . . represent an agreement at one point in time regarding a public issue. (Jones 1995: 1-8)

As Jones implied, but did not say clearly enough in my view, the stream of action would have to begin with the first efforts to translate desire into law, perhaps years or decades before enactment. If a law is to attain real standing, it must withstand repeated constitutional challenges. Supreme Court determinations may come only long years after enactment and are themselves not necessarily permanent. *Plessy v. Ferguson* (1896) established the "separate but equal" concept for segregation in public places, but *Brown v. Board of Education of Topeka* (1954) changed things for the public schools. Thus a policy was "legitimized" in 1896, and its opposite in 1954.

A "living Constitution," it follows, includes all statutes still in force. Many may fall into disuse long before they are *constitutionally* dead, but officials often rummage through legal attics in a search for old laws that might help them take actions not explicitly endorsed in recent laws, actions that the writers of the old laws did not foresee. In this sense, the "process of government," as Arthur Bentley described it, is not only interminable and ever changing, but honors no real distinctions among "insiders" and "outsiders":

> No sooner do we attempt to study [political institutions] than we find we must take into account the various grades of political groups . . . which

function through them. These range down from the political parties as organized in a "the government" through the parties outside of the government, to policy organizations, citizens' associations . . . [T]he governing body has no value in itself, except as one aspect of the process, and cannot even be adequately described except in terms of the deep-lying interests which function through it. (1908: 300)

Jones argues that by offering courses on "the presidency, Congress, the courts, the bureaucracy, political parties and interest groups," we lose sight of the interaction among these identifiable groups or institutions, and the most basic and fundamental product of that interaction—statutes that are effectively parts of the Constitution. Of these major institutions that are central to such fields as political science and public administration, only one is for practical purposes not subject to constitutional examination or review. As Harry V. Jaffa has reminded us, the American political system is "essentially unplanned" because "the party system," a "prime feature of the whole," was "no ingredient in the government envisaged by the Founding Fathers." That the party system we know ever would have developed or ever would have been praised "would have seemed incredible to them" (Jaffa 1964: 59-60). Yet the central feature of the party system remains virtually immune to challenge.

The Democratic Party was challenged in several state courts for the decisions of its Credentials Committee in choosing which state delegations to seat at the 1972 national convention when multiple delegations were disputing each other's legitimacy. In one instance, the Illinois Appellate Court held that the state's election laws had higher standing than the rules of the national party. Agreeing with the party, the Supreme Court declared that the integrity of Illinois' s presidential primary was not important enough to warrant restricting the party's First and Fourteenth Amendment rights of freedom of association. In Justice William Brennan's words, the "pervasive national interest in the selection of candidates for national office . . . is greater than the interest of any state," a view reinforced by a 1980 decision that overturned a ruling by the Wisconsin Supreme Court (Davis 1983: 94-99). Thus the "unplanned" party system is officially designated as an agent of a "pervasive national interest" that is constitutionally legitimate, but the means the parties use to fulfill that interest cannot be challenged.

An American political party, qua party, is a fundamental part of the political system even though it is not formally a part of the system. Party members, qua members, are not public employees but may control funds collected for electoral purposes. A party "boss" may or may not be an elected or appointed public official, and some of the most widely known "bosses" have been neither. Especially in the nineteenth century, a party was somewhat similar to what later became the political system of the Soviet Union; the Communist Party stood officially outside of the government but, at each level, instructed the government on a day-to-day basis. In the middle of the nineteenth century, the American public generally approved the party system:

> Parties are a necessity and organization is essential. It is the duty of the citizen . . . to support the party that stands for right policies and to adhere closely to its official organization. Loyalty should be rewarded by appointment to positions within the gift of the party; and disloyalty should be looked upon as political treason. . . . Positions constitute the cohesive force that holds the organization intact. (Lingley 1924: 118, quoted in Van Riper, 1958: 61)

The detailed history of the "spoils system" need not concern us here, but an important related factor often is overlooked. When "hordes of all sorts of people from the highest and most polished down to the most vulgar and gross" crowded Washington as Andrew Jackson took office, many were indeed hoping to find jobs, as were the 30,000 to 40,000 job seekers who showed up for William Henry Harrison's inauguration in 1841 (McDonald 1994: 317-319). These people had no jobs and had no place else to turn. Until well into the twentieth century, "the capitalist order was . . . incapable of guaranteeing [that] unemployment would lose all its terror if the private life of the unemployed were not seriously affected by their unemployment" (Schumpeter 1950 [1942]: 70). Most jobs paid what we would now call subpoverty wages, and there were frequent layoffs and no "safety nets." Similarly, many businessmen always needed help as well. The function of political parties was to provide jobs for loyal voters who were easily persuaded to pay unofficial taxes to their parties while doing whatever political work needed doing, and to help big donors with contracts and subsidies.

The nonpartisan civil service was invented in 1883 as a "check and balance" that would move the extraconstitutional function of allocating jobs and contracts inside the governmental structure, insulating that function from party control. The civil service was a morality-based reform that took the form that it did because there was no other immediately apparent way to counter or delete the functions of political parties. If, as suggested in 1964 (Storing, p. 151), and argued in 1986 (Rohr, pp. 181-186), we should consider the civil service a constituent part of the constitutional system of checks and balances, then the civil service was to be a fourth branch of the official government that would replace the external fourth branch that had come to dominate the system—the "unplanned" political parties. The argument to be made here, of course, is that the Pendleton Act of 1883, the act that created a civil service, is the instrument that legitimized professional administration, the modern administrative state, and morality in government.

Americans did not understand then, and do not now understand, the broad implications of this "party system" that the Founders did not at all intend to build. As a nongovernmental system that is not really subject to constitutional control or judicial review, it bears a striking resemblance to the system of the former Soviet Union that Americans criticized for so many years. In the communist system, the Communist Party stood outside the government but directed its every decision and action. In the U.S. design, a federal civil service was intended, in 1883, to wrest control of public management from party activists outside government, but this design never penetrated into state and local governments. Now that the federal civil service is effectively being dismantled, there is a visible move toward a return to party control at the federal level as well as a multilayered form of "spoils" control that is exemplified more and more by the extensive fund-raising and distribution activities of national party organizations. The resemblance to the old Soviet system is striking.

I turn again to Bentley to make another point too often rejected in academic circles. Bentley was terribly frustrated by the continuing argument that corruption occurred because "corrupt men have been in office or have controlled officials or both." He rejected the common solution, that is, "put in men who are not corrupt . . . and you will not suffer from corrupt acts." He argued that the standard approach did not take "nearly enough of the factors described as 'environment' into account" (1908: 191-192), but, even today, the idea remains dominant that corruption and other forms of cheating are related to character defects. My favorite example of how such arguments are made is drawn from my work on government regulation of business.

Economist Alfred E. Kahn, chairman of the Civil Aeronautics Board in the 1970s, worked hard to deregulate the airline industry and close the board. After leaving office, he publicly supported the continuation of a regulation he had issued while in office, one that required airlines to compensate passengers who were "bumped" from scheduled flights after their reservations had been confirmed. As a competitive strategy, airlines routinely overbooked flights because they knew that not every passenger would show up. Occasionally, of course, they found themselves with irate passengers who demanded compensation. As Kahn (1982) put it,

> When consumers are inadequately informed, competition may take the form of providing adulterated or unsafe products, with the least scrupulous among the competitors forcing the more scrupulous to cut corners

as well. It shouldn't be surprising that many ethical business people themselves are eager to have the government set limits on this kind of competition.

When all competitors cheat, the academic observer, the customer, the journalist, and the voter cannot determine which competitor initiated the cheating and with how much reluctance or eagerness each competitor decided to cheat. If "good men" feel they must cheat in some situations, then the category "good men" has no operational meaning. As Bentley suggested long ago, replacing all competitors with "good men" only erects "a set of problems in the background corresponding with the problems in the foreground, but not throwing any light upon the latter" (1908: 192). If corrupt behavior is to be changed, the operational environment must be changed, and Jones is correct. Law is the change agent.

The Moral Correction of
Constitutional "Flaws"

The reform movement was launched shortly after the Civil War, and it included lawyers, journalists, clergy, and academics, especially the members of the new American Social Science Association, who believed that a civil service was the social scientific solution to a crisis of authority. The reform took almost two decades to accomplish, bills being introduced in Congress as early as the 1860s. Two aspects of this history are worth close attention. As is now clear, today's academics are largely enemies of the civil service, not its friends. Second, it is incorrect to put the nineteenth-century American reform movement in the same category as the civil service initiatives in France, Germany, and Great Britain.

The European reforms "consolidated an evolving governmental order" in each case. The American reformers were *opponents* of the evolving order. They sought "nothing less than a reconstitution of the American state in its organizational, procedural, and intellectual dimensions" that would "break the hold of the party bosses over national institutions." If "reconstitution," the equivalent of a constitutional amendment, had the highest priority, "retrenchment" came in second, even though the 1880s were years of sustained reductions in the national debt. The third goal, of course, was "party maintenance," the perpetuation of "responsible" political parties that would "appeal to the public on the basis of great issues" but would not control government jobs. Admittedly, the reformers also had in mind the return to important administrative positions of the well-educated elites who viewed themselves as similar to the "genuine" statesmen that had been "produced in good measure a hundred years [earlier]" (Skow-ronek 1982: 47-68).

The reformers were helped by the spillover moral fervor generated by the abolition movement, the Civil War itself, Reconstruction, and the attack on the party-connected corruption of the era. In 1838, for example, the collector for the Port of New York made off with more than $1 billion, "a sum that, as a percentage of the federal budget, would have been equivalent to about $160 billion in 1992" (McDonald 1994: 323). The National Civil Service Reform League became a vigorous organization with chapters in many cities, flooding the country with monographs and other publications. The country was crying for reform and a professional administrative apparatus that could end the corruption.

When President Garfield was killed in 1881, and when corruption scandals led to Republican defeats in the 1882 elections and threatened more losses in 1884, a bipartisan agreement became possible (Van Riper 1958: 60-95). The task achieved by the reform movement was indeed monumental, that is, bipartisan agreement to surrender the power of spoils. The final road to reform was paved by a report to Congress prepared by Dorman Eaton (1976 [1879]), who had studied the British reform and had been assaulted by members of the New York Tweed Ring while he was involved in corruption litigation. His report, which Frederick Mosher made the first entry under "Management Movement" in his collection of basic documents, emphasized the moral dimension:

> Party government and the salutary activities of parties are superseded, but they are made purer and more efficient, by the *merit* system of office, which brings larger capacity and higher character to their support. . . . Government by parties is enfeebled and debased by reliance upon a partisan system of appointments and removals. . . . Patronage in the hands of members of the legislature, which originated in a usurpation of executive functions, increases the expenses of administration, is degrading and demoralizing to those who possess it, is disastrous to legislation, tends to impair the counterpoise and stability of government; and it cannot withstand the criticism of an intelligent people when they fairly comprehend its character and consequences . . . [A civil service] is proved to have given the best public servants; it makes an end of patronage; and . . . it has been found to be the surest safeguard against both partisan coercion and official favoritism . . . to reduce manipulation, intrigue, and every form of corruption in politics to their smallest proportions. (Eaton 1976 [1879]: 53-55)

Unfortunately and understandably, it was a practical impossibility to clearly outline in the statute the problem it was intended to solve. The defenders of spoils, or the more genteel concept of "rotation in office," argued that democratic principles require such rotation to ensure that those appointed are accountable to those elected to direct them, which is to say that "democratic principles" require blind obedience to those elected. The reformers could not really argue that a merit system was more democratic than a spoils system, and they hesitated to argue that "democratic" governments were inherently corrupt, even if that was true (Rohr 1989: 28-29). Yet the parties were indeed to be purified by "removal of the temptation" to be corrupt, this being "the principle of civil service reform" (Storing 1964: 141) that did not depend upon the innate character of individuals.

Only a few years later, Woodrow Wilson's famous essay (1887: 5, 8, 10) emphasized the moral basis of the reform:

> The poisonous atmosphere of city government, the crooked secrets of state administration, the confusion, sinecurism, and corruption ever and again discovered in the bureaux at Washington forbid us to believe that any clear conceptions of what constitutes good administration are as yet widely current in the United States . . . why have we but just begun purifying a civil service which was rotten a full fifty years ago? . . . flaws in our constitution delayed us . . . Civil service reform is thus but a moral preparation for what is to follow. It is clearing the moral atmosphere of public office as a public trust, and, by making the service unpartisan, it is opening the way for making it businesslike. By sweetening its motives, it is rendering it capable of improving its methods of work.

Declaring that "law should be administered with enlightenment [and] equity," Wilson added that while "politics sets the tasks for administration, it should not be suffered to manipulate its offices," and repeatedly emphasized the "discretion" that should be permitted career officials "serving during good behavior." He also foresaw how the 1887 invention of the Interstate Commerce Commission would lead to other "important and delicate extension[s] of administrative functions," as government made itself "master of masterful corporations" but without recourse to spoils management. Clearly, the "flaws in our constitution" were those that had permitted the unplanned dominance and corruption of political parties and their captive elected officials.

In historical context, a context that has been largely purged from textbooks in public administration, the nineteenth-century reform movement emphasized that "efficiency" could be achieved only within a system that provided every possible incentive for "moral" behavior. Put even more simply, "efficiency" was impossible in a spoils system, as even the simplest understanding of conventional politics has long made obvious. Patronage employees who are directed to work in political campaigns are not performing the duties for which they are paid. Tragically, textbook writers have chosen to emphasize "efficiency," and academics have vilified Wilson for his alleged overemphasis on "undemocratic" forms of administration (Ostrom 1989).

Obviously, the nineteenth-century "reconstitution" of the system created relationships that, in retrospect, had to become stressful and tension-filled. Civil servants subordinate to their elected or patronage superiors were to be the guardians of ethical standards, a function that could be performed only by giving them tenure. In a sense, civil servants were expected to be troublesome and to ask their superiors very tough questions. The politicians, moreover, were bound to look constantly for new ways to help their supporters as, for example, insisting again and again that they needed more patronage employees to direct the activities of resisting bureaucrats. Additional layers of patronage appointees, an American specialty, would make it easier for politicians to distribute "goodies" to friends. Inevitably, the politicians would seek to weaken or even destroy the civil service if they believed they could get away with it. Over time, the intellectuals would help less and less, for they disliked perpetuating the notion that democracies can be as innately corrupt as authoritarian regimes.

It has been very fashionable to invent histories that bear little relationship to what actually happened. Theodore Lowi, for example, has fashioned a top-drawer academic career out of attacks on civil servants, arguing that they are much more the prisoners of interest groups than are politicians, and putting a ludicrous twist on the original reform:

> Meritocracy was the late 19th century middle-class answer to the highly successful legitimizing theories of the Jacksonian democracy . . . [Administrators] could be entrusted with the great powers and responsibilities of government not merely because they were trained in their craft and would spend a lifetime in the agency dealing with the problems of that agency, but because they added to their professionalism and training a willingness to subordinate their abilities to the wishes of elected officials . . . [The reform was designed to] flesh out a more general theory or ideology of state consonant with the party or regime that was in power. (Lowi 1993: 262)

The reform, of course, was designed to *reduce* the power of whatever party happened to be in power. The dominant contribution of the intellectuals of this century has been the concept that there can be no real distinction separating "politics" from "administration," at least in the sense that the "discretion" given a civil servant to make decisions that allocate resources, or "values," gives that administrator the authority to make "political" decisions. This argument has the effect, intentionally or not, of obscuring the original concept that "politics" is inevitably corrupt while "administration" need not be.

The nineteenth-century reform movement remained alive and kicking well into this century, with the National Civil Service Reform League organizing yearly reminders and celebrations of the Pendleton Act. Surprisingly, in my view, it seems no longer considered very important at all, and this is most conspicuous in the academic circles that have designated Franklin Roosevelt's New Deal as the real beginning of the modern administrative state.

What About the New Deal?

Having emphasized in 1980 the moral arguments surrounding the Pendleton Act, Rohr republished the same analysis in 1989 but, in 1986, he awarded much higher status to the "Brownlow Report" (BR) of Roosevelt's Committee on Administrative Management, designating it a "constitutional statement of considerable significance" (1986: 137). In so doing, Rohr provided these supporting arguments:

1. The "political order that came into its own during the New Deal" features the "expert agency" that uses "loosely drawn statutes that empower unelected officials to undertake such important matters as preventing 'unfair competition,' granting licenses as 'the public interest, convenience or necessity' will indicate, maintaining, a 'fair and orderly market,' and so forth."

2. "The administrative state is in reality the welfare/warfare state [that] has provided the underpinnings of the free, decent, and prosperous society most Americans have enjoyed for the past half-century."

3. "[Political scientist] Rowland Egger has maintained that the Brownlow Report was the first comprehensive reconsideration of the Presidency and the President's control of the executive branch since 1787, and is probably the most important constitutional document of our time."

4. "No longer would it suffice to think of efficiency in government in terms of cost-cutting alone. A positive state demanded the effective delivery of promised services" (1986: xi, 136-137).

To look closely at these justifications is to immediately find problems in them. Significant regulatory agencies were the original contribution of the nineteenth-century reformers who began with the Interstate Commerce and Civil Service Commissions, to be followed shortly by antitrust and food and drug laws, and associated administrative machinery. Although the

Great Depression of the 1930s did indeed lead to regulatory expansion, a movement for "deregulation" swept away much of the apparatus for economic regulation of various industries, beginning in the 1970s. Airlines, trucks, buses, financial institutions, and telecommunications all were "deregulated." The "dismantling" was extensive (Tolchin and Tolchin 1983), and those of us who raised questions were ignored (Thayer 1984). Recent initiatives for economic deregulation have been wholly bipartisan in the tradition of real reform, but also as a rejection of both nineteenth-century and New Deal expansion. Initiatives for safety and health deregulation, on the other hand, have been matters of intense partisan dispute.

In Roosevelt's second inaugural in 1937, he declared that "tens of millions of [our] citizens . . . at this very moment are denied the greater part of what the very lowest standards of today call the necessities of life" (Burns 1956: 292). Prosperity did not arrive until the end of World War II and, unfortunately, was a by-product of the war, not the New Deal. Unemployment rates, moreover, have been unusually high since the mid-1970s, an indication that sustained prosperity is as elusive as ever.

The BR, especially in the context of the times, was a relatively minor exercise, perhaps an accident of history, out of touch with the history of earlier reforms and, worst of all, politically naive. Although Roosevelt had considered appointing a study committee as early as 1935, he did not establish the Brownlow Committee until the Senate had appointed its own special committee in February 1936, with Senator Harry F. Byrd of Virginia as chair. Roosevelt followed shortly thereafter, appointing Luther Gulick and Charles Merriam to his committee, less than a week after Byrd had appointed them consultants to his committee. The effort to replace Byrd's activity did not work; the Senate ultimately contracted with the Brookings Institution for a study that ultimately was at odds with the BR. With the economy then considered to be recovering, there was extreme pressure to reduce federal borrowing and spending, and to get rid of the emergency agencies created in Roosevelt's first term. Roosevelt himself promised again and again in his 1936 campaign that he would balance the budget for the fiscal year beginning in July 1937, and very nearly did so. The reality of the moment was "economy and efficiency"; any BR rhetoric to the contrary was meaningless.

At the time the Brownlow Committee presented its report in 1937, and Roosevelt transmitted it with a covering letter to Congress, his own attention was completely focused on his attempt to reorganize, or "pack," the Supreme Court. He managed the Supreme Court battle himself, giving Brownlow a much lower priority by assigning his son James to deal with it. Although the staff of the Brownlow Committee included "an honor roll of distinguished scholars in American political science, although most . . .

had yet to make their reputations," it remains the case that "there is little to suggest that, even in private, [Roosevelt] considered the [BR] as important as its framers did." The reorganization bill that finally was enacted in 1939 included only fragments of the original proposals, and Roosevelt moved very slowly even in filling the presidential staff positions that were authorized (Arnold 1986: 81-117; Brinkley 1995: 21-23; Burns 1956: 323, 382; Caiden 1984: 66-67). There is no reason to doubt the stories that Roosevelt casually mentioned the constitutional significance of the BR in meeting with the committee in late 1936 (Rohr 1986: 136), but I will suggest that Roosevelt may well not have even read the Brownlow Report.

The most famous aspect of the BR was its description of independent regulatory agencies as a "headless fourth branch" of government that should be brought at least partly inside the executive branch. This demonstrated a lack of awareness of the origins of these agencies in the nineteenth-century reform movement designed to keep active politicians out of allocation decisions. The device, still in use in such agencies as the Defense Base Closure Commission, was and is cumbersome but is useful in containing corruption. Indeed, the Supreme Court only a few years earlier had rejected Roosevelt's attempt to remove a member of the Federal Trade Commission (McDonald 1994: 329). Between the time the BR was submitted, and the reorganization bill was passed in 1939, Roosevelt and Congress agreed to establish the Civil Aeronautics Board to regulate the airlines, continuing the established regulatory principle.

Particular aspects of the BR suggest to me that Roosevelt, expending every ounce of energy on his Supreme Court fight, did not read the BR. At the time, members of Congress were being paid $10,000 per year, but the BR proposed salaries of $10,000 for lower level civil servants, and $12,000 to $15,000 for high-level careerists, which a politically astute and attentive president would not have proposed. Brownlow and his associates, all steeped in municipal reform experience, merely applied the "council-manager" form of municipal government to the legislative and executive branches. The municipal design assumed, of course, that an elected city council appointed a nonpartisan professional executive to oversee all agencies of the local government. The president of the country, of course, is in one sense the "implementer" of legislation, but is separately elected, has veto power, and is a political force of some magnitude. This simplistic copying of the council-manager formula caused accusations of a "dictator bill," and Roosevelt was forced to declare "I have no inclination to be a dictator" (Burns 1956: 344-345).

Because academic literature says as little as possible about the issue, the huge expansion of federal patronage in the 1930s remains even now largely unnoticed. Roosevelt, well schooled in New York politics, "took care" to keep his name alive there when, as assistant secretary of the Navy in World War I, he made sure the Brooklyn Navy Yard was "well sprinkled" with his appointees (Burns 1956: 73). The Great Depression almost compelled such quick invention of new agencies that Roosevelt "played the patronage game tirelessly and endlessly," with Postmaster General James Farley managing the patronage. As personal secretary to a Texas congressman, Lyndon B. Johnson was heavily involved in patronage and vote buying, mentored by a former postmaster general and congressman who had prevented Woodrow Wilson from getting patronage out of the Post Office (Burns 1956: 187-188; Caro 1982: 277, 285-286, 407-408, 411, 428, 430, 447-448).

The Democratic Convention that renominated Roosevelt in 1936 was "one of the most harmonious in party history . . . no floor debates . . . no roll-call votes" (*Presidential Elections* 1991: 91). It was reported that the delegates would "adopt a platform they have not seen and probably will not be permitted to discuss" (*New York Times* June 24, 1936: 15). A majority of the delegates were postmasters, U.S. marshals, internal revenue collectors, other federal officeholders, and close relatives. This collection of patronage beneficiaries, wholly dependent upon government in a time of severe unemployment, carefully instructed to cheer on cue and ask no questions, put on a performance that Farley orchestrated. Three old-time political bosses (Hague of Jersey City, Crump of Memphis, Pendergast of Kansas City) admired Farley's organizing skills as they looked on (Caro 1982: 568; Timmons 1948: 259-260). Small wonder that many in Congress, Democrat and Republican alike, were upset by what they saw as an emerging political machine under Roosevelt's personal control. Their suspicions deepened as Roosevelt mounted a strong but unsuccessful effort to defeat some Southern Democrats in the 1938 midterm elections and used federal employees to assist him.

At the time the Brownlow proposals were languishing in Congress, efforts were under way to halt Roosevelt's expansion of patronage. The Hatch Acts of 1939 and 1940, the sponsor a Democratic Senator, were designed to keep federal employees out of politics, and also state employees paid with federal funds. The first Hatch Act may have been "contrived" by Vice President Garner, then hoping to run for president in 1940 and wary of Roosevelt-controlled patronage delegates (Van Riper 1958: 340). Logically, the passage of any part of the BR proposals was held hostage to the first Hatch Act. The 1939 reorganization bill gave the president some additional administrative authority but cut off the patronage. The Hatch Acts actually were aimed at some additional constitutional "flaws" that had inadvertently been left behind by Pendleton. The original 1883 reform was designed to keep "politics" out of "administration." The Hatch Acts turned the tables by keeping "administration" out of "politics." The issue from then until much of the Hatch legislation was dumped in 1993 was whether this "depoliticization" infringed upon the constitutional rights of government employees.

Since the Roosevelt days, various such employees, principally teachers or union members, have managed to become delegates to national political conventions. CBS News estimated in 1980 that a third of the Democratic delegates were full-time government employees, while another study concluded that 21% of the 1980 Republican delegates were in the same category (Davis 1983: 73). Yet, when the first Hatch Act was passed, an approving editorial in the *New York Times* (August 1, 1931: 18) warmly quoted an opinion written by Oliver Wendell Holmes, then a member of the Massachusetts Supreme Court, about a policeman who had been fired for soliciting campaign funds. Wrote Holmes,

> The petitioner may have a constitutional right to talk politics, but he has no constitutional right to be a policeman. There are few employments for hire in which the servant does not agree to suspend his constitutional right of free speech, as well as of idleness, by the implied terms of his contract (*McAuliffe v. Bedford* 1892: 295, quoted in Leif 1931)

Holmes stated in so many words that political and civil "rights" do not extend to workplace relationships, a matter that in my view is not well handled in the academic literature. If your boss is an elected or patronage official, and if you are publicly campaigning and soliciting for an opposition candidate, you are publicly opposing your boss. If you are campaigning and soliciting on behalf of your boss, you are seeking to coerce those who may be affected by your superior's decisions, and it is also reasonable to conclude that your boss compelled you to campaign as a condition of retaining your job. If you report waste, fraud, or abuse on the part of your elected or patronage boss, your behavior can be labeled "political dissidence," "administrative insubordination," or "nonpartisan maintenance of ethical standards." Only the latter is compatible with the original design of the civil service.

The Hatch Acts were desirable additions, and the combination of these pieces of legislation and the Brownlow Report provide a more comprehensive view of the New Deal years. The idealistic young scholars who staffed the Brownlow Committee, my mentor Harvey C. Mansfield, Sr., among them, were so committed to a positive view of Roosevelt that they could not imagine that the expansion of his authority could be dangerous if linked closely with federal patronage. Because economic data for earlier decades were not as comprehensive as they should have been, they were unaware that patronage and vote buying always feed on poverty and depression.

After the Hatch Acts, Roosevelt brought many of the patronage appointees into the civil service, setting the stage for the long-term complaint by Republicans that Democrats had filled the civil service with those dedicated to Democratic policies. Following Roosevelt, administrations leaving office have tried to bring patronage appointees under civil service protection, and administrations entering office have claimed they needed more "loyal political appointees" to "control" a hostile bureaucracy.

The "informal" job descriptions of patronage employees always have included their availability for partisan tasks. Traditionally, the party-affiliated crew of a garbage truck is supposed to give higher priority to campaign activity than to garbage collection. It also was traditional for Secretary of State James Baker to suddenly abandon his Cabinet post in mid-1992 to become a campaign manager who might be able to salvage a faltering re-election effort by President George Bush. The Hatch Acts went as far as possible in furthering the professionalization of public administration that had begun in 1883.

The truly institutionalized modern presidency was a by-product of World War II and, later, the cold war. The attack on Pearl Harbor in 1941 immediately made victory in war so dominant a public purpose that "efficiency and economy" could indeed be set aside in favor of "effectiveness." Roosevelt had a free hand to borrow and spend whatever might be necessary because overspending for victory was much more acceptable than underspending to risk defeat. He was free to organize the executive branch as he chose, and this would have occurred with or without Brownlow. Almost predictably, the recent end of the cold war has brought demands for "balanced budgets" back to center stage, precisely the issue that Roosevelt was grappling with when the BR was issued in 1937.

The Murder of the Civil Service:
From Carter to Clinton

If, as I conclude, the Pendleton and Hatch Acts were designed to cripple the spoils system that had come to dominate the constitutional system through the political machines the Founders could not have imagined, it is reasonable to suggest that threatening the job security of civil servants and encouraging them to become political activists are likely to be connected with the resurgence of spoils systems, perhaps in slightly different forms than in the nineteenth century. While it has become popular for presidential candidates to campaign against the "Washington bureaucracy," the principal hatchet-wielders have been Presidents Jimmy Carter and Bill Clinton. The latter has clearly indicated why civil servants may well be in the way.

St. Louis radio interviewers asked President Clinton in mid-1994 to explain why he had raised $40 million in campaign funds after having promised during the 1992 campaign to work very hard to reform campaign financing. His answer:

> I justify it because of the opposition policies of the Republican Party and all the special interest groups that have raised and spent far more money against us, attacking me and my policies and spreading disinformation to the American people. . . . I don't believe in unilateral disarmament. The money that I have raised will be used to try to make sure that the Democratic Parties throughout the country in these fall elections and our candidates will at least have a fighting chance to talk about our record and the facts and what we've done. . . . it would be a mistake for the Democrats to just lay down and not raise any money, letting the Republicans and a lot of their allied groups have all the money in the world when they already have greater access to a lot of things like a lot of other media outlets than we do. (Clinton 1994: 1339)

The argument, of course, echoes Kahn's analysis of how "scrupulous" firms must cheat consumers if they are not to fall behind the "unscrupulous." Contemporary corruption is as clever as any yet devised in that the extensive fund-raising required of active politicians has thus far been treated as having nothing in common with outright bribery. It has even been given a scholarly label, "mediated corruption" (Thompson 1993: 369-381). "The Keating Five," Thompson's major example, are those senators who received significant campaign contributions from Charles Keating, a savings and loan operator whose conviction on racketeering charges was later overturned. The senators performed what has been known as "constituent service" by privately meeting with regulators and advising them that their constituent, Keating, was being harassed. In lengthy hearings held by the Ethics Committee, however, nobody could cite a close precedent for such meetings. Of interest, Thompson concludes that in cases of this sort, investigation should be turned over to an "outside body" that "would have at least the independence and respect of an institution like the Congressional Budget Office." Thompson thus implies that such cases are inevitable in the political system, and recommends the use of bipartisan or nonpartisan independent agencies.

It appears that so long as politicians do not make explicit promises in return for the money handed them to run campaigns, they are home free; the Supreme Court, sticking to such a very narrow standard, assumes that all such conduct is "unavoidable so long as election campaigns are financed by private contributions." In general, political science and public administration courses and textbooks treat corruption as systemic and inevitable in Third World countries but only an aberration in the United States. There is a considerable popular literature on the need for financial reform (Biersack et al. 1994; Jackson 1990; Stern 1992) but relatively little in academe (Kebschull 1992: 705-709). As Thompson notes, however, the major government scandals in recent years have involved a large measure of mediated corruption, that is., Iran-Contra, Housing and Urban Development, Bank of Credit and Commerce International, Banca Nazionale del Lavoro's Atlanta branch. To that list of Thompson's might be added "Ill Wind," an extensive Pentagon procurement scandal of the 1980s that involved bribery, particularly of political appointees, and illegal campaign contributions to a number of congressmen, who, of course, were able to deny that they knew of the contributions.

Paving the way for a final assault by politicians upon the civil service have been the academic communities of political science and public administration. With considerable help from economics, they have produced in recent decades a mountain of literature arguing that there actually is no difference in the functions of "politicians" and "administrators," except for the likelihood that the professional bureaucrats are *more* "resistant to change," *more* "addicted to red tape," *more* "subservient to special interests," and *less* "innovative" than their political counterparts and, because they are full-time employees, are engaged in "unproductive" work (in economics, making things to sell is all that is "productive"). These accusations nicely fit the "democratic" tradition, as far back as Aristotle, that the management of public affairs is an avocation of the rich, and that professional public management is wasteful.

What Presidents Carter and Clinton *intended* to accomplish with their "reforms" is less significant than the *consequences* that were easily predictable at the outset. In a retrospective look at Jimmy Carter's Civil Service Reform Act (CSRA) and his Reorganization Plan No. 2, Newland labels them a "landmark in U.S. history . . . epochal for fundamental governmental institutions." "With extraordinary strategy and skill," he adds, "public opinion was deliberately and brilliantly turned against the public service." The result was that "the president gained direct political control over the federal civil service" (Newland 1992: 87). A former dean of perhaps the leading graduate school of public administration in the country led the Carter Administration effort, sweeping away the pioneer independent agency, the Civil Service Commission, and replacing it with a single patronage appointee who was given increased authority to promulgate rules for "easy firing." The fact that virtually all of the academic community, well schooled in the ahistorical view that ignores ethical issues, supported a change that has forced civil servants to be loyal to political bosses, rather than to laws and institutions, must ultimately become a disgrace to my profession, itself a casualty of its own partisanship. My fellow academics deplore attacks on the "Roosevelt image" they idolize, but urge attacks on the "Nixon image" they deplore.

The many details of the CSRA need not concern us here, except for two examples of comic political opera. The CSRA created a "Senior Executive Service" (SES), presumably to comprise the most experienced and competent senior civil servants, who, by definition, would further upgrade professionalism. Yet the entire thrust of the CSRA was to make it easier to fire those who raised questions with their political bosses. The SES can be expected to perform well only if its members have job security; the SES created in 1978 is simply a bribery apparatus, that is, if you pay higher salaries to some civil servants, they will keep quiet about what you are doing. A second bit of foolishness was the CSRA promise to "protect" the "whistle-blowers" who report instances of waste, fraud, and abuse. There was even a small new agency set up to accomplish this function, but its real job turned out to be advising agencies on how to ensure that their firings could survive legal challenge. These contradictions were obvious when I outlined them as soon as the CSRA was introduced (Thayer 1978), foolishly believing that fellow academics could appreciate the need for tenure. Although Congress tried to add some paper protection for whistle-blowers in 1989, anyone who has talked with those courageous enough to "blow the whistle" knows that they are punished in many ways, mentally tortured in exquisitely painful ways, for daring to say anything.

It did not take long for the contemporary forms of corruption to reemerge, the Department of Housing and Urban Development being the classic example. The political hacks appointed to high positions in HUD, including the secretary's immediate assistants, made sure that contracts were awarded to developers who had been properly "certified" through Republican Party channels. Some of these appointees have since been convicted, and other cases are in progress. One of the patronage appointees testified to a congressional committee that "I never should have been hired at HUD . . . [Secretary] Samuel Pierce got loaded upon him a group of Young Turks who were on a must-hire list, and we had no housing experience whatsoever" (Moe 1991: 303). I have viewed many times a C-Span tape in which another of these "spoils" managers testified how the political leadership of HUD had maneuvered regulations to prohibit career administrators from evaluating proposals, how he and others were ordered by still higher political appointees to make the awards as dictated, and why he, operating about four levels from the top, did indeed worry that the process was "political." While the HUD corruption was being exposed, the Department of Defense was awash in large-scale procurement scandals and, as in the case of HUD, the independent inspectors general of these departments had much to do with assembling the evidence. The Clinton Administration, surveying the wreckage of the 1980s, decided that it should be made more difficult to uncover corruption.

Vice President Al Gore's National Performance Review (NPR), also known as "From Red Tape to Results" and "Creating a Government That Works Better and Costs Less"—a six-month effort to "reinvent" government—promised to get rid of 252,000 civil service positions, a number that has been increasing ever since. "Most" of these positions were to be taken from "the structure of overcontrol" comprising "supervisors, headquarters staffs, personnel specialists, budget analysts, procurement specialists, accountants and auditors . . . control structures [that] stifle the creativity of line managers and workers" (Gore 1993: iii-iv). Widely advertised as the work of career employees, the bookstore version of the report featured a Foreword by Tom Peters, typical of the gurus heavily involved in the effort.

As coauthor of the runaway best-seller *In Search of Excellence* (1982), Peters immediately became an industry of his own, operating five companies and grossing $4 to $5 million per year. By 1984, *Business Week* observed in a cover story ("Who's Excellent Now?") that of the 43 "excellent" companies listed in the book, at least 14 had "lost their luster," among them Atari, Texas Instruments, and Avon. In 1987, Peters mystified the *Business Week* editor who reviewed Peters's next best-seller because Peters now admitted that "there are no excellent companies" (Dobryznski 1987). Hiring such a guru to introduce the Gore Report posed something of a problem. Advertising him as the author of *Thriving on Chaos* would have been a bit much, so only the "excellence" book was mentioned, even though he had long abandoned its arguments. The Gore Report, and the slaughtering of the civil service that it initiated, is noteworthy for several reasons.

Without significant analysis, the civil service was selected as the victim, not political appointees, even though the significant "layering" of overhead that the NPR attacks is heavily concentrated in the "spoils" structures that sit on top of the civil service and are used to reward campaign workers. Second, the civil service positions being dumped are those that are most important in maintaining ethical standards in contracting, spending, and similar activities. Third, in what was and is an astonishing attack, the NPR scored the independent inspectors general for their "heavy-handed enforcement" that "inhibits innovation and risk-taking." The inspectors, the NPR added, should only "help managers evaluate their management control systems . . . and ensure efficient, effective service." Additionally, managers should be "surveyed periodically to see whether they believe IGs are helping them improve," and "criteria should be established for judging

IG performance." Along with this, all departments were to be given "authority over recruitment, hiring, and promotion" (Gore 1993: 23-25, 32). The fact that the attack on IGs has gone largely unnoticed demonstrates the soundness of the arguments that too little intellectual attention is given to the likelihood that corruption is systemic, especially given the importance of the IGs in the 1980s.

Understandably, there is no mention of the need to protect whistle-blowers; the authors of the NPR doubtless believe that there cannot be any waste, fraud, or abuse in a Clinton-Gore Administration. Then there is the interesting emphasis on making agencies "responsive" to their "customers." The examples so often used, in the NPR and in videotapes featuring the Vice President, are the Internal Revenue, Social Security, Customs, and Postal Service. I wonder why there are no references to the "customers" of the Departments of Agriculture, Commerce, and Labor? Would that raise questions about "special interests"? Nor can it be overlooked that the NPR seeks to "empower" employees, asking them to "take risks" while, of course, increasing the number to be removed and constantly warning those still on board that raising questions about the NPR will be taken as "cynicism."

The overall quality of the NPR can be indicated more precisely with two examples. After publication, Robert Stone, NPR project director, was asked how the initial downsizing figure of 252,000 had been developed. His explanation was as follows:

> We made a head count government-wide of supervisors, budget specialists, financial specialists, personnel specialists and headquarters people, plus regional offices. The total count was—I think the report says 690,000. We have a little later count that's about 670,000. We said, "This is twice as big as it ought to be."
>
> But if you cut that group in half, you have to substitute for them—for example, groups that measure progress, that set goals. So you just can't cut 335,000. The judgment was that maybe a quarter of what you cut out you ought to put back to perform these other functions. So half of the control and micromanagement force is 335,000, a quarter of the 335,000 is 85,000 or 83,000. That leaves you at about 252,000. That's roughly the arithmetic. (quoted in Kettl 1994b: 7)

The second example is the NPR's allegedly "genuine fresh notion that private-sector incentives ought to drive public-sector performance" (Kettl 1994b: 25), with ideas of "competition" and "privatization" leading the way. The NPR, concluding that the "monopoly" of the Government

Printing Office (GPO) should be ended, argues that the traditional role of the GPO

> may have made sense in the 1840s, when printing was in its infancy, the government was tiny, there was no civil service, and corruption flourished. But it makes much less sense today. We want to encourage competition between GPO, private companies, and agencies' in-house publishing operations. If GPO can compete, it will win contracts. If it can't, government will print for less, and taxpayers will benefit. (Gore 1993: 56)

So much for the precision with which those who produced the NPR went about their decision making, including their total lack of awareness about how competition actually works. If the GPO loses out in competitive bidding, is it to be closed down? What if all the bidders end up cheating, as Alfred Kahn described with airline behavior? Did they even consider that most of the corruption experienced in this country has been centered on the linkages of politicians, their patronage subalterns, and private contractors (Thayer 1987)? They clearly have acted forcefully to add some "temptation" for the reinvention of spoils, doubtless convinced that none of *their* appointees ever would be tempted to indulge in corruption.

From my perspective, it does not matter whether Presidents Carter and Clinton *intended* to reinvent a spoils system. They have had some reason to believe that because they assembled the "best thinkers" they could find on the subject of management, they have become the true experts on the subject, thus establishing the new principle that while the *politicians* know how to manage, the career *administrators* do not. Especially in the case of the NPR, it has also been a clever piece of work to hide what should be obvious to those who study government; the wholesale dumping of civil servants is a direct by-product of the "zero sum" and bipartisan budget policy. In the headlong drive to reduce federal borrowing and spending, any new initiatives must be financed by cutting other programs. The answer to finding money to finance Clinton initiatives, a "national service" program being one example, was to get rid of civil servants, and to do it as quickly as possible to meet financial goals. Thus anyone who believed that jobs would disappear only after careful study, as the academics hired by the Brookings Institution seem to have believed, was simply naive and unfamiliar with current trends. Kettl (1994a) expressed surprise and disappointment that "for most Federal employees, the threat to their jobs, not the focus on results, has been the defining reality."

Having successfully labeled itself as the partner of all the fashionable management gurus, the Clinton Administration took the obvious next step by agreeing to "reforms" of the Hatch Acts that now open the door to various forms of political participation by government employees. In vetoing such a bill in 1990, George Bush had strongly endorsed Hatch and merit principles:

> The Hatch Act has successfully insulated the Federal service from the undue political influence that would destroy its essential political neutrality . . . [I]t has been successful in shielding civil servants, and the programs they administer, from political exploitation and abuse . . . [T]he criminal justice process is ill-suited to the task of protecting Federal employees from subtle political coercion. . . . Overt coercion is difficult enough by itself to guard against and detect. The more subtle forms of coercion are almost impossible to regulate . . . [A]n appreciable lessening of the current protections . . . will lead to the repoliticization of the civil service. . . . We cannot afford . . . to embark on a retreat into the very worst aspects of public administration from the last century. (Bush 1990: 1988)

Bill Clinton, signing the "reform," reversed Bush's thinking:

> We've been supporting democracy throughout the world. . . . But here in our own country, millions of our own citizens have been denied one of the most basic democratic rights, the right to participate in the political process. . . . The original purpose of the Hatch Act was to protect Federal employees and other citizens from coming under improper political pressure. But now our Federal work force is the product of the merit system, not patronage. We have laws to protect our citizens against coercion and intimidation. We have guarantees that the administration of Federal laws must be fair and impartial. We have an exceedingly vigilant press and people more than eager to talk to them whenever they have been abused or think they have. (Clinton 1993: 2013)

To the political executive who has paid attention to his own speeches for years, the relationship with subordinates is not coercive but merely one in which the superior ensures that the subordinate will act in the public interest, and it can indeed be in the public interest to reward those who have contributed campaign funds. Any subordinate who disagrees is merely "incompetent." Typically, all of this is obscured by reference to political "rights."

What Is Left?

In political terms, the Carter "reform," the Clinton "reinvention," and, now, the election of a Republican Congress are indeed a return to old-time struggles between the legislative and executive branches for complete control of the "spoils." The struggle is intense because those who contribute the big money expect big rewards, especially when the marketplace does not provide nearly enough business for all. Seen in this light, the Republican initiatives that have followed the 1994 elections are efforts to "devolve" functions to the states so that friendly Republican governors can control the spoils, not the executive branch.

Democrats do not strongly oppose turning things over to the states because they understand that spoils systems still flourish in the states. In recent years, to cite a single example, Pennsylvania has been wracked by three scandals. The auditor general, not too long after keynoting a conference at the University of Pittsburgh on how to combat fraud, waste, and abuse, served a prison term for the selling of jobs by his office. The treasurer, about to be sentenced for fraud in connection with computer contracts, shot himself during a televised news conference, apparently so that his family would receive his pension. Now, the attorney general has resigned after pleading guilty to a felony charge connected with campaign finance and illegal slot machine dealers who managed to escape prosecution. Typically, he had denied all irregularities while running for governor in the 1994 primaries. These events, which involved both major political parties, are not unique in state government, even among officials such as these, primary guardians against corruption. The national media can report only a small fraction of the corruption and, of course, the local media cover only their individual areas. The result is that pervasive corruption remains largely unnoticed.

The Supreme Court rejected political affiliation and loyalty as the basis for hiring and firing at state level as recently as 1990, but there is every indication that the Court will accept whatever the politicians come up with in the future. It is obvious from watching conferences televised on C-Span that state governors have followed the leads handed them. They speak grandly of the *administrative* techniques they have mastered, and they know that filling personnel files with adverse appraisals will enable them to withstand legal challenges to firings. There is wide support for patronage in the intellectual communities of political science and public administration, always ready to endorse patronage even when the courts condemn it. After the 1990 decision, for example, Larry Sabato of the University of Virginia observed that "patronage is an accepted part of the landscape." Bernard Ross, chairing the Department of Public Administration at American University, added:

> You still need people to collect signatures, distribute literature, do the poll watching, serve on telephone banks and go to senior citizen centers and

> literally get out the vote. . . . the strength of a political party depends on
> its ability to both recruit people and raise funds. The question is, how do
> you stimulate people to work in campaigns? (Tolchin 1990: IV, p. 2)

Ross did not indicate whether such duties were explored in any of the courses in his department.

The designated academic cheerleader for NPR observes that changes made by Britain's Conservative government "heavily flavored" the NPR (Kettl 1994b: 34). The Clinton Administration's fascination with the Tory "reforms," which also have enabled the politicians to strike fear into the hearts of British civil servants, have even made the front page of the *London Times* (April 17, 1995), with one of the chief NPR gurus, David Osborne, being the spokesperson for the Gore project. Elsewhere, however, there are more than small hints that the British Conservative government is awash with corruption and has been forced to appoint a high-level investigatory commission on such matters.

President Clinton might do well to remember that the action of John Major's Conservative government that upset him so much in the 1992 campaign was the rummaging through the Home Office files to see if there was any dirt on Clinton that could help George Bush; the rummaging was done by civil servants at the behest of their political bosses. Other civil servants have been rewarded with plush private sector jobs for having joined with their political bosses in deceiving the public or otherwise keeping quiet. In 1994 and 1995, four members of Parliament were caught "selling questions," that is, in return for a cash payment, an MP will "table" a question for the prime minister to highlight an issue of concern to rich supporters (we all can wonder now who pays for the questions addressed to the prime minister when C-Span televises such sessions). One of the "privatized" functions was the sale of state-owned housing, and the Conservative Westminster City Council was later found guilty of "willful misconduct" in manipulating the sales to help the party at election time. The effect was to replace lower income renters with higher income buyers who, even if buying at discounted prices, were likely to be Conservatives. The losses were estimated at $31.9 million. The party recently achieved a "sleazy and disreputable" Gallup Poll rating of 61% (*Facts on File*, January 27, 1994: 51-52, November 3, 1994: 817-818; *London Times*, April 21, 1995: 1-2, 9).

A former high-level British civil servant who had become an adviser on administrative reform to a number of countries concluded that given the number of dubious actions taken by British governments in recent years, the single most important administrative reform in the United Kingdom since World War II is the public audit machinery, headed by a National

Audit Office and an Audit Commission, with wide powers of investigation (Stowe 1992: 393). It took a four-year investigation by this apparatus to uncover the housing corruption in Westminster City. The only hope in the United States is that, as in the nineteenth century, some politicians will expose others, a dangerous exercise if all of them have dirty hands.

And The Band Plays On

After the initial disputes over the control of White House tape recordings—a real issue that emerged from the Watergate scandal of President Richard Nixon's years—the archivist of the United States was made an independent position. The legislation specified that the archivist "shall be appointed without regard to political affiliation and solely on the basis of professional qualifications." Nevertheless, the archivist in office when George Bush left the presidency gave him control of computer tapes that a federal court later ruled to be government property not to be destroyed. There were millions of E-mail messages on tape, some of which already had been used in trials involving White House assistants. As of mid-1995, former President Bush was appealing the decision, and the Clinton Administration was supporting Bush.

In the meantime, President Clinton appointed as archivist a former governor of Kansas who had no relevant experience but who had helped the Clinton presidential campaign in 1992. The vice president of the American Historical Association, obviously speaking for many academics, responded to the appointment: "A political appointment is implicitly corrupt because it raises questions about whether the materials made available to the public constitutes the full record." The lawyer who challenged Mr. Bush's right to the tapes added that "the archivist is the custodian of the historical memory of the country," protesting the tendency to make the position a "political football." Predictably, the Clinton Administration denied any "politicization," and the appointment seemed likely to be approved (DeWitt 1995).

It is wholly understandable that as we return to the spoils system, the distributors of the rewards will do whatever is necessary to ensure that there are no paper or computer trails that become available to academic or journalistic researchers. The mention of "implicit corruption" signifies that a partisan appointee is not only likely to make archival decisions that will help his or her political mentors, but may well shield all politicians from whatever damage might be inflicted through document availability. The reinstatement of "temptation" is likely to have predictable results, no matter how difficult to ascertain.

Once again, as readers may note, the immediate recommendation from those who detect real or potential corruption is to remove political activists from the decision-making processes that are so tempting to such operatives. And, as in the nineteenth-century disasters that gave rise to the civil service, there is always the likelihood that political opponents will agree not to probe very deeply into each other's political machinations. If an archivist, for example, agrees to the request of one president for control or conceal-ment of historical documents, that same official is likely to feel compelled to accede to a similar request from a president of the other major political party. The point is that the recommendations for "independent" decision making have been so numerous over the years that the problems must be systemic enough to require systemic solutions. The civil service may not have been the best available solution, but its widespread use throughout the world suggests that nobody has yet been able to find a better solution to the obviously innate corruption of competitive politics and economic distress. In the U.S. case, neither political parties nor the civil service are creatures of the original Constitution. The United States now chooses to render impotent that institution established to maintain ethical standards while celebrating the organization and processes that guarantee corruption. The political logic is impeccable.

An earlier argument bears repeating. If I were involved in the contem-porary political game, I could not expect to remain in that game without playing according to its rules. I could not, that is to say, expect to remain "pure." The nineteenth-century reformers acted on the basis of many decades of evidence about systemic corruption, not innately sinful politi-cians. As the legendary Chicago political leader, Jacob Arvey, put it, "Politics is the art of putting people under obligation to you" (Tolchin 1990). Building upon Jimmy Carter's CSRA and using budget reductions as its hammer, the Clinton Administration declared open season on the civil service. Those who can so easily be dropped will not be asking questions, a wise decision on their part at a time when fired administrators do not easily find new jobs. A civil service that cannot ask questions is essentially dead. For practical purposes, the "administrative state" is now the pre-1883 model risen from its grave.

References

Arnold, Peri. (1986) *Making the Managerial Presidency: Comprehensive Reorganization Planning, 1905-1980.* Princeton, NJ: Princeton University Press.

Bentley, Arthur F. (1908) *The Process of Government: A Study of Social Pressures.* Chicago: University of Chicago Press.

Biersack, Robert, Paul S. Herrnson, and Clyde Wilcox, eds. (1994). *Risky Business? PAC Decisionmaking in Congressional Elections.* Armonk, NY: M. E. Sharpe.

Brinkley, Alan. (1995) *The End of Reform: New Deal Liberalism in Recession and War.* New York: Knopf.

Burns, James MacGregor. (1956). [Roosevelt] *The Lion and the Fox.* New York: Harcourt, Brace & World.

Bush, George H. (1990, June 15) "Memorandum of Disapproval."

Caiden, Gerald E. (1984) "In Search of an Apolitical Science of American Public Administration." In *Politics and Administration: Woodrow Wilson and American Public Administration.* New York: Marcel Dekker

Caro, Robert A. (1982) *The Years of Lyndon Johnson.* Vol. 1. New York: Knopf.

Clinton, William J. (United States). (1993) *Weekly Compilation of Presidential Documents.* Washington, DC: Government Printing Office.

Clinton, William J. (United States). (1994) *Weekly Compilation of Presidential Documents.* Washington, DC: Government Printing Office.

Davis, James W. (1983) *National Conventions in an Age of Party Reform.* Westport, CT: Greenwood.

DeWitt, Karen. (1995, May 21) "Hot Politics at the Hall of Documents." *New York Times,* sec. 4, p. 16.

Dobryznski, Judith H. (1987, December 21) "Tom Peters: Now 'There Are No Excellent Companies.' " *Business Week.*

Eaton, Dorman. [1879] (1976) "Report Concerning Civil Service in Great Britain." In Frederick C. Mosher, ed., *Basic Documents of American Public Administration 1776-1950.* New York: Homes & Meier.

Jackson, Brooks. (1990) *Honest Graft: Big Money and the American Political Process.* Washington, DC: Farragut.

Jaffa, Henry V. (1964) "The Nature and Origin of the American Party System." In Robert A. Goldwin, ed., *Political Parties: U.S.A.* Chicago: Rand McNally.

Jones, Charles O. (1995) "A Way of Life and Law." *American Political Science Review,* 89: 1-9.

Kahn, Alfred E. (1982, June 19) "Letters to Editor." *Washington Post,* p. A14.

Kebschull, Harvey G. (1992) "Political Corruption: Making It the 'Significant Other' in Political Studies." *PS,* 20: 705-709.

Kettl, Donald F. (1994a, September 6) "Did Gore Reinvent Government?" *New York Times,* p. A19.

———. (1994b) *Reinventing Government? Appraising the National Performance Review.* Washington, DC: Brookings Institution.

Leif, Alfred, ed. (1931) *Representative Opinions of Mr. Justice Holmes.* New York: Vanguard.

Lingley, Charles R. (1924) *Since the Civil War.* New York: Century.

Lowi, Theodore J. (1993) "Legitimizing Public Administration: A Disturbed Dissent." *American Public Administration Review,* 53: 261-264.

McDonald, Forrest. (1994) *The American Presidency: An Intellectual History.* Lawrence: University Press of Kansas.

Moe, Ronald C. (1991) "The HUD Scandal and the Case for an Office of Federal Management." *Public Administration Review,* 51: 298-307.

National Party Conventions, 1831-1988. (1991) Washington, DC: Congressional Quarterly.

National Performance Review [Al Gore]. (1993) *Creating a Government That Works Better and Costs Less: Report of the National Performance Review.* Washington, DC: Government Printing Office.

Newland, Chester A. (1992) "The Politics of Civil Service Reform." In Patricia W. Ingraham and David H. Rosenbloom, eds., *The Promise and Paradox of Civil Service Reform.* Pittsburgh: University of Pittsburgh Press.

Ostrom, Vincent. (1989) *The Intellectual Crisis in American Public Administration.* 2nd ed. Tuscaloosa: University of Alabama Press.

Peters, Thomas J., and Robert H. Waterman, Jr. (1982) *In Search of Excellence: Lessons From America's Best-Run Companies.* New York: Harper & Row.

Presidential Elections Since 1789. (1991) Washington, DC: Congressional Quarterly.

Rohr, John A. (1986) *To Run a Constitution: The Legitimacy of the Administrative State.* Lawrence: University Press of Kansas.

———. (1989) *Ethics for Bureaucrats: An Essay on Law and Values.* 2nd ed. New York: Marcel Dekker.

Schumpeter, Joseph A. (1950 [1942]) *Capitalism, Socialism, and Democracy.* 3rd ed. New York: Harper & Row.

Skowronek, Stephen. (1982) *Building a New American State: The Expansion of National Administrative Capacities, 1877-1920.* New York: Cambridge University Press.

Stern, Philip M. (1992). *Still the Best Congress Money Can Buy.* Rev. ed. Washington, DC: Regnery Gateway.

Storing, Herbert J. (1964) "Political Parties and the Bureaucracy." In Robert A. Goldwin, ed., *Political Parties: U.S.A.* Chicago: Rand McNally.

Stowe, Kenneth. (1992) "A Good Piano Won't Play Bad Music: Administrative Reform and Good Governance." *Public Administration,* 70: 387-394.

Thayer, Frederick C. (1978) "The President's Management 'Reforms': Theory X Triumphant." *Public Administration Review,* 38: 309-314.

———. (1984) *Rebuilding America: The Case for Economic Regulation.* New York: Praeger.

———. (1987) "Privatization: Carnage, Chaos, and Corruption." In Barry J. Carroll, Ralph W. Conant, and Thomas A. Easton, eds., *Private Means Public Ends.* New York: Praeger.

Thompson, Dennis F. (1993) "Mediated Corruption: The Case of the Keating Five." *American Political Science Review,* 87: 369-381.

Timmons, Bascom N. (1948) *Garner of Texas: A Personal History.* New York: Harper.

Tolchin, Martin. (1990, July 1) "Why Patronage Is Unlikely to Fade Away." *New York Times.*

Tolchin, Susan J., and Martin Tolchin. (1983) *Dismantling America: The Rush to Deregulate.* Boston: Houghton Mifflin.

Van Riper, Paul P. (1958) *History of the United States Civil Service.* Evanston, IL: Row, Peterson.

"Who's Excellent Now?" (1984, November 5) *Business Week,* pp. 76-88.

Wilson, Woodrow. [1887] (1978) "The Study of Administration." In Jay M. Shafritz and Albert C. Hyde, eds., *Classics of Public Administration.* Oak Park, IL: Moore.

Political Power and the Centrality of Administration

The Politico-Logic of Field Administration

Matthew Holden, Jr.

Purpose

I propose an approach to the relationship of "bureaucrats" and "politicians" in "modern systems of governance" somewhat different than that which my colleagues appear to adopt. My purpose is to revisit the subject of "politics and administration" to make the case that administration is the necessary form of action without which political power does not exist, and within those terms to propose a basis for further thinking about field administration.

Method

Before I proceed with the substance, I should say something on method. This chapter reflects some work on which I have been struggling too long but that is perhaps near its end. "The first step in undertaking political science research," to quote Manheim and Rich (1986: 5), "is the selection of an appropriate research question." This is very much the same as the staple of courses in methodology in which, to get the right answers, one must ask the right questions.

I am not sure we pay enough attention to this difficult problem. The clamorous ignorance that even the best educated people display on political matters suggests to me that, on the whole, we still see through a glass darkly. The issue, of course, is this: Whence cometh the right questions? Some questions are too trivial or foolish to be worth asking. On the other hand, some major questions are too big to miss. The discipline whose members are freed, by the investment of social resources to allow them to have much more autonomy over their projects, methods, and timing, has an obligation to take its self-policed responsibility seriously. But I have no formal prescription for this exercise in discovery. (This problem of "soft" methodology is discussed elsewhere.)

All that I have done here is to think about the literature of political science as I know it, to add to that some personal familiarity with administrative practice, and to assess the logic that seems mandatory. The chapter is an exercise in discovery, not of verification, although the discovery is taken very seriously. The level of confidence has no formal testing, but it is entirely judgmental.

Here I resort to the analogy of a legal trial. In the practice of law, the big difference is between establishing probable cause to take a case seriously and proving the case at trial. My chief aim is to argue probable cause about the role of "administration" in political systems. The forum to which I address the argument is the community of political scientists and others who make the study of politics a prime concern. To the political science audience, one makes the following statement: "Administration is the lifeblood of power"—no administration, no power. If we were able, I maintain, to conduct an orderly study of human governance, the situations we describe probably would fit what methodologists would regard as a normal pattern (Key 1966; Palumbo 1969; Tufte 1974). There are, of course, other audiences—both practitioners and scholars in other disciplines—who speak of the same phenomena in the terminology as "bureaucracy," "management," and "organization." Although I cannot explore the issue here, my contention is that the same argument applies to "private" organizations. My contention, from observation, is that it does apply to corporations, to churches, with which I am somewhat familiar as a participant and observer, and to universities, with which nearly all political scientists are familiar.

The Need for New Language

The very language in which political science speaks needs reconstitution. Linguistic convention commonly distinguishes between "bureaucrats" and "politicians," the latter category being limited chiefly to those who seek popular election to office. This convention makes conversation easier, but it reveals too little about the actual operations of power. Some political actors compete electorally; some have effective command over troops; some inherit office, even in this decade; and some get access to the process because of education and competitive examinations (e.g., higher civil servants). All who compete for the opportunity to coordinate the preferences of others, without the consent of others, and to decide what preferences will be supported and what overridden, are "politicians." The part of real experience to which I think attention is most worthwhile, and most neglected, is the actual organization of power. Without it, those who seek to comprehend political systems will persistently disguise from themselves some crucial aspects of the rules of politics. If the intellectual purpose were achieved, it would merge the "public administration" studied by those who concentrate on "American government" and that "public administration" studied in "comparative politics." It would also merge the "public administration" of those concerned with domestic politics and policy with the "public administration" of those concerned with foreign policy and international affairs, the most inclusive realms of administrative decision making.

Administration is neither separate from policies nor subordinate nor sequential to politics. Administration is a decision-making process, parallel to "legislation" and "adjudication."[1] Legislation as a process is very important in some systems of governance, and it may be imperative by standards of representativeness known to American political science. It is demonstrably not imperative, even to modern governments. Adjudication is important under various systems of law. Moreover, it may be that all are important to the criteria of *good* government that American political scientists are likely to consider. Administration is the third such process. *Among these three processes, it is central.* Such is the argument in bold relief. Moreover, in this chapter, I set forth some working propositions about how this might lead us to think of the politico-logic of field administration.

Discovering the Question

Thomas Hobbes, the symbol of autocracy, has a bad reputation, so that contemporary political scientists pay him little attention. But there is a level at which Hobbes raises a light that might yet help in the present darkness. "The skill of making and maintaining commonwealths . . . consisteth in certain rules . . . which neither poor men have had the leisure, nor men that have had the leisure, have hitherto had the curiosity or the method to find out" (Hobbes 1960: 136). The "rules" of politics we seek are not the moral norms but the explanatory principles or criteria that aid us to foretell, by means other than sheer prophecy, the essential sources of human conflict and resolution, the consequences of such conflict and resolution, and the mechanisms of common action and decision making. It is around the "making and maintaining of commonwealths" that political science finds questions that are unmistakably important.

The "making and maintaining of commonwealths" engages crucial issues about where conflict comes from and what its consequences are. It also engages issues of the mechanisms of power and decision making, which is what raises as well our contemporary concern about administrative decision making in human governance. Pendleton Herring might, if we could distill his work into propositions, come as close as anyone to being the Alfred Marshall of contemporary political science. So many ideas now important are found in his early work. His book in the 1930s unmistakably gave the corpus of political science an explicit basis for recognizing what was implicit in others.

Herring gave the explicit recognition that administrative decision making is an active element of policy making (Herring 1936). That idea is implicit in earlier work such as that of Frank Goodnow. Articulated by various others, it was given its sharpest formulation by Norton Long. Administration has to be politically engaged. "Power," said Long, "is the life blood of administration." He continued, "Its attainment, cultivation, maintenance, increase, dissipation and loss are subjects the practitioner and the student can ill afford to neglect" (Long 1949, 1962). Nonetheless, this understanding has not been incorporated into the whole discipline. Political scientists presume "administration" to be marginal to what they need to know. This presumption is exactly disabling to a political science purpose to discover, articulate, and test the basic rules of politics. It is from that point of view that this chapter takes up "political power," "administrative centrality," and "field control."

Administration as the Lifeblood of Power

Modern systems of governance, in the late twentieth century as we observe and the twenty-first century as we estimate, are comprehensible within fundamentals. The centrality of administration to power is such a funda-

TABLE 5.1 Summary of Resource Models of Administrative Decision Making

Hood	McGregor	Rhodes	Holden
Authority (law prescribing)	Rule of obedience	Legal authority	Coercive force
Finance (exchange)	Exchange (buying/selling)	Money	Money
Nodality (information)	Persuasion (informed behavior upon request)	Political legitimacy	Information
Organization (action with own re-sources)[a]		Organizational resources	

a. In American public administration, this used to be referred to, in some occasions, as "force account."

mental. No leader or ruler, actual or potential, reactionary or revolutionary, conservative or radical, can make many effective decisions without essential resources. Whatever is to be said of motives, strategies, skills, and luck, no one ever succeeds in power, over any extended period, without control of administration. This cannot be otherwise. It must be so because discretion must be exercised, on a continuing basis, about the actual use of the information, money and force, requisites, or necessary resources in governance to induce people to act jointly. Without these resources, people cannot be induced to act jointly over any extended period of time. At every "level" of government, and in every system of public government, control depends not upon the pronouncement of "rules" and "standards" merely but upon discretion about the actual use of information, money, and force. They may be interpreted as essentially equivalent to what Eugene B. McGregor, Jr., calls the "organization elements." The "organization elements" as expressed by McGregor refer to the rule of obedience, exchange, or buying and selling, and persuasion when informed behavior occurs upon request (McGregor 1981: 347-375). (They also are characterized by a substantial convergence with the "tools" of government as conceived by Hood or the power-dependence model as expressed by Rhodes.)

Dwight Waldo (personal communication) observed that no one ever seems to have followed up the implications of Long's famous and much cited article. Let us reflect on the verbs in Long's sentence. What *do* people do to *attain* power? To *cultivate, maintain,* or *increase* power? What acts do they *commit* that constitute dissipation and loss? When the answers are offered as to what people *do*, those answers will almost certainly allow the student to extend Long's hypothesis fundamentally.

Administration is power in practice. Austin Ranney once observed that most people "almost never see anyone or have dealings with anyone other than 'administrators' " (personal correspondence, March 25, 1969). Administration, as power in practice, reveals social realities, even when those who articulate social doctrine may wish to deny it. The more penetrating the study of administration becomes, the more it reveals things that, as in an Andrew Greeley novel, people would rather not know or be obliged explicitly to recognize (Greeley 1984). For example, to choose an example removed from present-day controversy, let us mention the administrative process associated with the United States as a slave society in the nineteenth century. An American scholar in public administration can live a whole life and hear no substantial discussion of the subject. The reason, apart from a bias against "history," is that the practices revealed violate most of the things now described as "American values." Movement, speech, and the use of the mails, as actually administered, all had to be far more constrained than any retrospective view of American values now is likely to admit. Yet the avoidance of inquiry into real experience is the avoidance of the task of political science.

Why "Administrative Centrality" Is Plausible

The Suggestion of "Pre-Political Science"

Administrative centrality was implicit in the learning that we may call "pre-political science." Two sorts of evidence are at hand. Handbooks for the instruction of royal rulers—"mirrors for princes"—were common in Asia from the distant past and in Europe from the fifth through the fifteenth centuries. It does not matter whether they deserve the sharp intellectual contempt that J. H. Hexter visits upon them—"singularly vapid (in) character," "dreary," "cliché-ridden" (Hexter 1973). The other evidence from "pre-political science" is in the writing of those who do command wide respect in the history of political thought. Political theory, understood as the history of political thought, is far closer to the identification of important problems for empirical inquiry than students of public administration normally maintain.

To aid the argument, I choose an illustration from Ibn Khaldun and a parallel illustration from John Stuart Mill. Ibn Khaldun, fourteenth-century administrator and scholar, lived and worked at various times from Tunisia (as it now is) to Cairo (Khaldun 1958: xxix-lxvii). His reported observation was that "the three basic pillars of . . . authority . . . are soldiers, money, and 'means to communicate with those who are absent.' " John Stuart Mill's nineteenth-century, English, rationalist concepts are not thought to have come from the same intellectual pool as the ideas of Ibn Khaldun, Arab and Muslim. Yet Mill, on the path to a quite different argument, finds it essential to acknowledge "muscular strength . . ., property, and intelligence" (Mill 1964: 245). They agree, in effect, that the resources necessary to enable joint action are simple and reducible to three: information, money or its surrogates, and force.

When the observers are, as Khaldun and Mill are, rather far apart, in time, culture, or intellectual background, we are entitled to suppose that the latter is not consciously or subconsciously copying from the former. We have some reason, thus, to give credence to the proposition asserted, as a point of departure for inquiry.

The History of Government

Administrative centrality is rendered plausible, as hypothesis, by what we currently know of the history of government. Representative institutions existed in Europe, in the Middle Ages, from Poland to the Atlantic Ocean until, as John Neville Figgis tells us, the mid-fifteenth century, when "it seemed to most practical statesmen, and all sovereigns that the tendency of advancing civilization is a tendency towards pure monarchy" (Figgis 1956 [1907]: 46). Monarchy was not merely a fact but increasingly the preference of the most educated of the time. It was the new idea. Because the parliaments had little to do with making actual decisions, they became, predictably, increasingly secondary to the administrative institutions.

We also have to deal with the *administration* of which most people seem to think when the word is used. That idea is of administration in terms of the secondary, essential, unglamorous routine. The dominant conception of *administration* may give the impression that there is an agreed "job" or "objective" in society, and that *administration* merely seeks the best methods to do that job or achieve that objective. The idea is that there is some domain within which the logic of action is governed solely by technical considerations and in which decisions are not made through conflict but through knowledge (Self 1972).

Routine and Micropolitics

The emphasis on a techno-logic equates presumed technical merit with "rationality" and construes "politics" as adverse to "rationality." As important as technical issues are, students of government will persistently go wrong without a fundamental understanding of the politico-logic of administration. Conflict of interest, and of disposition, must arise in groups. It is found in recognizable forms everywhere and, so far, found absent nowhere. Politics disappears only in the pure case of the true routine. We can find a few cases in which competing groups act as if their interests require the same service to continue without being taken over by themselves. Hugh Thomas wrote of the American-owned telephone system in Spain that "continued to serve both parties impartially" throughout the Spanish Civil War (Thomas 1961: 139, n. 1). Technical services were carried out, despite the fact that the services might have been seriously implicated in one or another phase of the war.

Even the most technical issues are not without value judgments and interests, however. No institution operates without people to do its work. We commonly, and correctly, associate "administration" with the procedures for recruitment, examination, selection, retention, promotion, and termination or retirement of personnel (Cayer 1986; Hennessy et al. 1991; Gladden 1972; Mattingly 1967; Tout 1920-1933). The discretion and decision-making capacity open to most people in a given agency may be "small," "narrow," and "officially" irrelevant to the policy ends that may be sought. Nonetheless, it is saturated with micropolitics (interpersonal politics) at a low level of visibility.

Within the very smallest cases, human transactions reappear in the exercise of power by one person over another, and the resistance of the subordinate to the putative superior. In the University of Virginia, in the early 1990s, a severe fiscal crisis appeared. Hardly anyone at the university's central level of authority would ever imagine the cleaning problem to be "political," but the authority tension could be seen in the buildings at night.

The problem seemed to be that wastebaskets did not get emptied fast enough. As a result, not enough gurneys were ready to go to the dumpster before some of the night supervisor's crew were to go home. The dumpster was not filled on time. Doubtless, this meant that the night supervisor expected (or received) complaint from her supervisor. Her instruction (or, maybe, merely nagging admonition) to the cleaning woman was, "Reach down in there and get it." The woman who physically mops the floors and empties the wastebaskets complained to the third party bystander about her supervisor. "She wants me to put my hands down in the wastebaskets." The tone of abuse, resentment, and defiance was obvious. But to this woman, the baskets were nasty, and she said, "I am not going to do that." This was a "political" transaction as much as others, but it simply lacked visibility to those at the highest levels. It would have visibility as soon as work disputes began to show up in overt labor resistance to management, expressed in financial demands, and in the unavailability of clean class-rooms on the next day.

Micropolitics in administration can take the form of slips or inadvertent failures in routine. Micropolitics also comes in petty authority (or face-to-face tyranny). The administrative functionary may teach the applicant—often by explicit instruction—that "in order to get what you want, you have to satisfy *me*!" Petty authority puts in basic human terms the idea that power is the capacity of X to induce Y to do something that Y would rather not do. The very week in which this chapter was finished, the world saw another revelation of administrative practice in the tapes of interviews between a former Los Angeles police sergeant, Mark Fuhrman, and a television scriptwriter. Face-to-face tyranny is often, although perhaps not always, grounded in the human tendency to retreat in the face of embarrassment and shame.

Finally, routine is politicized to the extent that dissatisfied claimants have unequal capacity to appeal beyond the initial level of decision, with some chance of having the original decision reversed. There is another side of the appeal problem. The category of pure routine (reproductive action) entailing no personal decision is a nearly empty set. The human being might become a mere animate object if all claims were to go to people "bound" by the "machinery" to render claims to the applicants' disadvantage.

The Requisites, Techniques, and Levels of Administrative Action

The Problem of What Is Absolutely Required

There are a variety of approaches that depend on a theory of what government "must" have in order to "function." I am a "functionalist" in this sense, following a path of thinking that goes back at least to Goodnow in American public administration and to others earlier and outside that tradition. In the varieties of human systems, there has to be some way for signals, desires, resistances, and problems to be communicated to the decisional center.

As these communications are aggregated, decision making transforms them into choices that are made and proclaimed. Decisions having been made and proclaimed, they must also be diffused into the body politic.

Discretion as the Collection, Use,
and Dispensation of Information

In the strictest sense, information is the ultimate requisite of government (Deutsch 1963; Brewer 1990). Information may be seen as cognitive (shared agreement as to what the facts are), particularly in the circumstances where there can be some objective indicators as to what is correct and what is not. Information may also be seen as morally and emotionally persuasive (shared values), so that one party has the ability to get another to believe that the first party is legitimate.

Those who would exercise leadership must have, at minimum, sufficient information about the rest of the world that they may keep themselves alive and free. If they are dead, they can govern nothing. If they are captive, they must be able to escape or, at minimum, give advice or orders that others will follow, despite the captivity.

The necessity of information does not make it easy to get. Indeed, some information is so fugitive or depends on the interaction of so many complex variables as to be impossible to obtain. On many occasions, there will be so many signals from the environment that it is almost impossible to tell in advance which are truly good indicators (Wohlstetter 1966). On other occasions, the organizational structure will block good information (Neustadt 1970). These are all occasions when people are ignorant but rational.

There is much room for empirical investigation into information and the administrative process. One of the instructive inquiries would be a political scientist's study of the development and use of statistical information in government. Perhaps there are more fragments from which to construct a "social archaeology of government information" than for any other purpose. Modern society treats as valid the information that is demonstrable within the criteria of contemporary science. But other forms of information are accepted, in one society or another. Gossip, seers and revelation, spies and school-trained experts, are all part of the information producing system. This means that are many important questions of discretion that turn up as conflicting expertise problems, as in natural science and physical technology (Fri 1995), in the criminal law process, and in the uses of psychology in testing and experimentation.

We have considerable need for some deeper understanding as to the exercises of discretion about money in all its aspects and discretion in the exercise of force in all its aspects.

There is also considerable need to differentiate techniques of administration (regulation, facilitation, and entrepreneurship as three distinguishable patterns) and levels of administrative action as to their generality— "policy" being the most general, "program" being the intermediate form, and "operational detail" being the final step without which the first steps remain unfulfilled.

Administration:
The Official Presumption of Command

Policy and, to some degree, program are the decisions likely to be articulated at the highest levels. Information, money, and sometimes force will be disposed or used to achieve what is desired. The giving and receiving of executive direction engages chief executives ("president," "prime minister," "general secretary," "pope"), executive entourages (sometimes called "staff"), and the operating entities to perform the ultimate work: "departments," "ministries," "boards," or "commissions." There is a persistent tension between the exercise of authoritative command by those formally invested with such authority and the actual need for some degree of bargaining with those who are their titular subordinates. Human physical weakness is the basic inducement to bargaining. No human being can do all that he or she is technically responsible for doing, and so must depend upon others.

From this point of view, public administration as a subject of study and a set of practices is logically quite closely connected with the variety of forms of executive politics that political scientists study. In another place, I have dealt with this as a question of the relationships between chief executives (or their functional equivalents, even in systems that do not depend on elections) and their entourages. The bargain between the chief executive and the entourage is critical. The former cedes some measure of power to the latter, in exchange for the latter's relieving the former of some degree of burden that is simply too much to carry continually.

There is also a set of bargaining relationships between chief executives and those principal subordinates (department heads, ministers, commissioners, and so on). The latter have both institutional roles and personal needs that are not in accord with the institutional roles and personal needs of the person who occupies the office of the chief executive at a given moment.

What Is Field Administration?

The "mechanisms" further emphasized in this chapter meet the problem of *field administration*. This is an old term that I here resurrect. The term comes from a recognition of another fundamental element. If decisions are to be more than sounds in the wind, they must be transmitted from "the highest levels" to the next lower levels and to the nth persons whose cooperation or compliance will be a part of making the decisions operative. The administrative political actors include not only top-level administrators at the center but also members of the network of field administrators operating in the territory away from the physical center of government—the capital—as well. Decisions at the highest level are seldom, if ever, self-executing. If the highest-level decision makers will act so as to achieve their purposes, then their decisions must be implemented by others throughout the territory or in the field (Smith 1967; Jacob 1963: 1). Gopal Krishan, an Indian geographer, refers to "approximately 200 national level territories, about 3000 regions analogous to French departments or the English counties, [and] about 40 to 50,000 units comparable to districts" (Krishan 1988). *Field administration constitutes the visible presence of government and is imperative to the organization of power.* Accordingly, *field administration* will tend to have a certain politico-logic (internal consistency) that is oriented to the problem of control in contrast, for example, to a techno-logic.

The term has little current name recognition in political science and cognate disciplines.[2] James W. Fesler and David B. Truman began to publish on this subject before World War II, Fesler continuing into the 1960s (Fesler 1936, 1943, 1949, 1962, 1965; Truman 1940). Earl Latham and others produced a deep research memorandum that ought to be at the center of the work at the end of World War II (Latham et al. 1947). In the context of social reform interests, Michael Lipsky's influential exposition gave us the caption "street-level bureaucracy" but remarkably little fresh thinking and/or empirical work has come forth on the phenomenon.

In American research, recognition has most recently been focused upon the regulatory process. "Much of the important work of administering the Clean Air Act," Melnick (1983) says, "takes place in the EPA's regional offices." Accordingly, regional offices constitute "bridges" between states and the Washington offices, explain federal regulations to the states, and express state and local concerns to Washington. There are a variety of fairly recent empirical studies along the same lines (Scicchitano et al. 1989; Scholz and Wei 1986; Schneider 1992; Thompson and Scicchitano 1987, among others).

As field administration plays a major role in these American regulatory institutions, so it also plays a role in other American administrative agencies. The Internal Revenue Service (IRS) and the Department of Health and Human Services (HHS) are among the major agencies whose regional directors have vast responsibility and authority regarding millions of Americans.

Perhaps field administration is not so well understood in regard to public order. Two illustrations may help. The mayor and Police Department of New York were severely criticized for their failure to intervene in a riot in the Crown Heights portion of Brooklyn in 1991. The Los Angeles Police Department was severely criticized for their failure to intervene in the portion of Los Angeles where riots were taking place in 1992. These two cases were probably the exaggerated version of the de facto withdrawal of field administrative action (policing) from many areas of cities. The residents of urban public housing projects, in the 1990s, are known to live with minimal likelihood that calling the police will produce a timely response, or that it will do any good at all. The folklore of many large cities is replete with expectations that tradesmen may be shaken down by an underworld, and that the police can or will do nothing. These are failures in the field.

Some failures in the field are endurable from the point of view of authority. However, there are limits. The presumption of government is that, to some extent, rulers will act to relieve distress. This cannot work if field administration does not work. Thus note an account from Wallo Province, Ethiopia, which the *New York Times* describes as "a remote northern province" ("Ethiopia Says" 1973: 3). There had been a disturbance in May in the provincial capital in which 17 students were killed. The provincial capital was in the heart of a famine area, with almost all people cut off from any form of transportation or communication. Six months later, the government was saying that it had been kept in ignorance of the famine as well as the circumstances in which the students were killed. The government said the shootings had been unnecessary, that the governor of the province should have met with the students, and that an inquiry was being conducted into why this was kept secret from the emperor. The governor said he had been too busy with other administrative matters, but some officials claimed he never left the provincial capital during his three-year tenure. The ability to produce food had gone, the ability to secure and distribute relief efficiently had not been created, and the ability of the central government to know in time the extreme circumstances was nonexistent.

The Downward Shift of Authority

Field administration has depended, historically, upon central decision makers allowing authority to shift downward, to be absorbed by subordinates. The field people, glamorized or not, down to the last (nth) person, participate in some of the flows of action that turn policies into programs, and programs into operational detail. Their actions diffuse governmental policies and authority (Latham et al. 1947). The downward shift of authority, planned or merely tolerated, does not mean that central decision makers give up all hopes of control. Indeed, central decision makers will attempt, all other things being equal, to keep field-level decision makers' choices in line with their own preferences (Kaufman 1967). Yet this can never quite work.

Hierarchy is virtually always imperfect to some degree. Field administrators' actions tend to deviate from what those actions would be if the field administrators followed their superiors' premises perfectly.

Reason 1 is that the field-level decision makers simply lack the physical or mental ability to perform what the central decision maker would require. The simplest case is that of physical fatigue.

Reason 2 is that the field administrator seeks to protect his (or her) self-interest, in the narrowest sense of that term. Physical survival is such a motive. Policemen's claims of physical fear become a different source of motivation to depart from overt policy forms. The police officer's use of violence on suspects, to whatever degree the police officer deems justifiable, is explained by the fear that the police officer has for his or her own safety. Financial self-interest, of course, is a worldwide source of deviation. This is illustrated in the parable in the Gospel According to St. Luke, Chapter 16. A steward was told that he would be fired for having "wasted (his master's) goods" (Luke 16:1-2). The steward, taking as his premise "*I cannot beg: to dig I am ashamed,*" quickly conspired to write down the debts of those who owed his employer, with the expectation that they would help to take care of him later (Luke 16:3, 16:5-7).

Reason 3 is that the field-level decision makers have been given some bigger job than they could possibly handle, no matter how alert they may be. If the field administrators are with an emergency service unit, and are told to see that everyone is fed after a hurricane has put the local stores out of business, it may be impossible. It may be that there are not enough supplies of wheat and rice, meat and fish, rice and potatoes, and so on for everyone to be fed.

Reason 4 is that field administrators modify their orders, or their own compliance procedures, to attract support from people who will not, in their opinion, comply with orders as initially issued or policies as initially pronounced. David Truman (1940) states in his report about the Chicago office of the Department of Agriculture half a century ago:

> The early experience . . . indicates that the field office of a new regulatory agency cannot expect to receive much voluntary co-operation from

persons in the trade until its activities have largely lost their controversial aspect—a result which can be influenced by the field men.

If this is a problem, then we should predict the field administrator would reinterpret instructions from above to the extent of achieving some compliance.

The first four reasons do not assume that field administrators disagree substantially with their instructions. *Reason 5 is that field administrators sometimes simply do not agree, for doctrinal, psychological, or ideological reasons, with what they have been told to do.* Field functionaries may, substantially but covertly, ignore, reinterpret, or implement their orders in ways that are more satisfactory by their own lights. The role of psychology should not be neglected. If policemen feel that violence is necessary to make others show respect, then the "real rules" allow a great deal of "acting out" the hostility that may build up within people whose normal experience on the job is that of immediate violence.

Field administrators may sometimes overtly defy the constituted authority under which they, in principle, work. This has been a common experience in military institutions. The United States, as a major country, is an unusual exception. The temporary display of imperfection in hierarchy was precisely the issue at stake in the removal of General Douglas MacArthur by President Harry S. Truman in 1951. Truman came to say that "the messages I sent him through other people he somehow or another seemed never to understand" (Miller 1973: 292).

Field administrators may, in these five ways, deviate from the premises of their superiors virtually to the extent of nullification of the public policy (Wallace 1933: 347-358).

Central Control, Devolution, and Negotiated Power Sharing

If a tendency for field subordinates to deviate is normal, so are observable efforts to limit deviation. This yields administrative relationships of central control, of devolution, and of negotiated power sharing. Central control exists to the extent all subordinate officials and employees act with perfect consistency upon the premises they have been given. Central control is most fully represented in systems where there is a territorial subdivision of authority. Some high-ranking field officer (provincial governor, commissioner, or prefect) is deemed "the" representative of the government in the field. Prefectoral administration is uniquely designed to support "current rulers' retention of central power" and to maintain control over field administration against the demands of outside pressure groups or against any disaffection of administrators themselves (Fesler 1965: 550). The prefectorate exists in most of the smaller Western European countries, Belgium, Denmark, Luxembourg, the Netherlands, Norway, and Sweden, in Italy, and in France, its most famous locale (Fried 1963: 3).

Perhaps the prefectorate is most noted, for Americans, in the French case. The conception that passed into American political science was that the French system was highly centralized, with very close control being exercised from Paris to the provinces. There was some basis to the lesson learned. The prefectorate had its precedent in the intendants as reorganized under Cardinal Richelieu in the 1620s (Gruder 1968: 1-10). When Napoleon Bonaparte created the French prefectorate, public order, the organization of local political support for Napoleon and his policies, and provision of information about the state of affairs in the department were high objectives. So it remained, when the prefects were agents and crucial to the coup in which Louis Napoleon made himself emperor (Forstenzer 1981). Central control is sometimes approximated, but central decision makers will virtually never achieve perfect central control. Even the French prefectorate was less centralized than the doctrine suggested.

Woodrow Wilson, as a young professor, when the Second Empire had disappeared and the Third Republic had come, glimpsed a different possibility. "I have learned . . . all that is necessary to know about what that autocratic person the French Prefect *may* do. . . . What I want to know is, what the Prefect does do" (Link 1966: Vol. 5, p. 417). Years later, Wilson concluded that the prefect was much more the "executive agent" of the council of the department to which he was assigned, that the office was a "party prize," the assignment of which hinged on support from the senators and deputies of the department. "This prefect was not the autocrat of Napoleonic government, but a trimmer to local opinion, of the sort too often found under popular governments" (Wilson 1911: 229).

Although the prefectoral form is identified with Europe, more people live under it outside Europe. The state governors appear effectively to be prefects, although they are elected in form. In reality, they are designated by the president, except in those states where the opposition party manages to win the governorship (Bernstein 1993). The prefectoral form was, so Gulick reported in the 1930s, "the general practice in territorial or colonial governments," although the nomenclature was different (Gulick 1937: 27). "The unit of administration throughout British India is the district," Sir Edward Blunt wrote in the 1930s, and "the district officer, whether known as collector, district magistrate, or deputy commissioner, is the responsible head of his jurisdiction" (Blunt 1937: 91). The relationship has continued in contemporary India, which is perhaps the most striking and largest scale example in the world today. The district officer, presiding over an area with about 2 million people (on the average), must be a person of some consequence.

Central control, although much discussed under various names, is the norm that administrative theory has come to adopt, especially in the twentieth century. It is, however, not what the world has most often practiced. Devolution has been the most common pattern and is widespread in the contemporary world. Devolution is the form of administration wherein the responsibility is placed upon officials of some lower level unit, with little central supervision of the manner in which they carry out this responsibility or even whether they do. As a structure, devolution reflects convenience or necessity quite as much as doctrine.

Devolution in contemporary situations is often advocated (even preached) as a means of participation and representation. Sometimes, it may serve that purpose. County government in the United States, for instance, is one of the stronger illustrations of contemporary devolution. The county still has the legal standing of being that of an administrative agent of the state. The sheriff has the duty to enforce these policies. Virtually all policies that have criminal penalties depend upon the action of local police officers, local sheriffs, and local prosecutors, normally elected locally or chosen by locally elected officials. Yet state officials often have little real power to review or redirect what these county-level officials do, as can be manifest in a jury proceeding. (Not only is devolution sometimes found in democratic regimes, but it is quite common in regimes of dominance, where one group rules over another, through an intermediate administrative elite) (Stevenson 1939). The remaining major pattern is negotiated power sharing. Negotiated power sharing arises when the "superior" level of government needs the cooperation of a lower level of government and lacks the ability to command obedience. Negotiated power sharing arises when neither the "superior" level of government nor the "inferior" level of government has the ability to act effectively without some degree of agreed cooperation from the other. Negotiated power sharing, though also of some vintage, has become particularly strongly developed in "intergovernmental relations" in the United States (Van Horn 1979; Levin and Ferman 1985).

Devolution and negotiated power sharing are more explicit and more common when the central government may operate primarily through the field agents of the "functional" units. Territorial assignments are made within the functions (Fesler 1949; Truman 1940). This is much more the American pattern. In the American case, presidents have overseas representatives in ambassadors. Ambassadors have often had great difficulty asserting control over the field representatives of the other American government entities that may have missions of one sort or another in the country to which the ambassador is accredited. Presidents do not normally have subnational officials who claim authority, in the president's name, over agriculture, commerce, interior, energy, and so on, at the field level. In American administration, the subordinate field officials generally are called representatives of the functional agencies. These are most often the "regional directors" or "regional administrators," and their geographic domains generally are the 10 standard federal regions based upon lines decided during the Nixon Administration.

To give some specificity, let us begin with one illustration of federal agencies in the United States. The Department of Health and Human Services embodies the large-scale income transfer programs in medicine and the social services. The latter is what Americans generally mean when they speak of "welfare programs." The U.S. Government Manual states that "regional directors represent the Secretary [of Health and Human Services] in their respective regions." HHS is a member of that family of agencies whose functions are mainly facilitative.

Many other agencies are mainly regulatory and they also have their field presence. The Environmental Protection Agency, the Occupational Safety and Health Administration (OSHA), and the National Labor Relations Board are examples of the regulatory agency. They are different than HHS in that they have more to do with assessing penalties and less with benefits.

Three Necessary Decisions From the Center: Areas, Agents, Authority

The approximation of central control, of devolution, or of negotiated power sharing is revealed, and produced, by the aggregate of decisions about the physical territories or administrative areas in which authority is to be exercised, the agents to be used or recognized, and the mission and authority to be recognized in those agents.

Areas

Area decision making will be dominated by the substantive work that has to be done. The demands for a given administrative area will, assuming technology to be constant, be governed by things that make people want to intervene and make claims, and the things that make it harder or easier for administrators to decide whom to support, what to approve, and when to make one choice or another. Area is not a concern of the highest level authorities under most circumstances.

It is very important, however, under the military circumstance. In the conduct of war, territory can be everything. What the field commander does, actively or by omission, about the movement into a territory will create "facts on the ground" that the top-level political executive cannot thereafter reverse. General Eisenhower's decisions about where to stop when moving into Germany had the important consequence of leaving politically strategic territory open to Soviet military control, and thus to Communist political control. General MacArthur's approach to the Yalu was feared, by American political leadership, because it might engage the Soviet Union or the Chinese. Civil War occupation of southern areas had the consequence of creating areas in which slaves would make themselves free, simply by escaping behind Union lines, regardless of whether policy on emancipation had been settled.

Territoriality, sometimes important in civil administration, is not important enough to similarly command the top-level decision makers' attention to the same degree as would military areas. In civil administration, the territorial issue may often be relatively removed from the view even of a department head. The relevant political groups will find that their major interests allow, or even require, them to ignore most debates about areas. Accordingly, the definition of administrative areas will be dominated by "professional" administrators or by those private interests encompassed in the "subgovernments."

Once administrative areas are established, they will tend to remain stable. Social demand will serve as a basis for opposition to change. Normally, existing arrangements will be perfectly satisfactory to the existing central executive, the existing career administrators, and all associated with each. In some unusual cases, various social interests are motivated to protect the agencies in which they have greatest interest, by protecting the territories within which those agencies operate.

Agents

Decisions about field agents are crucial. There must be situations in which the central decision makers do not have latitude to control field personnel selections. It has sometimes been the case that office was itself hereditary. It may be that some prescriptive criteria exist in one part of the world or other now. As a general rule, however, central decision makers will apply criteria in the following hierarchy: (a) regime loyalty, (b) personal loyalty to the appointing officer, (c) technical competence, and (d) ideas about the policies and programs of the agency or institution.

If there are no prescriptive criteria to limit human discretion, the demand for personal loyalty will tend to dominate all other considerations. The regime loyalty criterion will never be omitted, unless the person who can make the appointment also has ambiguous loyalties. He or she will take his or her own loyalty for granted and will take for granted that anyone he or she chooses is loyal. He or she cannot take for granted, however, that the appointee, while professing loyalty to the regime, will also be loyal to the appointing authority.

Personal loyalty is most acutely demanded when there is some question about the stability of the regime. If a regime is unstable, those who are formal colleagues at the central level will have many disagreements about long-range strategy and short-range tactics. If the disagreements reach the level of envious conflict, then the question of which ones the subordinate officials will sustain becomes critical.

Even in stable regimes, the chief executive (or those who use his or her authority) will try to make senior field appointments that will strengthen the chief's allies and weaken local adversaries. Field appointments become, at such times, not merely politicized but "partisanized" (Smith 1985: 161). At the higher levels, people on the winning side need to be assured that the people to whom their communications go will try to do as they are asked. They also need to be assured that those from whom information comes (these same people) will provide the advice and warnings that they need. In the local areas, or out at the periphery, people of the victorious party or side will always pressure their superiors and higher level counterparts for support in enjoying the fruits of victory. Moreover, they will benefit, sometimes in honor and sometimes in the material comfort in having the offices. The winners will have the need to psychologically show evidence of their triumph over the losers (Allen 1965: 172).

However, there are varieties in the level of intensity. The self-interested fights over patronage in the United States during the middle and later parts of the nineteenth century should be seen as one level. When political parties were new, the demand for personal loyalty was transformed into a demand for party loyalty, but loyalty then had little to do with ideology. In the economy of the time, financial fluctuations and panics were common. Thus the government job, with a relatively steady source of salary or fees, was a good job. The issue was chiefly a matter of monetary compensation to the supporters of the victorious party. Redistribution was stark. The Post Office Department, containing about three-fourths of federal jobs, was the leading example. From the time of Buchanan through that of Benjamin Harrison, the average rate of firing of postmasters was about 65% after each change of administration (Fowler 1943).

The more intense the social conflict, the more intense the demand for personnel change among "street-level" bureaucrats. People in whom new social forces are embodied will need to know by having their power verified in action.

Policy aspirations will also play some important role if the highest leaders think it troublesome to have too much change at once. The case of Tanzania is illustrative, at any rate. Independence meant that Africans took over the central government at once. Suffice it to say, as well, Africans in the villages and provinces wanted the honors and benefits of the offices they had not before gotten. Nonetheless, the new national leadership was able and willing to constrain the demands from their local supporters, because they felt the need for the experienced field administrators left from the British regime. A decade passed before they replaced the provincial commissioners (members of the Colonial Service) with new regional commissioners chosen from the political party, and then replaced the district commissioners (also British) with political area commissioners, who were to be assisted by the former civil servants (Tordoff 1965: 67).[3]

Public opinion can reach such a level of intensity that it imposes the functional equivalent of central control, even in a system that is formally decentralized. At such a point, the institutional distinction between "national" and "local," "federal" and "state," or, for present purposes, "central control" and "devolution" becomes trivial. In the most extreme cases, such as revolution or effective insurrection, change of leadership at the top is followed by systematic efforts to root out and destroy all who might be opponents beneath. This was something of the case when the Nazis took over in Germany (Allen 1965) and it had some of the same quality, it would appear, at the time of the French Revolution (Greer 1935; Gruder 1968).

The foregoing discussion applies most to personnel choices in situations that approximate central control. Devolution, where one elite has to operate through another elite, offers a somewhat different situation. If the central decision makers have to take the local decision makers more or less as they find them, then there is little personnel choice from the center—thus the American county government example, where officers are enshrined in statute and constitution, and no one at the center (state government) has much control over them. Virtually the same result was often to be found in premodern Europe, so that the kings' ambition was to be free of prescriptive local officials and to have designees of their own instead.

The other set of choices enters when some more powerful entity, such as a conquering power or a purchasing company in a takeover, enters an area where it needs the alliance of people who already have some weight. At that point, complexities are notable. Coercion is employed to exclude some groups, or some persons, from the personnel reservoir from which office holders may be recruited. Some groups are proscribed as absolutely unacceptable. Some individual persons may be similarly proscribed. The group may be proscribed on the basis that it is incompetent to perform the desired functions. It may also be restricted because, realistically, it is an independent source of power that the top elites wish to limit. Occasion may present itself for such persons to be reconsidered. Other groups may not be deemed absolutely unacceptable but may have their rights in some way restricted.

Devolution depends critically upon the coercion to accept office and to show deference or support. Coercion to participate, rather than exclusion, is also an important part of the personnel system under devolution. The dominant interest (the overlord) generally cannot afford to permit actions that are equivalent to resignation under protest or a disciplined and dignified abstention from service to the ruler. There is, however, a source of challenge to the dominant interest. Subordinate leaders, chosen for overlord purposes, tend over time to become more independent as they discover means of asserting themselves. Subordinate leaders do not see the world the same way as overlords do. They are likely to adjust to many facts differently. They will seek to become powerful themselves so as to no longer need to take orders. One of the first situations in which the subordinates' quest for their own independence arises is in the choice of the persons who are to be their subordinates. The administrative subordinate will almost certainly claim the right to select his or her own subordinates without control by the overlord (Apter 1961: 196). This will be accompanied soon by a claim, that may be stated as a "right" or sometimes merely as a matter of "efficiency," to have the overlord deal with those subordinates only through him or her.

Central decision makers will deem it necessary to, repeatedly, impose limits on the independence of those whom they have chosen. There should always be a prediction of a degree of personnel change in accordance with change of some central political office-holding group.

Authority

The overriding question always present is whether field administrators are to be given close instructions or whether instructions to them will allow wide latitude for their own decision making. No permanent and irrevocable decision can be made. Practice ultimately reveals both the problem of overload on the center, if latitude is not granted; it also reveals the tendency for deviations to occur, so lower-level (field) decision making often constitutes nullification of the policy sought.

From this comes three contingent problems in exercising authority: giving instructions, finding out what is going on below, and redirecting the courses that the field officials are to follow.

Authority Problem 1:
Means of Giving Directions

Control is sought, and sometimes exercised, through instructions for what must be done as to the content of policies, as to programs, or as to operational methods. The degrees of central control in large-scale departments vary. The U.S. Forest Service appears to have one of the strongest central control mechanisms in the federal government (Kaufman 1981). Several dozen statutes, scores of presidential proclamations and executive orders, hundreds of rules, regulations, and secretarial orders, and many court decisions provide the framework for "preformed decisions" for the work of individual forest rangers. Disputes are focused by staff assistants in offices above those of the ranger, and their resolution clarifies and controls policy. Moreover, financial and workload planning provides still other controls over what the field representatives do.

The process of instruction in part meant prescribing norms or standards by giving advice, offering counsel, and providing tutelage. It also involved threats to withhold both the means of action (such as money) and also the provision of assistance. *Tutelage* is a European term, and would be deemed offensive by American state and local officials. Nonetheless, something substantially akin to it is common practice in the contemporary United States and is revealed in the argument for professional performance norms as the means to induce state administrators to comply with "national policy."

Exercising control through finance, including giving financial support, was an integral part of the administrative process under colonial rule. It also has been an important part of the field administrator's dealings with local officials in France and has been important in the United States as well. It is common to have requirements established and assurances sought as to how funds will be spent and programs run (Van Horn 1979). Finally, in the American case, the requirements and assurances are structured in "the state plan," a formalized set of promises that state officials in a given policy area are required to make to the counterpart program officials in the federal government.

Authority Problem 2:
Finding Out What Is Going on Below

Direction is soon useless without means of finding out what is going on below. In a term introduced to common speech from cybernetics, this is *feedback*. Kaufman notes that the Forest Service's "preformed decisions" are reinforced (Kaufman 1967: 91-125): "Adherence to them is not treated as an automatic consequence of issuance. Deviation is consciously discouraged, conformity deliberately encouraged."

(1) Inspection, review, and reports. Inspection and review may be coercive, supportive, or even both. Inspection includes the truly open process in which the inspector and the person or agency being inspected are mutually aware of criteria, tend to accept the same criteria, and reciprocate confidence and respect for the same competencies, and inspections generally are conducted with full awareness.

The unknown personal inspection comes when the authority figure secretly investigates the domain. This is Haroun-al-Raschid's solution, represented in the claim that Haroun-al-Raschid, caliph (king) in Baghdad in the eighth century, used to disguise himself at night and go about the city to see if the reports of activity that came to him were accurate. *The known personal inspection is most highly developed in the military but also known in the civil administration.* In the military, at least under routine conditions, the visit of the commander from higher headquarters probably makes little difference to the enlisted personnel, although under adverse conditions it is a means of conveying reassurance that someone is interested in them. The personal inspection from higher headquarters is an instrument of control that Herbert Kaufman says is very influential in the federal administrative service in the United States (Kaufman 1977: 25).

In civil administration, there may sometimes be something of the same kind. Employees like to have some sign that someone of higher rank cares about what they do or about the circumstances under which they do it. They particularly like the possibility of breaking through barriers that others have imposed, namely, of being able to talk to their boss's boss.

Specific investigations, usually premised on supposition of error or misdeed, also provide means by which superiors learn something of what is going on among their subordinates. Investigations are perhaps a more drastic form of inspection, being either more focused in their inquiry or more broadly searching, as in the manner of the dragnet, and may often be oriented to finding something wrong. Secret investigations are a different form of inspection, and there is sometimes spying as well as reliance on a "grapevine," on informal reports, interest group complaints, and so forth.

(2) Audits. Audits, both of finances and of operational features, may be conducted as a part of regular procedure and premised on some special necessity or they may be for preventive purposes. Audits come after the fact and are intended as control measures, with the clear intention not merely to improve operations but to discourage malefactors and to detect those who have not been discouraged from wrong actions.

(3) Reports. Reports, both informal and formal, both systematic and occasional, by the subordinates to the superiors, constitute still another means of securing information that may be desired by those at the center.

(4) Complaints and hearings. Complaint and hearing procedures allow persons who object to various administrative actions to take their claims to some higher authority and, by implication, to inform the higher author- ity of things that the higher authority would otherwise not know.

Authority Problem 3: Means of Redirection

The significant problem for the central decision maker is, having learned something, finding a means to given an effective direction for change. One of the crucial means, in some cultures only, is institutionalized *self*-criticism. This seems to take the form of public exchanges of judgments about how well one is performing according to the relevant ideological, professional, technological, or other norms. When the persons involved internalize the values to which they refer, it amounts to voluntary accep- tance of authority. At this level, it is equivalent to the mobilization of values within the persons and groups who are participating.

Mobilization of affirmative self-interest is a vital measure in the reorientation of an administrative group. Most questions of conformity are settled by negotiation without recourse to formal hearing procedures. In the case of state plans in the welfare system, there was the potential for "conformity hearings." But it fit the interest of neither the federal partners nor the states to engage in a fight. Federal officials were, then, obliged to challenge their state counterparts more than they otherwise would have done. Financial sanctions and support are another party of the armory.

Career limitation sanctions (reprimands, nonpromotion, and so on) and threats of firing, or even actual firing, are sanctions to encourage the others. The fired person, being out of the organization, is beyond control or redirection from the second of being fired. Finally, of course, transferring a person, or the situation, from the administrative personnel system to the judicial system, as a matter of potential punishment, also becomes relevant.

Conclusion/Interpretation

This chapter is grounded in the premise that administration is the central political process. It is the exercise of discretion about the actual use of information, money, and force. Power is most fully organized when the results of aggregation and of high-level decision making are diffused through the instruments of field administration. On this basis, I believe that a deeper inquiry into the politico-logic of field administration is a crucial intellectual issue, and not one of mere casual interest.

1. Field administration constitutes the visible presence of government and is imperative to the organization of power.

2. Field administration has depended, historically, upon central decision makers allowing authority to shift downward, to be absorbed by subordinates.

3. Field administrators tend to deviate from what their actions would have been, if they had followed their superiors' premises perfectly, due to (a) lack of physical or mental ability; (b) self-interest, in the narrowest personal sense; (c) the fact that the job is bigger than they could possibly handle, no matter how alert they may be; (d) attempts to attract support from people who will not otherwise comply; and (e) their own disagreement.

4. The approximation of central control, of devolution, or of negotiated power sharing is revealed, and produced, by the aggregate of three decisions: territories or administrative areas in which authority is to be exercised, choosing of the agents to be used or recognized, and decisions about the mission and authority to be recognized in those agents. Exercise of authority over the field functionaries takes place by means of giving instructions to them, finding out what is going on below, and redirecting of the courses that the field officials are to follow.

Field administration ceases to be a relevant problem only when the political unit is essentially a face-to-face group, small enough that there is no logistical need for regular intermediaries between the center and the periphery (Fortes and Evans-Pritchard 1975; Mair 1962). If field administrators fail, central decision makers are left with no reliable structure to transmit back to themselves the desires, wishes, adaptations, and resistance within the body politic. Failures become part of the dissipation of authority (LaPalombara 1972: 208-209).

To this extent, the city may be the micro-scale model of the nation-state. In a given year, there are many nation-states in which there is some serious challenge to the functioning authority of the government. The drought in Wallo Province was a fact of physical nature, yet the administrative situation report was but an indicator of the crisis that, within a year, would displace the emperor and the entire imperial elite.

Failures in field administration are, ultimately, the failure of the whole structure that may anticipate governmental collapse. The challenge that insurgency or rebellion (R) always presents to authority (A) is that R would deny A routine access and acceptance and control over the persons and resources of physical territories (Leites and Wolf 1970). R diverts the flow of information to A from the subordinate population as it also diverts the flow of money and the use of coercive force. Open and notorious administrative collapse equals R's success. R takes the place of A by adverse possession.

Notes

1. Suffice it to say, there are a variety of debates one could have about the Almond and Powell formulation, which I here rephrase, but those have to be reserved for another time.

2. Vivian Thompson, now a doctoral candidate in political science at the University of Virginia, urged upon me the term *implementation*, but I declined. I advocate a stronger and more self-conscious connection to the intellectual history of the discipline and to connection with some concept of political control that can encompass more than one country or more than one period of time. However, the issue may be purely terminological, in which case I recall the statement by Charles E. Merriam: "What king cares what his sceptre is called?"

3. Michael G. Schatzberg has, in correspondence, challenged this interpretation of the Tanzania experience, and it is a point I have not resolved.

References

Allen, William Sheridan. (1965) *The Nazi Seizure of Power.* Chicago: Quadrangle.

Apter, David. (1961) *The Political Kingdom of Uganda.* Princeton, NJ: Princeton University Press.

Bernstein, Tao. (1993) *Fifty Years of State Governors in Mexico: Middle Elites and Political Stability.* Ph.D. Dissertation, Government and Foreign Affairs, University of Virginia, Charlottesville, VA, 29903.

Blunt, Edward. (1937) *The I.C.S.: The Indian Civil Service.* London: Faber and Faber.

Brewer, John. (1990) *The Sinews of Power: War, Money, and the English State, 1688-1783*. Cambridge, MA: Harvard University Press.

Cayer, N. Joseph. (1986) *Public Personnel Administration in the United States*. New York: St. Martin's.

Deutsch, Karl W. (1963) *The Nerves of Government*. New York: Free Press.

"Ethiopia Says Famine Was Covered Up." (1973, November 18) *New York Times*, p. 3.

Fesler, James W. (1936) "Standardization of Federal Administrative Areas." *Social Forces*, 15: 12-21.

————. (1943) "Criteria for Administrative Regions." *Social Forces*, 22: 26-32.

————. (1949) *Area and Administration*. University, AL: University of Alabama Press.

————. (1962) "The Political Role of Field Administration." In Ferrel Heady and Sybil Stokes, eds., *Papers in Comparative Public Administration*, pp. 117-142. Ann Arbor: University of Michigan, Institute of Public Administration.

————. (1965) "Approaches to the Understanding of Decentralization." *Journal of Politics*, 27: 536-566.

Figgis, John Neville. (1956 [1907]) *Studies of Political Thought from Gerson to Grotius, 1414-1625*. Cambridge: Cambridge University Press.

Forstenzer, Thomas R. (1981) *French Provincial Police and the Fall of the Second Republic: Social Fear and Counterrevolution*. Princeton, NJ: Princeton University Press.

Fortes, Meyer, and Edward Evans-Pritchard, eds. (1975) *African Political Systems*. London: Oxford.

Fowler, Dorothy Ganfield. (1943) *The Cabinet Politician*. New York: Columbia University Press.

Fri, Robert W. (1995) "Using Science Soundly: The Yucca Mountain Standard." *Resources*, 120.

Fried, Robert C. (1963) *The Italian Prefects*. New Haven, CT: Yale University Press.

Gladden, E. N. (1972) *History of Public Administration*. London: Cass.

Greeley, Andrew. (1984) *Lord of the Dance*. New York: Warner.

Greer, Donald. (1935) *The Incidence of the Terror During the French Revolution: A Statistical Interpretation*. Cambridge, MA: Harvard University Press.

Gruder, Vivian. (1968) *The Royal Provincial Intendants: A Governing Elite in Eighteenth-Century France*. Ithaca, NY: Cornell University Press.

Gulick, Luther. (1937) "Notes on a Theory of Organization." In Luther Gulick and L. S. Urwick, eds., *Papers on the Science of Administration*. New York: Institute of Public Administration.

Hennessy, Peter, Robert Maranto, and David Schultz. (1991) *A Short History of the United States Civil Service*. Lanham, MD: University Press of America.

Herring, Pendleton. (1936) *Public Administration and the Public Interest*. New York: McGraw-Hill.

Hexter, J. H. (1973) *The Vision of Politics on the Eve of the Reformation*. New York: Basic Books.

Hobbes, Thomas. (1960) *Leviathan*. Michael Oakeshott, ed. Oxford: Basil Blackwell.

Jacob, Herbert. (1963) *German Administration Since Bismarck*. New Haven, CT: Yale University Press.

Kaufman, Herbert. (1967) *The Forest Ranger*. Baltimore, MD: Johns Hopkins Press.

Key, V. O. (1966) *A Primer of Statistics for Political Scientists*. New York: Cromwell.

Khaldun, Ibn. (1958) *The Muqaddimah: An Introduction to History*. New York: Pantheon.

Krishan, Gopal. (1988) "The World Pattern of Administrative Area Reform." *Geographic Journal*, 154, 1: 93-99.

LaPalombara, Joseph. (1972) "Penetration: A Crisis of Government Capacity." In Leonard Binder et al., eds., *Crises and Sequences in Political Development*, pp. 208-220. Princeton, NJ: Princeton University Press.

Latham, Earl, with the assistance of William D. Carey, Arthur Svenson, Milton Mandell, and Wallace Sayre. (1947) *The Federal Field Service: An Analysis With Suggestions for Research*. Chicago: Public Administration Service.

Leites, Nathan, and Charles Wolf, Jr. (1970) *Rebel Lion and Authority*. Chicago: Markham.

Levin, Martin E., and Barbara Ferman. (1985) *The Political Hand: Policy Implementation and Youth Employment Programs*. New York: Pergamon.

Link, Arthur S., ed. (1966) *Papers of Woodrow Wilson*. Princeton, NJ: Princeton University Press.

Long, Norton E. (1949) "Power and Administration." *Public Administration Review*.

———. (1962) *The Polity*. Charles Press, ed. Chicago: Rand McNally.

Mair, Lucy Phillip. (1962) *Primitive Government*. Baltimore, MD: Penguin.

Manheim, Jarol B., and Richard C. Rich. (1986) *Empirical Political Analysis: Research Methods in Political Science*. New York: Longman.

Mattingly, Harold. (1967) *Roman Imperial Civilization*. London: Edward Arnold.

McGregor, Eugene B., Jr. (1981, November). "Administration's Many Instruments: Mining, Refining and Applying Charles E. Lindblom's *Politics and Markets*." *Administration and Society*, pp. 347-375.

Melnick, R. Shep. (1983) *Regulation and the Courts*. Washington, DC: Brookings Institution.

Mill, John Stuart. (1964) *Representative Government*. New York: Modern Library.

Miller, Merle. (1973) *Plain Speaking: An Oral Biography of Harry S Truman*. New York: Berkley.

Neustadt, Richard. (1970) *Alliance Politics*. New York: Columbia University Press.

Palumbo, Dennis J. (1969) *Statistics in Political and Behavioral Science*. New York: Appleton-Century-Crofts.

Schneider, Robert O. (1992) "Local Implementation of S.A.R.A. Title III: An Evaluation of the Disaster Management Problem." Paper, Southern Political Science Association.

Scholz, John T., and Feng Heng Wei. (1986) "Regulatory Enforcement in a Federalist System." *American Political Science Review*, 80, 4: 1249-1270.

Scicchitano, Michael J., David M. Hedge, and Patricia Metz. (1989) "The States and Deregulation: The Case of Surface Mining." *Policy Studies Review*, 9, 1: 120-131.

Self, Peter. (1972) *Administrative Theories and Politics*. London: Allen and Unwin.

Smith, Brian C. (1967) *Field Administration: An Aspect of Decentralization*. London: Routledge and Kegan Paul.

Smith, Brian C. (1985) *Decentralization: The Territorial Dimension of the State*. London: George Allen and Unwin.

Stevenson, George Hope. (1939) *Roman Provincial Administration Till the Age of the Antonines*. Oxford: Basil Blackwell.

Thompson, Frank J., and Michael J. Scicchitano. (1987) "State Implementation and Federal Enforcement Priorities: Safety Versus Health in OSHA and the States." *Administration and Society*, 19, 1: 95-124.

Thomas, Hugh. (1961) *The Spanish Civil War*. London: Harper Colophon.

Tordoff, William. (1965) "Regional Administration in Tanzania." *Journal of Modern African Studies,* 3, 1.

Tout, T. F. (1920-1933) *Chapters in the Administrative History of Medieval England.* Manchester, England: Manchester University Press.

Truman, David B. (1940) *Administrative Decentralization: A Study of the Chicago Field Office of the United States Department of Agriculture.* Chicago: University of Chicago Press.

Tufte, Edward R. (1974) *Data Analysis for Public Policy.* Englewood Cliffs, NJ: Prentice Hall.

Van Horn, Carl E. (1979) *Policy Implementation in the Federal System: National Goals and Local Implementors.* Lexington, MA: D. C. Heath.

Wilson, Woodrow. (1911) *The State: Elements of Historical and Practical Politics.* Boston: D. C. Heath.

Wohlstetter, Albert. (1966) *Pearl Harbor: Warning and Decision.* Stanford, CA: Stanford University Press.

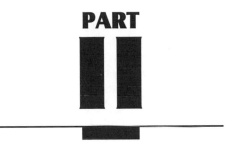

PART

II

Bureaucrats and Politicians in Presidential Systems

The four chapters in Part II focus on the relationship between politicians and bureaucrats in presidential systems of government. "System separation" here denotes the possible distinction between and significance of the relationship of politicians and their political appointees, on the one hand, and the career bureaucrats/civil servants, on the other, under the two different political systems of governance. A presidential system is generally characterized by a strong executive power, often vested in the president, with strong constitutionally granted authority, whereas the parliamentary system generally has a stronger legislature whose majority party leader is also the chief executive leader or prime minister or chancellor. Therefore, the nature of the relationship between bureaucratic elites and political elites may very well be different under the two political systems. Generally, there is more harmony in the relationship between the two administrative groups under the parliamentary systems, but this may not always be the case.

Chapter 6 by David Rosenbloom is a major contribution to the book. His analysis focuses on the fundamental issues of the separation of powers, the place and role of the bureaucracy, and its relations to democracy and democratic governance in the American presidential system. Rosenbloom argues that the constitutional separation of powers is *the* fundamental fact of American national administration and a major reason for its exceptionalism. He analyzes the contemporary constitutional doctrine regarding the separation of powers and the institutional dynamics of presidential, congressional, and judicial efforts to develop and maintain leverage over the bureaucracy. Citing numerous Supreme Court cases, Rosenbloom demonstrates how the different branches of government have tried to strengthen their control over the administration and its bureaucracy. The separation of powers, at the same time, has deeply affected the legitimacy of the American administrative state ever since its real rise in the 1930s. "Administrators are called upon to exercise executive, legislative, and judicial functions. They make rules, implement, and adjudicate." In practice, the competition between branches of government for control of the bureaucracy has led to continuing conflicts and problems for the American public administration, in general, and for higher level civil servants, in particular. Higher level bureaucrats often find themselves in no-win conflictual situations in which, for example, efficient execution of the law is frequently at odds with procedural fairness in adjudication. Citing Chief Justice Warren Burger, Rosenbloom states that higher level civil servants' (bureaucrats') honest and professional actions in preserving or promoting "constitutional integrity itself may be in conflict with governmental efficiency."

Chapter 7, by Francis Rourke, focuses on politics and bureaucracy and their impacts on professionalism, the professionalization of bureaucracy, and policy decision making; on escalating demands for responsiveness, conflicts between professionalism and responsiveness, and the politicization of bureaucracy; and the implications of all these for modern American governance. Reviewing the core literature on the two fundamental aspects of modern governance administration, the professional bureaucracy and its control by politicians, Rourke expertly addresses the debate. He begins with the statement that as a source of power within government, bureaucracy and professionalism have common roots—the public officials' "need for expertise in making the decisions and carrying out the manifold tasks for which public officials bear responsibility in modern society." He adds that the bureaucratization of modern government has contributed to the growth of professions and professionals, and that "government bureaucracy has been the birthplace of many new professions"—an observation as old as the ancient empires. Rourke's sound argument is that the increasing "tension between politics and professionalism in modern American bureaucracy" and politicization of the bureaucracy by politicians from all branches of the government have "expanded the number of situations in which professionals today take actions or make decisions that are inconsistent with their own standards of professional conduct." Professor Rourke then goes on to discuss in detail the escalating demands for responsiveness, conflicting views of responsiveness and professionalism, and politics, professionalism, and bureaucracy in American presidential government, which is, according to him, deeply divided by Congress and presidents over many issues, including a tighter control over the bureaucracy. Rourke concludes that the health of American democracy may be threatened when the voice of professionals is too strong but also when that voice "is too weak."

Professor Rourke's points are echoed by another expert on American government, Paul Van Riper in Chapter 8. His chapter focuses on the Pendleton Act of 1883 and the professionalization of the U.S. public service. Professor Van Riper's in-depth analysis shows the U.S. civil service reform of 1883 as the beginning of the professionalization of the U.S. government and administration. He includes almost all of the text of the Pendleton Act and then goes on to analyze its implications for the professionalization of modern American bureaucracy and government. His concluding points address recent criticisms by politicians and academic experts, discussed above, of the modern bureaucracy and professional state and their growing role in policy making and modern governance. Being critical of this political trend and the Civil Service Reform Act of 1978, which have had a politicization and deprofessionalization effect on the bureaucracy, Van Riper defends the professional role of the bureaucracy in the modern American presidential system of governance.

Chapter 9 by Lawrence Graham is another major contribution to this book. Focusing on the role of civil service and of political transients and career bureaucrats in Latin American presidential systems of governance, Graham compares and contrasts several Latin American governments and the frequent breakdown in presidential systems, namely, Brazil, Argentina, and Chile. He also compares the European countries of Portugal and Poland, with strong parliamentary systems of governance, with those of the former African colonies, Angola and Mozambique. Central to his analysis of all these countries, but with a focus on Latin America, are two key points: (a) the lack of attention by politicians who are reforming governments to the civil service and a professional bureaucracy in governance, and (b) a test of Fred Riggs's thesis of bureaucratic fatigue and bureaucratic dominance/excess. Drawing on his extensive personal experience as a consultant to these nations, as well as his broad knowledge of parliamentary and presidential systems, Graham analyzes the relationship between politicians (and their transients) and the career bureaucrats in the Latin American governments, particularly the way higher level bureaucrats react to regime changes, regime consolidation, and transitional situations. He finds supporting evidence for Riggs's hypothesis on bureaucratic fatigue in most Latin American countries experiencing frequent system breakdown; Chile is an exception, however, in which the professional state bureaucracy—identified as a semipowered bureaucracy—adopted itself, and so did not experience fatigue, and therefore survived its system type. Graham touches on issues of centralization, privatization, and professionalization as well as presidentialim and parliamentarism, and concludes that all governments need professional and institutional capacity in implementing economic, social, and political policies. And "somehow issues related to transients and careerist in public bureaucracies must come to be seen as being as mainstream as the current debate over presidentialism and parliamentarism."

The U.S. Constitutional Separation of Powers and Federal Administration

David H. Rosenbloom

Like much of U.S. politics, the federal administration is often viewed as an exception to the institutional and political patterns that normally prevail in Western nations (see Wildavsky 1991 for a review). The bureaucracy has long been highly permeable and penetrated by relatively large numbers of political appointees (see Silberman 1993). It has very low prestige and politicians find it a viable scapegoat for a wide range of governmental shortcomings. Agencies can be quite powerful, but the executive branch is in no sense independent or autonomous. It is subject to substantial legislative regulation and direction. Judicial involvement in federal administration is also quite pronounced. Indeed, studies of American bureaucratic politics often employ the concepts of "subgovernments" to denote coalitions between agencies and legislative committees and "partnerships" between agencies and the courts (Lowi 1969; Rosenbloom 1987). The premise of this chapter is that the constitutional separation of powers is *the* fundamental fact of American national administration and a major reason for its exceptionalism. The chapter analyzes contemporary constitutional doctrine regarding the separation of powers and the institutional dynamics of presidential, congressional, and judicial efforts to develop and maintain leverage over the bureaucracy.

The Constitutional Framework of Federal Administration: "Whose Bureaucracy Is This, Anyway?"[1]

Federal administration under the Constitution is an organizational theorist's nightmare. The Framers feared a strong, independent executive more than they foresaw the development of a vast federal administrative apparatus. It is worth remembering that there are now about as many civilian federal employees as there were people in the colonies on the eve of their independence. The Constitution is an eighteenth-century document into which it has been necessary to retrofit a modern administrative state.

Responsibility for taking care that the laws be faithfully executed is clearly vested in the president (U.S. Constitution, Article II, § 3). However, sufficient authority to carry out this charge is not. Constitutionally, the president has very limited authority over the administrative apparatus necessary for implementation. In fact, the text of the Constitution provides the president with only two specific domestic administrative powers that he can exercise on his own: (a) "He may require the Opinion, in writing, of the Principal Officer in each of the executive Departments, upon any Subject relating to the Duties of their respective Offices" (Art. II, § 2), and (b) "The President shall have the Power to fill up all Vacancies that may happen during the Recess of the Senate, by granting Commissions which shall expire at the End of their next Session" (Art. II, § 2).

By contrast, Congress has vast constitutional authority over the federal administration, although perhaps not sufficient responsibility for it. Congress is clearly in charge of budgets: "No Money shall be drawn from the Treasury, but in Consequence of Appropriations made by Law" (Art. I, § 9). It has vast authority over personnel as well:

> [The president] . . . by and with the Advice and Consent of the Senate, shall appoint Ambassadors, other public Ministers and Consuls, Judges of the Supreme Court, and all other Officers of the United States, whose Appointments are not herein otherwise provided for, and which shall be established by Law: but the Congress may by Law vest the appointment of such inferior Officers, as they think proper, in the President alone, in the Courts of Law, or in the Heads of Departments. (Article II, § 2)

In practice, the appointments clause has been interpreted as granting Congress broad legislative power over federal personnel and the organization of federal agencies. Congress also has vast constitutional authority to set the missions of agencies and to empower them. Among those policy areas specifically mentioned by the Constitution as part of the congressional domain are the regulation of commerce, post offices and post roads, raising and supporting armies, providing for a navy, and making rules for the "Government and Regulation of the land and naval Forces." Of course, Congress can do much more as the last clause of Article I, section 8, authorizes it "to make all laws which shall be necessary and proper for carrying into Execution the foregoing Powers, and all other Powers vested by this Constitution in the Government of the United States, or in any Department or Officer thereof" (see *McCulloch v. Maryland* 1819).

By the mid-1930s, if not earlier, it was evident that "the President needs help," as the U.S. President's Committee on Administrative Management (Brownlow Committee) put it (U.S. President's Committee on Administrative Management 1937 in Mosher 1976: 116). Although there had been some growth in presidential constitutional power vis-à-vis the bureaucracy, it was not enough to keep pace with vast changes in the scope and size of administrative operations. In *Myers v. U.S.* (1926), the Supreme Court held that the president had constitutional power to remove, on his own, executive officials appointed with the advice and consent of the Senate. In the Court's words, "Made responsible under the Constitution for the effective enforcement of the law, the President needs as an indispensable aid to meet it disciplinary influence upon those who act under him of a reserve power of removal" (*Myers v. U.S.* 1926: 132). A few years later, however, in *Humphrey's Executor v. U.S.* (1935), even this "reserve power" was restricted by the Court: "The necessary reach of the [Myers] decision goes far enough to include all purely executive officers. It goes no farther" (*Humphrey's Executor v. U.S.* 1935: 627-628). In a startling claim, the Court asserted that Federal Trade Commissioners occupy "no place in the executive department" and exercise "no part of the executive power vested by the Constitution in the President" (*Humphrey's Executor v. U.S.* 1935: 627-628). According to the Court, the commission "was created by Congress as a means of carrying into operation legislative and judicial powers, and as an agency of the legislative and judicial departments" (*Humphrey's Executor v. U.S.* 1935: 630).

The president's constitutional power to issue executive orders had also become well established (Cooper 1986). Further, separation of powers theory allowed Congress to delegate rule-making authority to the president for federal personnel management (Civil Service Act of 1883, also known as the Pendleton Act, upheld in *Butler v. White* 1897).

By the end of the 1930s, the president's managerial capacity had also been strengthened considerably by the creation of the Executive Office of the President, by the Reorganization Act of 1939 (which empowered the president to reorganize the bureaucracy subject to potential congressional veto), and by the firm expectation that the president, working through the Bureau of the Budget, would play a stronger role in budgeting. Politically, too, the post-New Deal presidency was supposed to be a source of policy initiative and leadership.

An impressive array of proposals for federal administrative reform have sought to augment the constitutional, legal, and political changes that had modernized the presidency. The Hoover Commission Reports of 1949 and 1955, the Ash Council (1969-1971), the creation of the Office of Management and Budget in 1970, the Civil Service Reform Act of 1978, and, most recently, the National Performance Review (1993) are examples. For the most part, discussion of administrative reform has been dominated by an effort to strengthen the president and the EOP and to reduce congressional involvement in administrative affairs (often labeled "micro-management"). Nevertheless, the Supreme Court's decision in *Morrison v. Olson* (1988) makes it clear that, constitutionally, Congress can still be very much in charge of administrative mission, structure, and process.

Morrison v. Olson: Where Are the Lines?

Morrison v. Olson (1988) demonstrates how entangled Congress and the judiciary can become in federal administration. The Ethics in Government Act of 1978, which expired in 1992, "allow[ed] for the appointment of an 'independent counsel' to investigate and, if appropriate, prosecute certain high ranking Government officials for violations of federal criminal laws" (*Morrison v. Olson* 1988: 660). The independent counsel was appointed by a special court, called the Special Division, which was also created by the act. The Special Division's appointment function was triggered by the attorney general's decision to undertake a preliminary investigation of possible criminal wrongdoing in the government. Upon completion of the investigation, or 90 days after the decision to conduct it, the attorney general had to report to the Special Division. If the attorney general informed the Special Division that no further action was warranted, then no independent counsel was appointed. On the other hand, if the attorney general believed there were reasonable grounds for further investigation or prosecution, then the Special Division was required to "appoint an appropriate independent counsel and . . . define that independent counsel's prosecutorial jurisdiction" (*Morrison v. Olson* 1988: 661). Once appointed, the Ethics Act granted the independent counsel "full power and independent authority to exercise all investigative and prosecutorial functions and powers of the Department of Justice, the Attorney General, and other officer or employee of the department of Justice" (*Morrison v. Olson* 1988: 662). These powers included appointing employees and engaging in prosecution.

To protect the independence of independent counsels, the act provided that

> an independent counsel . . . may be removed from office, other than by impeachment and conviction, only by the personal action of the Attorney General and only for good cause, physical disability, mental incapacity, or any other condition that substantially impairs the performance of such independent counsel's duties. (*Morrison v. Olson* 1988: 663)

The act also included procedural safeguards to prevent illegitimate dismissals of independent counsels. It also anticipated some level of supervision by Congress: Independent counsels were required to report to the legislature and be subject to congressional oversight.

Morrison was appointed under the Ethics Act in 1986 to investigate whether Olson, who was an assistant attorney general in the Justice Department, had given false and misleading testimony to a congressional subcommittee. After *Morrison* caused a grand jury to serve subpoenas on Olson (and others), he (and the others) challenged the constitutionality of the act in federal district court. That court upheld the act's constitutionality, but it was reversed by a court of appeals.

In an opinion of major importance to constitutional structure, the Supreme Court, per Chief Justice Rehnquist, held that the act violated neither the appointments clause nor the separation of powers, broadly construed.

The Appointments Clause

The first question was whether Morrison was an "inferior" or a "principal" officer. If the latter, then her appointment had to be by the president with the advice and consent of the Senate. The Court noted that "the line between 'inferior' and 'principal' officers is one that is far from clear, and the Framers provided little guidance into where it should be drawn" (*Morrison v. Olson* 1988: 671). Rehnquist's opinion identifies four factors that should be used in drawing such lines:

1. Can the officer be dismissed by a higher executive branch official?
2. Are the officer's duties certain and limited?
3. Is the officer's jurisdiction limited?
4. Is the officer's tenure limited?

Being able to answer "yes" to each of their questions, the majority had little difficulty determining that Morrison was an inferior officer.

The second issue was whether the appointments clause allows Congress to empower another branch of government to make appointments within the executive branch. Specifically, could the appointment of an inferior officer in the Department of Justice be vested in a court, albeit a unique one, the Special Division? The Court noted that the plain text of the appointments clause does not appear to prohibit interbranch appointments such as Morrison's. However, Rehnquist's opinion noted that the separation of powers could invalidate interbranch appointments that were "incongruous" because they "had the potential to impair the constitutional functions assigned to one of the branches" (*Morrison v. Olson* 1988: 675-676). In its view, though, this was not within the category of " 'incongruous' interbranch appointments" (*Morrison v. Olson* 1988: 677).

Article III

The next issue was whether the Ethics Act violated Article III of the Constitution, which restricts the judicial power to cases and controversies. In the 1976 case of *Buckley v. Valeo,* the Court had reiterated the long-standing principle that "executive or administrative duties of a nonjudicial nature may not be imposed on judges holding office under Art. III of the Constitution" (*Buckley v. Valeo* 1976: 123). On its face, the appointments clause would seem to anticipate that the courts would sometimes he called upon to make appointments. But here the Special Division had discretion to define the appointee's jurisdiction. Rehnquist reasoned that constitutionally such discretion must be "incidental" to its power to appoint: "The jurisdiction that the court [Special Division] decides upon must be demonstrably related to the factual circumstances that gave rise to the Attorney General's investigation and request for the appointment . . . in the particular case" (*Morrison v. Olson* 1988: 679). Although the Court found no infirmity in Morrison's jurisdiction, this standard is an open invitation to future litigation. It apparently places a significant burden of persuasion on the government rather than on the challenger.

The appointments clause undercuts the notion that interbranch appointments automatically violate Article III. However, it is irrelevant to other functions that the Ethics Act vested in the Special Division. Among these were granting extensions to the attorney general's conduct of preliminary investigations; receiving the attorney general's report; receiving expense reports from the independent counsel; granting attorney's fees to individuals investigated by the independent counsel, but not indicted; and determining whether to release the independent counsel's final report. The Court reasoned that the exercise of such "miscellaneous power" did "not impermissibly trespass upon the authority of the Executive Branch" (*Morrison v. Olson* 1988: 681). Nor did it require the Special Division to perform functions that are inherently executive.

Still, Article III could have been violated by the Ethics Act's provision that the Special Division terminate the independent counsel when his or her work was completed. Termination of an executive branch employee, other than by impeachment, is an administrative act and it is not typically considered to be judicial in nature. However, because the act severely circumscribed termination and did not give the Special Division broad power to remove the independent counsel, the Court found it did "not pose a sufficient threat of judicial intrusion into matters that are more properly within the Executive's authority to require that the Act be invalidated as inconsistent with Article III" (*Morrison v. Olson* 1988: 683).

Finally, the act could have violated Article III if the involvement of the Special Division with the independent counsel tainted the judiciary's independence. The Court found no such taint here but warned that

> the Special Division has no authority to take any action or undertake any duties that are not specifically authorized by the Act. The gradual expansion of the authority of the Special Division might in another context be a bureaucratic success story, but it would be one that would have serious constitutional ramifications. (*Morrison v. Olson* 1988: 684)

Specifically, the Court was concerned that the Special Division might supervise the independent counsel or seek to exempt him or her from conflict of interest or other laws.

The Separation of Powers More Generally

Having found that the Ethics Act violated neither the appointments clause nor Article III, the Court turned its attention to the separation of powers more broadly. The first issue was whether the restriction on the attorney general's power to remove the independent counsel, except for good cause, "impermissibly interfere[d] with the President's exercise of his constitutionally appointed functions" (*Morrison v. Olson* 1988: 685). The second was whether the act unconstitutionally reduced the president's "ability to control the prosecutorial powers wielded by the independent counsel" (*Morrison v. Olson* 1988: 685).

In addressing the restriction on removal of the independent counsel, the Court sought to clarify and consolidate constitutional doctrine. The *Myers* case held that the removal of executive branch officers is a presidential power under Article II of the Constitution. But Humphrey's and a subsequent case, *Wiener v. U.S.* (1958), tempered *Myers* by seeming to exempt executive branch officials exercising "quasi-legislative" or "quasi-judicial" functions from the scope of the president's constitutional removal powers. In *Morrison,* the Court flatly recognized that contemporary federal administration is so complex that trying to classify officials by the functions they exercise is a difficult—sometimes hopeless—task:

> Our present considered view is that the determination of whether the Constitution allows Congress to impose a "good cause"-type restriction on the President's power to remove an official cannot be made to turn on whether or not that official is "purely executive." The analysis contained in our removal cases is designed not to define rigid categories of those officials who may or may not be removed at will by the President, but to ensure that Congress does not interfere with the President's exercise of the "executive power" and his constitutionally appointed duty to "take care that the laws be faithfully executed" under Article II (*Morrison v. Olson* 1988: 690).

Using this approach, "the real question is whether the removal restrictions are of such a nature that they impede the President's ability to perform his constitutional duty, and the functions of the officials in question must be analyzed in that light" (*Morrison v. Olson* 1988: 691). On balance, the Court concluded that executive authority was not unduly trammeled by the good cause restriction.

Finally, the Court turned to the broader question of "whether the Act, taken as a whole, violates the principle of separation of powers by unduly interfering with the role of the Executive Branch" (*Morrison v. Olson* 1988: 693). The Court noted that "it is undeniable that the act reduces the amount of control or supervision that the Attorney General and, through him, the President exercises over the investigation and prosecution of a certain class of alleged criminal activity" (*Morrison v. Olson* 1988: 195). Nevertheless, the Court reasoned that the executive branch retained "sufficient control over the independent counsel to ensure that the President is able to perform his constitutionally assigned duties" (*Morrison v. Olson* 1988: 696). Specifically, there could be no independent counsel without a request by the attorney general, and if the independent counsel failed to faithfully execute the law, he or she could be removed for good cause.

Are There Any Lines?

The *Morrison* decision should put to rest any notion that the Constitution compartmentalizes powers into the categories of legislative, executive, and judicial. In *Buckley v. Valeo* (1976), the Court noted that the development of administrative agencies "has placed severe strain on the separation-of-powers principle in its pristine formulation" (*Buckley v. Valeo* 1976: 280-281). *Morrison* seeks to relieve the strain by recasting the separation of powers in terms of operational impact. The issue is not whether Congress or a court is deeply involved in the executive branch. Here the judicial branch appointed the independent counsel and established her jurisdiction while Congress, through the Ethics Act, restricted the executive branch's authority to remove her. Instead, the fundamental question is whether such legislative and/or judicial involvement unduly impedes the president's ability to perform his constitutional duties. The Court answers the question, "Whose bureaucracy is this, anyway?" by saying it belongs to all three branches insofar as the president can still faithfully execute the laws.

This answer runs counter to the broader thrust of *Myers* as well as executive reorganization in the 1930s, several recommendations of the National Performance Review, and much traditional and contemporary American public administrative theorizing. But it is in no sense ahistorical. The principle that Congress can legally direct executive branch officers was firmly established in *Kendall v. U.S.* (1838), in which the Supreme Court proclaimed,

> It would be an alarming doctrine, that congress cannot impose upon any executive officer any duty they may think proper, which is not repugnant to any rights secured and protected by the constitution; and in such cases, the duty and responsibility grow out of and are subject to the control of law, and not to the direction of the President. (*Kendall v. U.S.* 1838: 524)

But the outer limits set by *Morrison* for legislative and judicial involvement in federal administration may be too amorphous to yield much guidance. Justice Scalia complained bitterly of this in a dissent that argued for a much tighter compartmentalization of powers:

> There are now no lines. If the removal of a prosecutor, the virtual embodiment of the power to "take care that the laws be faithfully executed," can be restricted, what officer's removal cannot? This is an

open invitation for Congress to experiment. What about a special Assistant Secretary of State, with responsibility for one very narrow area of foreign policy, who would not only have to be confirmed by the Senate but could also be removed only pursuant to certain carefully designed restrictions? Could this possibly render the President "[un]able [sic] to accomplish his constitutional role"? Or a special Assistant Secretary of Defense for Procurement? The possibilities are endless. . . . As far as I can discern from the Court's opinion, it is now open season upon the President's removal power for all executive officers. . . . The Court essentially says to the President: "Trust Us. We will make sure that you are able to accomplish your constitutional role." I think the Constitution gives the President—and the people—more protection than that. (*Morrison v. Olson* 1988: 726-727)

Scalia concluded that "today's decision on the basic issue of fragmentation of executive power is ungoverned by rule, and hence ungoverned by law" (*Morrison v. Olson* 1988: 733). The shape of federal administration, then, is likely to be the product of political struggles for institutional power among the three branches.

Interbranch Competition
Over Federal Administration

Prior to the 1930s, for the most part, Congress was the dominant branch of government. Even if we date the rise of the federal administrative state from the 1880s, when the Civil Service Act (1883) and the Interstate Commerce Act (1887) were passed, it was not until the New Deal that the president's power truly rivaled Congress's. Since then, the president and Congress have both sought to gain greater control or leverage over the bureaucracy. Prior to the late 1930s, the Supreme Court had opposed the development of the administrative state (Rosenbloom 1989). Subsequently, it became an arbiter of efforts to control. The judicial branch has also developed leverage of its own by expanding the constitutional rights of individuals vis-à-vis administrative action and making administrators potentially liable for violating those rights.

The Managerial Presidency

The Brownlow Committee Report (U.S. President's Committee on Administrative Management 1937) established the intellectual and some of the institutional foundations for a presidentially centered federal administration. The report argued that it was Congress's function to set policy, provide appropriations, and then essentially let the president take over until it became reasonable to evaluate how programs and policies were working. In the committee's words, "Canons of efficiency require the establishment of a responsible and effective chief executive as the center of energy, direction, and administrative management" (U.S. President's Committee on Administrative Management, in Mosher 1976: 114). Consequently, "We hold that once Congress has made an appropriation which it is free to withhold, the responsibility for the administration of the expenditures under that appropriation is and should be solely upon the Executive" (U.S. President's Committee on Administrative Management, in Mosher 1976: 133). In practice, the establishment of the EOP, an outgrowth of the report's recommendations, solidified the president's role as the initiating force in the federal government, leaving to Congress the job of reacting. The EOP strengthened the president's ability to formulate policy, prepare an annual national budget, and propose administrative reorganizations.

Since 1939, several additional reforms have been introduced to strengthen the managerial presidency. Schedule C was added to the personnel system during the Eisenhower Administration to enable the president to make more political appointments within the federal service. Eventually, the number of Schedule Cs climbed to 1,700 (National Commission on the Public Service 1989: 17). The transformation of the Bureau of the Budget into the Office of Management and Budget in 1970, along with the creation of the Domestic Policy Council, "were distinctly centralizing in that they aimed at establishing greater capacity for policy formation, assessment and surveillance of administrative implementation" (P. Arnold 1986: 283). President Nixon's explanation of the reorganization indicated how normal it had become to view the chief executive as the primary source of both policy formulation and implementation: "A President whose programs are carefully coordinated, whose information system keeps him adequately informed, and whose organizational assignments are plainly set out, can delegate authority with security and confidence" (quoted in P. Arnold 1986: 283). Like Schedule C, the reorganization created new political appointments in the executive branch, most notably the heads of the operating divisions of OMB.

The Civil Service Reform Act of 1978 was another major reform. It was intended to enable the political executive to use personnel administration as a tool for managerial effectiveness rather than only as the mechanism for clean, efficient government that it had historically been (Ingraham and Rosenbloom 1992). Among other features, the act established the Senior Executive Service (SES). Career SESers are subject to greater direction by political executives than are other federal careerists. Moreover, up to 10% of all the positions in the SES can be political appointees.

The Reagan presidency left little doubt that these tools of presidential management could be effectively used to strengthen the political executive vis-à-vis the career service. The number of significant political appointees in the agencies rose to about 3,000 (National Commission on the Public Service 1989: 17) and the administration took considerable care to make sure they were in ideological agreement with the president's main policy thrusts (Lynn 1985). Efforts were made to cut careerists out of policy-making processes (Goldenberg 1985). Rhetorically, the administration railed against the bureaucracy and eventually seems to have seriously weakened and demoralized it (National Commission on the Public Service 1989: 1-9).

Despite considerable success in strengthening the managerial presidency, however, presidents continued to complain about congressional micromanagement and judicial interference. Presidential moves to strengthen executive control of the federal administration have frequently been met with congressional countermoves. Although the term seems currently out of vogue, *checks and balances* prevail.

Congressional Countermoves

In 1946, Congress laid the foundations for its modern role in federal administration by enacting the Administrative Procedure Act (APA) and the Legislative Reorganization Act. The APA, which regulates agency rule-making, adjudicatory, and enforcement processes, is premised on the belief that Congress will necessarily delegate much legislative authority to federal agencies. Rule making, in particular, is clearly a form of supplemental legislation and, in Congress's view, agencies engaging in it are acting as extensions of the legislature.

The need for reorganization flowed clearly from the view that whatever else they may be, federal agencies are agents of Congress. Hear, Robert M. La Follette, Jr., cosponsor of the Reorganization Act:

> Congress lacks adequate facilities today for the continuous inspection and review of administrative action. The time has long since passed when we could anticipate every situation that might arise and provide for it in minute regulatory legislation.
>
> With the expansion of Federal functions during the twentieth century, Congress has perforce created many commissions and agencies to perform them and has delegated its rule-making power to them. But it has failed to provide any regular arrangements for follow-up in order to assure itself that administrative rules and regulations are in accord with the intent of the law. . . .
>
> In order to strengthen Congressional oversight of administrative performance, the Legislative Reorganization Act authorizes the standing

committees of both houses to keep watch over the execution of the laws by the administrative agencies within their jurisdiction. Staffed with qualified specialists, these committees will conduct a continuous review of the activities of the agencies. (La Follette 1946:45)

The act established the broad framework for Congress's contemporary organization by standing committees and subcommittees. Over the years, the entanglement of (sub)committees and agencies has led many political scientists to focus on policy subsystems as a productive unit of analysis when studying the federal government (see especially, Lowi 1969; Ripley and Franklin 1976).

Another remarkable product of Congress in 1946 was the Employment Act. It incorporated Keynesian economic theory into law by making the government responsible for promoting "maximum employment, production, [and] purchasing power" (§ 2). Perhaps none but the most naive doubted that implementation would be "honey combed with political expediency" (Donnelly 1945: 665). Pump priming to create employment has often gone hand in hand with pork barrel to win votes (Fiorina 1977; R. Arnold 1979).

Together, these laws made it clear that Congress intended to be deeply involved in administration in the post-New Deal administrative state. Their import was not lost on Louis Brownlow, a major architect of the managerial presidency. Speaking in 1947, he realized the legislative potential for involvement in the executive branch and warned that

> the next step which we the people should take to meet the needs of the Presidency is to persuade the Congress not to yield to the constant temptation to interfere with the administration of the Executive Branch by needlessly detailed requirements for procedures in the execution of the laws it enacts; procedures sometimes so hampering that they almost have the effect of defeating the very purpose for which the Congress has enacted the law. The President is under the Constitutional obligation to "take Care that the Laws be faithfully executed," and if we mean to help the President to discharge this obligation we must be sure that his authority to do so is not usurped either by the Congress as a whole, by the House of Representatives or the Senate, and—most important of all—by particular committees of the Congress. (Brownlow 1949: 116)

Of course, one person's "micromanagement" may well be another's legitimate legislative control of administration (Mayer 1993).

Congress's action in 1946 was a response to changes in the executive, including the presidential office, during the New Deal. Similarly, in 1974, it enacted the Budget and Impoundment Control Act, partly in response to the establishment of OMB in 1970. The act established the Congressional Budget Office to strengthen Congress's role and information in budgeting. It also sought to control presidential impoundments, which became rife during the Nixon Administration. Further strengthening of Congress's institutional role in budgeting occurred in response to the growing deficit. The Budget and Emergency Deficit Control Act of 1985 (Gramm-Rudman-Hollings Act), the Balanced Budget and Emergency Deficit Control Reaffirmation Act of 1987 (Gramm-Rudman II), and the Budget Enforcement Act of 1990 all enhance Congress's capacity to respond coherently to the president's proposed budget.

The Government Performance and Results Act of 1993 (GPRA) has major potential to strengthen congressional influence over federal administration. It requires agencies to formulate strategic plans containing specific—and, preferably, quantifiable—goals for their various programs. The act requires that the plans be established in consultation with Congress (read: subcommittees). Eventually, budgetary appropriations are to be linked to agency performance. GPRA was a legislative initiative. It enjoyed executive support because of its results orientation, which fit nicely with Vice President Al Gore's National Performance Review (discussed below). It helps to solve a congressional collective action problem. Subcommittees will be able to supply the specificity in legislation that Congress as a whole is unable or unwilling to provide. The act is a license for subcommittees to define agencies' missions.

After the Republican Party took control of both houses in 1995, the extent of Congress's constitutional authority and political influence over the executive branch was fully evident. Its budgetary disagreements with the president caused two partial government shutdowns. Congress also sought deep programmatic cuts and major restrictions of federal regulatory rule making. As for micromanagement, among many other actions, congressional committees sought to impose travel restrictions on Department of Energy Secretary Hazel O'Leary and to force the Customs Service to pay more attention to combating drug traffic on the Mexican border.

The Federal Judiciary and Administration

The judiciary's response to the managerial presidency and congressional involvement in federal administration has had two main facets. First, the courts have adopted the role of umpiring according to the "rules" of constitutional integrity. The *Morrison* case is a clear example. Other leading examples are *Immigration and Naturalization Service v. Chadha* (1983), in which the Supreme Court found the one-house legislative veto in violation of the Constitution's "presentment" and bicameral clauses, and *Bowsher v. Synar* (1986), in which it held that Congress had unconstitutionally sought to vest an executive function in a legislative agent, the comptroller general. In *Chadha,* the Court set forth the logic of behind its commitment to strict constitutional integrity:

> The choices we discern as having been made in the Constitutional Convention impose burdens on governmental processes that often seem clumsy, inefficient, even unworkable, but those hard choices were consciously made by men who had lived under a form of government that permitted arbitrary governmental acts to go unchecked. There is no support in the Constitution or decisions of this Court for the proposition that the cumbersomeness and delays often encountered in complying with explicit constitutional standards may be avoided, either by the Congress or by the President. . . . With all the obvious flaws of delay, untidiness, and potential for abuse, we have not yet found a better way to preserve freedom than by making the exercise of power subject to the carefully crafted restraints spelled out in the Constitution. (*Immigration and Naturalization Service v. Chadha* 1983: 958-959)

The problem, of course, is that the Framers' document does not anticipate the contemporary administrative state. As Justice Robert Jackson once said, the agencies "have become a veritable fourth branch of the Government, which has deranged our three-branch legal theories much as the concept of a fourth dimension unsettles our three dimensional thinking" (*Federal Trade Commission v. Ruberoid Co.* 1952: 487). Still, without a commitment to constitutional integrity, it would be even more difficult to limit "the hydraulic pressure inherent within each of the separate Branches to exceed the outer limits of its power, even to accomplish desirable objectives" (*Immigration and Naturalization Service v. Chadha* 1983: 951)

Second, as the concept of "hydraulic pressure" suggests, the judiciary has developed leverage of its own over the administrative state. The most dramatic lever has been the constitutionalization of administrative practice since the 1950s. In a long series of decisions, the Supreme Court has used procedural and substantive due process, First and Fourth Amendment rights, and equal protection to regulate administrative behavior in dealing with clients (or customers), public employees, persons confined to public mental health facilities and prisons, and individuals involved in various street-level encounters (Rosenbloom 1983a). Further, the Court shifted away from a historic presumption of absolute official immunity to one of qualified immunity only. Today, most public officials and administrators may be held liable for money damages if their activity violated clearly established constitutional rights of which a reasonable person should have known (*Harlow v. Fitzgerald* 1982; Rosenbloom 1983a: chap. 6). Such liability provides individuals with a personal channel for vindicating their newly declared constitutional rights vis-à-vis administrators as well as giving the administrators a strong incentive to understand and respect individuals' rights.

These legal changes are of major magnitude. They overturned such major historical doctrines as "separate but equal" (allowing for racial segregation by law), "privilege" (defining government benefits, including occupational and other licenses, welfare, and public employment as privileges devoid of almost all constitutional protection), and, as noted above, official immunity at common law. Given that "constitutional law is what the courts say it is" (*Owen v. City of Independence* 1980: 669, quoting Justice Lewis Powell), placing constitutional constraints on administrative practices essentially enables the courts to tell administrators how to perform some aspects of their jobs. For example: Don't discriminate based on social characteristics such as race, ethnicity, and gender; use fair and reasonable procedures when depriving individuals of benefits or limiting their substantive rights; provide confined public mental health patients with humane physical and psychological environments; don't engage in barbaric treatment of prisoners, even though it may appear to be cost-effective; and make sure that law enforcement stops are supportable by reasonable and articulable premises (see Rosenbloom 1983a for a full discussion). Moreover, by shifting to qualified immunity, the courts have essentially told administrators to "do what we say or risk getting sued."

Although the record has been more mixed, since the 1970s the courts have also frequently probed the logic of administrative decision making with more vigor than earlier in the post-New Deal period (*Federal Trade Commission v. Sperry & Hutchinson* 1972; *Industrial Union Department, AFL-CIO v. American Petroleum Institute* 1980; *Motor Vehicle Manufacturers Assn. v. State Farm* 1983). By the mid-1980s, however, the Supreme Court had firmly established that agencies do have considerable discretion in choosing rule-making procedures (*Vermont Yankee Nuclear Power Corp. v. Natural Resources Defense Council* [NRDC] 1978), in interpreting statutes (*Chevron v. NRDC* 1984), and in deciding where to expend enforcement resources (*Heckler v. Cheney* 1985).

Taken together, these "hydraulic" judicial efforts to maintain institutional power in the age of the contemporary administrative state have enabled the courts to exercise substantial control over administrative practices and decision making. Litigation is now a normal part of the administrative process at some agencies (e.g., the Environmental Protection Agency; O'Leary 1993). The Supreme Court's umpiring in the name of constitutional integrity also enables it to check the efforts of Congress and the presidency to gain untoward power over administrative operations.

The Next Move:
"Reinventing" Federal Administration

The National Performance Review (NPR) is the latest move in the executive effort to dominate federal administration. The *Report of the National Performance Review* (the "Gore Report," after its author, Vice President Albert Gore), claims it "is not about politics" (National Performance Review 1993: iv). Rather, it seeks to cut unnecessary spending, serve customers, empower federal employees, help in solving problems at the community level, and foster excellence and entrepreneurial government. It asserts these goals will be achieved by creating a clear sense of mission within federal administration, delegating authority and responsibility, using incentives rather than regulations, basing budgets on outcomes, using market solutions, and relying on customer satisfaction as the measure of success (National Performance Review 1993: 7). Nevertheless, the report is a blueprint for far greater executive domination of federal administration.

It is noteworthy that the NPR seeks to reduce the impact of the separation of powers on federal administration by diminishing the roles of both Congress and the federal courts. Its view of the appropriate congressional role is reminiscent of the Brownlow Report's. Essentially, Congress is to develop clear goals, provide the requisite legal and spending authority, and then get out of the way until such time as it becomes appropriate to evaluate program implementation and other administrative activities. The Gore Report calls for the following: biennial budgeting, which would give Congress less flexibility and need to review administrative operations; giving agencies the authority to rollover 50% of unspent funding, thereby providing potentially vast sums of discretionary "no year" money and great relief from Congress's power of the purse; enhancing the recision powers of the president; eliminating congressionally imposed staffing *floors;* reducing requirements that agencies must report to Congress; minimizing line items and earmarks in budgets; and ending congressional involvement (micromanagement) in the establishment, closure, and consolidation of field offices and other administrative units. The NPR also proposes that the president develop and execute performance agreements with agency heads, whose duties are, of course, fixed by law. As mentioned above, though, GPRA can serve as a congressional counterweight.

Because the NPR favors greater discretion in federal administration, it necessarily would reduce the extent of available judicial review. The Administrative Procedure Act of 1946 excludes from judicial review "agency action . . . committed to agency discretion by law" (§ 701[a][2]). Among other features of the Gore Report that would promote discretionary government are phasing out central rules and controls, especially for personnel, labor relations, and procurement; allowing agencies to "manage to budget"; empowering employees to make decisions; using market-based approaches to solving public policy problems; and giving agencies greater freedom to set user fees and to determine how revenues derived from fees can be used.

It is far too early to assess the practical impact of the NPR. Implementation has been uneven, and many of the basic facts are in dispute (York 1996; "Forum on Reinventing" 1996). However, its relationship to the separation of powers bears watching. It may very well fall short of its goals precisely because Congress does not view its current role in federal administration as illegitimate, undesirable, or in need of reform. The courts, although recently permissive regarding agency exercise of discretion, may eventually find that the extent of discretionary government envisioned by the NPR threatens the rule of law.

Conclusion:
Consequences of the Separation of Powers
for American Public Administration

The separation of powers is far more than some hoary theory explicated in the eighteenth-century *Federalist Papers* and of interest mostly to constitutional historians. Its impact on American public administrative practice has been pervasive. It sets the framework for contemporary bureaucratic politics, administrative policy making, implementation, and oversight of agencies' activity. High-level federal administrators are perforce often called upon to coordinate the separation of powers, a role once played more strongly by political parties. Our presidentially centered literature speaks of a "government of strangers" (Heclo 1977), while congressionally oriented analyses find "iron triangles," "micromanagement" as a means of controlling policy, and strategic spending by administrators to build supportive legislative coalitions (R. Arnold 1979). These systems converge on agencies, and career SESers must often work to coordinate them, if they are to be coordinated at all. The courts have also been active players, and there is convincing evidence that their decisions can alter agency priorities (O'Leary 1993) and even systems of administrative practice, such as public personnel management (Shafritz et al. 1992).

American administrative legitimacy has also been deeply affected by the separation of powers (Rosenbloom 1983b). Administrators are called upon to exercise executive, legislative, and judicial functions. They make rules, implement, and adjudicate. They are also supervised by all three branches of government, each of which has a commitment to historic values associated with its work. In practice, this has meant that American public administration, which has always had a normative base (Waldo 1948; Dahl 1947), has been riven by conflicts among competing values. For instance, efficient execution of the law is frequently at odds with the procedural fairness favored in adjudication. Indeed, as Chief Justice Warren Burger pointed out in *Chadha,* constitutional integrity itself may be in conflict with governmental efficiency.

Under these conditions, it has been impossible to develop an all-encompassing vision of public administration. At the same time, anything less is subject to opposition on the grounds that it does not sufficiently protect or advance important values. Hence American public administration has suffered various crises of legitimacy and these can be expected to recur periodically. Relief comes when there is widespread agreement on what public administration should be. For instance, during much of the Progressive era (1890-1924), when the famous politics-administration dichotomy was in its heyday, there seems to have been strong political support for apolitical public administration. Whether a conception of public administration that becomes ingrained in the culture must be the ideology of a dominant political party, movement, or coalition is an open question. Historically, that was the case from the founding to 1828 (era of "gentlemen"), 1840s and 1850s (spoils period), and Progressive era (politically neutral expertise). Perhaps the kind of populistic vision of government underlying the NPR's emphasis on direct marketlike responsiveness to citizen-customers will eventually emerge as the dominant feature of public administration. Certainly, the NPR is well aware of the cultural change in administration that is necessary for its success (National Performance Review 1993: 8-9).

It should be evident that the separation of powers presents serious challenges not just to American public administrative practice but to administrative thought as well. The founders of the modern discipline of public administration, Woodrow Wilson (1887) and Frank Goodnow (1900), viewed the separation of powers as an obstacle to both good practice and clear administrative thought. Wilson suggested that the study of administration could potentially improve the constitutional distribution of authority. Goodnow struggled mightily to explain how two political functions, expression of the people's will and execution of it, could be melded with three branches. Both Wilson and Goodnow relied on a dichotomy between politics and administration as a means of resolving the quandaries they confronted in arguing for businesslike, efficient administration. Eventually, this dichotomy became a staple of advocacy for presidentially centered administration, from Brownlow to the NPR. Even though it is dysfunctional to theory building, the dichotomy serves useful political purposes and therefore perdures (Waldo 1984; Golembiewski 1984). The need for a theory of public administration that can encompass the functions and activities of all three branches is evident (Rosenbloom 1983b; Rosenbloom 1986; Brown and Stillman 1985). But the task of developing one appears no less daunting than that of integrating federal administration solidly into the constitutional separation of powers.

Note

1. Rourke (1993).

References

Arnold, Peri. (1986) *Making the Managerial Presidency*. Princeton, NJ: Princeton University Press.

Arnold, R. Douglas. (1979) *Congress and the Bureaucracy*. New Haven, CT: Yale University Press.

Bowsher v. Synar (1986) 478 U.S. 714.

Brown, Brack, and Richard Stillman. (1985, July/August) "A Conversation With Dwight Waldo: An Agenda for Future Reflections." *Public Administration Review, 45*: 459-467.

Brownlow, Louis. (1949) *The President and the Presidency*. Chicago: Public Administration Service.

Buckley v. Valeo (1976) 424 U.S. 1.

Butler v. White (1897) 83 F. 578.

Chevron v. Natural Resources Defense Council (1984) 467 U.S. 837.

Cooper, Philip. (1986) "By Order of the President." *Administration & Society, 18*: 233-262.

Dahl, Robert. (1947) "The Science of Public Administration: Three problems." *Public Administration Review, 7*, 1: 1-11.

Donnelly, James. (1945) Testimony Before Full Employment Subcommittee on Banking and Currency. Senate Hearings 763, August 30, pp. 665-668. Washington, DC: Government Printing Office.

Federal Trade Commission v. Sperry & Hutchinson (1972) 405 U.S. 233.

Fiorina, Morris. (1977) *Congress: Keystone of the Washington Establishment*. New Haven, CT: Yale University Press.

"Forum on Reinventing." (1996, May-June) *Public Administration Review, 56*: 245-304.

FTC v. Ruberoid (1952) 343 U.S. 470.

Goldenberg, Edie. (1985) "The Permanent Government in an Era of Retrenchment and Retreat." In Lester Salamon and Michael Lund, eds., *The Reagan Presidency and the Governing of America*, pp. 381-404. Washington, DC: Urban Institute Press.

Golembiewski, Robert. (1984) "Ways in Which 'The Study of Administration' Confounds the Study of Administration." In Jack Rabin and James Bowman, eds., *Politics and Administration*, pp. 381-404. New York: Marcel Dekker.

Goodnow, Frank. (1900) *Politics and Administration.* New York: Macmillan.

Harlow v. Fitzgerald (1982) 457 U.S. 800.

Heckler v. Cheney (1985) 470 U.S. 831.

Heclo, Hugh. (1977) *A Government of Strangers.* Washington, DC: Brookings Institution.

Humphrey's Executor v. U.S. (1935) 295 U.S. 602.

Immigration and Naturalization Service v. Chadha (1983) 462 U.S. 919.

Industrial Union Department, AFL-CIO v. American Petroleum Institute (1980) 448 U.S. 607.

Ingraham, Patricia, and David Rosenbloom, eds. (1992) *The Promise and the Paradox of Civil Service Reform.* Pittsburgh: University of Pittsburgh Press.

Kendall v. U.S. (1838) 12 Peters 524.

La Follette, Robert. (1946, August 4) "Congress Wins a Victory Over Congress." *New York Times Magazine,* pp. 11, 45, 46.

Lowi, Theodore. (1969) *The End of Liberalism.* New York: Norton.

Lynn, Lawrence. (1985) "The Reagan Administration and the Renitent Bureaucracy." In Lester Salamon and Michael Lund, eds., *The Reagan Presidency and the Governing of America,* pp. 339-370. Washington, DC: Urban Institute Press.

Mayer, Richard. (1993) "Policy Disputes as a Source of Administrative Controls." *Public Administration Review,* 53, July-August: 293-302.

McCollough v. Maryland (1819) 4 Wheaton 316.

Morrison v. Olson (1988) 487 U.S. 654.

Mosher, Frederick. (1976) *Basic Documents of American Public Administration, 1776-1950.* New York: Holmes & Meier.

Motor Vehicle Manufacturers Assn. v. State Farm (1983) 463 U.S. 29.

Myers v. U.S. (1926) 272 U.S. 52.

National Commission on the Public Service. (1989) *Leadership for America.* Lexington, MA: Lexington.

National Performance Review [Al Gore]. (1993) *Creating a Government That Works Better & Costs Less: Report of the National Performance Review.* Washington, DC: Government Printing Office.

O'Leary, Rosemary. (1993) *Environmental Change: The Federal Courts and the Environmental Protection Agency.* Philadelphia: Temple University Press.

Owen v. City of Independence (1980) 445 U.S. 622.

Ripley, Randall, and Grace Franklin. (1976) *Congress, the Bureaucracy, and Public Policy.* Homewood, IL: Dorsey.

Rosenbloom, David. (1983a) *Public Administration and Law.* New York: Marcel Dekker.

———. (1983b) "Public Administrative Theory and the Separation of Powers." *Public Administration Review,* 43, May-June: 219-227.

———. (1986) *Public Administration: Understanding Management, Politics, and Law in the Public Sector.* New York: Random House (2nd ed., 1989; 3rd ed., 1993, with McGraw Hill, New York).

———. (1987) "Public Administrators and the Judiciary: The 'New Partnership.' " *Public Administration Review,* 47, January-February: 75-83.

———. (1989) "Public Law and Regulation." In Jack Rabin et al., eds., *Handbook of Public Administration,* pp. 523-575. New York: Marcel Dekker.

Rourke, Francis. (1993, December) "The 1993 Gaus Lecture: Whose Bureaucracy Is This, Anyway." *PS: Political Science & Politics,* 26: 687-692.

Shafritz, Jay, Norma Riccucci, David Rosenbloom, and Albert Hyde. (1992) *Personnel Management in Government.* 4th ed. New York: Marcel Dekker.

Silberman, Charles. (1993) *Cages of Reason.* Chicago: University of Chicago Press.

Vermont Yankee Nuclear Power Corp. v. Natural Resources Defense Council (1978) 435 U.S. 519.

Waldo, Dwight. (1948) *The Administrative State.* New York: Ronald.

———. (1984) "The Perdurability of the Politics-Administration Dichotomy: Woodrow Wilson and the Identity Crisis in Public Administration." In Jack Rabin and James Bowman, eds., *Politics and Administration,* pp. 219-233. New York: Marcel Dekker.

Wiener v. U.S. (1958) 357 U.S. 349.

Wildavsky, Aaron. (1991) *The Rise of Radical Egalitarianism.* Washington, DC: American University Press.

Wilson, Woodrow. (1887) "The Study of Administration." *Political Science Quarterly,* 56: 481-506 (1941 republication).

York, Buyron. (1996) "Big Al's Big Scam." *American Spectator,* 29, February: 38-43.

7

Politics and Bureaucracy:
Their Impact on Professionalism

Francis E. Rourke

As a source of power within government, bureaucracy and professionalism have common roots—the need for expertise in making the decisions and carrying out the manifold tasks for which public officials bear responsibility in modern society. It is not a surprise, therefore, that these two phenomena have been joined closely together in their emergence and development in this country. As professionalism has grown in the United States, it has helped give rise to bureaucracies in all sectors of policy making and at the state and local as well as the national levels of government (Mosher 1982). Scientists have been among the first to see the need for strong national science agencies; doctors, for an improved state public health system; and teachers, for upgrades of local public school facilities. The growth of

AUTHOR'S NOTE: Research on which this chapter draws was supported by a grant from the Russell Sage Foundation, for which I would like to express my gratitude.

professionalism has thus been a major force driving the expansion of bureaucracy in the United States.

At the same time, the ongoing bureaucratization of government has created a growing number of career opportunities for professionals. Public organizations have provided settings in which a wide variety of existing professions have been able to work and thrive. Government bureaucracy has also been the birthplace of many new professions, including urban planners, state budget officers, and national policy analysts.

Moreover, in the wake of successive civil service reforms, the task of managing the everyday work of government agencies has itself become highly professionalized. One study concluded that "dual streams of professionalism have developed—the invasion of public administration by the professions, and the professionalization of the vocation of public administration" (Kearney and Sinha 1988: 572). It can, in fact, be argued that few things have benefited professionalism more in this country than the rise of the administrative state. A cynic might even suspect that professionals have been driven by the profit motive in helping to create many bureaucracies, which thereafter provide them with employment.

Because the interests of the professions and the bureaucracy dovetail in this way, these two spheres of human endeavor might well be expected to have had an amicable relationship throughout the course of their separate development in this country. But such has not been the case. When professions were first being organized in the United States, as Brian Balogh has shown (1991: 133), it was not uncommon for the members of many of these groups to look askance upon any connection with governmental activities.

> Unsure of their organizational and ideological solidarity, scientists, for instance, feared the corrupting influence of central government. In many instances they were prepared to forego its potential financial resources for what they hoped would be greater professional autonomy, secure in their belief that this was in fact the American way. Scientists and a host of other professionals did not actively seek Federal aid to produce experts, sustain their research, and pursue professional policy agendas until after World War II.

In those early days at least, many professionals appeared to believe that any ties with government agencies would subject them to political pressures that would eventually erode the independence needed to practice their craft in accordance with the scientific and ethical standards they were then developing. Of course, the attitude of professionals in this regard may also have been shaped by more self-serving considerations. One scholar who has examined the origins of the professions suggests that these groups sought autonomy not only out of concern for the integrity of their discipline but also as a strategy for preserving their exclusive authority over a body of knowledge they were just beginning to control (Larson 1977).

However, the opportunities that government bureaucracies provide for the exercise of expert skills eventually proved too attractive to resist, and professionals became increasingly visible in all areas of government employment, often holding key positions in administrative agencies like the Forest Service. But the conviction that professional work requires a large measure of autonomy for its effective performance remained an article of faith in large sectors of the professional community, and it has been a source of episodic conflict between professionals and their administrative superiors throughout this century.

One recent development on the political front has greatly strengthened the possibility of tension between politics and professionalism in modern American bureaucracy: the determined efforts of the White House and other centers of power in the American political system to bring the bureaucracy under tighter political control. Thus, even as American bureaucracy has become much more professionalized in recent years, with the number of professionals employed in government agencies constantly rising (Cigler 1990), it has also become increasingly politicized. These converging trends have greatly expanded the number of situations in which professionals today may have to take actions or make decisions that are inconsistent with their own standards of professional conduct.

Escalating Demands for Responsiveness

The growing demand for a greater degree of responsiveness in American bureaucracy is rooted in both political and organizational imperatives, drawing support as it does from the canons of both democracy and bureaucracy. From a political perspective, the drive for responsiveness is rooted in a basic assumption of democracy itself—that the policies of government should rest upon the consent of the governed, and that such consent can only be given by the people themselves or by the officials they elect to represent their views. Thus, in the traditional theory of public administration, bureaucrats belong to a subordinate category of public officials—charged with executing rather than formulating the policies of government.

In point of fact, of course, bureaucrats have usually played a much larger role in policy making than the formal theory of democracy might suggest. In the everyday workings of government, the information and advice civil servants give to elected officials go a long way toward shaping the character of national policy. Ultimately, however, it is elected officials who must give the stamp of approval to whatever decisions the government chooses to make, because these office holders are accountable to the public and can be removed from office at the next election.

Within the internal structure of bureaucracy, an organizational as well as a political imperative asserts itself. If public organizations are to be effective instruments for the achievement of policy goals, in democratic as in other forms of government, subordinate officials must abide by and faithfully carry out the orders and decisions of their superiors. Although the Nuremberg trials following World War II and other events in modern history have brought such dutiful obedience into great disrepute, "carrying out orders" is still the maxim that bureaucrats are normally expected to follow in the everyday work of government agencies. This hierarchical chain of command is a common feature of organizational life in the private sector as well. In fact, the obligation of subordinates to defer to their superiors' orders may well be described as a defining characteristic of a bureaucratic organization in modern society.

The subordination of bureaucrats in the governmental structure can thus be justified by the need for organizational efficiency as well as democratic accountability. In the United States, however, elected officials have never been altogether certain that they really control the activities of the bureaucrats who serve under them, and they frequently complain about the resistance they encounter when they try to bring about changes of any fundamental sort in the way in which government agencies operate.

It should not be surprising, therefore, that elected officials have stepped up their efforts in recent years to find new avenues of influence over the manner in which bureaucratic organizations carry out the policies placed under their jurisdiction. One of the landmark shifts in the modern development of the presidential office in the United States has been the emergence of the so-called administrative presidency, a regime chiefly characterized by intense efforts on the part of the chief executive to shape national policy not by the enactment of new laws but by interpreting existing statutes so as to tilt government programs in the direction in which the White House wants to go (Nathan 1975; Waterman 1989; Durant 1992).

Because this strategy relies on powers inherent in the administration of existing statutes rather than the passage of new legislation to achieve presidential goals, its success requires tight control over the behavior and actions of the bureaucrats responsible for enforcing the law. Under the administrative presidency, the discretionary authority that was once viewed as a central source of bureaucratic power in the policy process is transformed into an instrument through which chief executives can achieve their own policy objectives. As a result, a modern president often seems more concerned about the responsiveness of bureaucrats to political control than the extent of their professional skill. Moreover, during the presidency of Richard Nixon, the White House was often charged with using the administrative presidency as a covert device for initiating policy changes that Congress refused to support.

Presidents have not been alone in their attempts to manipulate the exercise of bureaucratic discretion to shape national policy. The rise of the administrative presidency has been paralleled in recent years by an expansion of congressional efforts to shape bureaucratic decision making. The legislature has done so in large part by spelling out in sometimes exquisite detail the way in which the statutes it enacts should be administered, even to the point of imposing deadlines for the achievement of some of its most important objectives.

Congress has also strengthened its ability to oversee the way in which the bureaucracy is adhering to its instructions, as conveyed either in the laws the legislature enacts or in the hearings and reports of the various committees through which Congress and the bureaucracy ordinarily interact. One of the most important factors contributing to this enhanced capacity for legislative oversight has been the great expansion in the size of congressional staff, especially in the number and professionalism of committee staff members. Having skilled experts of its own to assist it in carrying on its oversight function greatly strengthens both the incentive and the ability of Congress to keep itself informed on how well the executive agencies under its jurisdiction are carrying out the varied missions the legislature has assigned to them.

These efforts of the President and Congress to increase their control over the bureaucracy have been greatly energized by the advent of divided government in the United States in recent years. It has become increasingly common for each of the major political parties in this country to control one of the two policymaking branches of the national government. Beginning in 1948 the Republicans were very often in charge of the White House, while the Democrats remained the majority party in Congress. Since 1994, however, the reverse has been true, as the Democrats held on to the presidential office even as the Republicans gained control over Congress. This bipartisan system of government added a political dimension to the institutional competition that by itself has traditionally led these two branches of government to compete for control over the decisions and actions of bureaucrats.

Under divided government both the President and Contress have reason to look upon the bureaucracy with a high degree of suspicion. When, for example, the Democrats controlled Congress, they often saw the bureaucracy as the tool of Republican Presidents, while these same chief executives regarded bureaucrats as a hostile camp closely aligned with the Congressional Democrats who had given birth to the programs they administered. Such political concerns fueled the efforts of both the White House and Congress to tighten their control over the bureaucracy, in order to prevent bureaucratic discretion from being used to achieve the goals of both their political and institutional adversaries in the other branch of government.

The drive for legislative reform in recent years has also spurred congressional efforts to oversee bureaucracy. A major feature of this reform movement has been a desire to sharpen the cutting edge of legislative surveillance into bureaucratic activities. This has been especially true in areas where relations between a congressional committee and an executive agency have appeared to be excessively cozy in the past, as in the case of foreign intelligence operations (Kaiser 1992). Moreover, congressional reformers have been keenly interested in decentralizing power within legislative committees, and this has led to a proliferation of subcommittees. Although reformers may not have intended this result, such proliferation has multiplied opportunities for legislative intervention in the affairs of executive agencies.

Responsiveness and Professionalism: Conflicting Views

The growing pressure from both the White House and Congress for a more responsive bureaucracy has brought to the fore a question that has long haunted professionals working for a democratic government. Is responsiveness the only norm by which they should be guided in their role as bureaucrats, or do they have no less an obligation to uphold the ethical and technical canons that have traditionally guided the practice of their craft? As noted earlier, this question has taken on renewed importance today when the expanding demand for political responsiveness increases the likelihood that professionals may be asked to behave as bureaucrats in ways that their colleagues outside of government might regard as "unprofessional."

Just prior to World War II, a classic debate occurred between two leading political scientists who sought to reconcile the conflicting demands of professionalism and democracy. In an article published in 1940, Carl J. Friedrich made a strong case for tolerating and even encouraging a great deal of independence for professionals and their expert judgment in bureaucracy. "Throughout the length and breadth of our technical civilization," Friedrich (1940: 14) argued, "there is arising a type of responsibility on the part of the permanent administrator . . . which cannot be effectively enforced except by fellow-technicians who are capable of judging his [or her] policy in terms of the scientific knowledge bearing upon it."

Friedrich's argument could easily be interpreted as elevating professionals to the status of a privileged elite within government, free from any obligation to accept political control over their activities. A well-known student of comparative government, Herman Finer, was quick to read it in precisely this way. In a rejoinder that appeared shortly after the publication of Friedrich's article, Finer (1941: 335) wrote:

> My chief difference with Professor Friedrich was and is my insistence upon distinguishing responsibility as an arrangement of correction and punishment even up to dismissal both of politicians and officials, while he believed and believes in reliance upon responsibility as a sense of responsibility, largely unsanctioned, except by deference or loyalty to professional standards.

By fervently aligning himself with the cause of democracy, Finer (1941: 336) easily occupied the high moral ground in this debate. Few could disagree with his proposition that "the elected representatives of the public . . . are to determine the course of action of the public servants to the most minute degree that is technically feasible." Note, however, that Finer did introduce an important caveat to his argument when he suggested that elected officials have the authority to define the agenda of public servants only to the extent "that is technically feasible."

In a later essay, Friedrich sought to strengthen his argument for professional independence by seizing upon Finer's admission of the need for technical competence in government. He noted that governments are often asked to do "what the situation requires," and

> an understanding of the requirements of the situation may call for expertise, for technical knowledge which may be possessed only by a professional . . . a vast number of technicians of every variety, engineers, economists, agronomists, medical and natural scientists are continually confronted with situations which require the highest degree of technical knowledge and skill. (Friedrich 1960: 190-191)

Friedrich sought to underscore the risks a society may take when it denies professional knowledge the respect it deserves by citing the cases of two military professionals, Billy Mitchell in the United States and Charles de Gaulle in France, whose prophetic insights into impending changes in the technology of war were scorned by their political superiors.

In his earlier essay, Friedrich had, however, conceded that a democracy cannot justify a policy solely on the grounds that it has been designed in accord with professional opinion. "We have a right to call . . . a policy irresponsible," he wrote,

> if it can be shown that it was adopted without proper regard to the existing sum of human knowledge concerning the technical issues involved; we also have a right to call it irresponsible if it can be shown that it was adopted without proper regard for existing preferences in the community, and more particularly its prevailing majority. Consequently the responsible administrator is one who is responsive to these two dominant factors: technical knowledge and popular sentiment. (1940: 12)

Still, Friedrich was quite vague in identifying how responsiveness to something as vague as "popular sentiment" could be enforced upon technical and professional experts within government. He mentioned the fact that administrators commonly anticipate probable public reaction to their decisions during the course of their deliberations, and argued that civil servants commonly tailor their final judgments to fit such "anticipated reactions." Friedrich also borrowed from John Gaus the idea that there is an "inner check" or what Gaus also referred to as an "ideal of professional obligation," which can serve as a significant barrier against the possibility that professionals within bureaucracy might initiate policies in defiance of popular sentiment (Gaus 1936: 42).

This claim that the conscience of professionals could be relied upon to ensure their responsiveness to political control left both Friedrich and Gaus highly vulnerable to Finer's (1941: 336) trenchant comment that "reliance upon an official's conscience may be reliance upon an official's accomplice." Friedrich might be in a stronger position to defend his position today by pointing to the fact that some professions within government actually do incorporate the concept of deference to elected officials into their codes of ethics, thus trying to heighten the sensitivity of their members to the need to be responsive to higher authority while working in a political setting.

The use of a code of ethics in this way is primarily a characteristic of professions whose members occupy highly visible positions from which they can exercise a great deal of power in a democratic order, as is the case with military professionals or members of the city manager profession. To the extent that these groups allow their behavior to be shaped by such codes, the inner check of conscience that was extolled by both Friedrich and Gaus can still be said to play a useful role in reconciling professionalism and responsiveness in modern American bureaucracy.

Moreover, the utility of this concept of the "inner check" can be strengthened by giving it a quite different interpretation than that presented by Friedrich and Gaus. It can be looked upon not as a set of conscientious scruples limiting the way in which professionals exercise their power in a bureaucratic setting but as a description of the countervailing power that is inherent in the nature of professionalism itself—the fact that individual professionals seeking to advance their policy views within bureaucracy inevitably find themselves competing with other professionals advocating quite different policies.

It is this predictable division of opinion within their ranks that represents the real inner check limiting the power of professionals in modern bureaucracy: the variety of views that emerge as professionals debate policy issues. Here as elsewhere in American society, pluralism reigns supreme, foreclosing the possibility that the only voice heard in a policy debate will be that of one professional group or single point of view within any particular profession.

The strength of pluralism in this case points up the fact that professionals are as prone to disagreement as political office holders in both their analysis of the problems that beset American society and in the remedies they present as solutions. Although Friedrich and Gaus were on the right track in looking within professionalism itself for the key to maintaining its compatibility with the democratic ethos, they made the mistake of seeing ethical constraints within the conscience of individual professionals as the force that could be relied upon to accomplish this objective. They could have turned more profitably to James Madison's dictum in the Federalist Papers, and rested their case on the reliable certainty that, as he put it, "ambition" can be expected to counteract "ambition" within rival scientific and technical groups as well as among the political leaders and groups with whom Madison was concerned.

At the beginning of the century, it was common among leading figures in the Progressive movement to see the expertise of emerging professional groups as opening the way to a policy-making system in which professional experts would agree on solutions to all the problems spawned by urbanization and industrialism. It was faith in the possibility of such an expert consensus that led Progressives to push for the establishment of independent regulatory bodies in which skilled administrators rather than elected politicians would resolve policy issues for which American society was then grappling to find answers.

What many Progressives were reacting against was the discord and confusion that usually seemed to characterize policy disputes dominated by political parties and their leaders. It was their hope if not expectation that experts could find remedies for the social and economic problems of American society that every reasonable person would accept as the right solutions. What has emerged instead, as the previous discussion has tried to demonstrate, is a society in which the varied and conflicting suggestions of experts have become just as much a source of contention over how to cope with policy problems as was ever the case with political partisanship in the past.

Although this inevitability of dissension within professional communities put an end to the Progressive dream of a society in which expertise would function as a source of national harmony, it also allayed the concerns of people like Walter Lippmann, who feared that the domination of policy-making by experts would threaten the vitality of popular self-government. Prospects of a quite different future could now be entertained: A pluralist professionalism might actually have a beneficial impact upon the vitality of American democracy. The wide range of differences in expert perspectives would strengthen the sovereignty of the public over decisions on public policy. Moreover, the presence and advice of such experts in the policy-making process might even widen the range of choices available to the public, because these professionals were familiar with more policy options than might occur to either the ordinary citizens of a democratic society or their leaders.

Politics, Professionalism, and Bureaucracy

When they serve in a government bureaucracy, professionals are expected to comply with policies that are essentially political in origin, deriving their legitimacy from the outcome of the most recent election. As professionals, they may owe allegiance as well to some higher and more enduring commitment to the norms and standards governing the practice of their specialized craft. In the 1980s, physicians working in family planning clinics during the Reagan and Bush Administrations found themselves impaled on the horns of this dilemma when they were prohibited from giving information to pregnant women that might lead them to have an abortion.

The conflicting obligations that may beset professionals in American bureaucracy were by no means confined to physicians working in family planning clinics at that time. Lawyers working for the Social Security Administration were faced with a similar conflict of loyalties when they were required to deny benefits to disabled persons on grounds that the courts had clearly ruled to be illegal (Mezey 1988). A similar dilemma confronted scientists carrying on research involving the use of fetal tissue during this period, because they were denied federal support for such investigations, lest it create a market for fetal material that would encourage abortions.

Of course, not all professionals working in executive agencies or dependent upon government financial support face a crisis of conscience similar to that confronting professionals in these particular groups. Professions differ a great deal in the extent to which they perceive their integrity as being jeopardized by service in the bureaucracy. In her study of the extensive efforts of the Reagan Administration to secure the loyalty of civil servants to its policies, Marissa Golden found that such efforts met with considerably more resentment and resistance in the Civil Rights Division (CRD) of the Justice Department than they did in the National Highway Traffic Safety Administration (Golden 1992).

Much of the opposition at the Civil Rights Division was rooted in the fact that the policies toward which the administration was trying to steer the agency were regarded by many of the lawyers on its professional staff as being inconsistent with the civil rights statutes under which CRD had traditionally operated and that they had sworn to uphold. At the National Highway Traffic Safety Administration, on the other hand, the situation was, as Golden points out, quite different. At that agency, disagreement with the policies they were asked to carry out was seldom voiced by "engineers, physical scientists, highway-safety professionals, or economists. These professionals seemed more comfortable providing research evidence and data, presenting both sides of an issue, and leaving decision-making to others" (Golden 1992: 56).

There can also be substantial variations within a single profession as to whether service in the bureaucracy presents a challenge to professional integrity. These variations sometimes seem to be related to the location in the executive apparatus where the professionals are plying their trade. Economists, for example, have been known to complain about the extent to which they are reduced to "cooking data" that will lend credibility to the president's economic forecasts or policies while serving in staff positions on the Council of Economic Advisers or in other locations in and around the White House. On the other hand, such economists generally regard employment at an independent agency like the Federal Reserve Board as providing an organizational setting in which they can perform with the objectivity characteristic of a truly professional outlook rather than as "spin doctors" for the administration in power.

The experience of economists suggests that the more the work of a professional group is carried on within the orbit of the White House, the more its members are likely to become involved in activities that will sorely test their professional commitment. Support for this conclusion can also be drawn from the experience of the Office of Telecommunications Policy during the Nixon Administration. This office, after its initial establishment by President Truman, languished out of sight as a small unit within the

Office of Emergency Planning during the tenure of succeeding presidents. Much to the dismay of the telecommunication professionals on its staff, the agency's activities were underfinanced and largely ignored by the White House.

However, during the Nixon Administration, the fortunes of this telecommunication unit turned sharply upward. President Nixon saw the agency as a useful weapon in his constant skirmishing with what he viewed as a hostile media, and he proceeded to make it a full-fledged White House staff organization, the Office of Telecommunications Policy (OTP). The professionals in OTP initially welcomed this organizational promotion, because it brought both an expanded budget and greater leverage in bargaining with other executive agencies. But their enthusiasm soon waned, as OTP became a pawn in White House efforts to curb the power of the media in American politics rather than, as they initially expected, a vehicle for launching new departures in telecommunication policy making in such areas as cable television (Rourke and Brown 1996).

Thus there are substantial variations between and within professions as to whether service in the bureaucracy brings a challenge to professional integrity. Such challenges have, however, arisen in enough settings and with sufficient frequency in recent years to suggest that they represent a significant problem in modern American bureaucracy. As noted earlier, confrontations of this kind spring in large part from the expanding demand for responsiveness to which executive agencies are now subject. This demand mirrors a more general conviction on the part of the public, which has been strongly reflected in recent presidential elections, that government institutions in the United States fail to respond adequately to the problems of ordinary people.

If the debate between Carl Friedrich and Herman Finer over the role of professionals in bureaucracy were being conducted today rather than a half-century ago, Friedrich would be well advised to avoid any appearance of advocating what might be regarded as a position of autonomous authority for professionals within bureaucracy. In the context of contemporary politics, it would be much more persuasive to emphasize the benefits the public itself derives from allowing professionals within bureaucracy the independence needed to speak out strongly against policies that violate the ethical or technical canons of their calling, because these canons often serve to advance and protect the public interest rather than being merely a means of protecting the prerogatives of professional groups themselves.

To many foreign observers, the widespread concern in the United States over the responsiveness of bureaucracy to political control may seem quite puzzling, because Americans seem to have less reason to fear the power of bureaucracy than the citizens of any other country. The arrangements that have been developed here for heightening the sensitivity of executive agencies to the concerns of the people they serve seem to leave few stones unturned. In recognition of the value of redundancy in the pursuit of its objectives (Landau 1969), government in the United States has multiplied the ways and means through which the public can affect bureaucratic decision making (Kaufman 1981; Saltzstein 1992). American bureaucracy is subject today not only to growing and extensive oversight from the president and Congress, as discussed earlier, but to direction and sometimes capture by the groups it is set up to serve as well as to constant and intrusive scrutiny from a freewheeling set of media organizations.

It can, of course, always be argued that not even these multiple channels for achieving responsiveness provide a sufficient counterweighting power of professional expertise in modern bureaucracy. In *Democracy and the Public Service* (1982), Frederick C. Mosher wrote a powerful indictment of the dangers such power can represent. As Mosher notes, professional groups can define what expertise really is in each specialized field of knowledge, and their vision in this respect can be quite limited. As a result, professionalism may produce parochialism on the part of administrators, an inability to see beyond the assumptions and priorities of a somewhat narrow field.

Although other writers have argued that professionalism actually enhances the responsiveness of bureaucracy to public control (Kearney and Sinha 1988; Streib 1992), Mosher's concern was that "a professionally dominated agency might deny "the general public the opportunity for democratic direction and decision" (1982: 232). A similar fear was evident in the movement for a "New Public Administration" that flourished in the 1970s. It sought to have administrators emphasize values such as social equity and citizen participation rather than professional expertise in their policy decisions (Frederickson 1980).

A decade earlier, professionalism had also been the target of widespread criticism during the so-called revolt of the clients in the New Left movement of the 1960s (Haug and Sussman 1969). It was then charged that many professionals working in bureaucratic settings were indifferent to the needs of the population they were expected to serve, in plain violation of the traditional understanding that a professional orientation will be characterized by altruism as well as expertise. Up until then, it had been widely believed that "the professional can be trusted to apply or transmit his [or her] knowledge with the client's interest rather than his [or her] private concerns at heart" (Haug and Sussman 1969: 154).

Another critique of professionalism turned the tables completely. It charged that, rather than ignoring their clients, professionals have too much control over them, trespassing into areas of client behavior outside

the scope of their own professional expertise. In response to these complaints, a variety of efforts were made to enable client groups to play a
greater role in professional decisions affecting their interests. Teachers in
public schools, physicians in government hospitals, and urban planners
were among the prominent professional groups singled out for attack
during this period.

Clearly, the extensive power that professionals may exert over policy
making can well be an object of legitimate concern in any democratic
society. It must also be remembered, however, that the health of American
democracy may be threatened not only when the voice of professionals is
too strong in designing or carrying out the goals of public policy but also
when it is too weak.

References

Balogh, Brian. (1991, Spring) "Reorganizing the Organizational Synthesis: Federal-Pro-
    fessional Relations in Modern America." *Studies in American Political Development,*
    5: 119-172.
Cigler, Beverly A. (1990, November-December) "Public Administration and the Paradox
    of Professionalism." *Public Administration Review,* 50: 637-653.
Durant, Robert F. (1992) *The Administrative Presidency Revisited: Public Lands, the BLM,
    and the Reagan Revolution.* Albany: State University of New York Press.
Finer, Herman. (1941, Summer) "Administrative Responsibility in Democratic Govern-
    ment." *Public Administration Review,* 1: 335-350.
Frederickson, H. George. (1980) *New Public Administration.* University, AL: University
    of Alabama Press.
Friedrich, Carl J. (1940) "Public Policy and the Nature of Administrative Responsibility."
    In Carl J. Friedrich and Edward S. Mason, eds., *Public Policy,* pp. 3-24. Cambridge,
    MA: Harvard University Press.
———. (1960) "The Dilemma of Administrative Responsibility." In Carl J. Friedrich,
    ed., *Responsibility (Nomos III),* pp. 189-202. New York: Liberal Arts Press.
Gaus, John M. (1936) "The Responsibility of Public Administration." In John M. Gaus,
    Leonard D. White, and Marshall E. Dimock, eds., *The Frontiers of Public Adminis-
    tration,* pp. 26-44. New York: Russell & Russell.
Golden, Marissa M. (1992, January) "Exit, Voice, Loyalty, and Neglect: Bureaucratic
    Responses to Presidential Control During the Reagan Administration." *Journal of
    Public Administration Research and Theory,* 2: 29-62.
Haug, Marie R., and Marvin B. Sussman. (1969, Fall) "Professional Autonomy and the
    Revolt of the Client." *Social Problems,* 17: 153-161.
Kaiser, Frederick M. (1992) "Congress and the Intelligence Community: Taking the Road
    Less Traveled." In Roger H. Davidson, ed., *The Postreform Congress,* pp. 279-300.
    New York: St. Martin's.
Kaufman, Herbert. (1981, January-February) "Fear of Bureaucracy: A Raging Pandemic."
    Public Administration Review, 41: 1-9.

Kearney, Richard C., and Chandan Sinha. (1988, January-February) "Professionalism and Bureaucratic Responsiveness: Conflict or Compatibility?" *Public Administration Review*, 48: 571-579.

Landau, Martin. (1969, July-August) "Redundancy, Rationality, and the Problem of Duplication and Overlap." *Public Administration Review*, 29: 346-358.

Larson, Magali Sarfatti. (1977) *Rise of Professionalism: A Sociological Analysis*. Berkeley: University of California Press.

Mezey, Susan Gluck. (1988) *No Longer Disabled: The Federal Courts and the Politics of Social Security Disability*. New York: Greenwood.

Mosher, Frederick. (1982) *Democracy and the Public Service*. New York: Oxford University Press.

Nathan, Richard P. (1975) *The Plot That Failed: Nixon and the Administrative Presidency*. New York: John Wiley.

Rourke, Francis E., and Roger G. Brown. (1996, Spring) "Presidents, Professionals, and Telecommunications Policy Making in the White House." *Presidential Studies Quarterly*, 26: 539-549.

Saltzstein, Grace Hall. (1992, January) "Bureaucratic Responsiveness: Conceptual Issues and Current Research." *Journal of Public Administration Research and Theory*, 2: 63-88.

Streib, Gregory. (1992, May) "Professional Skill and Support for Democratic Principles: The Case of Local Department Heads in Northern Illinois." *Administration & Society*, 24: 22-40.

Waterman, Richard W. (1989) *Presidential Influence and the Administrative State*. Knoxville: University of Tennessee Press.

The Pendleton Act of 1883 and Professionalism in the U.S. Public Service

Paul P. Van Riper

The basic thesis here is that the Pendleton Act of 1883 has been the prime cause of the heavily technical and professional orientation of the U.S. civil service throughout the past century. This characteristic has been strongly criticized in recent years, going as far back as the two Hoover Commissions of four decades ago.

Efforts to reform the U.S. civil service in a more generalist direction have continued, culminating in the Civil Service Reform Act of 1978. Nevertheless, the substantive nature of the *Pendleton system* remains largely intact. The discussion to follow is designed to make it clear why those who would reorient our current civil service system into one more attuned to general management in the British manner face such a difficult task.

Professionalism

The nature of the Pendleton Act of 1883 is relatively fixed, but the concept of *profession,* hence professional or professionalism, is not. For the purposes here, I have adopted the broad definition found in the discussion of "Professions" in the *Encyclopedia of the Social Sciences* for 1933. Here the British authors A. M. Carr-Saunders and P. A. Wilson (Vol. 12: 478) write, "We recognize a profession as a vocation founded upon prolonged and specialized intellectual training which enables a practical service to be rendered."

You may object and ask for more qualifiers such as "licensed," "self-governing," "involving a degree," and so on. In fact, in 1964 another Britisher, Geoffrey Millerson, examined the literature and found some 23 such elements used by various authors to define the idea of profession. I am not wandering into this quagmire but am remaining on the modestly high ground of the simple and clear reference point of 1933.

Bear in mind also that qualifiers are largely a twentieth-century creation. During much of the nineteenth, even the classic professions of the ministry, law, and medicine hardly met my limited definition. In the early 1870s, Harvey W. Wiley, the distinguished chief chemist of the U.S. Department of Agriculture (1883-1912) and primary author of the Food and Drug Act of 1906, received his M.D. based on a summer's internship with a country doctor friend in Kentucky, followed (not preceded) by eight months' work at the Indiana Medical College in Indianapolis. He obtained his B.S. cum laude from Harvard based on five months' work in residence plus an examination. Indeed, in all his life he had a grand total of barely sixty months of classroom instruction of any kind (Van Riper 1992: 31-33). Up into the 1930s, in my state of Indiana, one could become a member of the bar if two worthy citizens would attest that you were honest and of good standing in your community. Even today, one can be a minister who calls him- or herself a minister.

The Birth of the Pendleton Act

This short statute, its essential provisions reproduced in the next section, was only four pages long. Nevertheless, in discussing federal legislation between the Civil War and the turn of the century, the historians Charles and Mary Beard (1940: Vol. 2, p. 341) have characterized the Pendleton Act as the first of "two or three acts which need long detain the citizen concerned only with those manifestations of political power that produce essential readjustments in human relations." The others of this distinguished group are the law creating the Interstate Commerce Commission of 1887 and the Sherman Anti-Trust Act of 1890.

Like most important laws, there is a history behind it, only a small portion of which is appropriate here (see Van Riper 1958, chaps. 4 and 5). From the late 1860s, there had been serious discussions of civil service reform in Congress. Committee reports dealt with British, French, German, and even Turkish and Chinese civil service systems, and there were several legislative proposals. Then, unexpectedly, and probably stemming from Republican reverses in the midterm elections of 1870, Senator Lyman Trumbull of Illinois succeeded on the last day of the short session of 1870-1871 in getting a reform rider attached to a sundry appropriations bill, which became law on March 3, 1871. This law is very short, consisting of one long sentence. In its entirety it reads (*U.S. Statutes* 1871, 16:514):[1]

> Sec. 9. That the President of the United States be, and he is hereby, authorized to prescribe such rules and regulations for the admission of persons into the civil service of the United States as will best promote the efficiency thereof, and ascertain the fitness of each candidate in respect to age, health, character, knowledge, and ability for the branch of service into which he seeks to enter, and for this purpose the President is authorized to employ suitable persons to conduct said inquiries, to prescribe their duties, and to establish regulations for the conduct of persons who may receive appointments in the civil service.

This law is still on the books and has remained an important source of presidential authority over the civil service.

To the surprise of nearly everyone, President Grant then appointed a commission of seven, chaired by the distinguished reformer George William Curtis, to draw up regulations for a real reform. Congress even appropriated $25,000. During a four-year period, the group, later known as the Civil Service Commission, then developed most of the examining terminology and procedures used a decade later (and still in place) by a more permanent, bipartisan Civil Service Commission of three members that lasted almost a century. Curtis carried on for two years, followed by Dorman B. Eaton, a well-known New York lawyer who was one of the founders of the National Civil Service Reform League. Grant did not persist, however, in support of the new agency when his party stalwarts complained, and Congress refused any appropriations for 1874. The commission was not abolished; it just faded away and went home. But the controlling of entrance into the U.S. civil service by way of examinations had been field tested on a few thousand applicants for positions in Washington, D.C., and was clearly feasible.

Meanwhile, another critical obstacle to permanent legislation that might mandate rather than just permit reform had been cleared away. This was a question of the legality, of the constitutionality, of any limits on the appointing power of top political officials. The Grant Commission put this question—one also raised by many senators and members of Congress—to Attorney General A. T. Akerman shortly after it had been formed. Akerman replied that, although an appointing power could alone make an appointment, either Congress or the president, by authority of Congress, could prescribe reasonable qualifications to be ascertained by tests (*Op. Att. Gen.* 1871, 13:516). Akerman's opinion still stands as the basic guideline for appropriate limitations on the power to hire in the federal government.

Despite the demise of the *first* Civil Service Commission, the reform pot continued to bubble. In 1877, President Hayes commissioned Eaton to report on the British civil service. He went to England at his own expense that year and in 1879 published a widely circulated volume, *The Civil Service in Great Britain*. To make a long story short, this was followed by the assassination of Garfield in 1881 by Charles Guiteau, a disappointed office seeker. Behind the scene were the endemic scandals of the Reconstruction Era. In 1883, General N. M. Curtis, an employee of the Treasury Department as well as treasurer of the Republican State Committee of New York, was convicted of illegal political assessments and his conviction was upheld by the U.S. Supreme Court. Assessments were a mainstay of the patronage system. Moreover, in upholding the assessments law, the Supreme Court also implied the constitutionality of civil service reform (*Ex parte Curtis* 1882). Even more significant were Republican losses in the midterm elections of 1882 and the prospect of losing the presidency in 1884.

By the early 1880s, a group of reformers, including Eaton, had prepared a draft of proposed legislation. Senator George H. Pendleton, a Democrat from Ohio, surprised them by introducing his own legislation. Eaton persuaded the senator to accept the reformers' version. This, Eaton's draft, was accepted by the House with no debate, but the Senate devoted considerable verbiage to the measure—enough to fill more than 200 pages of the *Congressional Record*—and made several amendments, two of which were of elemental and critical significance.

It is not surprising that Eaton's draft would have imported the British civil service system, largely intact, into the United States. But the Senate would have none of it. The guts of the system, competitive examinations for appointment to office plus partisan neutrality for those so appointed, survived intact. But there was concern about whether the exams might be too theoretical, and an amendment specified that they should be "practical in their character" (see Sec. 2, SECOND, in the act). There was even more opposition to a provision to allow entrance into the service only "at the lowest grade." Senator Pendleton himself introduced the amendment deleting this limitation. The House concurred in the changes and the bill became law on January 16, 1883.

As I wrote on the occasion of the centennial of the Pendleton Act (Van Riper 1983: 13),

> These two changes were enough drastically to revise the nature of the new system to be established. By fewer than a dozen words, a closed career concept on the British style was turned into the open program oriented system we have had for a century. In passing the two amendments there is no evidence whatever that Congress had any specific theory in mind. We are pragmatic rather than theoretical people.

Almost unconsciously Congress created a system superbly in tune with a classless (in any European sense) society and well oriented to the technological revolution even then in progress. Specialists could be recruited and brought into the service at any time and at any level they were needed.

As put forth at the beginning of this chapter, the working of the Pendleton Act system has been responsible for both the great technical competence of the U.S. civil service and also its limitations in terms of experience in and comprehension of what is today described as "general management." Uniformly the emphasis of the act's recruitment and promotion system—further supported by adoption in 1923 of the fine screen type of position classification procedure—has been on specialty, occupation, and profession for more than a century.

The Pendleton Act

Here is the 1883 act in its entirety except for Section 4, a housekeeping provision soon modified. Its four pages are as easily read and as comprehensible as the 116 pages of the Civil Service Reform Act of 1978 are opaque and incomprehensible (*U.S. Statutes* 1883, 22: 403-407):

> CHAP. 27—An act to regulate and improve the civil service of the United States. Jan. 16, 1883.
>
> *Be it enacted by the Senate and House of Representatives of the United States of America in Congress assembled,* That the President is authorized to appoint, by and with the advice and consent of the Senate, three persons, not more than two of whom shall be adherents of the same party,

as Civil Service Commissioners, and said three commissioners shall constitute the United States Civil Service Commission. Said commissioners shall hold no other official place under the United States.

The President may remove any commissioner; and any vacancy in the position of commissioner shall be so filled by the President, by and with the advice and consent of the Senate, as to conform to said conditions for the first selection of commissioners.

The commissioners shall each receive a salary of three thousand five hundred dollars a year. And each of said commissioners shall be paid his necessary traveling expenses incurred in the discharge of his duty as a commissioner.

SEC. 2. That it shall be the duty of said commissioners:

FIRST. To aid the President, as he may request, in preparing suitable rules for carrying this act into effect, and when said rules shall have been promulgated it shall be the duty of all officers of the United States in the departments and offices to which any such rules may relate to aid, in all proper ways, in carrying said rules, and any modifications thereof, into effect.

SECOND. And, among other things, said rules shall provide and declare, as nearly as the conditions of good administration will warrant, as follows:

First, for open, competitive examinations for testing the fitness of applications for the public service now classified or to be classified hereunder. Such examinations shall be practical in their character, and so far as may be shall relate to those matters which will fairly test the relative capacity and fitness of the persons examined to discharge the duties of the service into which they seek to be appointed.

Second, that all the offices, places, and employments so arranged or to be arranged in classes shall be filled by selections according to grade from among those graded highest as the results of such competitive examinations.

Third, appointments to the public service aforesaid in the departments at Washington shall be apportioned among the several States and Territories and the District of Columbia upon the basis of population as ascertained at the last preceding census. Every application for an examination shall contain, among other things, a statement, under oath, setting forth his or her actual bona fide residence at the time of making the application, as well as how long he or she has been a resident of such place.

Fourth, that there shall be a period of probation before any absolute appointment or employment aforesaid.

Fifth, that no person in the public service is for that reason under any obligations to contribute to any political fund, or render any political service, and that he will not be removed or otherwise prejudiced for refusing to do so.

Sixth, that no person in said service has any right to use his official authority or influence to coerce the political action of any person or body.

Seventh, there shall be non-competitive examinations in all proper cases before the commission, when competent persons do not compete, after notice has been given of the existence of the vacancy, under such rules as may be prescribed by the commissioners as to the manner of giving notice.

Eighth, that notice shall be given in writing by the appointing power to said commission of the persons selected for appointment or employment from among those who have been examined, of the place of residence of such persons, of the rejection of any such persons after probation, of transfers, resignations, and removals, and of the date thereof, and a record of the same shall be kept by said commission. And any necessary exceptions from said eight fundamental provisions of the rules shall be set forth in connection with such rules, and the reasons therefore shall be stated in the annual reports of the commission.

THIRD. Said commission shall, subject to the rules that may be made by the President, make regulations for, and have control of, such examinations, and, through its members or the examiners, it shall supervise and preserve the records of the same; and said commission shall keep minutes of its own proceedings.

FOURTH. Said commission may make investigations concerning the facts, and may report upon all matters touching the enforcement and effects of said rules and regulations, and concerning the action of any examiners or board of examiners hereinafter provided for, and its own subordinates, and those in the public service, in respect to the execution of this act.

FIFTH. Said commission shall make an annual report to the President for transmission to Congress, showing its own action, the rules and regulations and the exceptions thereto in force, the practical effects thereof, and any suggestions it may approve for the more effectual accomplishment of the purposes of this act.

SEC. 3. That said commission is authorized to employ a chief examiner, a part of whose duty it shall be, under its direction, to act with the examining boards, so far as practicable, whether at Washington or elsewhere, and to secure accuracy, uniformity, and justice in all their proceedings, which shall be at all times open to him. The chief examiner shall be entitled to receive a salary at the rate of three thousand dollars a year, and he shall be paid his necessary traveling expenses incurred in the discharge of his duty. The commission shall have a secretary, to be appointed by the President, who shall receive a salary of one thousand six hundred dollars per annum. It may, when necessary, employ a stenographer, and a messenger, who shall be paid, when employed, the former at the rate of one thousand six hundred dollars a year, and the latter at the rate of six hundred dollars a year. The commission shall, at Washington, and in one or more places in each State and Territory where examinations are to take place, designate and select a suitable number of persons, not less than three, in the official service of the United States, residing in said State or Territory, after consulting the head of the department or office in which such persons serve, to be members of boards of examiners, and may at any time substitute any other person in said service living in such State or Territory in the place of any one so selected. Such boards of examiners shall be so located as to make it reasonably convenient and inexpensive for applicants to attend before them; and where there are persons to be examined in any State or Territory, examinations shall be held therein at least twice in each year. It shall be the duty of the collector, postmaster, and other officers of the United States, at any place outside of the District of Columbia where examinations are directed by the President or by said board to be held, to allow the reasonable use of the public buildings for holding such examinations, and in all proper ways to facilitate the same.

SEC. 4. (Omitted)

SEC. 5. That any said commissioner, examiner, copyist, or messenger, or any person in the public service who shall willfully and corruptly by himself or in co-operation with one or more other persons, defeat, deceive, or obstruct any person in respect of his or her right of examinations according to any such rules or regulations, or who shall willfully, corruptly, and falsely mark, grade, estimate, or report upon the examination or proper standing of any person examined hereunder, or aid in so doing, or who shall willfully and corruptly make any false representations concerning the same or concerning the person examined, or who shall willfully and corruptly furnish to any person any special or secret information for the purpose of either improving or insuring the prospects or chances of any person so examined, or to be examined, being appointed, employed, or promoted, shall for each such offense be deemed guilty of a misdemeanor, and upon conviction thereof, shall be punished by a fine of not less than one hundred dollars, nor more than one thousand dollars, or by imprisonment not less than 10 days, nor more than one year, or by both such fine and imprisonment.

SEC. 6. That within sixty days after the passage of this act it shall be the duty of the Secretary of the Treasury, in as near conformity as may be to the classification of certain clerks now existing under the one hundred and sixty-third section of the Revised Statutes, to arrange in classes the several clerks and persons employed by the collector, naval officer, surveyor, and appraisers, or either of them or being in the public service, at their respective offices in each customs district where the whole number of said clerks and persons shall be all together as many as fifty. And thereafter, from time to time on the direction of the President, said Secretary shall make the like classification or arrangement of clerks and persons so employed, in connection with any said office or offices, in any other customs district. And, upon like request, and for the purposes of this act, said Secretary shall arrange in one or more of said classes, or of existing classes, any other clerks, agents, or persons employed under his department in any said district not now classified; and every such arrangement and classification upon being made shall be reported to the President.

Second. Within any sixty days it shall be the duty of the Postmaster-General, in general conformity to said one hundred and sixty-third section, to separately arrange in classes the several clerks and persons employed, or in the public service, at each post-office or under any postmaster of the United States, where the whole number of said clerks and persons shall together amount to as many as fifty. And thereafter, from time to time, on the direction of the President, it shall be the duty of the Postmaster-General to arrange in like classes the clerks and persons so employed in the postal service in connection with any other post office; and every such arrangement and classification upon being made shall be reported to the President.

Third. That from time to time said Secretary, the Postmaster-General, and each of the heads of departments mentioned in the one hundred and fifty-eighth section of the Revised Statutes, and each head of an office, shall, on the direction of the President, and for facilitating the execution of this act, respectively revise any then existing classification or arrangement of those in their respective departments and offices, and shall, for the purposes of the examination herein provided for, include in one or more of such classes, so far as practicable, subordinate places, clerks, and officers in the public service pertaining to their respective departments not before classified for examination.

SEC. 7. That after the expiration of six months from the passage of this act no officer or clerk shall be appointed, and no person shall be employed to enter or be promoted in either of the said classes now existing, or that may be arranged hereunder pursuant to said rules, until he has passed an examination, or is shown to be specially exempted from such examination in conformity herewith. But nothing herein contained shall be construed to take from those honorably discharged from the military or naval service any preference conferred by the seventeen hundred and fifty-fourth section of the Revised Statutes, nor to take from the President any authority not inconsistent with this act conferred by the seventeen hundred and fifty-third section of said statutes; nor shall any officer not in the executive branch of the government, or any person merely employed as a laborer or workman, be required to be classified hereunder; nor, unless by direction of the Senate, shall any person who has been nominated for confirmation by the Senate be required to be classified or to pass an examination.

SEC. 8. That no person habitually using intoxicating beverages to excess shall be appointed to, or retained in, any office, appointment, or employment to which the provisions of this act are applicable.

SEC. 9. That whenever there are already two or more in the public service in the grades covered by this act, no other member of such family shall be eligible to appointment to any of said grades.

SEC. 10. That no recommendation of any person who shall apply for office or place under the provisions of this act which may be given by any Senator or member of the House of Representatives, except as to the character or residence of the applicant, shall be received or considered by any person concerned in making any examination or appointment under this act.

SEC. 11. That no Senator, or Representative, or Territorial Delegate of the Congress, or Senator, Representative, or Delegate elect, or any officer or employee of either of said houses, and no executive, judicial, military, or naval officer of the United States, and no clerk or employee of any department, branch or bureau of the executive, judicial, or military or naval service of the United States, shall, directly or indirectly, solicit or receive, or be in any manner concerned in soliciting or receiving any assessment, subscription, or contribution for any political purpose whatever, from any officer, clerk, or employee of the United States, or any department, branch, or bureau thereof, or from any person receiving any salary or compensation from moneys derived from the Treasury of the United States.

SEC. 12. That no person shall, in any room or building occupied in the discharge of official duties by any officer or employee of the United States mentioned in this act, or in any navy-yard, fort, or arsenal, solicit in any manner whatever, or receive any contribution of money or any other thing of value for any political purpose whatever.

SEC. 13. No officer or employee of the United States mentioned in this act shall discharge, or promote, or degrade, or in manner change the official rank or compensation of any other officer or employee, or promise or threaten so to do, for giving or withholding or neglecting to make any contribution of money or other valuable thing for any political purpose.

SEC. 14. That no officer, clerk, or other person in the service of the United States shall, directly or indirectly, give or hand over to any other officer, clerk or person in the service of the United States, or to any Senator or Member of the House of Representatives, or Territorial Delegate, any money or other valuable thing on account of or to be applied to the promotion of any political object whatever.

SEC. 15. That any person who shall be guilty of violating any provision of the four foregoing sections shall be deemed guilty of a misdemeanor, and shall, on conviction thereof, be punished by a fine not exceeding five thousand dollars, or by imprisonment for a term not exceeding three years, or by such fine and imprisonment both, in the discretion of the court.

Approved, January sixteenth, 1883.

The essentials of the act of 1883 have been reproduced in full because in recent years there have appeared a number of misconceptions about it, leading one to believe that few current social scientists have ever read the act. The most common error is to attribute to it the development of the idea of political neutrality. I can be accused of quibbling, but I do not know what the meaning of *political* neutrality could mean. All the act did was to require that civil servants occupying competitive positions be *partisanly* neutral: They could not play a partisan role and they were not to be fired for partisan reasons.

The next most common error is to blame the Pendleton Act for giving career civil servants too much tenure protection against removal, and to hold the act responsible for modern difficulties with removals. The authors will be nameless but I have found such allegations in a recent book on no less than civil service law and in a recent addendum to the history of the U.S. civil service. The Pendleton Act provided no removal protection whatever except that career civil servants were not to be removed for partisan reasons. Even this protection was not buttressed by any civil or criminal penalty, and there was little the new Civil Service Commission could do for years other than report improper removals. For decades after 1893, there was still no removal protection for career civil servants. In the case of *Myers v. United States* (1926), the Supreme Court, through an opinion written by former President Taft as chief justice, suggested that there might be no way constitutionally to protect the tenure of any civil servant. It is said that the Pendleton Act "closed the front door" of entrance into the civil service, but no important efforts to "close the back door" of removal were successful until after World War II, and none of these derived in any way from the act of 1883.

It is also not well understood that the statute did not set up a complete personnel system in a modern sense. Indeed, there were none such in the United States at the time, public or private. In fact, the word *personnel* did not come into common usage until just before World War I. The civil service reformers were interested in bringing the spoils system to an end, a goal that their new statute was well designed to further. The development of personnel management in government, in any full sense of the function, had to wait until 1925 when the first federal departmental personnel office was created in the Department of Agriculture. Not until 1938 were all federal agencies required to have personnel offices by an executive order of Franklin D. Roosevelt.

Finally, the new statute was primarily permissive in nature, much like that of 1871. The 1883 law applied the new examination and appointment system only to the clerical offices in Washington, D.C., and to post offices employing 50 persons or more—in all perhaps 10% of a civil service of 125,000 to 140,000 persons. The president was authorized to expand the system or not, as he saw fit. As most presidents did not wish to be served by incompetents, most expanded the competitive offices by "covering in" more and more offices from time to time. By the end of Theodore Roosevelt's administration, more than 50% of the offices came under the *merit system,* a term that had come by then to characterize the Pendleton Act's procedures and thrust. Under Herbert Hoover, the figure rose to 80%, and under Franklin D. Roosevelt, after some backsliding, to the present figure of nearly 95%. Although the Civil Service Reform Act of 1978 superseded the Pendleton Act, and introduced a number of personnel innovations, the act of 1978 left the Pendleton system of examination and appointment essentially untouched.

The Pendleton System

The new job-oriented placement system of the Pendleton Act gradually became the norm rather than the exception. Can this system be described more precisely? I have made several efforts to do so, for the public personnel system of nearly all our governments in the United States—federal, state, and local—is unique in the world.[2] That is, the attraction and power of the Pendleton system have been such as to dominate not only federal personnel administration but also that of practically every U.S. state and local jurisdiction as well.

For analytical as well as descriptive purposes, I offer here a simplified chart (see Table 8.1), which I have used in my public personnel classes for the last 20 years or so, that appears here in public for the first time. Whenever possible, I like to be comparative, and this chart presents in a contrasting format the essential characteristics of our U.S. Pendleton system (designated an open, program staffing system) compared with the system of the British, of almost all other foreign governments, and of our uniformed military services and our foreign service (designated a closed, career staffing system).

Included in Table 8.1 are a few brief explanatory notes. The title of the table is meant to imply that fundamentally only two types of personnel merit systems exist, public or private. However, characteristics of the two types may be substantially intermixed, producing a third type. Most public systems are fairly pure types, while most business systems are mixed.

In comparing the systems, note that the advantages of one are the disadvantages of the other. For example, as the closed systems start with young people, such systems lack specialists. These systems are always engaged in enormous amounts of training. Open systems being staffed with specialists are traditionally tightfisted with money for training. Such systems can quickly respond to new technological developments, simply by hiring other specialists from outside the system. Almost by definition the

TABLE 8.1 A Typology of Personnel Systems

	Closed, Career Staffing	*Open, Program Staffing*
Career concepts	Life career in system Generalist beginning Rank in person whatever the job	Occupational career Specialist beginning Rank comes from the job
Classification system	Big pigeon holes, several large subservices Scientific, professional not eligible for general management posts No lateral entry, easy movement within big pigeon holes	Small pigeon holes but all in one or two big services Scientists and professionals eligible for general management posts Lateral entry, difficult to move outside original occupation
Entrance	Keyed to educational system (British and most officer systems) Enter when young Aptitude, arts examinations (obtain specialty in service, hence much training in service)	Keyed to achievement via education or experience, usually both Can enter at any age, any level Practical examinations of mastery of some occupational specialty, hence little training in service
Movement	Initiative with the government Deliberate selection out	Initiative with the person Peter principle, can stay indefinitely
Contraction and expansion	Handled like military—regulars and reserves (in contractions regulars stay, reserves go)	All on same basis—in RIFs probationers go first, career-conditionals next (both at whatever level they are)

career system produces competent generalists (general officers), for individuals can easily be moved around in the system and gain wide experience. The open system has great difficulty producing generalists; they don't come naturally as a result of the system. Rigid classification systems make it difficult to move personnel about and give them broad experience, and training is often too little, and too late. A federal training establishment was set up barely 30 years ago, and it is still a pale shadow of its military counterparts.

What proportion of federal civil servants can be reasonably described as professional, scientific, technical, specialist, and the like? If one goes by census categories, excluding blue-collar workers, the proportion is about 40%. If one includes all General Schedule employees above GS-10, then the figure is over 50%. In any event, the federal civil service has a considerably higher proportion of specialists than the U.S. workforce at large. This is in part because much of the federal civil service functions as a kind of general staff to all U.S. governments. Only in the U.S. Postal Service, the Departments of State and Defense, and a few lesser agencies does civil federal government *do* most of the work from top to bottom.

As a consequence of this specialist orientation stemming from the Pendleton system, what is bureaucratic life like in most federal agencies? This is perhaps best described in Hugo Heclo's *Government of Strangers.*[3] One of the most prominent consequences is the professional network phenomenon. Another is a kind of fractionalized ethos; loyalties are to professions and departments rather than to *the government.* It is a bit like the famous saying about French government: "Everything is centralized in Paris and nothing is centralized in Paris!"

There is considerable literature that is highly critical of the Pendleton system. The original work that started it all is probably Frederick C. Mosher's *Democracy and the Public Service,* published in 1968.[4] This is still one of the best analyses. For others, see the panel report of the National Academy of Public Administration, titled *Revitalizing Federal Management* (1983: chap. 5), the report of the Volker Commission, and much of the burgeoning literature on bureaucracy.

The main practical consequence of these criticisms has been the Civil Service Reform Act of 1978. From the point of view of this chapter, the main innovations were merit pay and the Senior Executive Service (SES), especially the latter, which represented an effort to develop a more unified—in terms of both experience and ethos—higher civil service at the former supergrades level. It was hoped this might help counteract the traditional separatist tendencies of the service.

What has in fact happened? The assessment most relevant here is one expressed by James E. Colvard, top civilian personnel officer in the Navy, who became Deputy Director of OPM under Constance Horner, in a May 1990 letter to me:[5]

> The SES has not lived up to expectations because the concept of the generalist manager is contrary to how the federal government really develops and uses managers. The cultures of individual agencies strongly

mitigate against mobility and the kind of development processes required to create, over time, the general managers envisioned for SES. With time the SES can become more effective. OPM has rejuvenated the executive manpower section. . . . As more agencies develop intra-agency mobility programs the federal government will eventually be able to generate an inter-agency program that works. I think it is the best way to develop executives, but we are about 10 years away from having the cultural understanding to make it work.

Conclusion

Can the Pendleton system be characterized more positively? From an examination of the congressional debate on the act, it is clear that the statute was not the product of any precise theoretical thrust or plan. Rather, members of Congress seemed to sense that a closed, career approach on the British model was not appropriate for a highly mobile society where capacity and experience ranked higher than formal degrees. Practical exams and lateral entry allowed any person qualified to enter the service and show what he or she could do. This, for example, allowed women and blacks to enter the U.S. public service in large numbers long before there were equivalent opportunities in much of private industry.

As I concluded in an essay celebrating the centennial of the Pendleton Act: "In recent years we have been critical of our federal bureaucracy, but it is the Pendleton Act which has kept us from forming any kind of closed bureaucratic system on the European or Oriental models. Thanks to this short statute, we do not yet know what bureaucracy really can be" (Van Riper 1983: 14).

Notes

1. This is referred to in the Pendleton Act as Sec. 1783, *Revised Statutes.*

2. For my various efforts to describe the Pendleton system, see the references under my name, below, especially Van Riper (1962) and the "Civil Service" entry in a late 1960s edition of the *Encyclopedia Americana.* See also Truman Benedict and others (1961).

3. (1977). See here and there, but especially chap. 4. See also Wilson (1989: 139-146) on the federal personnel system, and see his indexed pages under "Professionalism."

4. See especially chap. 4, "The Professional State," and chap. 5, "Three Systems of Merit."

5. See also his guest editorial in Colvard (1988), a first-rate critique.

References

Beard, C. A., and M. R. Beard. (1940) *Rise of American Civilization,* 2 vols., in 1 vol. edition. New York: Macmillan.

Benedict, Truman, and others. (1961) *Comparing Career Civil Service Systems: A Preliminary Study,* Personnel Report No. 621. Chicago: Public Personnel Association.

Colvard, James E. (1988) "Reflections on the Personnel Business." *Bureaucrat,* 7: 3-5.

Encyclopedia of the Social Sciences. (1933) New York: Macmillan.

Ex parte Curtis. (1882) 106 *U.S.* 371.

Heclo, Hugh. (1977) *A Government of Strangers.* Washington, DC: Brookings Institution.

Millerson, Geoffrey. (1964) *The Qualifying Associations.* London: Routledge and Paul.

Mosher, Frederick C. (1968) *Democracy and the Public Service.* New York: Oxford University Press.

Myers v. United States. (1926) 272 *U.S.* 52.

National Academy of Public Administration. (1982) "New Concepts for Personnel Management." Chap. 5 in *Revitalizing Federal Management.* Washington, DC: Author.

Van Riper, Paul P. (1958) *History of the United States Civil Service.* Evanston, IL: Harper & Row.

———. (1962) "The Tap Roots of American Public Personnel Management." *Personnel Administration,* 25: 12-16, 32.

———. (1983) "The Pendleton Act: A Centennial Eulogy." *American Review of Public Administration,* 17: 13.

——— . (1992) "Harvey W. Wiley: Pioneering Consumer Advocate." In T. L. Cooper and N. D. Wright, eds., *Exemplary Public Administrators.* San Francisco: Jossey-Bass.

Wilson, James Q. (1989) *Bureaucracy.* New York: Basic Books.

Transients and Careerists
in Latin America

Lawrence S. Graham

In the transitions literature and discussions related to democratic consolidation, a debate has emerged over the extent to which parliamentary systems are more conducive to the survival of democracy than presidential systems.[1] Rarely, however, has this debate engaged questions of institutional design beyond giving attention to presidents and parliaments. This is not to say that these issues have not been raised at meetings on the topic, only that they have not made it into print in books subsequently published. The case in point is the Linz and Valenzuela volume. There the editors acknowledge the outstanding contribution made by Fred Riggs at the May 1989 Georgetown symposium by introducing consideration of the U.S. case into these discussions, but they state that space considerations did not make it possible to include his paper in the final volume (Linz and Valenzuela 1994: xiii).

The problem with the exclusion of the U.S. case from the debate over presidentialism and parliamentarism is that it removes significant institu-

212

tional considerations. For, among presidential systems, not only is the United States the only instance where there has not been at least one coup designed to overthrow the system, it is also the most institutionalized. Coupled with exclusion of the U.S. case, which is frequent in the comparative politics literature, has been the movement of most public administration specialists at the cutting edge of their field into separate departments of public administration and policy schools, where policy issues such as civil service reform, merit versus partisan public personnel appointments, and size of the public service rarely, if ever, enter the debate over the consolidation of democratic regimes. Seen in the context of the debate over presidential and parliamentary constitutional design, these two developments have converged in the failure to consider the crucial role that public bureaucracy has played in the consolidation and survival of presidentialism in the United States when this form of government has had such a poor track record elsewhere.

Yet, central to this discussion is the issue of transients and careerists in the civil service and whether or not presidential and parliamentary systems can establish systems of governance through which policies elaborated by political leaders can be implemented effectively and efficiently. Conventional wisdom has long argued that a nonpartisan civil service is an essential component in consolidated democratic systems, and that transients, in the form of political appointees, should be concentrated in relatively small numbers at the senior level where partisans can ensure civil service compliance with the policies established by elected governments.

Latin American experience with democratic rule, presidentialism, and civil service reform is especially relevant to such discussions. There are three reasons that this is the case: the frequency with which the attempt to establish democratic regimes has led to breakdowns throughout the region, the long-term institutional commitment of these countries to presidentialism despite efforts to the contrary, and the failure of previous attempts at civil service reform to establish nonpartisan civil services.

In introducing consideration of public bureaucracy into discussions of democratization and the survival of democratic regimes, the argument developed here is that, if we are to examine the relationship between presidents and parliaments with their civil services, the question of governance—enhancing the capacity of elected governments to implement economic and social policy effectively—must be included. Although institutional choices regarding presidential and parliamentary regimes do constitute an important variable in determining the prospects for democratic consolidation, what has been missing from this debate is attention to the public bureaucracies through which economic and social policies linked to democratic survival must be implemented. If the whole state, then, is to be incorporated into this debate over presidential and parliamentary institutions, clarifying the issues and the choices to be made by policymakers in considering civil service reform and reductions in force can contribute to clarification of those factors that influence regime survival as opposed to regime breakdown.

The Record to Date
in Europe and Latin America

The most significant body of experience relevant to the problem of constituting viable democratic governments is to be found in the countries undergoing democratic transitions in Southern Europe during the 1970s, in South America during the 1980s, and in Eastern Europe during the 1990s. In these contexts, two major institutional concerns have emerged: how to impose constraints on executive power, so as to minimize bureaucratic excesses, and how to decentralize decision making, to ensure adequate representation of and responsiveness to regional and local interests. In the former, the emphasis has fallen on strengthening the role of legislatures either through the design of parliamentary systems in a limited number of cases (Spain, Greece, the Czech Republic, and Hungary), the creation of premier-presidential systems (Portugal, Poland, Romania, Bulgaria, Albania, and the successor states of the former Soviet Union and Yugoslavia), or the enhancement of legislative powers in reconstituted presidential systems (the Latin American cases).[2] In the latter, the responses have taken the form of guaranteeing local autonomy and increasing the power of subnational authorities. In those cases where pressures for regional autonomy have been the greatest, either regional autonomy statutes have been passed (namely, Spain and Portugal) or federalism has been revitalized (in the case of Brazil).

Despite these advances in designing institutional arrangements to reinforce democracy, policymakers in these countries have sidelined governance questions and largely ignored questions of civil service reform as a relevant issue in democratic consolidation. Why this is the case warrants attention. In the absence of a more general literature to draw upon, my own preliminary conclusion—based on an in-depth examination of democratic consolidation in one country (1980s Portugal) and the breakdown of democracy in another (1960s Brazil)—is that mass mobilization politics and the emergence of political parties incorporating expanded electorates create enormous pressures for patronage politics (Graham 1968, chaps. 7-9, and Graham 1993). These developments, in turn, have undercut attempts at civil service reform—especially efforts to hold down the number of public employees and to introduce merit criteria.

Advocates of presidentialism have defended the view that fragile new democracies, faced with fragmented and weak political parties, can best supersede stalemated legislatures and blocked social forces through the development of a strong executive, accountable to a national electorate and independent of legislative constraints. These arguments, present originally in the debates over how best to supersede the weaknesses of the Fourth Republic in France, surfaced in Portugal in the mid-1970s. In writing a new constitution, members of the constituent assembly wished to ensure the survival of democracy but were cognizant of the strength of support for presidentialism as a constant factor in Portuguese politics since the abolition of monarchy in 1910. In Poland, these arguments reappeared in the early 1990s as the Solidarity Movement disintegrated and a plethora of small parties emerged, none of which has had the capacity to create a majority coalition in the Polish Sejm. In both cases, where the identification of democratic rule with parliamentary traditions has been strong, the outcome has been semipresidentialism. But, whereas earlier experiments in Europe—namely, the Italian Republic—have produced presidential institutions that are weak in comparison with legislatures, in the new democracies of the 1970s and 1980s the separation of powers, divided government, and concepts of checks and balances have taken on new life as elected officials have sought to consolidate democratic rule and as strong presidents frequently have come to be seen as a counterbalance to stalemated legislatures.

In South America, transitions to democracy usually have been associated with the reaffirmation of presidentialism. This is not to say that advocacy of parliamentarism has not arisen. On the contrary, critics of presidential rule have emerged as awareness of the fragility of these countries' new democratic accords has increased. Conscious of past abuses of executive power throughout Latin America, especially under authoritarian rule, these people have advocated strengthening the power of legislatures and imposing constraints on executive authority by making heads of government more accountable to national congresses through requirements of majority support and the revival of such controls as interpolation (in Peru) and impeachment (in Brazil and Venezuela). In Chile, advocacy of parliamentarism, as the institutional design most conducive to the survival of democracy over the long term, has centered on analysis of the breakdown of democratic rule during the Allende government, new interest in the country's past history of strong legislative institutions, and the desire to remove as quickly as possible the constitutional constraints written into the country's new constitution by Pinochet and his supporters to secure continuing representation and voice in the new regime. In Brazil, the ineffectiveness of the country's first civilian president in 20 years (Sarney), coupled with the scandals surrounding the selection of his successor (Collor de Mello), and the inability of these presidents to work with the Congress have contributed to the revival of interest in parliamentarism. Still more interesting has been the first use ever of impeachment powers in Latin America, in the resignation not only of Collor de Mello but also of Carlos Andrés Perez (in Venezuela) in 1993.

In Brazil and Chile, reconsideration of the parliamentary option surfaced during the transition to democracy. But, despite advocacy of parliamentary solutions, especially by academics, both countries have remained presidentialist. In Brazil, the debate advanced the furthest, first in discussions over the content of the new constitution and later in a national referendum over regime type, in which citizens voted for presidential, parliamentarian, and monarchist options. But, when the time came to decide, legislators opted to exclude questions of system change from the prolonged discussions that followed on the specific provisions to be incorporated into the 1988 constitution, and voters later indicated their overwhelming preference for presidentialism in the April 1993 national referendum on the form of government.

Thus, whereas semipresidentialist solutions appear to be on the upswing in the European periphery, in South America politicians interested in breaking the past cycle of democratic breakdowns and the reversion to military rule have centered their attention on strengthening legislative powers and subsystem autonomy at the expense of the executive. This is especially true in those cases where there were instances of human rights violations, a record of unrestrained police action, and previous experience with the lack of accountability of military and civilian bureaucrats for actions taken during authoritarian rule.

Public Bureaucracies and the State in Transitions

Despite the primacy given to these larger institutional questions, how bureaucrats—especially those at the senior level—react to regime change constitutes an equally critical variable in regime consolidation. Seen from the vantage point of the transitions literature, Fred Riggs's chapter in this book, "Coups and Crashes: Lessons for Public Administration," stands alone in calling attention to the importance of this dimension in democratic consolidations. Correctly, at least from the standpoint of the cases I have been working with (Chile and Brazil in South America, Portugal and Poland in Europe, and Angola and Mozambique in sub-Saharan Africa), Riggs distinguishes between two different reactions on the part of bureaucrats in moments of major change and transition.

He writes:

> When bureaucrats feel pushed to the wall and see no solutions to their problems within the confines of constitutional rules and customary norms they may, in desperation, choose one of two contradictory options. The first involves a suspension of the rules and the imposition of bureaucratic domination—as commonly seen in contemporary *coups d'état*. The alternative reaction involves surrender, the abandonment of efforts to cope with current administrative problems, a choice that can contribute to regime *crashes*. I shall call the first *bureaucratic excesses* and the second *bureaucratic fatigue*. (Riggs, this volume)

The current concern with transitions to democratic rule and the breakdown of authoritarianism of the right as well as of the left has deflected attention from serious consideration of these dimensions of politics and policy. Although "the abandonment of efforts to cope with current administrative problems" is seen by many to be a consequence of single-party communist rule and is usually associated with the events of 1989, it is more appropriately a consequence of prolonged, centralized authoritarian rule in which major policy decisions are made within the regime or party and later ratified in society at large through public affirmation. Although this pattern certainly has been present in Poland, removal of its ideological content makes it clear that such patterns are equally characteristic of Portugal in the late 1970s (following the breakdown of its authoritarian New State), of Brazil in the late 1980s (in its protracted transition from authoritarian, military-dominated rule), and of Angola and Mozambique (in their rejection of Portuguese colonialism and the exit of nearly all the Europeans staffing the colonial service). In each of these cases, bureaucratic paralysis has followed immediately after the breakdown of institutionalized authoritarian rule in which civilian and military officials had "suspended the prior rules and imposed bureaucratic domination." Although the imposition of bureaucratic rule in Poland, despite the opposition of civil society, was a function of Soviet domination coupled with single-party communist rule, in the other cases—Portugal, Brazil, Chile, Angola, and Mozambique—the mechanisms of externally imposed, centralized bureaucratic rule and the presence of bureaucratic excesses were tied to conservative regimes, strongly anticommunist in their rhetoric and antidemocratic in their actions. In all six, however, the consolidation of bureaucratic authority under the governments in power before the transition to democracy was also linked to the forging of successful alliances between civilian and military officials. What is even more interesting in this range of cases is what occurred once their regimes were opened up. In Chile alone—in this range of cases—was there a sufficiently strong state apparatus not to encounter an instance of bureaucratic fatigue, once economic and political liberalization ensued.

The point of this reference to six very different country cases, with equally different mixes of regimes, is to confirm the importance of the bureaucratic variable as a factor influencing political outcomes, independently of structural choices linked to presidential or parliamentary systems and to authoritarian or democratic rule. In five of these cases, economic and political liberalization and the opening up of politics produced protracted transitions extending across years, if not decades. And in two of them—Angola and Mozambique—it is still premature to discuss democratization. To these considerations must be added the disintegration of several very different multinational states since 1990—namely, the Soviet Union, Yugoslavia, and Czechoslovakia—where bureaucratic paralysis not only hastened the demise of authoritarianism but contributed to their breakup. In each of these cases, the problem of weak national governments must be joined with those of paralyzed public bureaucracies unable to implement economic and social reforms. Certainly the older literature on state and nation building emphasized these institutional aspects. But somehow in the emphasis on political culture and socialization, the institutional component—the creation and maintenance of governmental institutions with the capacity to act effectively in the making and implementation of economic and social policy—has dropped out of discourse in the comparative politics literature.

South American Experience
With Bureaucratic Excesses and Fatigue

Three South American cases are especially relevant to this discussion: Brazil, Argentina, and Chile. Brazil is instructive because it is the sole Latin American case with meaningful experience with federalism and presidentialism (which Riggs has argued in an earlier paper is one of the variables present in explaining the success of American presidentialism as opposed to regime breakdown elsewhere; Riggs 1991: 22-23). Brazil also has experienced both bureaucratic excesses, derived from the development of coherent and effective military and civilian bureaucracies during its 20 years of authoritarian rule, and bureaucratic fatigue, in the economic and social crisis that has accompanied its transition back to democracy. Argentina provides contrasting case material of a paralyzed and "blocked" civil service, traumatized by 50 years of repeated regime breakdown and alternation between civilian and military rule. The failure of the Alfonsín administration to implement economic and social policy thus falls within a pattern common to previous Argentine regimes in which bureaucratic lethargy has characterized all governments, whether civilian or military. Chile's experience is relevant because of the ability of policymakers both to enact meaningful civil service reform and to make major structural adjustments in the state apparatus through the implementation of wide-scale privatization and reductions in force, while enhancing the professionalization of the civil service, without becoming identified exclusively with the authoritarian regime under which these changes were inaugurated.

Brazil. Despite the shift of power from the states to the federal government and the concentration of power in the presidency after 1930, Brazil has remained a federal republic. Furthermore, since 1930 it has moved through two distinct cycles of decentralization, notably the establishment of a limited democracy under the 1946 constitution (which remained in effect until a military coup in 1964), and, more recently, the return to democracy in 1985, accompanied once again by the attempt to empower state and local governments (this time under a new constitution promulgated in 1988; Lewandowski 1990: 26-30). The relevance of these developments is that, regardless of assertions to the contrary in the established literature limited to Brazilian experience, the concentration of power in the presidency during these two periods of democratic rule was no greater than that which has taken place in the United States (Graham 1990: 73-77). Nevertheless, despite the fact that in Brazil the combination of presidentialism and federalism reduced the weight of the presidency during these two eras (1946-1964, 1985-present) and these periods coincide with more independent legislatures, this particular institutional combination was not sufficient to head off regime collapse and military intervention in 1964.

In assessing the causes of democratic breakdown in 1964 and the current institutional stalemate and crisis, three of the other factors introduced by Riggs, in his paper on presidentialism, have greater explanatory power: the fluidity of the party system, coupled with party fragmentation and a multiplicity of parties; the rapid turnover of legislators as well as the absence of a seniority system among members of congress and of a strong committee system within congress; and the lack of a nonpartisan civil service below levels where political oversight authority is needed (Riggs 1991: 26-27, and Riggs this volume). Given that both Baaklini and Mainwaring have commented amply on the weaknesses of the Brazilian legislature, as well as the specific points mentioned by Riggs on parties and congress and how this is linked to the failure to consolidate a democratic regime, let me focus briefly on the absence of a nonpartisan civil service as an equally important contributing factor in regime breakdown (Baaklini 1989; Mainwaring 1990). The only period during which Brazil has had a nonpartisan civil service coincides with the first of its two periods of authoritarian rule, the New State era under the presidency of Getulio Vargas, 1937-1945. The subsequent era, one of limited democracy (1946-1964), was characterized by political party patronage coupled with personalism in determining many civil service appointments and extensive inroads into the merit system set up under the auspices of a centralized public personnel office, the Administrative Department for the Public Service, during the Vargas era.

Under bureaucratic-authoritarian rule (1964-1985), serious but unsuccessful attempts were made once again at global civil service reform. But, although political party patronage was ended once the old party system was abolished, it was never possible to reintroduce a full-fledged merit system, and patronage through personalism continued in major sectors. Ultimately, the need to have qualified technical personnel in key program areas was resolved by confining merit appointments to those ministries and agencies central to financial and economic management, planning, and security affairs and by bypassing the rest of the state apparatus. Consequently, when the transition back to democracy was initiated in 1985, what the new government encountered was a mixed system, staffed by competent technocrats in the aforementioned areas, designated as priority ones by the previous regime, and a multitude of agencies and ministries staffed according to nonmerit criteria. Since 1985, little or no attention has been given to the question of civil service reform, other than to express rhetorical interest in debureaucratization, civil service cutbacks, and reorganization. In such an environment, the public service has simply drifted, with little or no attention to the state apparatus. Thus, to use the categories suggested by Riggs for characterizing nonmerit civil services, Brazil has moved during the last 28 years from a public service characterized by bureaucratic excesses, during which technocrats in economic and financial management, planning, and security affairs had extensive power, to one dominated by bureaucratic fatigue and a directionless civil service since the return to democratic rule in 1985.

Argentina. Argentine experience under the military, until the shift back to democratic rule in 1984, is essentially one of direct military rule combined with economists directing various economic projects through the finance ministry. There, bureaucratic excesses fall more within the domain of military officers engaged in the arbitrary use of power than within the domain of an alliance of civilian and military bureaucrats, as was the case in Brazil. The devastation left by prolonged military rule, combined with the economic crisis facing the country at the time the transfer of power took place, required a much more frontal attack on the problems of the civil service than was the case with Brazil. Yet, despite serious endeavors to the contrary initiated through the State Secretariat for Administrative Reform (1983-1985), it has proven to be as difficult to change the inertia of the Argentine civil service since the return to democracy as before. The words of Oscar Oszlak, former undersecretary of state for administrative reform (1983-1985), sum up this state of affairs most effectively.

> The inherited bureaucracy—an "administrative widow" of countless political regimes—becomes a ballast for the new government, especially when the nature of the regime also changes. Both ephemeral and prolonged incumbency tend to crystallize bureaucratic institutions, regulations, and practices. When these turn out to be incompatible with the orientation of a new regime, they become institutional remnants, unburied administrative corpses. They may remain in the structure of the government's apparatus, still competing for valuable resources, but usually deprived of any useful function. The historical reiteration of this trend has converted the state bureaucracy into a true "cemetery" of political projects. (Oszlak 1991: 6)

The Argentine case thus provides an extreme example of bureaucratic fatigue, where repeated governmental change, instability, and the appointment of new persons of confidence by each government has led to a cumulation of bureaucratic strata that provide a historical record of each successive change in government. In such a context, inertia predominates in which each subsequent change has left a further layer of employees over and above those of the previous government. The net result of this situation is a compartmentalized bureaucracy in which the primary motivation for employees is survival and assurance of the continuity of one's position rather than performance. In this regard, while the reorientation of the role of the state under Menem, Alfonsín's successor, continues to move ahead, as he has implemented a vigorous privatization policy, the isolation of individual employees and the compartmentalization of work in the public sector remains as impervious to change as ever. Oszlak's pessimism over the intractability of the Argentine state to reform in terms of its personnel, expressed in the foregoing citation and more extensively in his full paper, is a case in point. Argentina, consequently, is one of the clearest instances on record of an institutionalized, non-performance-oriented bureaucracy in a society with ample numbers of skilled human resources in which the primary interest within the state apparatus is survival, through securing one's future through a limited but sufficient salary to live on, when so many others have failed to find viable means of support.

Chile. The Chilean case stands in marked contrast to Brazilian and Argentinean experience. In fact, within the Latin American region, there are only two instances of well-developed state apparatuses with an established record in the implementation of economic and social policy once national governments have resolved to take action: Mexico and Chile. Mexico is excluded here because, as an institutionalized authoritarian regime, it has yet to open up politics sufficiently to fall within the democratic category. Not only is the dynamic between the ruling PRI party and opposition groups very different, the prospects for a successful democratic transition do not remain at all clear, given the outcomes of the last round of elections in 1994 and the assassinations of two prominent PRI party leaders identified with political reform (José Francisco Ruiz Massieu and Luís Donaldo Colosio). The relevance of the Chilean case is its early structuring of a state apparatus with considerable capacity for implementing policy and the conversion of various policy initiatives into concrete projects and programs. The civil service before the military coup of 1973, which overthrew the government of Salvador Allende, was a semipowered bureaucracy, with a mixture of merit and partisan civil service appointments. Not immune to the political appointments made with each change of government, bureaucratic strata reflecting the preferences of each president intersected with program areas in which politicians recognized that competent technical personnel were needed. This meant that during the turbulence of the 1970s—with the unsuccessful attempt first to bring about a peaceful transition to socialism and then the violence of military action, designed to remove the advocates of state socialism by force—the state apparatus continued to function effectively as middle-and lower-level public bureaucrats complied with the dictates of the government in power and continued to carry out their responsibilities. The closest Chileans came to seeing this state apparatus dismantled occurred during the early Pinochet years, in which political purges coupled with a militant commitment to the implementation of a Friedman-style free market economy shrank the state to a point where public administrators were limited to the provision of minimal public services. Only in the face of economic disaster in 1982-1983 did the government abandon this stance. Having engaged in extensive privatization and opened up the economy to international market forces, conservative political leaders found themselves so vulnerable to the volatility of the global economy that the Pinochet regime nearly collapsed.[3]

The reconstitution of the Chilean state and the creation of a small, but effective professional, nonpartisan civil service is one of the major accomplishments of the 1980s. Beginning in 1983 and extending through the 1989 transition under the democratic government of Patricio Aylwin to the present government of Eduardo Frei (the son of the president who preceded Allende), what has reemerged is a semipowered public bureaucracy, professional and nonpartisan at the middle and lower levels and partisan and transitory at the top. Whereas the first phase of the economic reforms of the Pinochet government relied on Chileans trained in the United States and applications of the free market prescriptions of U.S. economists to Chile, the second phase—dominated by the so called Santiago boys—represented an adaptation of structural adjustment, privatization, and market economics to fit Chilean reality. The key innovation was realization by the right that regime survival and the capacity of the government to act independently required bringing the state back in as an active participant in economic and social policy, to regulate and modify the extremes in market economics and protect domestic private sector interests against the uncertainties of the international economy. By 1989, when the opposition successfully negotiated the return to democracy, so solid were the changes in economic policy and in the development of a corresponding state capacity to implement and sustain this policy, and so clear were the economic benefits for a majority of Chileans (despite persistent pockets of poverty), that the opposition committed itself to maintaining this economic strategy and a smaller, but more professional civil service. As a consequence, Chile stands alone today in South America as an instance of sustained successful economic reform, structural adjustment, privatization, and economic productivity under competitive market conditions. The significance of the Chilean case is great in this regard. Where there is a tempering of political forces and when domestic politicians, spanning the political spectrum from right to left, can demonstrate the ability to pragmatically lay aside past ideological differences, it is quite possible to reform the state apparatus. In so doing, political leaders, inside and outside government, can facilitate a smooth democratic transition and make a major contribution to creating the appropriate conditions for sustaining democracy in the long term.[4]

The Significance of the State Apparatus in Successful Transitions

The lessons learned from working with these developments in Southern Cone South America must be joined more successfully with the development management and policy literature that has emerged out of the experience with structural adjustment and policy reform in sub-Saharan Africa. This writing is often presented as the more relevant body of experience and new thinking about the necessity of both dismantling the state apparatus in power prior to economic and political liberalization and reconstituting the state to make market reforms work. Yet, seen in terms of results, this is a literature essentially of policy failure when issues of persistent poverty and the consequences of constrained resources for social policy are examined. When the aforementioned Latin American cases are joined with more recent writing on societal conditions in sub-Saharan Africa, the reencounter with the state in development work and recognition of the importance of devoting attention to institutional development, within and outside government, take on a significance that is much wider and that extends beyond any single world region. What all these materials make clear is that, although there is no predetermined role for the state to play in these new policy initiatives, how governments respond to market reforms and democratization through the design of social and economic policies becomes a major factor influencing policy outcomes.[5]

The central issue in such discussions has become not whether one is enamored of the state and is simply advocating new forms of state intervention, but that issues of governance are central to discussions of how governments can develop a greater capacity to implement economic and social policy effectively. Although institutional choices regarding presidentialist and parliamentary regimes do constitute an important variable in determining the prospects for democratic consolidation, broader considerations such as these, which involve rethinking the public-private interface, embrace state and society as a whole. Regarding achieving greater policy coherence and donor coordination in economic and financial management, the centrality of the state in these reform initiatives cannot be ignored.[6] Nor can it be assumed that the setting of rigorous economic and financial guidelines for a country alone will automatically be converted by host governments into a set of market prescriptions that will operate effectively simply by the declaration of a policy preference for free markets. On the other hand, in social policy a strong argument can be made for giving a minimal role to the state and encouraging governments to work through and with national and international nongovernmental organizations (NGOs) in providing social services and in meeting basic needs, especially in countries with poor majorities. This is because of the established track record of many NGOs in effective service delivery in such areas as the distribution of food and medicines, care for abandoned children, and creation of institutions better able to respond to the needs of the poorest of the poor.

Seen from this perspective, issues of civil service reform become secondary to the development of capacity-building initiatives designed to enhance the ability of nationals to assume greater participation in the determination of policy preferences and in the design of programs and projects directed at target populations within their own societies. In such a setting, the question of the appropriate public-private mix becomes situation specific, according to the human resources available and how these resources can be better developed, organized, and managed. In this regard, the publication of the first U.N. Development Program's *Human Development Report 1991* has called attention to this shift in development policies and programs in the direction of focusing attention more effectively on the human dimension. This concern with rethinking the appropriate mix between the public and private sectors as well as the role of the state is to be found in that report's Chapter 3, "Financing Human Development" (U.N. Development Program, 1991). What is so important about this report is its refocusing of the debate over appropriate development priorities around broader questions of human development and human resources.

In considering both the U.N. and the World Bank reports for 1991 and surveying economic and social policy outcomes since, it becomes clear how important it is not only to look at these issues cross-nationally, irrespective of world region, but also to introduce civil service questions into the debate over the consolidation of democratic regimes. Only with a broader perspective, incorporating consideration of the state as a whole and comparing and contrasting individual country experience, can the issues and choices facing policymakers in civil service reform be made more relevant to the current larger institutional debate.[7] Somehow issues related to transients and careerists in public bureaucracies must come to be seen as being as mainstream as the current debate over presidentialism and parliamentarism. To date, identifying the appropriate mix of civil service employees according to the situation encountered, involving both careerists (dedicated to public service careers and oriented toward the execution of government programs) and transients (representing the changing priorities of governments and linking the policy preferences of a given administration with the execution of activities by a continuous staff of public employees), has been seen by comparativists to be of secondary importance. The point in all this is that the design of feasible public personnel policies conducive to more effective implementation of governmental policies and programs must be understood as an indispensable ingredient in the consolidation and maintenance of all democratic regimes, whether presidential or parliamentary.

Notes

1. Although this literature is extensive, for the purposes of this chapter the most relevant sources that have brought this debate into focus are Linz and Valenzuela, *The Failure of Presidential Democracy* (1994), Shugart and Carey, *Presidents and Assemblies: Constitutional Design and Electoral Dynamics* (1992), and Liebert and Cotta, *Parliament and Democratic Consolidation in Southern Europe: Greece, Italy, Portugal, and Turkey* (1990).

2. The scholar who has done the most to clarify this debate by introducing semipresidentialist options is Matthew Shugart. In examining semipresidentialism, he has distinguished empirically between two types of regimes: premier-presidential systems, in which presidents retain substantial executive and legislative powers, and presidential-parliamentary systems, in which the balance of power lies with parliaments. The Portuguese case is particularly relevant here in its shift from a premier-presidential system to a presidential-parliamentary one, as its democratic regime has become consolidated. Shugart suggests presidential-parliamentary systems are more conducive to democratic consolidation than premier-presidential ones (Shugart and Carey 1992, especially chap. 3).

3. The most extensive discussions of, first, the strength of Chile's state apparatus and, second, the failure of Pinochet's initial reforms and the subsequent necessity of bringing the state back in to make a market economy function effectively are to be found in Valenzuela, "Parties, Politics, and the State in Chile" (1984), and Stepan, "State Power and the Strength of Civil Society in the Southern Cone of Latin America" (1985, especially pp. 319-324).

4. A succinct statement of these developments, and how they have become compatible with redemocratization, is to be found in Windhausen, "Democracy Is on Track in Chile" (1992: 18).

5. The basic point of reference in this literature is chapter 7, "Rethinking the State," in the *World Development Report 1991* (World Bank, 1991: 128-147). Indicative of this new thinking regarding the importance of enhancing policy management capacity is Gelase Mutahaba and M. Jide Balogun, *Enhancing Policy Management Capacity in Africa* (1992). A perusal of the table of contents suggests the kinds of issues to be confronted in this debate over the introduction of policy management concerns into the design of more comprehensive and appropriate development policies and programs in which civil service reform is mandatory. These materials, plus the various policy papers on structural adjustment, management capacity, and poverty alleviation prepared under the auspices of the bank, however, must be contrasted with the emerging literature that questions the capacity of the sub-Saharan African states to respond to these demands. See in particular the work of Catherine Boone, especially *Merchant Capital and the Roots of State Power in Senegal, 1930-1985* (1992). For more succinct discussions of these problems in the press, see "Latin American Economic Speedup Leaves the Poor in the Dust" (1994: 1 ff.) and "Africans Breaking Down Under 'Structural Adjustment' " (1994: 38A).

6. This point is central to the governmental reorganizations under way in Angola and Mozambique and to the brokering of these transitions after years of sustained civil conflict. For a summary statement of this perspective, see the *Report of the Inter-Agency Programming Mission on Support to Economic and Financial Management and Planning in Mozambique* (1992, especially p. 34) for the U.N. Department for Economic and Social Development, the U.N. Management Development Program, the Swedish International Development Agency, the International Monetary Fund, and the World

Bank. A relevant background paper dealing with the centrality of the state in such cases is Graham, "The Dilemmas of Managing Transitions in Weak States: The Case of Mozambique" (1993).

7. Indicative of this new interest in human needs and human development as the focus for development work is Doyal and Gough, *A Theory of Human Need* (1991).

References

"Africans Breaking Down Under 'Structural Adjustment.' " (1994, September 25). *Dallas Morning News.*

Baaklini, Abdo. (1989). "Presidentialism and Brazilian Politics" (unpublished paper). Albany: SUNY, Department of Public Administration and Policy.

Boone, Catherine. (1992) *Merchant Capital and the Roots of State Power in Senegal, 1930-1985.* New York: Cambridge University Press.

Doyal, Len, and Ian Gough. (1991) *A Theory of Human Need.* New York: Guilford.

Graham, Lawrence S. (1968) *Civil Service Reform in Brazil: Principles vs. Practice.* Austin: University of Texas Press.

———. (1990). *The State and Policy Outcomes in Latin America.* New York: Praeger.

———. (1993) "The Dilemmas of Managing Transitions in Weak States: The Case of Mozambique." *Public Administration and Development,* Special Issue, "Reforming Public Sector Management in Centrally-Planned and Transitional Economies," 13, 4: 409-222.

"Latin American Economic Speedup Leaves the Poor in the Dust." (1994, September 7) *New York Times,* p. 1.

Lewandowski, Enrique Ricardo. (1990) "Local and State Government in the Nova Republica: Intergovernmental Relations in Light of the Brazilian Political Transition." In Lawrence S. Graham and Robert H. Wilson, eds., *The Political Economy of Brazil: Public Policies in an Era of Transition,* pp. 26-38. Austin: University of Texas Press.

Liebert, Ulrike, and Maurizio Cotta, eds. (1990) *Parliament and Democratic Consolidation in Southern Europe: Greece, Italy, Portugal, and Turkey.* London: Pinter.

Linz, Juan J., and Arturo Valenzuela, eds. (1994) *The Failure of Presidential Democracy.* Baltimore: Johns Hopkins University Press.

Mainwaring, Scott. (1988) "Brazilian Party Underdevelopment in Comparative Perspective." Working Paper No. 134, Helen Kellogg Institute. Notre Dame, IN: Notre Dame University.

———. (1990) "Presidentialism in Latin America: A Review Essay." *Latin American Research Review,* 25, 1: 157-179.

Mutahaba, Gelase, and M. Jide Balogun, eds. (1992) *Enhancing Policy Management Capacity in Africa.* West Hartford, CT: Kumarian.

Oszlak, Oscar. (1991) "Redemocratization and the Modernization of the State: The Alfonsín Era in Argentina" (unpublished paper). Buenos Aires: IPSA XV World Congress of Political Science, July 21-25.

Report of the Inter-Agency Programming Mission on Support to Economic and Financial Management and Planning in Mozambique. (1992) New York: U.N. Department for Economic and Social Development.

Riggs, Fred W. (1991, November) "Presidentialism: An Empirical Theory" (unpublished paper). Honolulu: University of Hawaii, Political Science Department.

Shugart, Matthew S., and John M. Carey, eds. (1992) *Presidents and Assemblies: Constitutional Design and Electoral Dynamics.* New York: Cambridge University Press.

Stepan, Alfred. (1985) "State Power and the Strength of Civil Society in the Southern Cone of Latin America." In Peter B. Evans, Dietrich Rueschemeyer, and Theda Skocpol, eds., *Bringing the State Back In.* New York: Cambridge University Press.

U.N. Development Program. (1991) *Human Development Report 1991.* New York: Oxford University Press.

Valenzuela, Arturo. (1984) "Parties, Politics, and the State in Chile." In Ezra N. Suleiman, ed., *Bureaucrats and Policy Making,* pp. 242-279. New York: Holmes and Meier.

Windhausen, Rodolfo A. (1992, August 11) "Democracy Is on Track in Chile." *Christian Science Monitor,* p. 18.

World Bank. (1991) *World Development Report 1991: The Challenge of Development.* New York: Oxford University Press.

PART

III

Bureaucrats and Politicians in Parliamentary Systems

The discussion of parliamentary systems provides a broad view of these governance systems and the role of bureaucracy in their administration. Not all parliamentary systems are alike, just as not all presidential systems are not alike. For example, postrevolutionary Iran represents both a semipresidential and a semiparliamentary system plus additional institutional arrangements based on Islamic principles; Brazil represents a semipresidential system, as Graham discusses in his chapter in this book; and France represents both strong presidential and strong parliamentary system.

Chapters 10 and 11 discuss in detail the theoretical and empirical aspects of parliamentary systems of governance, particularly in Continental Europe, and the relationship between bureaucrats and politicians. First, in Chapter 10, Guy Peters makes a major contribution to the book by analyzing these forms of government and the relationships between higher level civil servants and politicians. He compares them with the presidential systems, especially the United States, and indicates that there generally is a more harmonious relationship between career and political appointees in the parliamentary systems in which both political appointees and career civil servants are found in both the executive and the legislative institutions. Peters's analysis encompasses both theoretical/conceptual and developing hypotheses as well as empirical discussions of the place and behavior of the professional career bureaucrats and their political counterparts in the governance of major political systems in European democracies. He also discusses the extent of politicization of the civil service, plus the role of civil servants in the policy-making process in European democracies. First, he presents a five-model scheme of relationship between the two groups and relates them to various parliamentary governments of Europe. His five models include the Weberian/Wilsonian notion of the politics-administration dichotomy, at one end, and the "administrative state," with bureaucracy being the dominant partner in this dichotomous relationship, at the other end. In between are the "adversarial model"; the "village life" model, which assumes that both should have no conflict with each other but be "two components of a single group serving the state and the public"; and the "functional village life" model, which assumes the same integration but only within specific functional areas of government. Peters adds that this kind of functional relationship becomes increasingly important as governments have become more professionalized, and states that "although the 'functional village life' model appears more compatible with a Continental, fused model of administrative and political careers, it may also appear in presidential regimes as well." In the sections that follow, Peters discusses parliamentary and presidential government in detail, differentiates the various parliamentary systems with elite recruitment, and concludes "in particular, any simple division between presidential and parliamentary systems does not appear to be valuable in making predictions."

Chapter 11, by Francis Terry, explores the British case. As Peters noted, the United Kingdom represents the ideal-type of generalist civil servants and generalist political appointees in the European democracies. In "Getting on in Government: Political Priorities and Professional Civil Servants," Terry examines in detail the relationship between the two groups as "the heart of successful policy making in democratic government." He explores the contrasting perspectives from which politicians and civil servants in the United Kingdom deal with the business of government. First he reviews the principal requirements that politicians in the British parliamentary system seem to have for their civil servants, and then compares these with the collective and individual characteristics that civil servants display.

Analyzing the nature of the British civil service, Terry identifies two main groups of civil servants: a small group of about 4,000 at the top chiefly concerned with "policy making" at the center, and a much larger group of about 500,000 "operational" management and administration personnel at the middle; with a third miscellaneous group of 533,350 (as of April 1994) U.K. civil servants. Terry's discussion covers the reforms and changes that have occurred in the civil service and bureaucracy before and during the 1980s. He concludes that the reforms of the 1980s have "shaken up many traditional patterns of civil service structure and procedure, but these reforms have had much greater impact in operational areas than in policy making. The resistance to change in culture among the policymakers appears to be deeply entrenched, and has been successfully maintained through much of the reform process."

Bureaucrats and Political Appointees in European Democracies: Who's Who and Does it Make Any Difference?

B. Guy Peters

Scholars and practitioners of government working within the Anglo-Saxon tradition are accustomed to making, and assuming, a relatively clear and sharp distinction between the political and the administrative aspects of government. This distinction is assumed to exist both for actions—making versus administering public policies—and for the personnel who perform those actions. This distinction is enshrined both in our empirical analysis of government (Aberbach et al. 1981; Heclo 1977) as well as in our normative analysis of what constitutes good government (Wilson 1887; but see Appleby 1949). The assumption (and to a lesser extent the reality) is that individuals in government positions must be career neutral, civil servants, or political appointees (Peters 1994).

The additional assumption contained in this Anglo-Saxon conception of government is that the motivations and behavior of the two groups of public officials are quite different, and that they are therefore locked in an institutional struggle over power and policy within government. Of the two groups, the elected political officials generally have been assumed to have the better motives and to be serving the public interest, while the dedication of the public bureaucracy to the public is generally questioned (Niskanen 1971; Bodiguel and Rouban 1991). This assumption remains operative even when political institutions are also facing a substantial loss of confidence by the public.

For most other democratic systems in the world, the distinction between civil servants and political appointees is less clear and less meaningful. First, it is less clear given that many civil servants are also active politicians, and, further, many career appointments depend upon, or are heavily influenced by, political considerations (Christensen 1991). The same individual may play both types of role several times during his or her career (Derlien 1988, 1990; Chevallier 1985). The distinction between civil service and political appointees is also less meaningful given that both groups (if they can be identified clearly) tend to operate with a common conception of their careers as being in service to the state. Thus any attempt to make a clear differentiation between the two groups would probably appear artificial and a fundamental misinterpretation of the jobs of both groups. Whether serving as a political appointee or as a career official, the ultimate tasks of the members of both groups (or really one group) are the same. This absence of a clear differentiation between civil servants and politicians in most European executive systems is to a large extent a function of having a clear concept of the state, something notably lacking in most Anglo-Saxon thinking about government (Stillman 1991).

As well as these broad cultural patterns, structural factors can affect the relationships between civil servants and their nominal political masters. There are a large number of such possible institutional impacts, but the one of greatest saliency for this chapter is the distinction between parliamentary and presidential systems (Shugart and Carey 1992; Weaver and Rockman 1994). Although presidentialist systems are relatively rare in the industrialized world, there are some notable examples of presidential or at least semipresidential (Duverger 1980) regimes in both Anglo-Saxon and Continental democracies. Likewise, there are several examples of Anglo-Saxon parliamentary regimes, although examining more than one of these will extend the purview of this chapter outside West Europe to include North America and the Antipodes. Still, we can get examples of countries that

TABLE 10.1 Institutional Formats and Cultural Groups

Institutional Format	Cultural Group	
	Anglo-American	Continental
Presidential[a]	United States	France
Parliamentary	United Kingdom, Canada	Germany, Sweden

a. Including "semipresidentialist" regimes.

would fill all four cells of a simple 2 × 2 table linking political culture and institutional format. (See Table 10.1.)

In this chapter, we will look at the impact of several factors on the behavior of public administrators and their relationship to political leaders. In particular, we will be interested in the extent to which the civil service has been politicized, both de jure and de facto (Meyers 1985). That is, political factors either may be a formal part of the appointment of a public employee, or they may be smuggled in under the table but still be a part of the final determination. We are also concerned with the role that civil servants are accorded in the policy-making process. These two dimensions may be related, but countries need not be in the same category for both dimensions. For example, a highly politicized civil service could be extremely Weberian. Its members simply might follow the directions of their political superiors, with whom they would be expected to agree, even if they do have political values of their own. On the other hand, a neutral civil service may be able to exert substantial policy-making power through their "neutral competence" (Sayre and Kaufman 1960) in a system that is deficient in such competence among its ministers. The civil service in one-party-dominant regimes (even those with parties in power by totally democratic means—Sweden for most of the past 60 years) appears to be an example of the former case, while that of the United Kingdom has for much of recent history appeared to be an example of the latter (Hennessy 1989).

Explaining Variations

In this section of the chapter, I will attempt to outline the two principal "independent variables" for the analysis. Although I will be using the positivist language common in the social sciences, I will not be able to follow through with the type of precise measurement that would be assumed from that language. This failing is to some extent a function of the nature of research in comparative administration and comparative executive politics (Peters 1988; Derlien 1992). Attempting, for example, to devise measures for the influence of the public bureaucracy in policy making can be an extremely slippery exercise. It can be approached by asking about perceived influence (Aberbach et al. 1981) or by careful observation of a few actors (Kaufman 1981), or it can be done from the diaries of ministers and civil servants (Crossman 1977; Bruce-Gardyne 1986), but generalizable measures of real influence over policy by civil servants are more difficult to obtain. Still, we will be able, by examining a range of cases and attempting to characterize patterns of interaction in these cases, to develop some preliminary working generalizations about the topic.

Of interest, both of these explanations would fit rather easily under the broad umbrella of the "new institutionalism" in political science (March and Olsen 1989; Ostrom 1991; Peters 1996). On the one hand, we can hypothesize that structural elements of a political system are crucial to determining its performance and the behavior of major actors within it. On the other hand, we could assume that the principal values contained in the "political culture" of the system, and particularly of organizations within the political system, may be crucial in determining the pattern of behavior. Both of these are central tenets of contemporary institutional thinking and are assumed in those theories to covary (Peters 1992). In the case of these executive and administrative systems, it appears that they may not.

Dimension 1:
Cultural Separation Between the Two Groups

The first dimension we will use for classifying administrative systems is the separation between administrative and political careers. The distinctions among the different concepts of administrative and political interactions are reflected in the five models of such relationships I developed earlier (Peters 1987; see also Rose 1987). On both ends of this assumed continuum are cases drawn from a relatively unadulterated Anglo-Saxon perspective. At one end is the Weberian/Wilsonian notion of the almost complete separation of politics and administration, with civil servants willingly taking the direction of their nominal political "masters." At the other end of the continuum is a model referred to in the analysis as the "administrative state," with the same separation between politics and administration but with the bureaucracy being the dominant force (Wilson 1975). Another model located toward the second end of the continuum, the "adversarial model," assumes a substantial separation between the two groups of decision makers but also that there is no clear resolution in their struggle for power. It should be stressed that all of these models must be considered ideal types (Giddens 1971) with empirical cases only approximating these mental images of bureaucrats interacting with politicians.

The other two models developed in this earlier analysis fit better with the Continental variants of the relationships between civil servants and their political leaders. The first of these models—"village life"—assumes that civil servants and politicians are both parts of a unified state elite and that they therefore should not be considered as being in conflict over power or policy.[1] Rather, they can be seen more clearly as two components of a single group serving the state and the public, with relatively common goals and a common set of rewards (Derlien 1992). France and Germany are obvious cases in which there is such a merger of the two branches of an executive elite. Further, in both cases, many civil servants are also parliamentarians (over half of the Bundestag in Germany are civil servants of one sort or another[2]) and ministers (Birnbaum 1985) so that there is a similar merger of careers across the major institutions of government.

The final model developed in that analysis—"functional village life"— assumes some of the same integration of civil service and administrative careers but within specific functional areas of government. Thus, rather than having a single, all-purpose elite at the top of government, government can be seen as consisting of a number of different elite groups defined by their policy area and perhaps also by their professional training. Thus a politician and a civil servant in a ministry of education or health, as examples, would be hypothesized to have more in common than would a political leader from the health sector and one from defense. This type of functional relationship has become increasingly important as governments have become more professionalized (Slayton and Trebilcock 1978; Bjorkman 1982) and their tasks have become more technologically complex. Each policy area will have its own jargon and its own methodologies that unite the actors within it and can be used to exclude outsiders from effective participation.

Although the "functional village life" model appears more compatible with a Continental, fused model of administrative and political careers, it also may appear in presidential regimes as well. For example, in the United States, the archetype of the presidential regime, "issue networks" (Heclo 1978) and "policy communities" (Rhodes 1988) flourish. These networks are composed of political appointees and civil servants, and also include people working outside government entirely. Those outsiders may be merely awaiting a change of partisan control of the White House to become insiders again (McKenzie 1987), but they stay in touch with the issues and with the community. If anything, the existence of these policy communities has helped to break down the barriers between political appointees and civil servants because of their common interest in the subject matter of the policy area.[3] The real difference in this analysis may be not so much the political culture of the political system as a whole as it is the nature of the particular policy area, with technical areas approximating the "functional" model more closely than less technical areas.

Dimension 2:
Parliamentary and Presidential Government

The second dimension of importance for this analysis is institutional, specifically the difference between presidential and parliamentary systems. This has been one of the classic distinctions in comparative politics (Wilson 1956; Price 1943) and has been receiving increased attention recently, in part because of its presumed relationship to the stability of regimes (Linz 1990; Riggs 1991). Also, especially in the United States, the dysfunctions associated with "divided government" have been argued to create numerous governance problems (Fiorina 1991; see also Pierce 1991; but see Mayhew 1991). We will not enter the debate over presidentialism and the stability of regimes in this chapter but will focus on the possible relationship between the form of government and the nature and performance of administrative systems. More specifically, we will want to determine if there is any relationship between this structural characteristic of democracies and the manner in which civil servants and politicians interact with one another.

Just how should the form of government affect the relationship between politicians and civil servants? In the first place, it could be hypothesized that the integration between the executive and legislative branches in a parliamentary regime should be related to a more cooperative relationship between political leaders and administrators. Rather than looking for loyalists who can be engaged in the ongoing conflict with the political party or parties in the other branch, a common pattern of service to the state could be more possible. Partisan loyalty might be hypothesized to be less important than competence and experience. Further, there would be little need to replace administrative personnel if there is a change in government given that all parties appear committed to relatively common standards of service. This hypothesis of civil service neutrality in parliamentary regimes appears to be supported in some regimes (the United Kingdom) but not in others (Germany).

In presidential regimes, there is a need for civil service loyalty not only to the political party but also to the institution of the presidency at the head of the executive branch. The independent legislature represents a clear rival for the loyalty of civil servants, especially given that the legislature is as important or even more important in the budgetary process. It also constitutes another point of access for agencies that may be unsuccessful with their executive branch leadership. As Aberbach and Rockman (1988) argued, the logical equivalent of the parliamentary "Yes, Minister" statement in a presidential system might be, "Yes, Congressman." Presidents and their top appointees must therefore be very jealous of the loyalty and commitment of their civil servants lest they become too committed to their congressional friends and collaborators.

The contrary hypothesis might also be entertained. That is, the nature of parliamentary government is more about seizing control of the entire apparatus of government, and then using that apparatus to implement a party program (Rose 1974; Katz 1986), than is presidential government. Whereas partisan and institutional responsibility for policy can be diffused in a presidential regime, it is substantially clearer in a parliamentary regime (Pasquino 1986). As a consequence, the party loyalty of administrators is much more important than in a presidential system. The government must be sure that any failures in their program are not a function of sabotage or mere lack of commitment by their civil servants. Similarly, the supportive involvement of a civil servant with the program of one strongly partisan government may make it difficult for him or her to work effectively with any subsequent government of a different political complexion. Again, the case of Germany and the "early retirement" of civil servants with a partisan affiliation is a useful example.

Another way in which the form of democratic government may affect the relationship between civil servants and politicians is through the form of accountability employed. The typical way to enforce accountability in a parliamentary regime is through ministerial responsibility. This concept is perhaps most clearly defined in the British case, where the tradition is that civil servants are anonymous and ministers must take full responsibility for the actions of their departments, even if errors are committed by the permanent staff (Marshall 1989). This constitutional convention has been eroded substantially, both through the actions of ministers (Turpin 1985; Woodhouse 1994) and through the creation of the parliamentary select committees to oversee departments (Drewry 1985), but the basic elements of the convention survive. In other parliamentary regimes, the notion of ministerial accountability is somewhat less stringent, and individual civil servants can be called to account for their actions. Mechanisms such as the ombudsman in Scandinavian parliamentary regimes (Stacey 1978) serve to reinforce the individual responsibility of public servants. Even in those cases, however, one principal means of bureaucratic accountability remains through their ministers to parliament (Lundqvist 1988).

The accountability of public administrators is handled substantially differently in presidential regimes. In those cases, the administration is responsible both to their organizational superiors in the department or agency and through them to the president, and also directly to congressional committees and subcommittees (Aberbach 1990). The appointed political leaders of an agency are certainly responsible for policy, but administrators are often subpoenaed before Congress and committees to respond to questions about management as well as perceived mismanagement. This form of accountability may weaken the civil service as an institution and make it spend much of its time looking over its collective shoulder. Further, an emphasis on personal responsibility may make the individual members of the public service less likely to follow orders they believe to be illegal, immoral, or just stupid.[4] Not only is the minister responsible for any harms arising from those orders, the individual civil servant also might be in a presidential regime.

It may be, however, that the distinction between presidential and parliamentary regimes is misspecified. The fundamental difference may be the degree to which the regimes are divided in practice rather than whether they are presidential or parliamentary in constitutional theory (Laver and Shepsle 1990; Laver and Shepsle 1991). As I will point out below, there may be factors in parliamentary regimes that make them behave very much as a presidential regime. The division usually associated with presidential regimes may occur in parliamentary regimes that have to form coalition governments, especially when those coalitions must bridge a range of ideological views. Likewise, it may be that a presidential regime that had strong agreement on fundamental political values and both political branches of government[5] dominated by the same political party might function very much like a parliamentary regime. The limited empirical analysis I will perform toward the end of this chapter will address this question more directly, although the difficulties of measurement involved will prevent anything like a definitive answer.

Summary

In summary, we have so far identified at least two important factors that can influence the relationship between civil servants and their political "bosses." On the one hand, there is the extent to which the two groups are conceptualized as being fundamentally different sets of actors, as opposed to a part of the same governmental elite in common service to the state. This is largely a cultural variable, although there may well be some structural manifestations of this presumed separation of roles (Page 1985). The second variable is the form of government, classified broadly as either presidential or parliamentary. There may be a great deal of variation within these broad categories. This is true for presidential regimes (Moulin 1978) but is especially true within parliamentary regimes (Lijphart 1989). Therefore, I will undertake in the next section to analyze some of those significant differences among parliamentary regimes to determine what their possible impacts may be on the performance and accountability of the civil service.

Differences Among Parliamentary Regimes

As noted above, there may be important differences among parliamentary regimes that will influence how political leaders and civil servants will interact with one another in making policy. Lijphart (1984, 1989), for example, classifies these systems as either "majoritarian" or "consensual," after advancing an earlier (1968), more complex classification scheme. Richardson (1982) advances another classification based upon policy-making styles, but still argues for important differences among parliamentary regimes. Some of these observed differences in parliamentary systems will be a function of the nature of the personnel laws establishing the civil service and of the structure of the administrative system. Other differences will be more a function of the structure of the political aspects of the system as well as the way in which the "game" of politics is played within the individual country. We will start by looking at those latter types of differences.

Coalition Government

One of the most crucial political factors affecting the role of the civil service in parliamentary regimes is the existence of a coalition government, and associated with that the number of parties involved in a coalition. Everything else being equal, being a coalition will weaken the governing capacity of a government. Further, the more parties that are involved in the coalition, the weaker that government likely will be. Multiparty governments can operate to some extent like presidential regimes with the civil service having several alternative groups to whom to be loyal and responsive. They may also be receiving demands for patronage positions from several different parties in government. Stated another way, coalition governments may permit the civil service much greater autonomy and power than might be true in single-party regimes. This is true for their own institutional politics and the ability to play one partisan group off against another as well as for their role in making public policy. The very fact that forming a government may take weeks or even months in a coalition regime, and the difficulties often encountered in reaching decisions within a coalition once formed, will allow the civil service the latitude to make decisions on their own or to structure the decisions that will be made by their nominal political masters.

Also related to the question of coalition government is alternation in office. If a single party dominates in a parliamentary regime, it has been argued that the interests not well represented by that party—business if a left party dominates, for example—find alternative mechanisms for exerting influence. Rokkan (1966) argued, for example, for the existence of an alternative path of influence through corporate pluralist structures for interests not represented through the electoral process during a reign of almost two decades by the Labor Party in Norway. In such a situation, a parliamentary regime begins to function very much like a divided presidential regime, with formal institutions being balanced by the less formal ones. Further, civil servants will have to be connected to the two alternative forms of governance, and an informal set of checks and balances will develop.[6]

The Lijphart (1984) differentiation between consensual and majoritarian systems helps to clarify the role of multipartyism in parliamentary regimes. A two-party system is almost inherently majoritarian, while multiparty systems tend to be more or less consensual. If a regime tends toward a minimum winning coalition, or toward minority governments (Norway), then it may behave much as does a two-party, majoritarian regime. Further along this continuum are party systems in which there are two clearly defined blocs of parties, with alternation between them, or with one or two center parties serving as swing members of a coalition. Sweden, for example, has had two clear blocs for most of its recent history with the left bloc winning most of the time, while in Germany the Free Democrats have served as the swing member of coalitions for almost the entire history of the Bundesrepublik.

We would therefore expect a continuum of policy-making power by the bureaucracy ranging from single-party governments with a long tenure at one end to multiparty governments with short tenures at the other. Table 10.2 arrays the parliamentary systems of West Europe, Japan, the Antipodes, and North America along such a continuum. Everything else being equal, we would expect Japan and Luxembourg to have the weakest public bureaucracy relative to its political masters, and Belgium, Finland, and Italy to have the strongest.

These few cases would make one believe that this variable may have little real relationship between coalition governments, continuity, and the power of the public bureaucracy. Certainly the Japanese bureaucracy is frequently cited as among the most powerful in industrialized democracies (Koh 1989), although the power of interest groups (Schwartz 1993) and

TABLE 10.2 Multipartyism and Duration of Coalitions

| | Moderate | Extreme | Extreme |
One Party	Multiparty	Multiparty (Long)	Multiparty (Short)
United Kingdom	Germany	Finland	Italy
Ireland	Sweden	the Netherlands	Belgium
Austria	Norway	Switzerland	Denmark
		Spain	

the importance of factional politics within the ruling Liberal Democratic Party may be understated. Likewise, although the Italian bureaucracy appears powerful and well organized relative to some of the political institutions in that country (LaPalombara 1987; Cassesse 1980), it still may not be such an effective institution when contrasted to other administrative systems. Much the same would be true for the civil service in Belgium, although there is a case that the Finnish bureaucracy has been a major force in policy making in that country (Ståhlberg 1983).

Parliaments as Variables

Another manner in which we tend to think of parliamentary regimes as all the same is to assume that all their parliaments are the same. This is far from the case. One of the important dimensions of variation among parliamentary governments is the extent to which the cabinet, and especially the prime minister, dominates parliament. If a parliament can develop sufficient independence from its executives, then the system may begin to appear somewhat presidential in behavior, if not in constitutional structure. There can never be the degree of separation that occurs when a president has an independent electoral mandate for a fixed term, but some of the dynamics associated with opposition and division may exist. Even in systems such as that of the United Kingdom in which the parliament lacks power relative to the executive, there have been attempts on the part of the parliament to reassert its powers to forestall, or at least delay, the "presidentialization" of the system (Jones 1991; Peters 1994; Foley 1993).

Parliaments vary along a number of dimensions that may influence their capacity to act independently of the executive. For example, parliaments differ markedly in the extent to which they initiate their own legislation (Table 10.3). A parliament such as that of Ireland or Belgium[7]

TABLE 10.3 Sources and Success of Legislation

	Government Bills as Percentage of Total	Percentage of Bills Passed[a]	
		Government	Private
Austria	65	96	50
Belgium	23	137[b]	7
Denmark	59	84	6
Finland	48	102[b]	1
France	22	82	3
West Germany	74	101[b]	58
Greece	87	77	0
Ireland	9	90	10
Italy	29	51	9
Luxembourg	94	100	24
The Netherlands	98	85	16
Norway	90	99	12
Portugal	70	14	48
Spain	58	81	13
Sweden	app. 99	—	app. 1
United Kingdom	92	92	10
Average	58	86	17

SOURCE: Based on data from the Inter-Parliamentary Union, *Parliaments of the World* (New York: Facts on File, 1986).
a. Percentage of bills introduced in each category that are passed into law.
b. Greater than 100% because of bills coming from upper house.

appears likely to be a more powerful foe of executive dominance in making policy than would one of the type in the Netherlands, Sweden, or the United Kingdom. Parliaments also differ in the extent to which they have staffing and the other analytic resources that enable them to conduct policy analysis autonomously and contend with the resources of both political executives and the bureaucracy. Table 10.4 points to some of the differences that exist in this regard, with Germany having a capacity for the Bundestag to behave more like a "transformative legislature" than would the Irish Dail.

We would hypothesize that to the extent that a parliament is able to function autonomously, the relationship between civil servants and political executives will appear more like the one we would expect in a presidential

TABLE 10.4 Staff Support for Parliaments

	Personal Staff[a]	Committee Staff	Legislative Reference and Research
Austria	from party	no	very limited
Belgium	no	yes	yes
Denmark	from party	yes	yes
Finland	yes, also from party	limited	very limited
France	yes	yes	yes
West Germany	yes	yes	yes
Greece	limited	limited	no
Ireland	limited	limited	very limited
Italy	from party	yes	yes
Luxembourg	yes	very limited	no
The Netherlands	limited, also from party	yes	very limited
Norway	from party	yes	limited
Portugal	no	very limited	very limited
Spain	from party	yes	very limited
Sweden	limited	yes	yes
Switzerland	limited	yes	limited
United Kingdom	limited	very limited	limited

SOURCE: Data from Inter-Parliamentary Union, *Parliaments of the World* (New York: Facts on File, 1986).
a. Paid for by government.

regime. Further, to the extent that parliament is autonomous, we would expect the patterns of policy making to be less capable of domination by either the political executive or the bureaucracy. This is especially true if the parliament is differentiated into functional committees that provide a place for specialized interests and agencies to gain greater access. The game becomes more of a free-for-all and less of a structured match.

Elite Recruitment

In addition to the nature of the coalition that will run a government, another important factor in determining the relationship between civil servants and politicians is the nature of the political and civil service elites themselves. The differences in civil service recruitment have been relatively well documented (Peters 1989; Kingdon 1990). On the one hand is the classic "talented amateur" so prominent in the myth and reality of British government. On the other is the highly specialized education received by many American civil servants. The generalist training (albeit of different sorts) specifically directed toward government service experienced by French and German civil servants resides someplace in the middle of this continuum (Page 1985). These differences in the backgrounds of civil servants can be expected to be a significant factor influencing their effectiveness in the policy-making process.

In addition to the initial recruitment of civil servants, their career patterns are also likely to have an influence on their capacity to serve as effective policymakers as well as on the conception they hold of their role within government. A career pattern such as the French or British, with relatively free movement among posts in government,[8] can be hypothesized to create a sense of being part of an all-purpose administrative elite that has a greater commitment to the public service as a whole than to any individual department or agency. A career within a single organization such as often occurs in Germany or Sweden, on the other hand, is likely to generate loyalty to that organization and a narrowed conception of the public interest. The latter career pattern is also likely to make any politician coming in to "direct" the ministry appear to his or her staff to be an outsider who should be resisted, regardless of the political legitimacy of his or her mandate to govern.

Differences in the recruitment patterns of political leaders tend to be less well documented (but see Dogan 1989; Rose 1987). There are very great differences among parliamentary regimes in how they choose their ministers. In the first place, there are differences in the educational backgrounds of ministers. These differences to some extent are similar to those that exist for civil servants. In some instances, the ministers are well trained; either they have training in the subject matter that they will have to administer (Austria) or they will have relevant, all-purpose training such as in economics or law (Germany). In other instances (the United Kingdom, Belgium), ministers may have generalist backgrounds, have been full-time politicians, or have worked in public service careers that may or may not be relevant to the performance of their ministerial job. Obviously, a minister with an educational and/or professional background relevant to the ministry that he or she will direct is a more worthy adversary for the career civil service than is a generalist or someone with a less relevant specialty.

Another basic question is whether the political executives come from inside or outside of the legislature. Riggs (1991), for example, makes a great deal of the point that ministers (or their equivalents) in presidential regimes (the United States in particular) generally come from outside the legislative body, and that this is presumed to make them less capable of coping politically. Some scholars of parliamentary regimes (Heady 1974), on the other hand, have argued that recruitment from inside parliament unduly restricts the talent base available to government and also tends to produce ministers who do not have an adequate understanding of the policy area that they must manage. Further, by remaining in parliament, a minister also retains a huge number of demands on his or her time that are likely to diminish the effective conduct of the executive post (Marples 1969). Indeed, some parliamentary governments have decided that it is better to recruit at least some ministers from outside of parliament, and those regimes that do appear to function as well as or better than those that keep to the traditional practice of having all ministers come from parliament (Blondel 1988). France and Norway may have stumbled on the best of both worlds by having most ministers elected to parliament— thereby proving their political connections and their links to the governing party—but then having them resign from their legislative seats once chosen as ministers.[9]

In addition to their elective status, ministers may also differ in their career patterns. Those executive systems that depend upon ministers being sitting members of parliament have a tendency to move ministers around frequently among offices. They, like administrators who move frequently, may not have any firm commitment to an organization and almost certainly will lack any substantial knowledge base about the policies for which the ministry is responsible. The civil service often can provide a rather complete knowledge base (if a biased one) for them. Put another way, a generalist minister who is moved frequently from post to post is unlikely to be able to contend effectively with civil servants who have better training and has spent a career mastering the subtleties of the policy area that he or she is administering. It would not even be a fair fight.

Governments do vary substantially in the extent to which they move their ministers among positions. Some may cycle and recycle ministers among a number of posts, while others assume that a particular minister may be effective only for particular types of policy areas. For example, the British government tends to move ministers rather frequently and to have them work up a ladder of seniority of positions (Searing 1989). On the other hand, countries such as Austria or, to some extent, Germany, tend to pick "horses for courses." They tend to bring in new, specialized executive talent if a sitting minister fails, rather than simply shuffling the ministries among existing cabinet ministers. Coalition governments may have to do some of that shuffling of posts to preserve their coalitions (Laver and Schofield 1991) although there the agreement may be about which party gets what posts, not just how many posts.

If we think about the factors involved in recruitment and selection for positions of both civil servants and their ministers, and break those patterns

TABLE 10.5 Recruitment and Career Patterns of Ministers and Civil Servants

	Ministers	
Civil Servants	Generalists	Specialists
Generalists	Muddling (United Kingdom)	Politicized (Spain)
Specialists	Bureaucratic (Italy)	Technocratic (Austria)

into two broad categories—generalist and specialist—for each, we can derive a simple 2 × 2 table (Table 10.5) that can be used to classify political systems. By *specialist* I refer to the education and training of an executive (political or administrative) as well as to the pattern that he or she is likely to follow during a career. Such a table is almost inherently too simplistic for the complex underlying reality it attempts to depict, but it still provides a place to start for a comparative analysis within parliamentary regimes.

The United Kingdom is a "pure" case of generalist ministers and generalist civil servants. In terms of backgrounds and careers, most members of both groups lack any specific justification to be occupying the particular posts that they may occupy. On the other hand, in Austria and Finland, there is a tendency to select highly qualified ministers (often from outside parliament) and to match them with rather specialized civil servants to create a "technocratic" style of government. The cases in the off-diagonal cells are less clear, although the cases of both Sweden and Italy with a civil service recruited by department and ministers with substantial mobility (especially in Italy) make for a very compartmentalized style of governing.[10] Finally, in Spain and Switzerland, rather specialized ministers (perhaps especially in Spain) confront a more generalist bureaucracy, with the probability of what we refer to as a "politicized" governing pattern.[11] Any number of other factors may have to be taken into account in determining what will happen when civil servants actually confront their political masters across their respective desks, but this simple typology provides one place to begin to look for the answers.

The question now becomes whether this typology explains behavior and performance any better than did the earlier attempt to break down that large category called parliamentary governments. The answer appears to be a tentative and partial "yes." First, the case in which the two groups of executives were relatively evenly matched and neither (usually) can claim any particular expertise in the subject matter is the case associated with the greatest apparent conflict over power and policy. Sir Humphrey may be a fictional character, but his role models have existed in the British civil service for some years (Hennessy 1989). At the other extreme, the governments of Austria and Finland have been able to govern what might otherwise be very fractious regimes through a technocratic executive that relies heavily on expertise and sectorization.

Again, the off-diagonal cases are much less clearly defined. The Swedish case has been one with a strong civil service but also one of a rather stable one-party democracy. The relationship between civil servants and their ministers appears much less clear under the current right-wing regime.[12] It could well be that civil servants will have a less pronounced role under this current government, even given the decentralized agency structure that tends to enhance the capacity of civil servants to supply direction to policy. The capacity of the Swedish civil service is further enhanced by the practice of recruiting by ministry or agency rather than centrally. This allows for greater specialization by the organizations and for them to socialize their members somewhat more readily than they might otherwise be able to do in the "folkways" of that particular agency.

The Spanish and Swiss cases are somewhat less clear. The Swiss government tends to be extremely stable and to have ministers survive in office for a long period of time. Also, several of the ministers in the government tend to be expert in the fields for which they are responsible—especially the economy. The bureaucracy is also extremely capable but tends to be recruited on more general grounds and to move around among ministries. In Spain, ministers are often recruited from outside the parliament and bring with them specialized skills. These ministers work with a bureaucracy that is frequently argued to be in need of fundamental reorganization if it is to be a part of a successful modern government (Vallalva 1990).

It therefore does appear that this old "chestnut" (Ridley 1968) in the study of civil service systems—generalists versus specialists—does have some utility for understanding how civil servants and ministers relate to one another. Examining the variable in respect to either group itself may not have a great deal of utility, but when the two are combined, they appear to make some useful predictions about patterns of interaction between these two groups.

We might be able to elaborate this "generalist and specialist" dichotomy somewhat more by looking at the extent to which ministers can call on assistance in the development and implementation of policy. Especially important would be the capacity to call on assistance from outside the career public service, or if from within the career service, from individuals who share some of the same political convictions as the minister. We have noted that at least in one presidential regime (the U.S.), the president and his ministers (or equivalents) are provided with huge staffs and can obtain almost all forms of policy advice they might need. Despite that, they may still depend upon the civil service for some information, especially about the procedural elements of policy making.

The executives of most parliamentary regimes do not have the advantage of such a level of support for policy and must depend more upon the civil service. Still, there are marked variations in their access to independent (non-civil service) policy advice (Weller 1987). In some countries, ministers are able to appoint *cabinets* to provide them with assistance (Gaborit and Mounier 1987). These bodies of advisers and aides are often composed of civil servants but they need not entirely comprise officials. Even if there is not a formal *cabinet* structure, a minister may be able to bring in personal advisers to assist him or her in implementing a particular vision[13] of policy. At the other end of this dimension would come the United Kingdom in which ministers have funds for a very few (but increasing) advisers and must depend largely upon their civil servants for policy advice (Gaffney 1991).

The above paragraph has to some extent made the civil service the bogey man, seemingly offering "biased" advice to naive, defenseless ministers. Such a characterization would overestimate both the power and the venality of the civil service and underestimate the capacities of their ministers. Still, if we are concerned about patterns of interaction between ministers and their civil servants, we must remember that most ministers start their jobs at a disadvantage relative to the civil servants and that policy advice is one means of leveling the playing field. Further, the notion of "independent" policy advice may be something of a misnomer. Most ministers will tend to recruit policy advisers who are in agreement with their party programs. Thus any advice the adviser provides would be in the policy direction that the minister wants to hear rather than in the direction that the ministry has tended to follow in the past. This difference has been especially important for the change-oriented governments of the right and left that were in power in many countries during the 1980s (Peters and Barker 1992).

There does appear to be some relationship between the level of advice available to ministers and their effectiveness in governing their departments, or at least in their serving as effective foils to their civil servants. In general, ministers are more effective when they do have sources of advice in which they have greater confidence and over which they have greater control. This knowledge base does not provide any guarantee that the minister will be effective, but it does at least provide him or her with a fighting chance.

Summary

This chapter has been an attempt to address the question of the impact that the form of government has on the behavior of public administrators and their relationship to their nominal political masters. We have examined a number of factors for which reasonable hypotheses could be generated about the relationship of the two. These in general are various institutional and cultural factors but cover a range of alternatives within that broad category.

If, on the basis of these "data," we had to make a choice about how to predict behavior and the relationship between civil servants and ministers, there are two factors that appear especially relevant. One is the political, and especially the administrative, culture of the country (Peters 1989). It appears that the fundamental value statements concerning the role of civil servants and their separation from partisan political life will have at least as strong an influence over our "dependent variables" as will structural considerations. In particular, any simple division between presidential and parliamentary systems does not appear to be valuable in making predictions.

There does, however, appear to be some relationship between recruitment patterns of both civil servants and ministers and their relative powers and success in policy making. The old familiar statement about specialization of training and of career patterns does appear to offer a good deal of insight into how the two groups of actors will deal with each other in making policy. More and more, policy making involves a great deal of substantive expertise and professional knowledge. If either participant lacks a significant knowledge base (or cannot have independent advisers), he or she will be at a significant disadvantage in any battles over public policy.

Given the difficulties of measurement of the concepts involved in this analysis, these conclusions must be seen as extremely tentative. Still, the concepts do provide us first with a background against which to begin searching for alternative explanations for the phenomena we have observed. Also, these preliminary findings should provide an incentive to investigate means for measuring the phenomena in question more precisely so that more definitive answers to the important questions raised can be provided.

Notes

1. This term obviously is used somewhat differently than it was by Heclo and Wildavsky (1974).

2. This number is somewhat inflated given that schoolteachers are counted as civil servants.

3. Even in the Reagan Administration, the people brought in to reduce the size of programs often were members of the policy community. They simply had different ideas about "good policy" as compared with the modal member of the community who favored program maintenance or expansion.

4. The contrary hypothesis is that an emphasis on personal responsibility would make civil servants even more likely to "pass the buck" and evade responsibility than they otherwise might.

5. Yes, the courts are political, but not in the sense of being involved directly in the passage and implementation of legislation.

6. I am indebted to Tom Christensen for reminding me of this point.

7. Or we could include France if we want to assume that for these purposes France is parliamentary.

8. In the case of France, this movement also includes movement to and from the private sector (see Rouban 1994).

9. This provision appears to have been adopted in France less to recruit executive talent than to attempt to prevent the governmental instability that plagued the Third and Fourth Republics in France.

10. The marked differences in the political cultures of these two countries would, however, make us expect somewhat different styles of governing even given the similarities in intraexecutive relationships.

11. Again, the marked differences in cultures and styles might be expected to produce different patterns of governing.

12. This is especially true because of the presence of a new Democracy party as a part of the coalition. Under a previous bourgeois regime, there was little tension between the civil service and the government.

13. The "vision thing."

References

Aberbach, J. D. (1990) *Keeping a Watchful Eye*. Washington, DC: Brookings Institution.

Aberbach, J. D., R. D. Putnam, and B. A. Rockman. (1981) *Bureaucrats and Politicians in Western Democracies*. Cambridge, MA: Harvard University Press.

Aberbach, J. D., and B. A. Rockman. (1988) "Mandates or Mandarins? Control and Discretion in the Modern Administrative State." *Public Administration Review*, 48: 606-612.

Appleby, P. H. (1949) *Policy and Administration*. University, AL: University of Alabama Press.

Birnbaum, P. (1985) "The Socialist Elite, 'les Gros,' and the State." In P. G. Cerny and M. A. Schain, eds., *Socialism, the State and Public Policy in France*. London: Frances Pinter.

Bjorkman, J. W. (1982) "Professionalism in the Welfare State: Sociological Savior or Political Pariah." *European Journal of Political Research,* 10: 407-428.

Blondel, J. (1988) "Ministerial Careers and the Nature of Parliamentary Government: The Cases of Austria and Belgium." *European Journal of Political Research,* 16: 51-71.

Bodiguel, J. L., and L. Rouban. (1991) *Le fonctionnaire détrôné?* Paris: Presses de la fondation nationale des sciences politiques.

Bruce-Gardyne, J. (1986) *Ministers and Mandarins.* London: Sidgwick and Jackson.

Cassesse, S. (1980) "Is There a Government in Italy?" In R. Rose and E. Suleiman, eds., *Presidents and Prime Ministers.* Washington, DC: American Enterprise Institute.

Chevallier, J. (1985) *La haute administration et la politique.* Paris: PUF.

Christensen, T. (1991) "Bureaucratic Roles: Political Loyalty and Professional Autonomy." *Scandinavian Political Studies,* 14: 303-320.

Crossman, R. (1977) *The Diaries of a Cabinet Minister.* London: Hamish Hamilton.

Derlien, H.-U. (1988) "Repercussions of Government Change on the Career Civil Service in West Germany: The Cases of 1969 and 1982." *Governance,* 1: 50-78.

———. (1990) "Continuity and Change in the West German Federal Executive Elite, 1949-1984." *European Journal of Political Research,* 18: 349-372.

———. (1992) "Observations on the State of Comparative Administration Research in Europe: Rather Comparable Rather Than Comparative." *Governance,* 5: 279-311.

Dogan, M. (1989) *Pathways to Power.* Boulder, CO: Westview.

Drewry, G. (1985) *The New Select Committees.* Oxford: Clarendon.

Duverger, M. (1980) "A New Political System Model: Semipresidential Government." *European Journal of Political Research,* 8: 165-187.

Fiorina, M. (1991) "Coalition Governments, Divided Governments and Electoral Theory." *Governance,* 4: 236-249.

Foley, M. (1993) *The Rise of the British Presidency.* Manchester: University of Manchester Press.

Gaborit, P., and J.-P. Mounier. (1987) "France." In W. Plowden, ed., *Advising the Rulers.* Oxford: Basil Blackwell.

Gaffney, J. (1991) "The Political Think Tanks in the United Kingdom and the Ministerial Cabinets in France." *West European Politics,* 14: 1-17.

Giddens, A. (1971) *Capitalism and Social Theory.* London: Cambridge University Press.

Heady, B. (1974) *British Cabinet Ministers.* London: Allen & Unwin.

Heclo, H. (1977) *A Government of Strangers.* Washington, DC: Brookings Institution.

———. (1978) "Issue Networks and the Executive Establishment." In A. King, ed., *The American Political System.* Washington, DC: American Enterprise Institute.

Heclo, H., and A. Wildavsky. (1974) *The Private Government of Public Money.* Berkeley: University of California Press.

Hennessy, P. (1989) *Whitehall.* London: Secker and Warburg.

Jones, G. (1991) "Presidentialization in a Parliamentary System?" In C. Campbell and M. J. Wyszomirski, eds., *Executive Leadership in Anglo-American Systems.* Pittsburgh: University of Pittsburgh Press.

Katz, R. S. (1986) "Party Government: A Rationalistic Concept." In F. G. Castles and R. Wildenmann, eds., *Visions and Realities of Party Government.* Berlin: de Gruyter.

Kaufman, H. (1981) *The Administrative Behavior of Federal Bureau Chiefs.* Washington, DC: Brookings Institution.

Kingdon, J. (1990) *The Civil Service in Liberal Democracies.* London: Routledge.

Koh, B. C. (1989) *Japan's Administrative Elite.* Berkeley: University of California Press.

LaPalombara, J. (1987) *Democracy, Italian Style.* New Haven, CT: Yale University Press.

Laver, M., and N. Schofield. (1991) *Multiparty Government: The Politics of Coalitions in Europe.* Oxford: Oxford University Press.

Laver, M., and K. A. Shepsle. (1990) "Coalitions and Cabinet Government." *American Political Science Review,* 84: 873-890.

———. (1991) "Divided Government: America Is Not 'Exceptional.' " *Governance,* 4: 250-269.

Lijphart, A. (1968) "Typologies of Democratic Systems." *Comparative Political Studies,* 1: 3-44.

———. (1984) *Democracies.* New Haven, CT: Yale University Press.

———. (1989) "Democratic Political Systems: Types, Cases, Causes, Consequences." *Journal of Theoretical Politics,* 1: 33-48.

Linz, J. (1990) "The Perils of Presidentialism." *Journal of Democracy,* 1: 51-69.

Lundquist, L. (1988) *Byråkratisk etik.* Lund, Sweden: Studentlitteratur.

March, J. G., and J. P. Olsen. (1989) *Rediscovering Institutions.* New York: Free Press.

Marples, E. (1969) "A Dog's Life in a Ministry." In R. Rose, ed., *Policymaking in Britain.* London: Macmillan.

Marshall, G. (1989) *Ministerial Responsibility.* Oxford: Oxford University Press.

Mayhew, D. (1991) *Divided We Govern.* New Haven, CT: Yale University Press.

McKenzie, G. C. (1987) *The In and Outers.* Baltimore: Johns Hopkins University Press.

Meyers, F. (1985) *La politisation de l'administration.* Brussels: Institut International des Sciences Administratives.

Moulin, R. (1978) *Le présidentialisme et la classification des régimes politiques.* Paris: Librarie Generale de Droit.

Niskanen, W. (1971) *Bureaucracy and Representative Government.* Chicago: Aldine-Atherton.

Ostrom, E. (1991) "Rational Choice Theory and Institutional Analysis: Toward Complementarity." *American Political Science Review,* 85: 237-243.

Page, E. C. (1985) *Political Authority and Bureaucratic Power.* Brighton, United Kingdom: Wheatsheaf.

Pasquino, G. (1986) "The Impact of Institutions on Party Government." In F. G. Castles and R. Wildenmann, eds., *Visions and Realities of Party Government.* Berlin: de Gruyter.

Peters, B. G. (1987) "Politicians and Bureaucrats in the Politics of Policymaking." In J. E. Lane, ed., *Bureaucracy and Public Choice.* London: Sage.

———, (1988) *Comparing Public Bureaucracies: Problems of Theory and Method.* Tuscaloosa: University of Alabama Press.

———. (1989) *The Politics of Bureaucracy.* 3rd. ed. New York: Longman.

———. (1991) *European Politics Reconsidered.* New York: Holmes and Meier.

———. (1992) "The Policy Process: An Institutionalist Perspective." *Canadian Public Administration,* 35: 160-180.

———. (1994) "Are Parliamentary Regimes Becoming More Presidential?" In K. Von Mettenheim, ed., *Presidential Government: An Evaluation.* Baltimore: Johns Hopkins University Press.

———. (1996) "The New Institutionalism: Is It New and What Makes It Institutional." In R. E. Goodin and H.-D. Klingemann, eds., *The New Handbook of Political Science.* Oxford: Oxford University Press.

Peters, B. G., and A. Barker. (1992) *Advising West European Governments.* Edinburgh: University of Edinburgh Press.

Pierce, R. (1991) "The Executive Divided Against Itself: Cohabitation in France, 1986-88." *Governance,* 4: 270-294.

Price, D. K. (1943) "The Parliamentary and Presidential Systems." *Public Administration Review,* 3: 317-334.

Rhodes, R. A. W. (1988) *Beyond Westminster and Whitehall.* London: Unwin Hyman.

Richardson, J. J. (1982) *Policy Styles in Western Europe.* London: Allen and Unwin.

Ridley, F. F. (1968) *Specialists and Generalists.* London: Allen and Unwin.

Riggs, F. W. (1991) "Presidentialism: An Empirical Theory." In M. Dogan and A. Kazancigil, eds., *Comparing Nations: The Pendulum Between Theory and Practice.* Oxford: Basil Blackwell.

Rokkan, S. (1966) "Votes Count But Resources Decide." In R. A. Dahl, ed., *Political Oppositions in Western Democracies.* New Haven, CT: Yale University Press.

Rose, R. (1974) *The Problem of Party Government.* London: Macmillan.

———. (1987) *Ministers and Ministries: A Functional Analysis.* Oxford: Clarendon.

Rouban, L. (1994) *Les cadres supérieurs de la fonction publique et la politique de modernisation administrative.* Paris: Direction Générale de l'Administration et de la Fonction Publique.

Sayre, W., and H. Kaufman. (1960) *Governing New York City.* New York: Russell Sage.

Schwartz, F. (1993) "Of Fairy Cloaks and Familiar Talks: The Politics of Consultation." In G. D. Allison and Y. Sone, eds., *Political Dynamics in Contemporary Japan.* Ithaca, NY: Cornell University Press.

Searing, D. D. (1989) "Junior Ministers and Ministerial Careers in Britain." In M. Dogan, ed., *Pathways to Power.* Boulder, CO: Westview.

Shugart, M. S., and J. M. Carey. (1992) *Presidents and Assemblies: Constitutional Design and Electoral Dynamics.* Cambridge: Cambridge University Press.

Slayton, P., and M. J. Trebilcock. (1978) *The Professions and Public Policy.* Toronto: University of Toronto Press.

Stacey, F. (1978) *The Ombudsman Compared.* Oxford: Clarendon.

Ståhlberg, K. (1983) "De stätlig anställda i Finland." In L. Lundquist and K. Ståhlberg, eds., *Byråkrater i Norden.* Åbo: Åbo Akademi.

Stillman, R. J. (1991) *Preface to Public Administration.* New York: St. Martin's.

Turpin, C. (1985) "Ministerial Responsibility: Myth or Reality." In J. Jowell and D. Oliver, eds., *The Changing Constitution.* Oxford: Basil Blackwell.

Vallalva, M. B. (1990) "La administracion publica y los funcionarios." In S. Giner, ed., *España: Sociedad y Politica.* Madrid: Espasa Colpe.

Weaver, R. K., and B. A. Rockman. (1994) *Do Institutions Make a Difference?* Washington, DC: Brookings Institution.

Weller, P. (1987) "Types of Advice." In W. Plowden, ed., *Advising the Rulers.* Oxford: Basil Blackwell.

Wilson, J. Q. (1975) "The Rise of the Bureaucratic State." *Public Interest,* 41: 77-92.

Wilson, W. (1887) "The Study of Administration." *Political Science Quarterly,* 2: 197-214.

———. (1956) *Congressional Government.* Cleveland: World.

Woodhouse, D. (1994) *Ministers and Parliament: Accountability in Theory and Practice.* Oxford: Clarendon.

Getting on in Government: Political Priorities and Professional Civil Servants

Francis R. Terry

The relationship between bureaucrats and politicians goes to the heart of successful policy making in democratic government. Politicians are elected to office with a variety of commitments and pledges—sometimes inconsistent or impractical, always and necessarily designed to attract public support. Overnight, it becomes the responsibility of bureaucrats to play a major part in turning these promises into reality or, at any rate, a version of reality that somehow reflects credit on the politicians.

This chapter explores the contrasting perspectives from which politicians and civil servants in the United Kingdom deal with the business of government, and it points to an inherent paradox that the British system has been struggling for a long time to resolve: The characteristics that are traditionally valued highly in the making of an obedient and impartial civil servant obscure many of the other qualities that politicians need to secure

255

the implementation of their policies. We begin by reviewing the principal requirements that politicians in the British parliamentary system demand from their civil servants, and then compare these with the collective and individual characteristics that civil servants display. The picture is complicated and rapidly changing because the sweeping reforms affecting the U.K. civil service over the past decade have sought to break down its traditional culture and to supply, from the business world as well as from within, additional qualities that appear to be needed. There have also been shifts in the respective roles and responsibilities of civil servants and ministers, as a result of the reform process, that were probably unforeseen.

In the United Kingdom, the constitutional position of ministers and civil servants has traditionally had a strong basis in historical convention (rather than written rules) and in what amounted to a "pact of secrecy." The convention of ministerial responsibility assumed that each minister was accountable to Parliament for the conduct of his or her department, and that the act of every civil servant was in principle the minister's act. Ministers would therefore, until quite recently, take the ultimate responsibility for them. Nowadays, this is not invariably so: The more positive distinction introduced into civil service organization between "policy making" and "implementation" has enabled ministers to avoid automatically having to resign when their officials blunder. Traditionally, also, dealings between the civil servant and minister have been seen as privileged, and not for open discussion in Parliament or the media. But a number of recent crises have revealed a great deal about the working relationships of ministers, civil servants, and Parliament. These include the examination of standards in public life by Lord Justice Nolan (Nolan, 1995), problems with the operations of the Child Support Agency, the sacking in late 1995 of the director of the newly formed Prison Service Agency, Mr. Derek Lewis, and the Inquiry by Lord Justice Scott into the supply of arms to Iraq. Evidence brought to light by the Parliamentary Select Committee on the Civil Service, and the ensuing debate on an explicit code of conduct for civil servants, have added further insights into the workings of the restructured government machine. A further aspect that is changing rapidly is the impact of European Union policy making. The banning of British beef exports in 1996 fueled a debate on the United Kingdom's constitutional position in Europe and the roles of ministers, civil servants, and expert advisers in this wider arena.

Politicians and Priorities

In the first week or so after an election victory, it is the task of an incoming prime minister to appoint suitable members of his or her party to all the main offices of state. Under the British system, there are about 15 principal departments of state, each headed by a secretary of state and each assisted by a small group of junior ministers. Not all ministers hold a seat in the House of Commons: Indeed, it is essential for the government to have competent spokesmen and women in the House of Lords on all important issues as well as in the Commons. It may occasionally happen that a secretary of state is a peer, sitting in the Lords, with a more junior minister acting as spokesperson in the Commons. (This occurred in 1979-1982 when Lord Carrington was foreign secretary, and Douglas Hurd was the minister of state responsible for foreign affairs.)

In addition to the secretaries of state for the principal departments, there are up to 100 other minor offices to be filled, most of them by parliamentarians. Given that the House of Commons consists of 651 seats, and that British governments rarely command a majority of more than 100, there is a fairly good chance (about 1 in 3 or 4) that an MP will also hold some form of government position. Many of these MPs are ambitious and keen to achieve "results" (with attendant publicity) so that when there is a reshuffle of ministerial portfolios, they will be promoted to a more senior position or a department with greater prestige. There is an informal hierarchy of departments: Below the prime minister and chancellor of the exchequer (in charge of the Treasury), a post at the Foreign Office or the Home Office carries more status than one at the Environment or Social Security Department, even though the latter dispose of very much larger budgets, and those in turn are generally rated more highly than posts at Agriculture or Northern Ireland.

In pursuing their political ambitions, ministers want to shine not only with the media but on the floor of the House, in comparison with their party colleagues, and not least with their constituents who elect them. They also, although they may not fully realize it, need to command the respect and allegiance of their departmental civil servants. By convention, however, civil servants are excluded from helping directly to fulfill ministerial ambitions in a number of important respects. They may arrange press interviews and brief the minister on what the current policy is, in dealing with various questions, but they cannot do much to help if he or she fumbles his responses or appears inarticulate. They will, of course, ensure that any damaging interview is counteracted as much as possible through briefing of journalists, distribution of authoritative and ready-prepared materials, and other publicity. Although civil servants may draft speeches for use in Parliament, they cannot much help the way they are delivered or how the minister deals with interventions and points made in the ensuing debate. Civil servants do not help with the minister's constituency business either, this being looked after usually by a local agent or by party workers.

In other respects however, ministers have a great deal of help from their civil servants: In the development of policy, they command enormous resources in terms of intellectual skill, experience, research, and sheer hard effort. In delivering programs, civil servants typically show tact and dedication, although they may lack technical knowledge to meet all the demands placed upon them and, perhaps, a certain flair that ministers may wish for. Since the reforms of the 1980s (see below), this has been less of a problem because the use of external consultants is much more widespread now, replacing the best amateur efforts of officials. In terms of managing the department, ministers have little to worry about: The permanent secretary and his colleagues take care of all the routine functions in a well-oiled machine.

The constraints that ministers find, when they take up office, lie not so much in the alleged bureaucratic evils associated with the civil service (procrastination, formalism, and undue deference to higher ranks) or in the overt obstruction for which civil servants are sometimes blamed. The constraints more often lie in other, unexpected areas. First, a minister may be surprised at the extent to which he or she is forced to depend on officials at so many key points. Ministers are literally surrounded and insulated from the outside world. Officials will set up public appearances, media communications, and meetings on behalf of the government; they will offer drafts of speeches in the House and elsewhere; they will brief the minister on the answers to be given to questions in Parliament or in front of select committees inquiring into current policies and expenditures; and they will recommend a policy line to be taken in Cabinet or committee discussions.

Ministers vary greatly in the extent to which they follow the texts drafted for them, or the prearranged program or the policy line that is proposed for them. But it is certain that the civil servants will have checked and prepared everything as it should be, because their jobs depend on it. Ministers may also underestimate the extent to which any pronouncement that they make will have ramifications or repercussions in other programs and other branches of government. It is the civil servants' responsibility too to ensure that their minister does not unintentionally offend his or her Cabinet colleagues or unwittingly depart from what has been established as the government's line on any particular issue. The penalty for this emphasis on circumspection and consistency is that ministers often feel constrained by their civil servants, and may suspect they are being deliberately manipulated when they cannot see an obvious reason why officials act as they do.

This dependence on officials is accentuated by pressures of time: British Cabinet ministers frequently work a 12- to 14-hour day, six days per week. The House of Commons sits for considerably longer than most other parliaments, and it often sits late into the night. Ministers, as members of the government, may be called to vote at any time, or they may have to develop and steer through Parliament a major piece of legislation while maintaining regular contact with interest groups, local authorities, political colleagues, and their electors. Unlike their counterparts in the Netherlands, for example (where ministers of the Crown automatically suspend their role as constituency representatives), British ministers also have to keep pace with a variety of local demands and interests. These can be all the more important if the minister's seat is a marginal one, where neglect may spell failure when an election is called, as (unlike the preset timetable for elections in the United States) it may be at any time.

Aside from the physical pressures of the role, ministers ultimately succeed through political skill—because they know the importance of tactical advantage, of the need for electoral support, the value of putting the best possible interpretation on present circumstances, and handing out or repaying favors. This is not, of course, the currency in which civil servants normally deal. As Blackstone and Plowden (1988: 13) observe,

> The more nearly Ministers or advisers are professional politicians the less likely they are to have managerial skills or experience. Nor are they likely to possess the skills of analysis and scientific problem solving. . . . The conclusions of analysis can be totally convincing in every sense except a political one, and for that reason alone can be set aside.

Officials, on the other hand, have powerful advantages—not least in terms of knowledge—over an incoming minister, but they must never be seen to exploit these, even though a minister may not know the most elementary facts about his or her department's work, or about the distribution of resources among its various functions and for which they are formally responsible. That is perhaps why the initiative of Michael Heseltine, in introducing his Management Information System for Ministers (MINIS) while environment secretary in 1981, was such a landmark reform. But it was more significant for the intention that lay behind it than the results that followed. The first outputs from MINIS, when lodged in the Library of the House of Commons, were little more than a vaguely worded list of activities with a record of achievements whose significance was unclear. In some divisions, establishing a new advisory committee was marked as an "achievement" because it signaled better informed decision making; elsewhere, the winding up of a committee was an "achievement" because it marked a simplification of bureaucracy.

The MINIS initiative was important, because it represented a challenge to the civil servants' control of information and a desire on the part of the secretary of state to exert his authority in a more informed and comprehensive way over the bureaucracy. It was followed by a series of other reforms in the Thatcher governments of the 1980s, aimed at transforming the traditional role of the British civil service in much more radical ways, by stimulating greater efficiency, innovation, and accountability. These reforms have been surveyed extensively by other writers (Levitt 1987; Richards 1989; Collins 1991; Terry 1996); for present purposes, the key point is that the reshaping of the British civil service in the 1980s was cast primarily in terms of better value for money. This fitted in with the Conservatives' enduring need for reductions in public expenditure as a proportion of GDP, for reasons of economic management; but as it became clearer that lasting reductions were impractical or politically unsaleable, the drive for efficiency became an end in itself. It became tinged with the implication that politicians were being held back from making faster progress toward their objectives by the inappropriate and wasteful methods of the civil service. We shall see how these specific policy aims affected the structure and culture of the civil service in a later section of this chapter.

One further general point needs to be made, however, about the characteristics of the ministerial role. Ministers are "birds of passage," often seeing their current portfolio as a step toward some more important post. This feeling may be strengthened where, as we have noted, their knowledge or interest in the subject is limited. Civil servants, on the other hand, can afford to take a longer view. They may have spent years developing a policy, through research, consultation, and refinement of the various possible options. In the period while any new minister is finding his or her feet and clearing his or her mind about priorities, civil servants are at their most influential. It is noteworthy that in countries such as Italy after 1945, or France under the Fourth Republic, where political stability was at a premium, the business of government continued in many respects quite satisfactorily. The point is that where holders of political office change frequently, and coalition compromises rule the day, civil servants take charge—almost *faute de mieux*. Here is Richard Crossman, a leading figure in the Labour governments of the 1960s:

> Too many job changes . . . means a tremendous decline in the power of the politician over the Civil Service machine and a tremendous growth in the power of the Whitehall Departments, both to thwart central Cabinet control and to thwart departmental Ministers' individual control. The truth is that a Minister needs eighteen months to get real control of his Department. (Crossman 1975: 614)

Thus the fulfillment of political ambition only partially coincides with the priorities that civil servants themselves may have. Civil servants are supposed to have the welfare of the state at the root of their professional ethic; as a result, they feel obliged to grapple with issues that need to be resolved as well as those that carry votes (see Shonfield 1965 and Coombes 1970). A good illustration is the problem of disposing of radioactive waste. For many years, the nuclear industry in the United Kingdom, as in the United States, has been generating huge quantities of radionuclides that are potentially damaging to human health and the environment. Most expert opinion, inside government and outside, believes that safe and effective methods of disposal for the wastes have to be found. But the identification of any specific disposal site inevitably provokes a storm of public protest. Since the early 1950s, officials have been developing policies and approaches, backed up with extensive research, that they periodically put before ministers for decision. The outcome is invariably the same: Ministers do not see any votes in provoking a public outcry about the choice of a specific disposal site if the issue can be postponed. The priorities of the politicians simply do not coincide with those of the bureaucrats, or even with what is apparently in the national interest.

The Nature of Civil Service Work

The work of civil servants in the United Kingdom is typically thought of in two main types: a relatively small group of about 4,000 senior officials at Grade 5 and above, who are chiefly concerned with *policy making* at the center and with the development of new legislation, and a much larger group, numbering over 450,000, whose job largely consists of other kinds of *operational* management and administration. In addition, there is a miscellaneous group of specialists, industrial staffs, and others, making up a total of around half a million U.K. home civil servants.

The central policy-making group is traditionally recruited from the older established universities, carries high status, and is quite well paid by public sector standards. Its members are mostly clustered in the principal departments of state, in central London, and they monopolize contact with ministers. This "Whitehall club" (named after the main street lined with government buildings) is a powerful informal network, assessing, informing, and influencing the tone of government policy. To some extent, it substitutes for one of the most important formal mechanisms for reviewing the interrelationships of policy, the Central Policy Review Staff (CPRS), abolished under Mrs. Thatcher's premiership. Although the practice is changing now, many people in policy work have little experience of anything else during their careers and little formal training; their function chiefly involves supporting ministers' work in Parliament and setting or adjusting the frameworks within which the mass of other public servants carry out their work, but without directly supervising them.

Civil servants in operational roles comprise a wide diversity of officials administering welfare, defense, education, employment, and other programs. They also include taxation and excise officials and regulatory, scientific, and research personnel. Their function is largely to carry out instructions within a framework of policy expressed in legislation and regulation and to respond to public demands in various ways. Much of this work is quite routine in character; it nonetheless requires a good educational standard and often specialist training and retraining as policies and procedures change. Staff in operational roles typically work in directorates or agencies with a "flat pyramid" structure, and advancement to the top management positions is a lifelong process achieved by the very few.

For many decades, staff of the British civil service have been grouped into occupational classes; Table 11.1 gives a current summary. Each class has its own grading structure, salary scales, and entitlements. Although the situation has become a great deal more flexible in recent years, it was traditionally difficult to move between classes, and there were (sometimes unwritten) penalties affecting salary or promotion prospects in doing so. For present purposes, we shall focus on the Administration Group and the Open Structure that between them cater to people in the great majority of both policy-making and operational management jobs.

Up till the reforms proposed, but never fully implemented, by Lord Fulton (1968), the Administration Group (previously the Administrative class) was considerably smaller than it is now, because staff in the more junior executive and clerical grades, whether serving in the policy or nonpolicy divisions within departments, were in separate classes. Senior administrative civil servants originally were trained by serving a kind of apprenticeship to a Principal Officer in the grade above the one to which they were recruited, namely, the Assistant Principal (AP). Within a period of around three to five years, an AP could expect to progress to Principal (now Grade 7), with the prospect of perhaps one or two further promotions before retirement, unless he showed exceptional skill and potential for the very highest office. Women were very rarely recruited to the AP grade.

From the late 1960s onward, when the Fulton reforms began to take effect, the distinction between Executive and Clerical classes was abolished and the two were gradually merged with the Administrative class in a unified grading structure. Establishment of the Open Structure in the early 1980s also allowed senior vacancies to potentially be filled by officials from

TABLE 11.1 U.K. Civil Service Occupational Groups, 1994

Category	Number of Employees
Open Structure (Grade 1-3)	630
Open Structure (Grades 4-7)	16,812
Administration Group	216,881
Economist Group	212
Statistician Group	225
Information Officer Group	843
Librarian Group	448
Professional and Technical	15,299
Science Group	9,782
Secretarial Group	6,167
Social Security Group	44,041
Curatorial/Conservation	141
Graphics Officer Group	335
Legal Group	180
Research Officer Group	243
Training/Industrial Officers	2,969
Communications Officers	593
Mapping and Charting Offices	2,791
Pharmaceutical Officers	86
Photographers	252
Process & General Supervisory Officers	693
Psychologists	268
Stores Officers	1,330
Support Officers	13,458
Telecoms & Technical	1,476
Other Nonindustrial	141,280

SOURCE: *Civil Service Statistics 1994* (Her Majesty's Treasury 1994).

any class; thus senior members of the Scientific class, for example, became eligible for top administrative posts on a par with their colleagues who had come up through the ranks of the Administrative class. Initial recruitment became more open, too, with the abolition of the AP grade and the opportunity for members of the former Executive grades to make the transition to the "fast stream," which led to more rapid promotion. The rising numbers of graduates, entering the job market from the newly created universities of the 1960s, also made it possible to recruit graduates directly into the Executive grades.

It is tempting to see in this process of reform a reflection of wider social trends in Britain at the time. The distinction between Administrative and other classes broadly mirrored the social and educational divide between the middle-class elite and the working classes. (The aristocracy were very rarely interested in the civil service as a career.) With the move toward a more egalitarian society in the 1960s, the Fulton reforms enabled talented people from a wider range of backgrounds to be drawn into senior posts. Sir Terence Heiser, permanent secretary at the Department of the Environment (1987-1992), had originally joined the civil service in the most junior clerical grade; his elevation (although hardly typical) would have been almost unthinkable in the pre-Fulton era.

Yet in other ways, the old-style class distinction has persisted. Despite liberal-minded policy initiatives at various times in the past 20 years, ethnic minorities remain underrepresented in the Open Structure and many senior grades below it; the proportion of women in senior posts is not much better (although not much worse either) than is the case in private sector organizations. The civil service remains very hierarchical; age and experience are highly important factors in achieving promotion, whether in policy work or operational management.

For the "fast-stream" civil servant bound for a senior job in policy making, the career progression follows a distinctive pattern. Training is now more precisely tailored to the needs of particular departments, but there is considerable emphasis on the correct style of relationships between officials and ministers and on the requirements of parliamentary accountability. The stages in the legislative process must be understood in detail, along with the annual public expenditure planning cycle, the etiquette of drafting answers for ministers to correspondence and parliamentary questions, the different types of parliamentary debates, some European Union matters, and a selection of topical issues on the agenda of the government of the day. A recent review (Efficiency Unit 1994) confirmed the present scheme of recruiting about 100 high-caliber graduates to the "fast stream" each year, but criticized the bias toward Oxbridge and diluted the promise of almost automatic advancement to the top positions. Instead, fast-stream entrants will have to compete with others who have come up "through the ranks" and with outsiders. Already, 9 out of the 35 most senior posts at the top of departments (Permanent Secretaries) are held by people who were not originally career civil servants.

Once appointed, the civil servant who has joined in the fast stream, or shows exceptional promise in a more ordinary line position, needs to build up experience. The personnel division within each major department of state will periodically move this aspiring senior official to a variety of jobs, at about two- to three-year intervals, so that some familiarity is acquired with each of the key policy areas for which ministers are responsible. As a rough generalization, the shorter the intervals, the more rapid the prospect of advancement. These tours of duty in different parts of the department will often include a spell in one of the regional offices of government and perhaps also a secondment to industry, business, or another branch of government. Indeed, it is a strong indication of forthcoming preferment if an official is posted to the Treasury or the Cabinet Office, where the workload is more than usually onerous and the levels of responsibility higher.

One further type of experience is highly desirable before promotion is guaranteed: a posting to the private office (personal staff) of a minister or to the office of the department's top official (the Permanent Secretary). This is quite likely to be the first occasion on which a civil servant, probably now of several years' standing, actually comes face-to-face with a politician. It can be a testing and sometimes discomforting experience, but to pass through it with credit is a sure route to success. This is a rather odd convention: The skills required for working in a private office are an ability to demand papers and advice from other officials who may be considerably more senior, and to harass them if they do not oblige; an ability to monitor a large number of issues and arrange the relevant documents into the right order at the right time; to keep track of the minister's movements and know where he or she will be, who will accompany him (or her), and what papers should be sent with him (or her). But the skills do not include any real management ability in planning or marshaling resources, communicating or fulfilling objectives; nor do they include familiarity with the issues in any depth. Nevertheless, the experience is important, because it gives a few privileged officials an insight into how politicians actually think and operate. Having gained that experience, the British civil servant can expect to be promoted to a senior policy or management position with little further training or qualification.

The situation in the United Kingdom is in marked contrast to the way in which personal staffs are organized around ministers in other European countries and in the European Commission. There, each minister appoints a "cabinet" of key advisers who work with him or her on developing policy. They may frequently undertake special studies or inquiries and offer advice in parallel with what is put forward by the line divisions of the department. They serve without any particular promise of advancement within the mainstream of a department, having a personal loyalty and a political sympathy with the minister, and they usually depart from the Cabinet, and even from the civil service, when the minister is replaced. Although British ministers do appoint specialist advisers from outside government, their function is at best to provide alternative input to policy from the permanent officials, and their position as interlopers is inclined to be resented or undermined.

In much of the British civil servant's training and experience, there is a strong emphasis on written expression. Any document going before a minister is likely to be drafted and redrafted several times or, at any rate, "covered" by a memo from a senior official that summarizes the key points. There is a recognizable style for civil servants to follow: always clear, concise, unemotional, and well argued. Overtly political points are taboo; they are more likely to be couched in terms of attracting credit for the policy, achieving the government's objectives, and so on. Not a surprise, civil servants learn to keep their own political feelings deeply submerged and indeed suppressed. This is perfectly reasonable because quite often they are called upon, like civil servants in other democracies, to find ways of fulfilling policies to which they privately do not necessarily subscribe.

It is important to recognize that the civil service in Britain is also "nonexecutant" in a number of important areas of work. That is, it does not deliver programs directly but relies on local authorities, the National Health Service, the remaining nationalized industries, or professional bodies such as the police to implement government policies. It is sometimes frustrating for politicians coming into office to find that many of the goals they set themselves are not actually within the competence of civil servants to deliver. Civil servants, who have understood their limitations in this regard long ago, have tended to turn it into a virtue: The skills they traditionally value are those of analysis and appraisal of options together with judicious defense of the status quo rather than executive action. The instruments they could offer ministers, aside from legislation (with its attendant sanctions for noncompliance), were persuasion, incentivization, demonstration by example, and sometimes, with Treasury and parliamentary approval, selective allocation of new expenditures. For much of the time, "getting results," as the politicians see it, means (for the civil servant) finding some other body that will take on the task. The perceived weakness of civil servants in the techniques of policy implementation, alongside the quest for value for money, seems in retrospect to have been a powerful impetus behind the reforms imposed in the 1980s.

But there are other limitations on the civil servant's ability to fulfill his or her master's expectations. Departments of state are also sectional interests and are influenced in turn by other interests (many of them not necessarily political) outside government. The advice they give is not constrained by current political considerations, even though it may be designed to fit in with them. It is quite likely to reflect wider consultations or representations that have been made, and that is probably advisable, because ministers may otherwise underrate the resistance they face. On the other hand, it may not seem as helpful to them as they would wish.

With any major policy initiative, there are also the more general problems of changing a long-established organization with large numbers of staff. Most civil servants are employed on terms that more or less guarantee them work to retirement age (at present, 60) and, like bureaucrats everywhere, they cling to established ways of working. It was this sense of a protected and complacent workforce, apparently draining the public purse, that fired Mrs. Thatcher and her ministers to impose a series of sweeping reforms on civil service structure and working practices in the later 1980s and 1990s.

Reforms of the 1980s

Perhaps the most striking of these is the creation of a large number of "executive agencies" to streamline the nonpolicy work of departments. Beginning with a report from the Prime Minister's Efficiency Unit in 1988 (Jenkins et al. 1988), over 120 agencies have now been established in a role independent or semi-independent from their parent departments. The aim of the reform is to

strengthen accountable management for the delivery of government services;

achieve greater precision about the results expected of people and organizations;

focus activity on outputs, as well as inputs;

reduce the "handicap" of imposing a uniform system in an organization of the size and complexity of the civil service; and

sustain the pressure for improvement in value for money (economy, efficiency, and effectiveness).

Subsequently, the government has decided that before any function would be converted to agency status, it would be subject to a "prior options" test. This would determine whether the function could in fact be abolished, transferred to the private sector, contracted out, "market tested" (rigorously assessed against private sector practice), or made into an agency.

The majority of agencies are quite small and all but a very few operate as "satellites" of conventional departments. Eleven of them have fewer than 100 staff, 41 of them have fewer than 500 staff; 63 fewer than 1,000 staff, and 76 fewer than 2,000. At the other end of the scale, the five largest agencies have more than 10,000 staff each and account for two-thirds of the civil servants in agencies. In an effort to strengthen ministerial control, the chief executives of agencies are directly accountable for their organization's performance. A number of these chief executives have been recruited from outside the civil service. But the large numbers of small agencies attached to some departments, such as Trade & Industry, has meant that in practice ministers have tended to delegate direct control back to their top departmental officials. In other departments, the pressures (or political attractions) of dealing with other, more important work has tended to "crowd out" direct contacts between chief executives and ministers.

The development of executive agencies reflects a more business-orientated, managerialist ethic now being imported into the civil service. It has replaced the concern of 20 years previously to widen opportunity, to level-up employment conditions, and to improve access to senior positions. It has stimulated a culture of decentralization and diversity, with more "freedom to manage" in certain limited respects. From April 1994, agencies with more than 2,000 staff (and a few with less than that) have been given delegated responsibility for pay and conditions of staff. (There are a few exceptions in the Defense area.) Although the practical effects of this have been slow to emerge, a number of agencies seem keen to adopt pay structures and conditions that are distinctively different than in the rest of the service.

These rather centripetal tendencies in the civil service have created new tensions, and in the view of some commentators (for example, Stewart 1996) are fundamentally flawed. The logic of creating executive agencies is that ministers are expected to set the policy agenda, determine departmental priorities, specify the outcomes of policy, and monitor performance. For their part, chief executives are expected to ensure the agencies satisfy ministerial requirements and take responsibility for implementation, including any failures thereof. The traditional role of the policy-making group of civil servants has thus been enlarged by taking on new responsibilities for monitoring, regulation of, and evaluation of agencies' performance, while chief executives of agencies, who concentrate on "delivering the goods," are not expected to have much policy competence.

The reality, however, is that chief executives have found themselves embroiled in policy debates arising from the treatment of particular cases and, consequently, in potential conflict with ministers and policy civil servants. Ministers meanwhile, for various reasons, have been unable to resist intervening in the day-to-day decision making of agencies. A graphic example of the confusions that have now arisen over policy versus operational issues is in the report of Justice Learmont (1995), who was called upon to investigate relationships between the Home Secretary and the Prison Service Agency. It was apparent that the agency's director general was subjected to constant pressure from ministers, with more than 1,000 documents having to be submitted in a four-month period (October 1994 to January 1995) and ministerial questions running at over 600 per year. The Learmont Report observes, "The Director General has not assumed [this] task voluntarily: it is assigned to him, as to Chief Executives of all Agencies. It occupies too much of his time, to the detriment of the efficient running of the Prison Service" (Learmont 1995: 93).

Creation of executive agencies has also produced friction with the Treasury, which has been reluctant to delegate much financial independence to agencies, and also with the trades unions. There is a new kind of class distinction reemerging too. In 1993, a long-awaited report on career management and succession planning in the civil service was released by the Efficiency Unit (it was known as the "Oughton Report" after its principal author). It is clear that around 90% of the senior posts in the Open Structure will remain in traditional departments of state, even though these will shortly account for only 25% of total staff in the service. Only about 10% of top posts will be with the executive agencies. This suggests that policy work will continue to attract the elite, being highly paid and separated from operational management issues. As Harrow and Talbot (1994) say, " 'Traditional policy skills,' despite the whole agency program, remain the pinnacle for civil service careers."

Conclusions

We have seen how the belief spread among government ministers in the 1980s that private sector methods and approaches would be more effective in implementing policy than traditional ways while discussion about policy alternatives tended to be downgraded and even discouraged after the abolition of the CPRS. The reforms of the 1980s shook up traditional patterns of civil service work but have so far had the greatest impact in operational areas rather than in policy making. The resistance to change in culture among the policymakers appears to be deeply entrenched and has been successfully maintained through much of the reform process. Indeed, the latest White Paper (government policy statement) on the civil service, titled *The Civil Service: Continuity and Change* (Major et al. 1994), tends to confirm this view. After a brief acknowledgment of the value of opening senior posts to people from outside the civil service, and a promise to reduce layers of top management, the White Paper says, "Most of the top Civil Service posts will continue to be filled by those with substantial previous experience within the Service."

The traditionally exclusive control that Whitehall civil servants have had over policy making is nevertheless becoming eroded. Their view is increasingly diluted by policies formulated in Brussels for the European Union as a whole (most obviously in agriculture but also in a variety of other social and economic contexts), and they are suffering an uneasy tension with agency chief executives who find themselves unavoidably making decisions that have policy implications. Movement between civil service posts and the outside world is now much more common, with a rise in secondments and midcareer entrants into departments. Business areas with interests close to government, such as defense procurement and financial services, have seen exchanges of personnel with departments; joint work with business in a whole range of functions including education, health, transport, and economic development has become commonplace. The Private Finance Initiative (PFI), intended to supplement or replace government spending on new projects, has resulted in major resource decisions being shared with the private sector.

The reforms of recent years have fundamentally altered the relationships of bureaucrats and politicians in the United Kingdom. But in attempting to resolve the paradox outlined in the opening of this chapter, the values that civil servants should espouse have been thrown into doubt without any clear replacements being identified; meanwhile, the imperative of achieving political programs more effectively has raised new problems, for which privatization or partnership with business are seen as the solutions. While these changes progress, policy civil servants seem to be holding on to their traditional place in government administration; agency civil servants meanwhile are increasingly developing the habits of private sector managers, although they remain generally lower in status and less well paid.

References

Blackstone, T., and W. Plowden. (1988) *Inside the Think Tank: Advising the Cabinet, 1971-1983*. London: William Heinemann.

Collins, B. (1991) "Central Government: A Review of 1991." In F. Terry and H. Roberts, eds., *Public Domain 1991*. London: Public Finance Foundation.

Coombes, D. (1970) *Politics and Bureaucracy in the European Community*. London: Allen and Unwin.

Crossman, R. H. S. (1975) *The Diaries of a Cabinet Minister*. Vol. 1. London: Hamish Hamilton.

Efficiency Unit. (1994) *Review of Fast-Stream Recruitment*. London: Her Majesty's Stationery Office.

Lord Fulton, Chairman. (1968) *Report of the Committee on the Civil Service* (Cmnd 3638). London: Her Majesty's Stationery Office.

Harrow, J., and C. Talbot. (1994) "Central Government: The Changing Civil Service." In P. Jackson and M. Lavender, eds., *The Public Services Yearbook*. London: Chapman & Hall.

Her Majesty's Treasury. (1994) *Civil Service Statistics 1994*. London: Her Majesty's Stationery Office.

———. (1995) *Civil Service Statistics 1995*. London: Her Majesty's Stationery Office.

Jenkins, K., K. Caines, and A. Jackson. (1988) *Improving Management in Government: The Next Steps* (Ibbs Report). London: Her Majesty's Stationery Office.

Justice Learmont. (1995) *Review of Prison Service Security in England and Wales and the Escape from Parkhurst Prison on Tuesday 3 January 1995* (Cm 3020). London: Her Majesty's Stationery Office.

Levitt, M. (1987) "Central Government: A Review of 1987." In P. Jackson and F. Terry, eds., *Public Domain 1989*. London: Public Finance Foundation.

Major, J., K. Clark, and W. Waldegrave. (1994) *The Civil Service: Continuity and Change* (Cm 2627). London: Her Majesty's Stationery Office.

Nolan, J. (1995) *First Report of the Committee on Standards in Public Life* (Cm 2850[I]). London: Her Majesty's Stationery Office.

Oughton, J. (1993) *Career Management and Succession Planning Study* (Oughton Report) (Efficiency Unit [OPSS]). London: Her Majesty's Stationery Office.

Richards, S. (1989) "Central Government: A Review of 1989." In P. Jackson and F. Terry, eds., *Public Domain 1989*. London: Public Finance Foundation.

Shonfield, A. (1965) *Modern Capitalism*. Oxford: Oxford University Press.

Stewart, J. (1996) "A Dogma of Our Times: The Separation of Policy-Making and Implementation." *Public Money & Management*, 16, 3: 33-40.

Terry, F. (1996) "Private Management of Public Enterprise: How Services in the UK Have Been Transformed." In A. Farazmand, ed., *Public Enterprise Management*. Westport, CT: Greenwood.

PART

IV

The State of the Current State

The concluding chapter in this book is by Bert Rockman. His analysis is focused on the broadest aspects of modern governance: the state in general and the administrative state in particular, as well as the current controversial trend toward—and debate over—the shrinking government or state, public bureaucracy, and civil service professions around the globe, including the United States, with the implications for public administration. Rockman's analysis is comprehensive and strategic; it covers political, economic, social, and administrative aspects of modern governance around the world. But he also discusses significant micro issues concerning the management of the economy and administration as well as the public-private division of policy and administrative affairs. More specifically, Rockman tells us in his conclusion how the modern state in general and the administrative state have expanded, what functions they have performed, and what has been happening to them since the 1970s drive against their expansion. He then reviews the literature and focuses on the pivotal aspects of modern administration, bureaucracy and civil service, privatization (marketization) and contracting out, and professionalization of the modern state, and what these have meant to various viewpoints on democracy and governance. In this regard, he discusses the major political issues of accountability, responsiveness, and responsibility, values that are often regarded by critics to be in conflict with professionalism and the professional bureaucracy. His analysis of the current global trend in reshaping the state and the ensuing ideological approach of "managerialism" leading governments to become a "competitive market" is extremely useful in understanding the profound changes that are taking place in societies and their governments around the world. Under these newly defined boundaries of state functions worldwide—with major variations, of course—the relationship between bureaucrats and politicians is also being reshaped. But, just as guidance in governance—read: the politicians' task—is important, so is discretion. That will require "cooperation and collegial relations between political leaders and between them and civil servants. And it will require the involvement of civil servants." Rockman concludes that "a shrunken government will work no better than a swollen one."

12

"Honey, I Shrank the State"

On the Brave New World of Public Administration

Bert A. Rockman

Changes in the Nature of the Governing Problem

The first two-thirds of the twentieth century witnessed the development and enlargement of the administrative state, though, to be sure, the administrative state had its genesis far earlier in many places. Armstrong (1973), for instance, locates the development of the French civil service in the sixteenth century and Farazmand (forthcoming) shows that a developed administrative state existed in ancient Persia. Certainly, several other states, such as Sweden and Japan, had for centuries developed a substantial professional corps of public servants to serve their respective crowns. What is profoundly different, however, about the twentieth century (and in some settings, the latter part of the nineteenth century) is the expansion of the scope and activity of the state (Rose 1976). This expansion of activity has fueled debate about the appropriate size of the state, its functions, and its centrality in the lives of the citizenry. And it is also this expansion that has led us to speak of the phenomenon we call "the administrative state."

The dominant motif of thinking through the first two-thirds or so of the twentieth century was predicated on the notion that government would play a positive force in society in providing for collective goods and securing the well-being of citizens through the provision of services. In this sense, the state grew as a corrective against the imperfections of market forces and, to some extent in Europe, as a prophylactic against the threat to regimes posed by revolutionary Marxism. A favorable conception of the positive state was accompanied especially after 1945 by a number of other factors—a growing prosperity and thus a form of social surplus represented as slack in governmental budgets, an expectation that governments and bureaucrats were competent and worthy of trust (a condition that varied, however, quite a bit from one setting to another), and a belief that public problems required public solutions. Above all, the generation of social security and welfare programs created constituencies who clearly benefited from the programs, while the costs of those programs had yet to become fully apparent.

By the 1970s, it was becoming clear that the expansionary era in government was soon to end. Articles emphasizing an overloading of governmental responsibilities became prominent (King 1975; Brittan 1975; Rose and Peters 1978). Limiting expansion of the welfare state by the recession-prone 1970s no longer was in doubt; indeed, by now, its contraction rather than its consolidation is in the throes of becoming realized. As well, in the past 20 or so years, the social and economic costs of regulation became more prominently advertised.

These concerns grew more salient precisely because, by comparison with the growth rates of the previous two and a half decades after World War II, the rate of economic growth began to pale. Stagnant macroeconomic conditions were not conducive to expanding the government agenda. In fact, they would lead to a concern that businesses were being too greatly restricted by the regulatory hand of the state, thus stifling economic growth, and that capital was being too heavily taxed to generate productive investment. The slack available to an expansion of the public agenda thus diminished, and the prospect of raising taxes brought forth taxpayer revolts, especially in the United States, where voters, perhaps unknowingly, voted to cripple the capacity of their local governments to raise revenues. Like the famous shot at Concord advertised to have been heard around the world, the popular approval of Proposition 13 in California in 1978 signaled a change in the rhetoric of political debate in the United States—a change that would begin to resonate in other contexts as well. The new focus would be on fiscal restraint, cutbacks, and management efficiency within a diminished public sector. The allergy to taxes would not change the immediate demand for government services, but it would inevitably affect the capacity of government to supply them.

The Keynesian ideas still prominent in the early 1970s (when Richard Nixon reputedly claimed that "we are all Keynesians now") came to be overshadowed by neoliberal market ideas. Neoliberalism provided the intellectual driving force for downsizing government and privatizing a number of its functions (Self 1993). Government programs came to be viewed merely as the product of one set of more powerful interests acquiring rents (subsidies) from some set of more numerous but less politically powerful citizens. William Niskanen (1971), a neoclassical economist, provided a great deal of the intellectual wherewithal for this argument in his frequently acclaimed if abundantly controversial book, *Bureaucracy and Representative Government*. The neoliberal argument regarding the positive state was that it was bloated, inefficient, unrepresentative, and thus unfair.

An interesting question is why neoliberal ideas became so prominent, the answer to which, unfortunately, may be more a matter of speculation than of certainty. I have suggested some of the conditions leading to pressures for government belt-tightening—the loss of the fiscal dividend stemming from economic growth and decreasing confidence in government itself. But it may be that the fundamental impetus for rethinking the state was produced by two factors. One was the emergence of outsized budget deficits as the costs of the welfare state expanded even as the level of welfare per capita did not. The other was the victory of right-wing political coalitions committed not merely to being more efficient managers of the welfare state but to rolling back the welfare state itself. Such coalitions were the symbiotic hosts for the resurgence of neoliberal economic ideas.

Rhetoric, of course, has outpaced action, although the gap between the two has been closing notably. As we head into the twenty-first century, there can be little doubt that the shape of government is changing and, with changes in its scope, the administrative state also will change. Indeed, it already has in some instances. And as it does, it will raise numerous questions and challenges. Among these are ones about what the role of the professional civil servants will be.

The changing shape of the state and the diminution of its functions may or may not by themselves greatly shape the character of the civil service. There remains much uncertainty in this regard. Obviously, a diminution in the responsibilities of government and a downsizing of government is likely to affect personnel and the number of civil servants. Beyond that, not much else is clear. Thus, despite the relatively small public sector and the highly decentralized features of the Swiss confederacy, the depoliticized character of government in Switzerland enables its civil servants to play an influential role. Clearly, how the civil service is affected depends upon how the downsizing is done. Furthermore, as Fred Thayer's provocative chapter in this book suggests, the historic role of the civil service is, as a general matter, to safeguard the integrity of public transactions. If so, then the scope of the state may be less relevant to altering this role than are changes in the context through which managing the state and accounting for its (and the civil servants') performance are conceived. In other words, a smaller state need not be an unfriendly one to civil servants. For the civil service, what is crucial is whether or not there is a change in the nature of its role and responsibilities.

Such changes, though, could be foreshadowed by changes in the scope and functions of government. A currently fashionable way of viewing government, for example, is in terms of a market analogue wherein agencies are conceived of as suppliers of services and citizens as consumers thereof (NPR 1993; Kettl 1994; Kettl and DiIulio 1995). The implication appears to be that unless government agencies change their ways of doing business, their monopoly of supply will be threatened. Civil servants, in other words, may find their conduct to be governed more by shifting patterns of taste than by principles of legal accountability.

The Profession of the Civil Service:
Accountability, Responsiveness, Responsibility

When one speaks of the *professionalization* of administration, there are several senses in which the term can be, and indeed is, used. For Max Weber (1946), professionalization meant the development of a full-time corps of officials selected by merit and committed to the fulfilment of the law. Defined in such a fashion and behaving accordingly, such a professional permanent officialdom is, at least theoretically, incorruptible. It is committed to the impersonal application of the law and resistant to the entreaties of those who would seek to deviate from that standard. Herbert Kaufman (1977) notes in this regard that the buildup of red tape that limits the opportunity for discretionary behavior and makes government appear to be unresponsive, sometimes even silly, is a function of the need to ensure that official behavior is held to formal account and can be defended as lawful. The more government seeks to do and to hold to account, the more it proliferates red tape. That is especially true in the United States, where the web of accountability is unusually complex owing to the separation-of-powers system.

Red tape is so disconcerting because it is inherently inconvenient and impedes seemingly sensible behavior. By definition, it limits discretion, which understandably conflicts with the reality that discretionary behavior may be needed to produce timely results. Furthermore, discretionary behavior is made necessary when laws are ambiguous or conflicting—a condition that is likely to be produced by a more expansive state and, again, one that in the case of the United States also tends to be produced by the separation of powers.

The standard of commitment to law often denies to civil servants the power to make their own judgments, but by virtue of that, in principle, also provides protection from the necessity of following the dictates of unlawfully behaving superiors. Strictly speaking, then, there is a potentially large clash between the principle of neutral commitment to the law and that of the chain of command. Of course, legal accountability and the chain of command are not so easily distinguishable in reality mainly because those commanding responsiveness higher up on the chain are also constituted to do so by election or some other lawful form of principal-agent relationship. Nonetheless, in a system governed by law, civil servants owe their ultimate loyalty to the law rather than to their superior in the event of a clash. Notably, civil servants in the United States are required to swear fealty to the law (the Constitution) rather than to their superiors. In constitutional monarchies, loyalty typically is given to the crown, which symbolically represents the sovereignty of the state. In each case, ultimate loyalty is supposed to be rendered to a principal (and thus also a principle) higher than the next rung on the chain of command.

One thing, then, that we learn about accountability is that, for the most part, it is the enemy of discretion and judgment.[1] Another thing we learn about it is that it will likely contribute to the advancement of red tape and often therefore to frustration with bureaucracy and government. Judgment, timeliness, and accountability are rarely mutually compatible. Accountability requires reporting to ascertain whether or not there is compliance with the law(s). Reports piled on top of one another lead to the conclusion as well as the reality that a government of laws quickly becomes a government of lawyers (and accountants and auditors as well). When society moves from personal to impersonal encounters and from particularistic to universalized relationships, it brings forth laws and regulations—the currency of distrust.

As we note, of course, compliance itself is often not a straightforward matter. Laws are frequently silent or unclear; legal principles are not always consistent or in accord; nor are the dictates of political leaders consistent with one another, or always clearly in accordance with legal precedent. Ambiguity often provides the context for choice, and ambiguity necessitates discretion. In the absence of ambiguity, the rote application of procedure dominates. When that occurs, the space available for judgment is circumscribed. Thus Charles Goodsell (1981) describes the condition that often exists at the field level as being one of "compression," wherein the field bureaucrat is given little discretion to bend the rules despite facing situations that give compelling reasons to do so. Goodsell describes a situation, in short, in which the system of legal accountability, that a professional civil service is committed to uphold, clashes with the civil servant's sense of professional responsibility. The clash is between what professional norms teach civil servants is the responsible thing to do and what the law requires them to do. Therein we have yet another interpretation of what it might mean to call the civil service professional. Such an interpretation stresses the technical competence of the civil servant and the civil servant's expert knowledge. This conception of professionalism also incorporates the professional and ethical norms that stem from the civil servant's trained expertise. In this sense, the civil servant is obligated to provide his or her best advice or to find the most felicitous (or least calamitous) outcome within the legal or political constraints. Hence there may be a clash between accountability and responsibility. Discretion at the point where the government meets its citizenry optimizes the prospects for professional judgment and, alas, also for capricious behavior. Discretion limits, moreover, the mechanisms for enforcing both the chain of command and accountability. Delegation is, as Matthew Holden astutely observes in his chapter, a grant of power, and power is what administration is about. To whom shall such discretion be provided? And how can it be monitored? These are topics of current and also perennial debate in the context of governmental and thus administrative reform.

Expertise, particularly of a substantive sort, suggests that there is a need for the government to know something about what it is doing or what it plans to do so that it may do it judiciously. It is worthwhile to note, if in passing, that substantive expertise in bureaucracy implies a preference for a positive state that needs to know how to properly engage the problems it has been empowered to deal with—or, from a more skeptical perspective, those it has been empowered, if unintentionally, to create. A laissez-faire state, by contrast, has little need as such for substantive expertise.

In addition, there is an expertise that comes from experience. By working in a specific jurisdiction dealing with a specific set of problems over time, the civil servant gains superior knowledge not only about the substantive problem but also about the politics that define its feasible solution set. This experiential-based knowledge provides a form of expertise that often comes in handy when mediating between what political leaders want to do and what they might be able to do.

The classic precept of the administrative state presupposes that commitment to the impersonal workings of the law, responsibility to the chain of command (assuming there to be one), and the application of professional substantive or procedural judgment are consistent. The problem is that they frequently are not. In fact, different principles are at work behind each of these notions of a professional bureaucracy. Commitment to the law reflects the principle of accountability, as we have noted. The chain of command represents the principle of responsiveness. And the use of professional knowledge connects to the principle of responsibility. The second of these principles, responsiveness, is typically demanded by the political rulership, sometimes in memorable and colorful ways such as expressed in Nixon deputy John Ehrlichman's memorable dictum, "When we say jump, their answer should be 'how high.' " Efforts to produce unrestrained responsiveness are complicated or eased by the constituted structures of political authority. The difficulty attached to producing unrestrained responsiveness toward the political executive in the United States is complicated by the very nature of the separated system (Jones 1994). The separated nature of political supervision of administration, in fact, sometimes leads to aggressive efforts on the part of both executive and legislative political actors to structure responsiveness exclusively to them (T. Moe 1985; Aberbach and Rockman 1976). It provides some impetus to managerialist ways of shaping the executive branch even as it so often inhibits managerialist designs from being consummated. For, in the end, managerialist measures cut Congress out of the picture (R. Moe 1994)—a condition that for understandable reasons Congress finds less willing to accept than do the political managers of the executive branch.

What is currently only speculative is how the shrinkage of government may be—if it is at all—altering the accepted precepts of a professional civil service and the principles under which it purportedly operates. A genuine empirical exploration of this linkage, if such there be, constitutes a vital and commendable research agenda. When that mission is largely accomplished, it should tame speculations of the sort I offer here.

Reshaping the State

There are a number of ways in which the modern state is being reshaped. The safest thing to be said is that they are not all consistent with one another. Moreover, most assuredly, the reshaping of the state is being undertaken differently in different places and at different paces. One should not underestimate variety and difference in tradition here as shapers of response. A few basic themes are apparent, however. One is that the state not only needs to be reshaped, it needs to shape up and act more responsively to its citizens. This is not exactly a new idea, although it is being expressed through new forms. Bottom-up administration also motivated such programs as "Model Cities" more than a quarter century ago with results not likely to commend themselves to the current ahistorical advocates of performance-based management. A second is that the state not only needs to be responsive, it also needs to be leaner and do less. More of its functions, in this view, can be farmed out to the private sector—some of them to be regulated by the state in the form of contracts, such as running prisons or parks; others simply to be left either to the private marketplace or to eleemosynary organizations, such as funding for culture and perhaps even subsistence for the poor. Yet a third form with which I begin here has much less directly to do with the gross output of the state or its scope of activity than with the organization of relationships between the civil service and its political overseers, between the civil service and the citizenry, and between spending and controlling units of government.

The rubric of managerialism speaks to many of these issues. *Managerialism,* as a fashionable term, implies that something is afoot in rethinking the traditional roles of civil servants. And indeed something is, but it is hard to pin down in terms of a single syndrome. Much of the rethinking emphasizes the role of the managerial and fiscal discipline necessary to keep governments from becoming hopelessly centrifugal in their tendencies. But other elements emphasize instead qualitative improvements in the performance of government organizations as evaluated by external constituencies. One stream tends to emphasize the logic of managerial rationality, whereas the other tends to highlight the logic of consumerism.

Managerialism

Luc Rouban (1995: 35) defines *managerialism* as an "attempt to rationalize society with managerial tools, that is, with cultural tools coming from the business world." Strictly speaking, the rise of managerialism has little directly to do with the growth or contraction of the state, per se. Its techniques and modes of operation can be associated with expansionary or contracting regimes, although of late it has been more connected to the latter (because almost no one is in an expansionary mode). Managerialism does, however, have a good bit to do with restructuring power relationships within the state. It is principally focused on the question: "Who controls?" From this standpoint, managerialism emphasizes organizational rationality as that is determined by the chain of command.

Because the current dominant management problem of government has become so heavily linked to matters of fiscal control, the development of managerialism seems to have been associated with conservative governments that have been assiduously seeking to find ways to control the growth of public expenditure (Savoie 1994). In this regard, managerialism has been associated with a trend toward greater financial centralization and control over agency behavior, the generation of a set of central monitoring agents with the authority to regulate the actions of agencies, a decline in agency-specific clientelism, and an alteration in the balance of discretion in favor of central authorities. But managerialism in the age of public expansion stood for the same things, only with a different twist.

The concept of managerialism, as the tag suggests, implies salvation through technique and procedure. It represents ultimately the triumph of what Karl Mannheim (1936) called "functional rationality" over what he termed "substantive rationality." From this perspective, systems override substance. The reality, of course, is that proponents of managerial reforms often want systems to serve substance. By definition, proponents of managerial reform are enemies of the status quo regardless of what the status quo actually represents. In recent years, managerialism often has meant producing the discipline and generating the diagnostics to allow the financial cutters to wield their scalpels. It sometimes has meant, as it certainly has in the United States, the micromanagement of agencies from central monitoring units. Yet it was only a generation ago when Allen Schick (1969) applauded the development of budget-policy analytics as a means of breaking through the torpor of subsystem politics to promote systematic and comprehensive policy making—buzzwords then of the political left.

The one thing that is clear about managerial reform is that almost always it has been in the service of a logic of greater central control, with the intent of increasing responsiveness to central executive actors. It does so by emphasizing accounting and reporting procedures. Managerialism, by virtue of its link to the chain-of-command principle, provides a pathway for those at the top to break through the blockage represented by subsystem politics and clientelism. The implications for civil servants are twofold: Those involved in actually managing agency programs will have their discretion and authority circumscribed, whereas those in positions of monitoring and controlling the behavior of agencies from the center are likely to find themselves with enhanced authority.

More recently, however, a different form of managerial reform has arisen. It derives from a "consumerist" logic, whereby local discretion is extended even as resources are tightened. Budgetary scarcity, a condition that is often thought to be at the root of centralized management control (Peters 1995), also provides a logic for political authorities at the center to escape the risks attached to making decisions under budgetary duress. Instead of necessarily being driven to seek maximum control from the center (T. Moe 1985), choice and responsibility may be farmed out locally so that blame is diffused. Good management, consequently, is taken to mean pleasing the agency's consumers—a new conception apparently of agency clienteles.

Borrowing the language and symbols of "total quality management," or TQM, the Clinton Administration's contribution to this reformist tack is to extend discretion and to analogize government as a business operating in a competitive marketplace of suppliers for its services. Thus governmental service delivery would have to be something it rarely can be, given its logic of accountability, and that is to be entrepreneurial. Competing for market share should emphasize rapid adaptation and inventiveness in the field relatively unhampered by managerial constraints. These aspects of the National Performance Review headed by Vice President Al Gore (1993) emphasize a market rationality (rapid adjustment to demand and preference) rather than a managerial rationality responsive to a chain-of-command logic. This vacuum of authority, and thus of accountability, is noted by Donald Kettl (1994) in his appraisal of the NPR initiative:

> *If empowerment drives the NPR, and empowerment means delegating far greater discretion to bureaucrats, what glue will unify governmental policy and prevent it from spinning off centrifugally into thousands of directions?* This is the core problem of accountability in the NPR. (p. 30, italics are in the original)

Government as a Competitive Market

The new path of managerial reform, as indicated above, is designed to reverse tendencies toward micromanagement by higher authorities. The idea is that it may then lead to the possibility of letting a thousand flowers bloom. Without a landscaping strategy, however, chaos results. The ultimate grounding for government and the civil service, after all, is to provide regular, predictable, and authoritative responses on the basis of law. The logic of entrepreneurship, of pleasing the "customers," and of responses wholly adaptive to the case or the claimant certainly will reduce the strangulating effects of red tape. That is no doubt a good. Flexibility is a virtue. But if there is no gyroscope to guide specific administrative decisions, they, in turn, will be devoid of the regularity of law by which accountability is measured. And that is bad. Ironically, then, this latest in a line of management reforms (NPR) seems to minimize management altogether and to devolve discretion to the point where government and the marketplace will seem nearly indistinguishable from one another. Jon Pierre (1995: 69-75) refers to this phenomenon as "the marketization of the state."

Treating government in accordance with market principles seems to be especially in favor in the Anglo-American democracies. The United States, of course, has had a long-standing attachment to unfettered market principles. In some ways, however, the rush to market principles has been even swifter in Britain. The Thatcherite revolution in Britain has created a distinctly more sympathetic view—at least among Tory elites and their supporters—to the idea that markets are the wave of the future. Accordingly, in this view, the civil service left to its own devices would reinforce a past anchored in economic decline and the loss of enterprising spirit. Competition may be thus viewed as providing the basis for a more responsive, inventive, and open civil service made less comfortable in its traditional privileges of exclusive access to the political decision makers. Graham Mather, a Conservative member of the European Parliament and an enthusiast for competitive advice giving via contracting out, has argued in accordance with the underlying theory of competitive markets that "insecurity by keeping everyone on their toes is likely to produce better advice."[2] The alternative consideration of the role of the civil service is that security based on the monopolistic advisory role of the civil service breeds frankness and informed skepticism—vital but not easily marketed elements of policy advice.

By virtue of being an open system, the competitive marketplace for policy advice may appeal to those who have been excluded by the class barriers imposed by the insularity and exclusiveness of the civil service itself—a condition that, to be sure, is much less pertinent in the American case (Rockman 1995). In Britain and no doubt elsewhere, demystifying the civil service elite may be seen as a way of opening government and making it more accessible to those less traditionally cultivated to serve in it. In this sense, the marketplace is a great democratic leveler. It is kind to neither tradition nor élan, nor even necessarily to merit. Competitors in the marketplace must adapt to prevailing tastes to survive or prosper. Although there is always some demand for merit, it is usually in limited supply.[3] Open entry among suppliers is the ingredient that allows a marketplace to be fully responsive to its range of demands.

By contrast, exclusivity is the hallmark of an elite that defines its own qualifications and thus indispensability—an elite that by virtue of its meritorious qualities is given a privileged position in the corridors of policy making (Suleiman 1974, 1978; Savage forthcoming). Almost everywhere the civil service aspires to that status. Yet, increasingly, the assumptions underlying this special elitist claim are under attack. Democracy unpeels the layers of insulation that traditionally have provided the civil service with its special status and its privileges (the American case excepted). One way of responding to this claim is for any set of rulers to assert managerial control and seek to politicize the civil service or at least the conditions of its service (Rourke 1992; Aberbach and Rockman 1994). Another option is to make the civil service simply less relevant by placing its traditional functions within a competitive marketplace. Civil servants always have one trump card that can be played in any system—namely, that they have been there before. They have knowledge and experience that is indispensable and that (at least the experiential-based knowledge) is unlikely to be replicated on the outside. But experience is more likely to lead to caution rather than undaunted vision, and more likely to lead to advice that inhibits rather than liberates choices.

The traditional role of the civil service is founded on a quite different set of ideas altogether than those on which markets are predicated. The professional civil service represents a bond to the past as well as to the legal authority of the government. This constrains adaptability because knowledge of the past ties present behaviors into a web of past commitments, this being an inconvenient matter for those intent on reinventing the present. The legal authority of the government also provides the basis for the lawful, accountable, and even neutral or universalistic behavior of the civil service.

The implications of marketplace approaches for the civil service are far reaching. In a competitive marketplace, there is no institutional sanctity. Everything is up for grabs. When advice to the government is for sale, it is likely to be aimed at the receptivities of the current governors; advice to the ministry ineluctably will be designed to please the current minister. That is the central difference between two competing worldviews—the permanence of institutions and the transience of tastes. The most essential role of a professional civil service, after all, is to balance transience with permanence and temper the enthusiasms of the present with the anchor of the past. Without the past, there is no ballast, and without ballast, choices are apt to be unstable. But caution is the stuff of caricature, which ultimately leads to an erosion of the credibility of the civil service. And that, in turn, leads to an available market for management faddists and government reinventors.

The formality by which a government of laws unfolds its time-consuming procedures is yet a different source of dissatisfaction with government, leading to an emphasis on "consumerism" through marketplace ideas. Law is the medium through which social distrust is expressed. No doubt more trusting and communal societies resolve potential conflicts more through the medium of social adjustment (Kelman 1981), but such social processes can easily exclude those who are seen to lie outside of the community. Social adjustments are more easily arrived at the less sharply differentiated are the preferences of the population.

Whenever the sphere of legal rights is widened, legal protection and due process claims grow, and with these comes a mountain of paperwork to assure accountability to the law and to protect or defend against litigation. The longer term evolution of modern democracies has been in the direction of expanding rights and legality and therefore regulation. That evolution—and, above all, the mountain of red tape it yields—produces sufficient negative externalities to create the belief that government ought to be made more efficient, responsive, and user friendly.

These concerns do not lack legitimacy. They may contribute some to popular dissatisfaction with government. Above all, they help contribute to a burgeoning industry in management nostrums that run the gamut from strategic control to bottom-up management—the latter implying virtually none at all. Most of the problems they are invoked to deal with are inherent in varying degrees across modern constitutional governments. This does not mean that management nostrums, such as the NPR, are without redeeming merit. They are all designed to address some problem that results from the underlying pathologies attendant to a government of laws and a civil service responsible for implementing them. At particular moments, some types of management reform will seem especially appealing as the pathologies they address become particularly salient. They usually address these problems, however, in narrowly focused ways without due regard to legal and political complexities. There is, after all, a market in management schemes too, and contingency does not play well in that market.

The NPR, for example, tries to increase agency-level discretion and lessen the stranglehold of central agencies and the role of micromanagement. It tries to do so by locating discretion at the bottom of these organizations, in their field operatives, and implicitly at the top, in their political appointees. It is unclear in its legal guidance precisely because it wants government and management to respond flexibly and to minimize the red tape problem. A flexible response risks, however, the danger of being a capricious and legally unaccountable one (Lowi 1969).

Ultimately, the power of the market analogy derives from the growing sources of competition to what once had been regarded as the sole legitimate monopoly of government. Policy advice flows like water now in every country capable of financing think tanks or consultancies. The global expansion of capital, the speed of technological innovation, the deepening and diffusion of knowledge, and the decline of deference toward public authority perhaps all conspire to make governments seem less relevant and less capable. The impact of this may be to make the civil service less powerful because the states they serve are becoming less so.

The principles based on legalism by which the classic administrative state arose are by no means likely to vanish. But they clearly are coming under pressure from a combination of forces that compel states to adopt mechanisms to react more adaptively, driven by the logic of markets and sometimes even by common sense. The expansion of rights and the growth of regulation drive legalism. And that consequent in turn drives a counter-reaction toward speedier and more adaptive responses. The two logics—legal accountability and flexible response—are, in principle, clashing and incompatible with one another. Managerial reform typically emphasizes the latter. Responsiveness to the chain of command is one form for achieving flexible response, that is, managerial rationality, in a fashion that at least pleases the political rulers of the executive. More recently, the shift has been to a form of consumerism or commonsense response dictated by a market rationality. Here, the idea is to please the consumers of governmental goods.

Contracting Out and Privatization

Governments always have contracted out some services mainly because of the costs of various sorts attached to building up their own full-time apparatus. Mercenary soldiers, for example, come quickly to mind as one such service that traditionally has been much in demand. These days, the management of prisons, parks, and many municipal services are given over to private contractors. Although the nature of their contracts can vary widely, it is clear that once a service is given over to private hands, the private contractor is likely to be appraised on the basis of performance and cost efficiency. But who will do these appraisals and under what criteria? Who will supply the information? And how accountable will privately contracted employees be to legal norms prevailing for government employees? Furthermore, who can vouch for their training? Kettl (1993) notes that the rush toward privatization does not always produce satisfactory answers to these questions because the principal-agent relations have not been carefully thought through. Here, Kettl notes that in spite of the market logic for privatizing, that logic does not always prevail. Frequently, instead, monopolistic sources of supply have been created under privatization without adequate oversight.

Contracting out and *privatization* sometimes are synonymous, but they are not necessarily so. Contracting out is essentially a public service or function that has been leased to private management under a term contract. As noted, governments have been doing this sort of thing for a long time.

The arguments for doing it largely focus on cost efficiencies, especially in labor-intensive activities. (Cost efficiencies here may also include political costs, which presumably drove rulers to hire nonsubject forces to help with the military work.) It is not surprising, therefore, that service activities such as garbage pickup, prison management, facilities security, and the like seem suitable for contracting out because the overhead costs of hiring directly in the public sphere are otherwise greater. (In the United States, it also is likely to mean that nonunion employees can be hired through private auspices to counter the only prospering union sector—government employees.) Presumably also, contracting out can be gauged by performance during the period of the contract, although how clearly the contractors will be held to account is likely to vary with the terms of the contract and the willingness to enforce them. As with other performance- or outcome-based processes, a lot depends upon how clearly the performance criteria are specified. Kettl's excellent book on this subject (1993) shows how infrequently such criteria are made clear.

If the form of privatization that contracting out assumes is more typically in the form of a lease than a sale, governments also have been engaging, especially within the past decade or so, in divesting themselves more permanently of a number of assets they have held. As Guy Peters notes (1995), an old yet urgent reason for this is the financial stress affecting the public sphere. Assets that lose money are not assets; they are liabilities. One can see, of course, how this conception also links to managerialist perspectives toward administration. Whereas an interventionist view of government is that it should compensate for market failures by undertaking activities that lose money but provide social good, the managerialist view of government seems consistent with the idea that government also should be disciplined by market incentives and costs. Thus railroads, national airlines, and real estate, among other things, are up for sale (or have been sold) to private bidders at a greater or lesser pace in different national contexts. The costs of their subsidy have become too expensive for governments trying to tame budgets and hold the tax line. Moreover, in the case of some types of assets, new global or regional trade regimes can even make governmental subsidies problematic in negotiations.

Still, in regard to privatization, one should not discount the role of ideology on either side of the debate. How big the state should be and what it should do are essentially matters of political taste, not ones of scientific assessment. What functions belong in the private or public spheres or some mix thereof is a matter of political judgment and policy preference rather than a matter amenable to purely scientific analysis. The assumption that markets will do it better depends mightily upon what the "it" is. Until that is specified and analyzed with respect to marginal value, not just cost, the assumption that markets will do it better is mostly just that, namely, an assumption. Certainly, where public monopolies are simply being replaced by private monopolies, the latter are neither economically nor politically responsive. Nevertheless, one thing seems clear enough, and that is that governments at varying rates are liquidating many of their assets, especially those they deem to be a financial burden.

Some Final Thoughts

In its newly slimmed down profile, the state likely will have less to manage. It is probable that this situation will last for a while; it is unlikely that it will last indefinitely. Deregulation of industries and markets is likely at some point to produce demands for re-regulation. Even the meltdown of the social service state will have its limits. Political rationalism, at least in democratic systems, will in the end, I suspect, not be dominated by economic rationalism.

Important issues of accountability and even quality of performance are raised by the new conditions enveloping governance and changing its traditional modalities. These conditions also raise new issues about what functions a modern civil service should be prepared for—indeed, even what its roles are to be. It is likely that the civil service will not be as secure and independent as it has been accustomed to being in the past, and that it will be in competition with service providers from outside of government ranging from garbage collectors to policy advisers. These are not absolutely new conditions, it is essential to reiterate. There are lots of examples of outside suppliers to provide for government service well before the current privatization craze kicked in. But in the current cycle of thinking about governmental performance, outside competition is likely to become even more legitimate until its own deficiencies and abuses are revealed. A slimmer and smaller government imbued with the ethic of managerialism probably will place civil servants more frequently in the role of monitors and overseers of government contracts. Where public services are privately managed, the link to accountability is potentially weakened. Presumably as well, the key to attracting government contracts will be to demonstrate how much less privately managed services will cost rather than how much better those services will be performed. In the age of managerialism, it appears that civil servants will have less to manage.

Above all, however, the current trends in reshaping the state may bring into conflict in a more noticeable way the competitive logic of markets versus the institutional logic of government, especially as that is embodied through the civil service. Markets are about adjusting supply to demand

and shaping response to prevailing tastes. Institutions, on the other hand, shape the present through the past. Civil servants represent a past that limits the repertoire of present response. They provide experience and memory. Presumably, these qualities help to clarify feasible pathways and specify judicious options. Such options, however, often dampen enthusiasm for bold new strokes. In any competition for policy advice likely to emphasize radical options, civil servants are at a disadvantage (Aberbach et al. 1981). Boldness, imaginativeness, and appealing recommendations are easier to come by when the responsibility for implementing them is absent (Rockman 1981, 1990).

The issue of how the role of the civil service will change, brought about by the changing nature of the governing problem itself, remains very much open. For those who cling to the quaintly old-fashioned belief that the public sector has unique responsibilities not susceptible to market logic and that the civil service has unique responsibilities to ensure that the public interest is served, these are challenging times. If the challenge cannot be met by mindless bashing of either government or bureaucrats, it also cannot be met by denying the reality of the emphases on managerialism, performance, competition, and downsizing that are being placed on the public sector, especially in the English-speaking democracies. Leadership and cooperation are essential if the demands for greater market responsiveness and managerial efficiency are to be reconciled with the professionalism and neutrality that civil servants bring to the process of governance.

That these possibilities exist, however, is not merely a flight of fancy. Two experts in Australian government who have closely followed the way these matters have been played out there indicate that when faced with the same austerity drives affecting other governments, the Australian political leadership moved the civil servants directly into engaging these needs and responding to them (Campbell and Halligan 1992). That experiment remains incomplete, and potential contradictions are still to be ironed out between the managerialism and fiscal controls deriving from the age of austerity, on the one hand, and the traditions of policy influence and neutral competence of the civil service, on the other. A key to the Australian experience has been trustworthy relations between the political leadership and the civil service to promote mutual engagement. That it can be done, of course, does not mean that it will be. Without mutual collaboration and trust between political leaders and civil servants, chances are that destructive disengagement is a lot more likely to occur than is constructive engagement.

Whether shrinking the state is a good or bad idea is not really the issue here. No doubt, there is no clear or simple answer to that except in the minds of ideologues. The impetus for shrinking the state and for a market logic to govern its responses has come from real life problems, not just from the abstract designs in the heads of neoliberal economists. The real issue is whether these responses can be made to work in a manner consistent with traditional principles of legal accountability—no easy task, especially in a system such as the American one in which different political principals are likely to have varying definitions as to what that constitutes. Coherent guidance will be necessary. Yet, so will discretion—indeed, discretion becomes acceptable only in the context of guidance. That will require cooperation and collegial relations between political leaders and between them and civil servants. And it will require the involvement of civil servants. The smart money says "no way" —but that is likely to ensure that a shrunken government will work no better than a swollen one.

Notes

1. The exception, ironically, has to do with equating professionalism and accountability, the logic of which is that professionalism inherently dictates that judgment will be used to enhance accountability in a substantive rather than procedural way (Friedrich 1940). Such an equation appears, however, to confuse the concept of accountability, which is a legal notion, with that of responsiveness or even responsible behavior, which are, respectively, political and moral notions.

2. Comments made at a symposium, Nuffield College, Oxford University (February 8, 1995).

3. This conflict is often expressed in terms of the neutral competence ideal versus a demand from the political leadership for responsive competence. Neutral competence is frequently endangered because there is little demand for it whereas there is lots of demand for the latter, as Francis Rourke notes in his chapter in this volume. See also Aberbach and Rockman (1994).

References

Aberbach, Joel D., Robert D. Putnam, and Bert A. Rockman. (1981) *Bureaucrats and Politicians in Western Democracies*. Cambridge, MA: Harvard University Press.

Aberbach, Joel D., and Bert A. Rockman. (1976) "Clashing Beliefs Within the Executive Branch: The Nixon Administration Bureaucracy." *American Political Science Review*, 70: 456-468.

———. (1994) "Civil Servants and Policymakers: Neutral or Responsive Competence?" *Governance*, 7: 461-469.

Armstrong, John A. (1973) *The European Administrative Elite*. Princeton, NJ: Princeton University Press.

Brittan, Samuel. (1975) "The Economic Contradictions of Democracy." *British Journal of Political Science*, 5: 129-159.

Campbell, Colin, and John Halligan. (1992) *Political Leadership in an Age of Constraint: The Australian Experience.* Pittsburgh: University of Pittsburgh Press.

Farazmand, Ali. (forthcoming) "Administration of the Persian Achaemenid World-State Empire: Implications for Modern Public Administration." *International Journal of Public Administration.*

Friedrich, Carl J. (1940) "Public Policy and the Nature of Administrative Responsibility." *Public Policy,* 1: 3-24.

Goodsell, Charles T. (1981) "Looking Once Again at Human Service Bureaucracy." *Journal of Politics,* 43: 763-778.

Jones, Charles O. (1994) *The Presidency in a Separated System.* Washington, DC: Brookings Institution.

Kaufman, Herbert. (1977) *Red Tape: Its Origins, Uses, and Abuses.* Washington, DC: Brookings Institution.

Kelman, Steven. (1981) *Regulating America, Regulating Sweden: A Comparative Study of Occupational Safety and Health Policy.* Cambridge: MIT Press.

Kettl, Donald F. (1993) *Sharing Power: Public Governance and Private Markets.* Washington, DC: Brookings Institution.

———. (1994) *Reinventing Government? Appraising the National Performance Review.* Washington, DC: Brookings Institution.

Kettl, Donald F., and John J. DiIulio, Jr., eds. (1995) *Inside the Reinvention Machine: Appraising Government Reform.* Washington, DC: Brookings Institution.

King, Anthony. (1975) "Overload: Problems of Governing in the 1970s." *Political Studies,* 23: 284-296.

Lowi, Theodore J. (1969) *The End of Liberalism: Ideology, Policy, and the Crisis of Public Authority.* New York: Norton.

Mannheim, Karl. (1936) *Ideology and Utopia: An Introduction to the Sociology of Knowledge.* New York: Harvest.

Moe, Ronald C. (1994) "The 'Reinventing Government' Exercise: Misinterpreting the Problem, Misjudging the Consequences." *Public Administration Review,* 54: 125-136.

Moe, Terry M. (1985) "The Politicized Presidency." In John E. Chubb and Paul E. Peterson, eds., *The New Direction in American Politics.* Washington, DC: Brookings Institution.

National Performance Review [Al Gore]. (1993) *Creating a Government That Works Better and Costs Less: Report of the National Performance Review.* Washington, DC: Government Printing Office.

Niskanen, William R. (1971) *Bureaucracy and Representative Government.* Chicago: Aldine-Atherton.

Peters, B. Guy. (1995) "Introducing the Topic." In B. Guy Peters and Donald J. Savoie, eds., *Governance in a Changing Environment.* Montreal: McGill-Queen's University Press.

Pierre, Jon. (1995) "The Marketization of the State: Citizens, Consumers, and the Emergence of the Public Market." In B. Guy Peters and Donald J. Savoie, eds., *Governance in a Changing Environment.* Montreal: McGill-Queen's University Press.

Rockman, Bert A. (1981) "America's 'Departments' of State: Irregular and Regular Syndromes of Policy Making." *American Political Science Review,* 75: 911-927.

———. (1990) "Initiating a New Policy: Issues of Consensus and Implementation." Paper prepared for the annual scientific meeting of the International Society of Political Psychology, Washington, DC.

————. (1995) "Continuité et Changements: Les Elites Politiques et Administratives Américaine." In Ezra Suleiman and Henri Mendras, eds., *Le Recrutement des Elites en Europe*. Paris: La Découverte.

Rose, Richard. (1976) "On the Priorities of Government: A Developmental Analysis of Public Policies." *European Journal of Political Research*, 4: 247-289.

Rose, Richard, and B. Guy Peters. (1978) *Can Governments Go Bankrupt?* New York: Basic Books.

Rouban, Luc. (1995) "The Civil Service Culture and Management Reform." In B. Guy Peters and Donald J. Savoie, eds., *Governance in a Changing Environment*. Montreal: McGill-Queen's University Press.

Rourke, Francis E. (1992) "Responsiveness and Neutral Competence in American Bureaucracy." *Public Administration Review*, 52: 539-546.

Savage, Gail L. (forthcoming) *The Social Construction of Expertise: The English Civil Service and Its Influence, 1919-1939*. Pittsburgh: University of Pittsburgh Press.

Savoie, Donald J. (1994) *Thatcher, Reagan, Mulroney: In Search of a New Bureaucracy*. Pittsburgh: University of Pittsburgh Press.

Schick, Allen. (1969) "Systems Politics and Systems Budgeting." *Public Administration Review*, 29: 137-151.

Self, Peter. (1993) *Government by the Market? The Politics of Public Choice*. Houndmills, England: Macmillan.

Suleiman, Ezra N. (1974) *Politics, Power, and Bureaucracy in France: The Administrative Elite*. Princeton, NJ: Princeton University Press.

————. (1978) *Elites in French Society: The Politics of Survival*. Princeton, NJ: Princeton University Press.

Weber, Max. (1946) "Bureaucracy." In H. H. Gerth and C. W. Mills, eds., *From Max Weber: Essays in Sociology*. New York: Oxford University Press.

Author Index

Subject Index

About the Editor

Ali Farazmand is Associate Professor of Public Administration at Florida Atlantic University, where he teaches core courses in the M.P.A. and Ph.D. programs: Organization Theory and Behavior, Personnel/HRM, and Conceptual Foundations of Public Administration. His research interests also include civilization and administration, organization/administrative theory and behavior, bureaucratic theory and politics, the political economy of state, administrative state, revolution, elite theory, and comparative and development PA. He holds a Ph.D. in public administration from the Maxwell School of Syracuse University. He has published numerous journal articles, book chapters, and books. His recent publications include *The State, Bureaucracy, and Revolution in Modern Iran* (1989), *Handbook of Comparative and Development Public Administration*, and *Handbook of Bureaucracy* (editor, both with Marcel Dekker, 1991, 1994), *Modern Organizations: Administrative Theory in Contemporary Society* (1994), and *Public Enterprise Management* (editor). His forthcoming books include *The New American Administrative State* and *Handbook of Crisis and Emergency Management*. He is an active member of the American Political Science Association, American Society for Public Administration, International Political Science Association, American Academy of Management, Eastern Regional Organization of Public Administration, and others.

About the Contributors

Lawrence S. Graham is Professor of Government, University of Texas at Austin. He is a specialist in comparative politics whose interests concern issues in public policy and management. His publications on politics and bureaucracy have focused on Latin America (especially Brazil and Mexico) and Southern Europe (especially Portugal). His more recent work has involved the study of development policy and programs in Latin America as well as in Southern and Eastern Europe. Illustrative of these publications are *The State and Policy Outcomes in Latin America* (1990), *The Political Economy of Brazil: Public Policies in an Era of Transition*, edited with Robert H. Wilson (1990), and *The Portuguese Military and the State: Rethinking Transitions in Europe and Latin America* (1993).

Matthew Holden, Jr., a native Mississippian, is the Henry L. and Grace M. Doherty Professor of Government and Foreign Affairs, University of Virginia, where he has also been a member of the Center for Advanced Studies. In 1996, he was the Newman Visiting Professor of American Civilization at Cornell University. He has written, from the conceptual viewpoint that politics is a universal human process, in various fields of political science (particularly urban politics, ethnic conflict and politics, American government, law and politics, and "soft" methodologies, such as reflection and participant observation). His most recent book is *Continuity and Disruption: Essays in Public Administration* (1996), based upon the predicate that administration is the central political process. This is one of three studies in a long-term project toward a political theory of administration. He is also engaged in a major work on the reorganization of the electric power industry. He has been a Vice President of the American Political Science Association and has been active in the Midwest Political Science Association, the Southern Political Science Association, the American Society for Public Administration, and the National Academy of Public Administration. He was the second editor of the *National Political Science Review* and is a member of the Working Group on the History of Public Administration of the International Institute of Administrative Sciences. He has for many years been interested in the reciprocity between practice and theory. In the nonacademic environment, he has been a commissioner of the Federal Energy Regulatory Commission as well as the Wisconsin Public Service Commission and a member of the President's Air Quality Advisory Board. He has also been a private arbitrator and has served as an Alternate to the House of the Deputies, General Convention of the Episcopal Church of the United States. As a private citizen, he is actively involved in the promotion of child care services, particularly for poor children.

Renu Khator is Professor of Government and International Affairs at the University of South Florida in Tampa. Her areas of interest include environmental politics, Asian politics, and Indian politics. She is the author or editor of three books: *Environment, Development, and Politics in India; Forest Policy in India: People and the Government;* and *Public Administration in the Global Village.* In addition, her articles have appeared in major national and international journals.

B. Guy Peters is Maurice Falk Professor of American Government at the University of Pittsburgh. He previously taught at Emory University, the University of Delaware, and Tulane University and has had visiting positions in Britain, Sweden, Norway, Switzerland, and the Netherlands. He also was the founding coeditor of *Governance.* His published works include *The Politics of Bureaucracy, Comparing Public Bureaucracies, American Public Policy, Policy Dynamics* (with Brian W. Hogwood), *The Pathology of Public Policy* (with Brian W. Hogwood), *Advising West European Governments* (with Anthony Barker), and *The Future of Governing.*

Fred W. Riggs is Professor Emeritus of Political Science at the University of Hawaii. The American Society for Public Administration gave him the Dwight Waldo Award for distinguished service in research and publications in 1991, and he was honored by the Eastern Regional Organization for Public Administration in 1983. During the 1960s, he led ASPA's Comparative Administration Group, predecessor to SICA, ASPA's Section for International and Comparative Administration. In recent years, he has focused on the special problems of presidentialist regimes, looking at the American constitutional system in a comparative perspective. In the context of the modern world system, he views the rise of ethnic nationalism as an urgent problem for democratic governance and world peace. More details about his life and intellectual adventures can be found in the Festschrift produced in his honor in 1992: *Politics and Administration in Changing Societies,* edited by Ramesh K. Arora (New Delhi). More details can also be found in *Who's Who in America* (1997).

Bert A. Rockman is University Professor of Political Science and Research Professor in the University Center for International Studies at the University of Pittsburgh, where he also holds an appointment in the Graduate School of Public and International Affairs. He has most recently published *The Clinton Presidency: Early Appraisals,* with Colin Campbell, and *Agenda for Excellence 2: Administering the State,* with B. Guy Peters. He is currently working on *The Changing U.S. Federal Executive,* with Joel D. Aberbach.

David H. Rosenbloom is Distinguished Professor of Public Administration in the School of Public Affairs at The American University. He received his Ph.D. in political science from the University of Chicago in 1969. In 1970-1971, he was an American Society for Public Administration Fellow in the U.S. Civil Service Commission. He was elected to the National Academy of Public Administration in 1986. He became editor-in-chief of *Public Administration Review* in 1991 and served until 1996. In 1992, he received the Distinguished Research Award of the National Association of Schools of Public Affairs and Administration and the American Society for Public Administration. His published work focuses on the politics, law, and personnel of public bureaucracy. Titles include *Federal Service and the Constitution* (1971), *Federal Equal Employment Opportunity* (1977), *Public Administration and Law* (1983), *Bureaucratic Government, USA* (with David Nachmias, 1980), *Representative Bureaucracy and the American Political System* (with Samuel Krislov, 1981), *Essentials of Labor Relations* (with Jay Shafritz, 1985), *Toward Constitutional Competence: A Casebook for Public Administrators* (with James D. Carroll, 1990), and *Public Administration: Understanding Management, Politics, and Law in the Public Sector* (1993).

Francis E. Rourke is the Benjamin Griswold Professor of Public Policy Studies at Johns Hopkins University (Emeritus). He also has taught at the University of Minnesota, Yale University, and the University of California at Berkeley. In 1987, he was designated the John Gaus Distinguished Lecturer at the annual meeting of the American Political Science Association. Among the books he has written are *Secrecy and Publicity: Dilemmas of Democracy; Bureaucracy, Politics and Public Policy;* and *Bureaucracy and Foreign Policy.*

Francis R. Terry is Professor and Head of Research at Nottingham School of Business, Nottingham Trent University, United Kingdom, where he teaches business and public management. He has published extensively on the British public enterprise management and civil service system as well as on comparative public management. Author of numerous articles and book chapters, he is also the editor of the journal *Public Money & Management.*

Frederick C. Thayer is Professor Emeritus, Graduate School of Public & International Affairs, University of Pittsburgh. He has published extensively on civil service "reform," government regulation of business, and organization theory. He deeply regrets the return to the federal government of a nineteenth-century spoils system.

Paul P. Van Riper is Professor Emeritus of Political Science at Texas A&M University, where he was formerly department head and directed the M.P.A. program. He has recently been appointed a faculty member of the new Bush School of Government and Public Service of the university, which opens in the fall of 1997. He has taught at Cornell and Northwestern and has served as a visiting professor at Chicago, Michigan, Oklahoma, Utah, and the University of Strathclyde in Scotland. He was a civilian management analyst in the Department of Defense during the Korean War and is a retired Lt. Colonel, army reserve. He has published many articles on the civil service and is the author of the *Handbook of Practical Politics* (1952) and *History of the United States Civil Service* (1958), coauthor of *The American Federal Executive* (1963), and editor and coauthor of *The Wilson Influence on Public Administration* (1990). From the American Society for Public Adminstration, he received the Dimock Award in 1983 for the best commissioned essay in its journal for 1983, and in 1990 he received its Dwight Waldo Award for his lifetime contribution to the literature of public administration.